Paradigms Regained
The Uses of Illuminative, Semiotic and Post-Modern Criticism as Modes of Inquiry in Educational Technology

A Book of Readings

Paradigms Regained

The Uses of Illuminative, Semiotic and Post-Modern Criticism as Modes of Inquiry in Educational Technology

A Book of Readings

edited by

Denis Hlynka
University of Manitoba

and

John C. Belland
The Ohio State University

Educational Technology Publications
Englewood Cliffs, New Jersey 07632

Library of Congress Cataloging-in-Publication Data

Paradigms regained : the uses of illuminative, semiotic, and post
  -modern criticism as modes of inquiry in educational technology : a
  book of readings / edited by Denis Hlynka and John C. Belland.
    p.   cm.
  Includes bibliographical references and index.
  ISBN 0-87778-223-7
    1. Educational technology. 2. Instructional systems. I. Hlynka,
  Denis. II. Belland, John C.
  LB1028.3.P26 1991
  371.3'078–dc20   90-39819
                                                               CIP

Printed in the United States of America.

Library of Congress Catalog Card Number:
90-39819.

International Standard Book Number:
0-87778-223-7.

First Printing: January, 1991.

PREFACE

The paradigm shift which Thomas Kuhn identified in his 1962 landmark work titled *The Structure of Scientific Revolutions* has been slowly drawing attention to the possibilities of alternative methodologies of research. It is somewhat ironic that educational technology, a field which prides itself on being within the vanguard of change, suddenly appears instead to be lagging behind other fields and disciplines. While these other fields have already spent a decade or more questioning and exploring genuine research alternatives, educational technology appears to have become stuck fast in a technological, means-ends model which goes by a variety of names including the *systems approach*, *instructional development, instructional systems design*, or just plain *educational technology*. Inquiry in the context of this positivistic conception of the field seems then to be limited to formal experiments which seek to provide information which would predict and control the learning outcomes from technologically-based instructional systems.

Yet it would be erroneous to assert that educational technologists have been totally remiss in exploring these alternatives. It is just that the literature has not yet systematically recorded such explorations. Phrases and concepts such as "qualitative methodologies," "semiotics," "the post-modern condition," "reader response theories," and "post-structuralism," have begun to permeate even the literature of educational technology. It is the purpose of this book of readings to pull together from divergent areas some of the literature which is beginning to explore such options.

The single word which seems to encompass the trends reported here is "criticism." Saying that, however, we need at once to withdraw and point out the inadequacy of such a term. Most important, criticism is most often misconstrued as "negative judgment." We, however, take the broader approach to criticism, a view derived from the arts and humanities. In this larger view, criticism is the "study concerned with defining, expounding, and evaluating works of literature" (Abrams, p. 36). In educational technology, then, criticism, by extension, is that study concerned with defining, expounding, and evaluating processes and products of educational technology.

The purpose of this book is to make available under one set of covers several of the key documents and papers which reflect such critical study. The first set of readings, *Criticism as a way of looking at educational technology,* provides an introduction to three (out of many possible) types of critical inquiry which have been conducted in the field of educational technology. The second set of readings, *From critical theory to educational technology,* documents five papers which attempt in various ways to relate critical thinking to educational technology. Section three, *Case studies,* deals either with specific research studies, using different critical methodologies, or with the explication of specific theoretical stands. Section four, *Computers and the critical view,* focuses explicitly on the domain of computers as an area which has received perhaps more critical commentary than any other aspect of educational technology. This section concentrates on critical analyses applied to this sub-domain of educational technology. The penultimate set of readings, *Foundations,* covers contributions which are outside the field of educational technology, but relevant to our discourse. This section includes several historic and classic papers, some of which have been forgotten by educational technologists in their rush towards technicist-oriented progress. We conclude (Section six) with a warning that criticism is not the only paradigm, and that it is open to misuse, abuse, and inappropriate interpretation.

As always, when one begins to select, it immediately becomes obvious what is left out. We regret that there are no contributions here from Elliot Eisner, Roland Barthes, Umberto Eco, Ferdinand de Saussure, and a wide range of other writers, both inside and outside the educational technology domain. Even after we stopped our selection process, new papers continually appeared which would have made further contributions to the general direction of this book. In short, the further we explored, the more we left out. Nevertheless, we feel that this book should have three major values. First, it should provide an introduction for further exploration into critical methodologies as appropriate to educational technology. Second, the book presents an international collection of authors including scholars from Canada, France, Great Britain, and the United States. The spellings in each of the works have been retained in original form to serve as a reminder of the national diversity of authors and translators. Third, and perhaps most important, this set of readings should be tangible evidence which gives a clear trace of work which has been done and needs to be done in a yet unexplored direction. Educational technology has not yet moved broadly in the directions indicated in these readings. Perhaps that time has come. Perhaps this book takes that first step.

It may be useful to provide a comment on our title. *Paradigms Regained* is our attempt at intertextuality, uniting Milton's *Paradise Lost/Paradise Regained* title syntagmatically to the popular contemporary term, "paradigm." We believe that the critical paradigm is not new. It has been largely ignored, however, in educational technology. Our aim is to encourage the discourse and debate which will help the field regain the contribution of this sort of inquiry.

The two quotations on the frontispiece provide further focus. The quote from Milton is our attempt to show direct relevance between our book and his poems, especially since we have corrupted the title of a real work of art. Milton reminds us that scholars (including critics) must be humble. Inquiry is such a vast and diverse enterprise that the advocacy of a single method or particular ideation is absurd. The Gablik quote reinforces that view but places it within a contemporary perspective.

If these quotations help the reader focus on the essence of this book, their use is justified. The other reason we used them is that they state their message (and ours) with elegance. That is one of the major strengths of aesthetic paradigms in educational technology. Not only do we wish to make a statement, but we want to make it with elegance and style.

Acknowledgments

No book ever provides adequate honor to the many persons who encouraged, enlightened, chastened and sustained the authors and editors. We do, however, want to acknowledge herein the important help of Tillman Ragan who, while president of the Research and Theory Division of AECT, sponsored a presidential session which introduced the two author/editors of this book to each other. Barbara Martin and Randy Kotting, in their continuing sponsorship of the Forum, have provided a venue in which criticism in our field could be presented. The Professors of Instructional Design and Technology group meetings held every Spring at Shawnee Bluffs Indiana have provided not only an annual occasion for us to converse in depth but also the opportunity to engage in sustained dialogue with many esteemed colleagues. The graduate students at the University of Manitoba and The Ohio State University tested our intellects and our communication. In particular, Linda Mlodzinski at the University of Manitoba became the first single-student evaluator to "walk through" the entire project.   Also at the University of Manitoba, we acknowledge the invaluable assistance of Jill Winship who made complicated tasks seem easy. In this era of desk-top publishing, we must provide special recognition to Ms Connie Dow at The Ohio State University who was able amongst innumerable interruptions to enter most of these articles into the computer, and to keep track of the correspondence related to seeking permissions.   Ms Nadine Denton also assisted with keying, proofing and a myriad of other related tasks.

Finally, our families tolerated our many hours at the computer and on the telephone. We know that they wondered many times about our absentmindedness as we "participated" in family activities with our minds far away in the worlds of criticism and post-modernism.

> Thank you, all.
> D. Hlynka
> J. Belland

REFERENCES

Abrams, M. H. (1971). *A glossary of literary terms.* New York: Holt, Rinehart and Winston.

Belsey, C. (1980). *Critical practice.* London: Methuen.

Kuhn, T. S. (1962). *The structure of scientific revolutions.* Chicago: University of Chicago Press (second edition, 1970).

TABLE OF CONTENTS

Paradigms Regained
The Uses of Illuminative, Semiotic and Post-Modern Criticism as Modes of Inquiry in Educational Technology

A Book of Readings

The first and wisest of them all professed
To know this only: that he nothing knew . . .
John Milton, *Paradise Regained*

The role of criticism today is to engage in a
fundamental reconstruction of the basic
premises of our whole culture . . . It is not just a
matter of seeing things differently, but of
seeing different things.
S. Gablik. (1984). *Has modernism failed?*
NY: Thames & Hudson

Introduction

> "The value of a scientific idea lies not in whether
> it turns out to be right or wrong; instead it lies in
> whether it is fruitful, whether it leads us to new
> ideas, whether it leads us to progress."
>
> D. Goodstein,
> Kepler's Three Laws, *The Mechanical Universe.*

Critical Study of Educational Technology

Denis Hlynka & John C. Belland

While the dominant current paradigm for educational technology research is quantitative, the rise of qualitative methodologies has already been recognized as an acceptable contrasting paradigm. Guba and Lincoln (1981) put the distinctions clearly in perspective. In quantitative methodologies:

> there is a single reality on which inquiry can converge; in qualitative methodologies there are multiple realities. In quantitative methodologies, inquirer and respondent are independent, while in qualitative approaches they are interrelated, each influencing each other. Finally, quantitative truth statements are nomothetic, allowing, expecting and demanding generalizations to be made. Qualitative truth statements are idiographic, such that generalizations are neither possible nor expected.

The battleground between quantitative/ qualitative opponents has been clearly set, and the qualitativists have won a first victory in the sense that their views have become accepted as an

alternative approach.   But a curious danger has
arisen. The well known syndrome of winning the
battle but losing the war has provided a shift in the
deployment of resources. Now that the qualitative
methodologies   have   become   part   of   the
mainstream, that is, have themselves become
paradigmatic, it appears that in an attempt to gain
legitimacy, qualitativists desire to be perceived as
being scientific. A different kind of science, it is
true, but nevertheless, science. The original debate
of art vs science turns out to be one kind of science
vs a second kind of science.(p. 54)

The Third Paradigm

This book is built on the premise that the field of
educational technology needs to bring back the original dichotomy
described by Guba and Lincoln: qualitative in contrast to
quantitative; art in contrast to science.   To do this requires
different paradigms. If the first paradigm is quantitative and the
second is qualitative, then this book argues for a third paradigm,
which we shall call the "critical" paradigm. Perhaps yet a fourth
paradigm would be historiographic and a fifth paradigm would be
philosophic/analytic.

At first glance, the term "critical" might be perceived as
simply another synonym for part of the second, qualitative,
paradigm. But the critical paradigm is neither quantitative nor
qualitative. It does not follow any traditional statistical or
experimental methodology derived from the behavioral sciences,
nor is it based on anthropological participant observation or
sociological data-gathering models. Rather, this third paradigm
focuses on criticism in the sense of art and literary criticism
models within the humanities.

Perhaps the simplest way to order the three paradigmatic
alternatives is to turn to Habermas. Rather than beginning from
the methodological issues of qualitative/quantitative, Habermas
develops his theory of knowledge which he calls "knowledge-
constitutive interests." Knowledge is not one simple value-free
construct. Rather, knowledge is constituted in different interests,
of which there are three. The first and most well known of these is

the technical interest. Key words associated with this interest are science, positivism, objectives. Extrapolating beyond Habermas' theoretic concerns into the practical field of education, this model is exemplified in curriculum theory by the well known Tyler Rationale. Tyler (1949) asked four simple questions which have proven to be the cornerstone of the technical paradigm:

1. What educational purposes should the school seek to attain?
2. What educational experiences can be provided that are likely to attain these purposes?
3. How can these educational experiences be effectively organized?
4. How can we determine whether these purposes are being attained? (p. 1)

Extrapolating this paradigm beyond curriculum theory into educational technology, one can easily see parallels in models and paradigms of instructional systems design (ISD). Just about all ISD models include processes for determining purpose (goals, objectives, etc.), analyzing learners, tasks, contexts, etc., and constructing a prototype—all guided by formative evaluation. Thus, this sort of process description is most familiar in educational technology.

The second of the knowledge-constitutive interests Habermas names the "practical." Habermas in introducing this second type of knowledge is saying that technical knowledge is important, but is not the only legitimate knowledge. For Habermas, practical understanding involves a consideration of interpretive sciences for and within a given situation. In curriculum theory, this view is most clearly stated in the work of Joseph Schwab who suggests that the four "commonplaces" of learning, namely the teacher, the student, the content, and the milieu form the starting point of developing a true "practical" knowledge, significantly different from an objectives-driven technical model.

The third knowledge-constitutive interest is the "critical," and forms the basis for Habermas' so-called "critical theory." It is this latter domain which forms the basis for our book of readings. However, we choose to broaden our discussion of the "critical" to include what at this stage can only be described as a "grab bag" of often different interests, procedures, and viewpoints. Nonetheless, all are connected by a series of common views. Critical methodologies:

- put their trust in a thinking person, rather than in a procedure;
- tend to focus on "the work" and how it relates to the entire contextual system;
- are empirical to the extent that they refer to "the work" which can be examined by other critics and by the public;
- are public in that the body of critical work is disseminated and cross-referenced so that other critics and the public can examine the range of critical thought for themselves; and
- treat a work not as a closed text, from which readers are expected to extract the single true meaning, but rather as an open text, subject to a multiplicity of meanings, sometimes even contradictory ones, with those meanings residing in the text, in the author, and in the reader.

Critical approaches. Among the variety of critical approaches (that grab-bag mentioned above), the following should be singled out:

- Critical theory, represented by the theoretic work of Habermas;
- Criticism and connoisseurship, advocated most strongly in curriculum theory by Eisner, and in educational technology by Belland;
- Reconceptualism and currere, represented in curriculum theory by William Pinar;
- Semiotics, represented by a wide variety of cross-disciplinary scholars, and in educational technology by Muffoletto, DeVaney and Hlynka; and

  - Post-modern and deconstructionist approaches represented theoretically by names such as Derrida, Foucault, and Barthes. In this book papers by Taylor and Swartz, and Fox attempt to apply post-modern concepts to educational technology.

Even if an instructional developer is striving mightily to be scientific and systematic in the design of an instructional system, many of the decisions made in the course of development will be aesthetic, intuitive, experiential and phenomenological. Scientific inquiry can provide information about the ultimate effectiveness of these decisions in terms of intended learning outcomes. However, seldom are all the learning outcomes of an instructional system intended. Incidental learning could also be measured scientifically, but not until the researcher is able to determine what the incidental learnings might be. Critical paradigms provide a mode of inquiry which can provide insight and information which goes beyond the possibilities of scientific inquiry. As such, they are useful in dealing with the incidental, the aesthetic, and the subtle. As Gage (1978) reminds us, when one or two variables are examined, then scientific models are appropriate, but when there is a multiplicity of variables, one is working in the realm of art.

Concerns

There are many concerns one might have about the infusion of critical method into educational technology. There is the argument over whether the practical arts should be subject to criticism. There is also the dissonance caused when epistemologies clash—in this case the logical positivism of science and the relativism or constructivism of criticism. Another is the practicality of educating critics in educational technology since it is probably impossible to separate method from content in criticism. Each of these concerns will be addressed below.

Fine vs. practical art

One such concern is that the works of educational technology are not intended to be fine art or classic literature.

Rather, instructional systems are designed to be practical systems for the purpose of helping people learn. Just as there is a continuing debate in the arts and humanities as to whether practical arts and popular writing are appropriate stimuli for critical analysis, so in the field of educational technology there will be ongoing concern about the use of criticism as a way of knowing about instructional systems.

Some may argue that a major national or international broadcast television series, *e. g.,* "Sesame Street" or "Nova," are appropriate works to be studied using the processes of criticism. After all, these works have been produced by teams of persons, many of whom are artists. Instructional technologists who have worked on these teams often complain that their analyses are ignored by the producer/directors as planning and production decisions are made on aesthetic criteria. Such creative works are the sorts of things studied by literary, art, film or television critics all the time.

On the other hand, a mathematics lesson for primary-grade learners has not been designed aesthetically. It may have been the product of systematic instructional design or may have resulted from less formal lesson planning. It may be intended for use by many learners, but it may be focused on one particular group of learners in a single school building. While there is surely creativity involved in designing such a lesson, some scholars will claim that the creative/aesthetic aspects are of such a minor consequence that criticism is irrelevant.

Other scholars will respond that even designers who use all the scientifically-derived knowledge available to them have to make inferences which are beyond the data and which involve judgment of aesthetic criteria. The resulting decisions form an important determinant of the form and substance of the lesson. Such phenomena are the proper grist for the critical mill.

Relationship to science

A second domain of concern which will probably be expressed involves the varied way people define scientific inquiry. In its broadest sense, science can be defined as any systematic inquiry. In the context of this definition, a large portion of criticism is stipulated to be in the domain of science.

For example, most semiotic studies are rigorously systematic. To argue about these conceptual borders is likely to distract from the conduct of inquiry in any mode. In order to estimate the value of criticism for the field of educational technology, a substantial body of criticism must be written. In addition, intense efforts using scientific methods must continue. Over a period of time, we assume that the knowledge derived from all modes of inquiry will be complementary.

In attempting to awaken the field of educational technology to a variety of critical inquiry possibilities, we hope that attention to critical paradigms increases the critical study of the scientific methods themselves. Romiszowski (in conversation with the authors) said that he believes that while there are many practitioners of "hard science," those who study human behavior are involved in "really difficult" science. Thus, criticism can be symbiotic with science as it seeks to illuminate and interpret scientific methodologies and findings. At the same time, science can provide data to be included in the sources of critical analysis.

Education of critics

One of the comfortable delusions in educational technology is that one can become a scientist by taking a sequence of courses in methodology and statistics. There is substantial danger in this delusion, but there would probably be greater danger if the field assumed that critics can be prepared in a similar manner.

The development of critical thinking begins even before entering formal schooling. Students who continue in a liberal arts tradition experience continuing development of critical methodologies in their undergraduate courses in the arts and humanities. Persons who enter the field of educational technology from undergraduate majors in literature, art history, film and television studies and the like are likely to begin graduate study with well developed, disciplined critical inquiry skills.

For criticism to develop in depth in educational technology, students must be exposed to a much larger body of work than is the case today. They will have to analyze many instructional systems, view innumerable films and television programs, try out a range of courseware, read textbooks, handbooks and manuals, and scan work-sheets and tests. They will need to experience these works from multiple points of view simultaneously—student, developer, teacher, and evaluator. In addition, they will need to develop the ability to focus on the most salient attributes rather than on surface features. In these ways, students and scholars will have sufficient experience to be able to focus on those works which need critical study as well as be able to bring normative criteria to bear in the critical process.

In addition, students and scholars will have to study a significant body of criticism. These activities probably cannot be separated from the regular course sequences in instructional design, computer applications, video in education, etc. Instead, critical processes will have to be infused into every course.

The Readings

The following brief notes outline the basic contributions of each of the following readings to the use of "criticism" as a way of inquiry in educational technology.

Section One—Criticism as a Way of Looking At Educational Technology

It is appropriate to begin by exploring the potential of critical methodologies derived from a variety of critical traditions. Consider for a moment the following idea. What if what we call educational technology was indeed considered an art, rather than a science. What would be the techniques by which we would conduct scholarly inquiry? For one, art criticism relies on the notion of the connoisseur. Following that line of exploration, **Belland** examines the connoisseurship model, derived from the curriculum theory of Elliot Eisner, and suggests ways in which the educational technologist might become a connoisseur. Just as one talks of a canon of great works in literature and music, so we might consider a canon of best works in educational media; just as trained perception is a hallmark of the art critic, so one might similarly develop educational technology critics.

A second methodology found in contemporary art criticism is semiotics. Semiotics, the science of signs, focuses attention of the art object as a sign. We ask what is a sign? What laws govern the creation and interpretation of signs? Where does meaning reside? In a similar vein, **Hlynka** examines the traditions of semiotics as a second critical area of which educational technologists need to be cognizant. It would seem obvious that educational technology is a field in which signs and their meaning are paramount but are largely ignored or misconstrued. If there exists a theory of signs (and there does in semiotics), then it would seem that such a theory should be a cornerstone in the development of theory for educational technology. This is a theme on which Muffoletto will focus in a later chapter.

    Taylor and **Swartz** look at post-modern world-views in educational technology. This paper challenges the Heinich paradigm and suggests that answers lie in the realm of post-modern analytic methods and deconstruction techniques. In particular, suggest Taylor and Swartz, we need to take a "new pragmatist" approach to educational technology, beginning with the claim of Rorty that all knowledge is a social construct. The result of "new pragmatism" is that it "allows for the empowerment of alternative knowledge communities," focusing on the status of alternative world views, and the role of educational technology in supporting or denying these views.

Section Two—From Critical Theory to Educational Technology

    The second part of this book bridges the gap from critical theory to educational technology. **Aoki** provides a clear educational agenda derived from the critical theory of Habermas. Aoki is not an educational technologist, but rather a curriculum theorist. His tripartite distinction presented here deals with curriculum theory, not educational technology. Nevertheless, the distinctions he makes are very important for placing the critical paradigm into perspective, alongside the other modes of inquiry. Aoki's three paradigms are (1) the technical, (2) the situational interpretive, (3) the critical-theoretic. Aoki serves an important role in making the philosophic arguments of Jurgen Habermas practically relevant to curriculum. Aoki would probably argue that educational technology falls clearly into the technical paradigm. We agree, but in this book, our hope is to suggest that

educational technology should equally well incorporate the other
two domains.

   Boyd is placed next, since his paper provides a convenient
transition from Aoki and is also derived from the philosophic
ideas of Habermas. Boyd sees technology of education not as
conformist and controlled but, to use a keyword of Habermas,
"emancipative." His point is forcibly stated, yet this view might
normally not be accepted by more traditional educational
technologists, who consider that a primary purpose of educational
technology is as a mechanism for control.

   Our focus to this point has been on either a general
conception of educational technology, or else a concept of
educational technology as hardware, software, and media.
Davies adds instructional development to our discourse. While
instructional development represents a clear example of the power
of the systematic method for the design, development, delivery and
evaluation of instruction, Davies argues that instructional
development is, in fact, an art. Based on Collingwood's 1938
distinction between art, science and craft, Davies shows how
instructional development draws on all of these and should be a
common meeting place where art, science and craft co-exist and
complement each other.

   Hlynka and **Nelson** present their argument based in part
on the Davies paper presented above. They explore the concept of
metaphor and suggest that the way we normally perceive
educational technology is already as a "dead" metaphor. What we
need are new metaphors to give new meaning to what we do. Such
metaphors may be found in the domain of "art." This at the very
least should keep our field in a state of wide-awakeness.

   Nichols provides a simple but powerful perspective from
which to examine educational technology. First, he says, we know
from studies in the history of technology that technology begets
negative aspects. These are sometimes unexpected, sometimes
underestimated, and sometimes simply ignored. Indeed a whole
body of literature has been built on such negative dimensions of
technology.   Nichols then takes the next obvious step: "If
educational technology is a subset of general technology, then one
must expect that educational technology also has negative

consequences."(p. 117) What then are these potential negative dimensions? From a philosophic perspective, Nichols attempts to isolate several key points.

Section Three—Case Studies

The third section presents a series of case studies, or practical examples which move us from theory into praxis, that is, practice informed by theory.

Muffoletto uses semiotic theory to explain the importance of understanding meaning in instructional films. He shows how semiotics can be a useful tool for media producers and users in understanding the impact of an instructional product. He suggests that readers who hold that instructional messages are simply "common sense" do not understand the constructed nature of mediated reality.

Belland, Duncan and **Deckman** provide yet a different way of doing criticism. Beginning with a theoretic paper stating their position, which is based in the tradition of Dewey and Eisner, **Belland and Taylor** then present a short scenario dealing with self learning via a technological tool. This scenario has been passed to a "connoisseur," **Alger,** for critical analysis. Alger in turn presents a detailed multifaceted commentary on the meaning of technology in education.

One of the needs in developing a canon of educational technology criticism is a body of methodological tools. **Hudak** provides us with one such study which attempts to generate a grounded theory from a specific situation involving a high school course in media literacy. The methodology is qualitative. He asks, "What do students learn when they are presented with a project to produce a video?" Hudak's careful and thoughtful analysis provides some insightful conclusions.

Several of the papers noted so far have provided us with what to some readers must seem to be an elusive "post-modern perspective." In particular, the word "post-modern" and its near synonym "deconstruction" have been referred to so far by Hlynka, and Taylor & Swartz. The paper which appears next, by **Fox,** is one which consistently applies post-modern thinking to open learning and distance learning. Fox exemplifies this methodology which allows one to deconstruct the normally conceived concepts of "knowledge," "information," and "learning." Of course we know what knowledge is, but what is the nature of post-modern knowledge? Of course we know what information is, but what does "information" mean from within a post-modern observation point? Fox shows how the seemingly esoteric theories of Derrida, Foucault and Lyotard have direct and powerful implications for educational technologists in the 1990s. If Fox is right, we have much work to do.

There are many other critical methodologies which can and have been applied to the study of educational technology. **DeVaney** combines semiotic methods with constructivist theory from the social sciences to provide a framework in which one can examine media in general and educational television in particular.

Section Four—Computers and the Critical View

It is perhaps inevitable that the microcomputer revolution would stir up the most controversy. Thus it is not really surprising that there is already a substantial body of critical literature dealing specifically with the computer.

The set of four papers from *Educational Communication and Technology Journal,* beginning with **Streibel's** "A critical analysis of computers in education," is an especially telling example of conducting critical inquiry. The four papers together provide an example of the scholarly debate which is an essential part of scholarly inquiry. First, Streibel presents a critical analysis of the use of computers in education. This carefully argued analysis examines three approaches to computers, namely as drill and practice, as tutorial programs, and as intellectual tools.

Streibel's analysis has evoked critical commentary from two scholars—**Heinich** and **Damarin**. Heinich makes four key counter arguments. First, one cannot assume that there is only one operative instructional mode. Second, one should not underestimate students. Third, one should not overestimate the potential impact of the teacher. Fourth, philosophical position does not dictate instructional methods.

At this point Damarin enters the debate. Damarin extends Streibel's position and focuses on the important dimension of context, in particular the implications of contextualization or lack of contextualization of computer-related instructional activities. She concludes by bringing into the discussion the famous "two cultures" debate of Snow and Leavis of the late 1950s. This in turn raises the question of whether science or the arts are at the center of our societal philosophy, or whether there is a clear split of two distinct cultures.

To conclude what has by now become a debate, **Streibel** is given the opportunity for rebuttal. This he does taking up each of the respondent's points in order. Ordinarily in journals of criticism, the debate would be ongoing; but at least this group of chapters illustrates the essential place public discourse has in criticism.

Rothe looks specifically at educational software and suggests a six part categorization of social criteria which provide hidden assumptions in software production and utilization.

Murphy and **Pardeck** claim that "technology does not merely represent a set of devices that teachers may choose to use, but more importantly advances a world-view that shapes social existence." Based on the philosophies of Merleau-Ponty, Heidegger, and others, they show some of the dangers posed by a technological world view advanced by computers.

Section Five—Foundations

Here we move back in history to pick up some of the works which have become classics in the area of critical interpretation.

Feldman presents a model which is well known, in one variant or another, by art educators and art critics. This critical framework for aesthetic analysis consists of four steps: description, analysis, interpreation and evaluation.

Langer uses semiotics as a tool for explaining art, but she considers a work of art to be a single symbol, not a system of elements which may be analyzed. Langer identifies two primary forms of communication which she names discursive and presentational. Linguistic communication provides discursive forms. Aesthetic communication provides presentational forms. These latter contain forms of imagination and forms of feeling. The idea of two oppositional communicative forms is a significant one and occurs repeatedly in literature under a variety of parallel

if not synonymous names. For example, Umberto Eco, literary
theorist and author of the best selling novel, *The Name of the Rose,*
uses the terms "open text" and "closed text." Hughes (1986) prefers
the term, "underdetermined discourse," to refer to the plain prose
style considered the language of science. In opposition, Hughes
uses the term, "overdetermined discourse," to describe fiction—
discourse replete with slippery signifiers, metaphoric
construction, and deliberate ambiguous meaning. Lyotard (1979)
introduces the concepts of narrative knowledge and scientific
knowledge.

        Whichever   dichotomy   we   prefer—underdeter-
mined/overdetermined, open/closed, scientific/narrative—the
concept seems to be derived from Langer's initial attempts to
distinguish presentational and discursive. Indeed, Langer's
paper reprinted here is so replete with implications for educational
technologists that it is difficult to note them all. But at least a
passing reference must be made to her argument that language
belongs to the discursive realm and not the presentational.
Following this reasoning, Langer would surely argue that terms
which extend the concept of literacy to computer literacy, media
literacy or television literacy are inappropriate or even
misguided.

        Contemporary discourse in interactive video provides
opportunities to simulate realistic situations. Indeed, a major
promise of interactive video lies in its simulation capabilities.
What is missing in so many analyses of interactive video
potential is the idea that the technology is not value neutral.   But
saying that, we need to explore the nature of reality and the nature
of simulations. **Baudrillard** does just that in a paper which has
been hailed as one of the landmarks of post-modernism. What is
the nature of the simulacrum, or the simulated reality, asks
Baudrillard? The answer is not what one might expect. In the
post-modern world, a double coding comes into play in which an
object is deconstructed by the weaknesses of its own foundations.
In a curious twist, argues Baudrillard, a simulation is what
happens when one attempts to copy reality. But then there occurs a
post-modern turn in which reality copies the simulation!
Baudrillard provides a provocative analysis of the nature of

reality and those who attempt to simulate it. If he is right, his ideas cut across every aspect of educational technology. "The merging of the medium and the message is the first great formula of this new age."(p. 466)

Kliebard, working from the perspective of curriculum theory, suggests in his short paper three specific metaphors: production, growth and travel. Educational technology might well tap into these metaphors for a useful examination of how its products and processes provide different meaning.

Section Six—Towards a Critical View: A Dissenting Statement

With all the promise of critical methodologies, there nevertheless needs to be a warning issued that we are not yet precisely sure of where critical methodologies will take the field of educational technology. At worst, researchers express a fear that such critical and qualitative work is sloppy, inappropriate, and of no specific value. Such objections may well be justified. Most difficult of all will be the task of scholars to be able to accept different ways of knowing, and their attendant different ways of inquiry. The meaning of Puccini's "Madame Butterfly" cannot be expressed in terms of technical objectives. The art of Picasso's "Three Musicians" cannot be reduced to a verbal description. Yet, we are probably a long way off before a thesis in educational technology might be written in the form of a novel. Recognizing these concerns, we approach our final section, not with a "let's go get 'em" attitude, but rather with a need to stop and consider where we are headed. The final reading points us in this direction. **Gibson**, while sympathetic to critical methodologies, nevertheless issues a warning that such approaches are often based on shaky theory, ill-advised practice, and fuzzy thinking. He suggests some specific guidelines which are necessary if curriculum criticism is to be taken seriously as a viable mode of inquiry. Educational technologists would do well to heed Gibson's warning, and to approach criticism thoughtfully.

REFERENCES

Gage, N. L. (1978). *The scientific basis of the art of teaching.* New York: Teachers College Press

Guba, E. & Lincoln, Y. (1981). *Effective evaluation.* San Francisco: Jossey-Bass.

Hughes, K. (1986). *Signs of literature: Language, ideology, and the literary text.* Vancouver: Talonbooks.

Kuhn, T. (1962). *The structure of scientific revolutions.* Chicago: University of Chicago Press (second edition, 1970).

Lyotard, J. (1979). *The postmodern condition: A report of knowledge, theory and history of literature, vol. 10.,* Minneapolis: University of Minnesota Press.

Tyler, R. (1949). *Basic principles of curriculum and instruction.* Chicago: University of Chicago Press.

Section 1

Criticism as a Way of Looking At Educational Technology

1

Developing Connoisseurship in Educational Technology

John C. Belland
Instructional Design & Technology
The Ohio State University

Many people can recall events in either their personal or professional lives in which they realize that they were perceiving that event in complex, subtle ways—ways which might not be understood initially by others. Such an experience represents connoisseurship. Or perhaps one's most vivid remembrances about connoisseurship are those of observing a connoisseur in action seeing, hearing, smelling and tasting things which seemed beyond the capabilities of an ordinary mortal. Most have experienced both sorts of events. Eisner (1985) contends that anyone with a great deal of experience can develop connoisseurship. He also points out that connoisseurship is the private "act of knowledgeable perception . . ."(p. 219). Connoisseurship, then, is the sophisticated internal preparation an individual brings to her/his experience of anything. The connoisseur can be relied upon to absorb a great deal of information about her/his experiences. This information can be interrelated with that resulting from earlier experiences resulting in the accumulation of a great systematic reservoir of knowledge. Other such information can be isolated and savored for special effect even though all the previous experience of the connoisseur is guiding such reflection implicitly. All these experiences are empirical and since most of them relate to works which have permanence or which can be documented accurately with a medium, they can be checked and verified by repeated exposure.

Thus connoisseurship is empirical; it must be possible to observe the phenomenon directly.

The word connoisseur connotes to many people ideas of snobbism or other dimensions of elitism. On the other hand in this paper, I propose that being a connoisseur in any field allows one to cut through all the distracting trivial details and to get to the heart of most matters. In addition, being a connoisseur enables one to make such experience known through the process of criticism so that a body of knowledge can be developed. "The major difference between connoisseurship and criticism is this: connoisseurship is the art of appreciation, criticism is the art of disclosure"(Eisner, 1985, p. 219). If there is to be developed an extensive effort to understand educational technology through criticism, there must be a concerted effort to develop connoisseurship among its scholars and researchers.

In order to illustrate the concept of connoisseurship as a basis for criticism in educational technology, I will offer a personal example. It is offered humbly in the knowledge that the effort resulted in neither reflection nor action.

Audiotutorial Biology

Eighteen years ago, there was a minor fad in higher education science teaching called the audio-tutorial laboratory. This laboratory concept, developed by Sam Postlethwaite at Purdue University, was installed in many college and university campuses and focused on the teaching of introductory life sciences. At The Ohio State University, a three million dollar, 110 station laboratory was installed. It allowed the laboratory and the presentational portions of the beginning freshman biology course to be integrated. Each student was supplied with a work space outfitted with a sink, gas jet, laboratory tools, a transparency viewer, and audiotape playback with both hand and foot controls. Each student was able to spend whatever time she/he needed to work through both the laboratory exercises and the associated curriculum. The laboratory served 12,000 students per year in Biology 100 at a cost of approximately $0.30 per student hour of instruction (an unbelievably low sum since elementary classroom instruction at the time cost about $0.50). It also served the 400 students in Biology 110.

The faculty operating the laboratory were very well prepared and efficient. They had developed a system to ensure that all the components for the course were in constant readiness. Lab instructors and discussion section leaders were trained. The audiotapes were recorded and duplicated for each learner station. The laboratory specimens were ready when each student needed them (the production of chick embryos was especially impressive in this regard) and data were being collected on the performance of learners in the course. In general, the finding was that learners who spent the most time with the materials scored highest on the tests and received the highest grades. Had educational technology reached a utopian height? Had a process been found which was more effective, efficient, and less costly? All the indicators above suggested that.

Of course, there is another side to this story which has resulted in the abandonment of the audiotutorial system for biology at Ohio State (and I presume at most other universities). Eventually, the College of Biological Sciences faced that even though several courses in science were required as part of the general education of all OSU undergraduates, it was a rare student who took a second course in biology. In fact, most of the enrollment for the second and higher courses in biology came from those persons who were required to take this additional work for pre-med or other majors.

I sensed the flaws in this elaborate system for instruction within a few weeks of the opening of the laboratory. I suggested corrections for most of them. Had the staff for the course heeded these suggestions, some portion of 150,000 students might have chosen to take additional work in life science fields. I now know that my behavior at the time was that of a connoisseur of instructional systems and technology.

What did I observe? First, I noticed that the senior instructor for the course referred to the audiotape recordings as lectures both in the lab manual and in conversation. I placed the student headphones on and listened for a while and found the senior instructor to be orating as if he were speaking to a class in a large lecture hall. His tone of voice, his overcareful enunciation, and his exaggerated emphasis were irritating to me as they surely were to the students. I also found that the lectures on audiotape were fully 90 minutes long (an artifact of filling up an 1800 foot reel of tape) with no obvious breaks (the lecturing went on even when students were to be simultaneously performing laboratory experiments), and found that the senior instructor's voice was the only one on the tapes. Thus, the audio was not tutorial in tone or content, and listening to it on headphones was uncomfortable if not painful. Of course, each learner could stop and start the tape at will. He/she could rewind and replay portions. However, he/she had no easy way to find a place on a tape. If the learner took a break, he/she had to waste a lot of time to find just where she/he left off (to take a break, the learner had to abandon his/her lab space to another student and then would resume work in the next available space). I observed that when a problem developed, the lab assistant was instructed to ask the learner to re-listen to the tape and seldom offered an explanation in some new or paraphrased form.

From the course staff, I found out that the discussion sections were the site for the testing. Since the discussion section leader had some latitude in assigning grades, learners really didn't want to discuss. They wanted to appear to be reasonably smart to the instructor.

What did I do? I discussed these experiences and observations with the instructional staff for the course and told them that audio through headphones is a very intimate medium (especially in monophonic form in which the speaker seems as if he is in the middle of one's own head). I said something like this: "The concept of a lecture is simply not appropriate. On the other hand, since the medium is not interactive, true tutorial mode is impossible. However, the style, tone, structure, and ambiance should be that of a tutorial conversation. The voice level should be kept conversational in quality, and the length of each section should be limited to no more than 10-20 minutes."

I also addressed the roles of the lab and discussion section instructors. I pointed out that one of the main functions for these instructors should be to attend to the affective needs of the learners. Instructors needed to encourage learners in the use of the technological environment, to remind them to reflect on what they had been listening to and doing, to provide them with thoughtful substantive assistance or elaboration, and to know them as people not just as the "kid in station 86." In the discussion sections, I pointed out that the instructors either should have been trained to lead real discussions concerning content which is at issue or that which is indeterminate or realize that they were not really conducting discussions at all. I offered an alternative recommendation for these sessions—use them as settings in which learners could present reports on a biological investigation or special laboratory project.

Many of these suggestions sound like ones which should have been made *a priori* (*i.e.,* during the design process) by a knowledgeable instructional designer. No instructional designer was a member of the planning team, however, so such advice would have not been available. In addition, many instructional designers are so data driven, that they would choose not to provide such advice until a formal scientific study could be conducted. Other designers, after reviewing the data, would probably not find anything wrong with the course as it was planned and produced—after all, the learners learned the content. In the instance described above, the course staff chose to ignore my comments saying that they would wait until they had seen the data.

In developing the idea of the connoisseur below, I will attempt to show why a person is able to perceive salient elements in any work (the instructional system in this example) without the need for a great deal of data or formalistic modes of inquiry.

The Connoisseur

It is my belief that it is essential to develop sensitive connoisseurship in persons who work in educational technology. Such a capability will enable the development and refinement of technology-based instructional systems without subjecting learners to design flaws and other subtle factors which affect both cognition and affect. Becoming a connoisseur requires the development of: fine discrimination, a hierarchical system of concepts, organizing principles to structure the relationships among the concepts, and strategies so that one can focus on the salient aspects and ignore the myriad array of other aspects present in any complex phenomenon. These requirements are

strikingly similar to Gagné's (1984) conception of higher-order
thinking in general and thus are familiar to most educational
technologists.   The intensity and sophistication necessary to
develop connoisseurship may be greater than that required for
ordinary learning in courses and seminars, and the application
of such ideas to a technologist's own development may be more
difficult than applying them to others in the process of
instructional design.

Perceptual discrimination. At the first level, there is the
process of perceptual discrimination.   In the domain of
connoisseurship, the discriminations are fine and subtle—
approaching the physical limits of the sensory organs and nerves
and the processing power of the perceptual system. An example of
discrimination which would be connoisseurlike and yet not too
sophisticated would be perceiving the type font that text is set in.
The connoisseur would recognize that setting some text in the
Font, New Century Schoolbook, as opposed to Bookman is an
attempt to induce an aura of authenticity and permanence to the
information conveyed. Another example would be that of noticing
that a review section in a computer tutorial used a fresh approach
instead of just putting the learner through the same old frames one
more time. A third example might be finding that the producer
used a brighter then usual key light in a video to draw the
learner's eye to an important object.

Such discriminations may be the natural reactions to
sensory experience of some people. For most people, however, such
reactions must be tutored or mentored. From the first example
above, the novice print materials designer should sit with the
layout people as they discuss type fonts. There the novice will be
overwhelmed with the level of detail discussed by the experts. At
first the novice will react that the experts are engaging in a whole
lot of sophistry. He will wonder what it is that they are really
seeing. Later on, he will see some of the detail himself. He will
still miss a lot, and he will "kick himself" every so often in
conversation when he misses an important feature or detail.
Later on, he will be able to compare and contrast type font styles in
a professional way with just about anybody. Then others will be
amazed to hear about the complexity of selecting a style of type.

The same sort of process must be provided in each area in which perceptual discrimination needs to be developed. This suggests that classes in which instructional technologists are taught should be infused with examples of mediated symbol systems. Instructors and students should discuss not only the content and structure of these systems but also should discuss and examine the subtle differences among production qualities, coding systems—including forms of discourse, metaphor, iconographics, symbolics, formal features of the medium(a), and exemplary practices. Again, at first, the learner will be overwhelmed with the array of interesting things to be learned—things which go way beyond the student's expectations. Yet these discriminations will be learned quickly just so that the learner can appear to be conversant with educational technology professionals.

It is still relatively easy for the student of educational technology to experience a large portion of the linear media produced for education and training. That student may not have seen all the films or videos of a particular producer, but could have viewed a significant representative sample of her/his work. (In the simplest case from the "olden" days, one or two viewings of films produced by ERPI Classroom Films was sufficient to establish the basis for discriminations between other works of that production house and for discriminations among the work of other producers. On the other hand, the work of Norman McLaren or Julien Bryan evolved so substantially over the years that considerably more experience is required to grasp the range of nuance in those films. Of course, the student of educational technology would have been curious to view as much film and video as possible both with senior faculty and among their graduate student colleagues. I believe that most graduates of educational technology programs before 1970 could say that they had developed connoisseurship for the educational film and perhaps also for instructional video. Some more recent graduates have managed to attain widespread and deep experience with these media, but the number so qualified seems to be dwindling.

Few students and professionals in educational technology have ever become connoisseurs of interactive media. In probably

the simplest example, that of computer based tutorial systems, it is
unlikely that anyone has experienced all the paths a learner may
take through the system. It is difficult to remember just whether a
particular sequence of responses has been tried and to judge how
the programmed feedback to those responses might affect a
learner. An educational technologist who is an expert in computer
languages and programming can look at the program object code
and begin to put together a picture of the ways the authors have used
to handle the many different possible learner responses, yet
finding a technologist skilled enough to interpret the computer
code simultaneously with considerations of the learner is
extremely rare. It may in fact be tantamount to impossible to train
anyone to have these dual capabilities. Therefore, it is necessary
that students in educational technology spend a substantial
amount of time observing students actually using the
programmed tutorials, recording the patterns of response and
noting the effects of the computer feedback on the student learners.
Eventually such student observers will be able to make the
discrimination between a statement of helpful learning guidance
and a patronizing attempt to intimidate or control the learner.
When one begins to deal with simulation systems or intelligent
tutoring systems, the level of complexity increases dramatically.
Yet there is no substitute for experience. The educational
technology connoisseur will need to spend many hours, whether
required by coursework or not, reading, viewing, observing,
participating and otherwise accumulating a vast range of
perceptual experience with instructional products and systems.

   Developing concepts. While the development of a simple
concept is not particularly useful in the development of the
connoisseur, the development of concepts with indeterminate
limits and hierarchies of concepts is central. By concepts with
indeterminate limits, I am referring to ideas like kindness—
where does kindness leave off and obsequiousness or patronizing
begin—or to phenomena like color—what is the relationship of
scarlet and crimson? The connoisseur knows that in the former
example, culture, gender, age, context, social status, tone of voice,
body language, and a myriad of other qualities impact on whether
an act can be judged to be kindly. There may be some differences

among connoisseurs in making these judgments, but there is often an amazing degree of unanimity.

For subtle or nuance-rich concept learning, one cannot rely on the findings from experimental research in scientific concept learning—several examples of the concept followed by a non example—or on the articulation of definitions. Such concept learning is a form of social learning which involves the interaction of both highly experienced and novice learners. The highly experienced learners must be present to use their finely tuned powers of perception and discrimination to observe the subtleties. The novices are needed both to try to emulate the experienced ones and to ask the sorts of unexpected questions which often shock the deliberations into a new direction or a new focus. In a way, the novice asks, "Why is the emperor not wearing any clothes?" Eisner (1985) minimizes the importance of concept learning in connoisseurship by stating that concept learning is just simple classification. In many cases, he is correct. But in the types of concepts examined above—types which occur often in technological works—he is wrong. These concepts are more like placing identifiable markers in a complex array of continua.

Concept hierarchies. In the broad concept of instructional film, there is the narrower concept of the narrative film. Within the concept of narrative film is the concept of the dramatic narrative film. Within dramatic narrative, stream of consciousness, particular approaches to stream of consciousness, and so on. The educational technology connoisseur needs to experience these narrower and narrower concepts which are parts of the larger ones. Again an extensive and intensive set of experience is required.

Within computer-based tutorial instruction, learners need to be able to relate the concepts of learner control, program control, pacing, review, remediation, feedback, reinforcement, screen complexity, screen layout, and many others. Within each one, for example screen layout, they need to be able to interrelate the size, font, arrangement and presentation rate of text with its nature, its placement, the sequencing, the use of cueing devices and so on which can impact the pictorial elements (if any are used). All of these concepts become a complex array of possibilities for the connoisseur to observe.

Principles. In the realm of principles, the fruits of scientific inquiry can help inform the connoisseur. Knowledge from research, conjecture from theorizing, analysis from philosophers, critical essays, and reflective thought all become a basis for selecting which elements out of the infinitude available to observe and for applying criteria to those observations. One operating principle in connoisseurship is that the observer is never finished learning. While she/he may have seen similar things before, each creative work (in this context, a work is most often an instructional system) has unique nuances. Some of these nuances may not make very much difference in the effectiveness of the work, but others may in fact account for most of the results. An example of this is the crude attempt made at updating Braverman's *An American Time Capsule* by adding the pictures of presidents Ford and Carter with two additional cymbal crashes. I doubt if this change has much overall effect on learners, but it destroys the artful ending of the film. Of course, extending the line of presidents may convey the idea that the United States is continuing on the same course, or it may convey that there was nothing unique about the Nixon presidency—neither idea is very useful.

A second general principle which guides the connoisseur is courage in one's convictions. He/she must remain convinced that the experiences one has had and the taste that one has cultivated are valid. They may be in conflict with the taste of others, but the connoisseur must hold her/his system of subtlety and focus dear and subject only to the change imposed by new experience.

There may be many other general principles which can be applied to connoisseurship, but there are also many specific knowledge principles which must be employed in particular. It is the application of knowledge from all other modes of inquiry which provides the balance and restraint in the process of criticism. And while this paper does not deal with the public act of criticism, it seems reasonable that the connoisseur's cultivation of taste would be disciplined in private in preparation for any public disclosure which might ensue.

Strategies

The development of intellectual strategies by the connoisseur is complex. It is like problem solving in general in that the connoisseur must be able to keep an open mind or "break set." She/he must be able to apply different collections of previous experience in order to be sure that she/he has been able to attend to the essentials of the experience. However, it is unlike problem solving in general in that it begins with an experience which calls for interpretation rather than one which evokes the sense that there is a problem. In addition, there is no process similar to that of defining the problem. Rather, connoisseurship strategies focus on: 1) ensuring that the connoisseur's involvement with the experience of a work is extensive and intensive, 2) interrelating the experience with previous similar experiences, 3) assuring that critical dimensions have been observed and analyzed, and 4) reflecting on the meaning of the new experience in the context of all previous experience.

Implications for Instructional Technology Programs

If it is important to develop connoisseurs in instructional technology, several actions must be taken by both faculty and students. Most on the list below are obviously and simply derived from the discussion above. All need to be fleshed out in detail, but that can be the body of another paper.

1. Instructional technologists need to experience the "classic" works in the field—especially instructional films.
2. Instructional technologists need to review and critique instructional systems in all media forms.
3. Instructional technologists need to interact with a heterogeneous array of individuals who are in various stages of developing connoisseurship for the field.
4. Instructional technologists need to read critical literature in the curriculum field as

well as general artistic criticism published in
the popular press.

5. Instructional technologists need to develop
    courage to hold and express unique
    observations and analyses and be able to
    interact with others based on them.

6. Professors of educational technology will need
    to study the extent to which connoisseurship can
    be developed in general. In this way, the
    profession can decide whether it can continue
    to prepare scholars capable of observing
    educational technological phenomena in
    general or whether sharp specialty divisions
    will be required.

7. Researchers will need to examine the extent to
    which connoisseurship will improve the
    gathering of data even under traditional
    experimentalist paradigms.

Rorty (1987) was addressing philosophic criticism not
connoisseurship in a review of Habermas' *Der Philosophische
Diskurs der Moderne* when he compared first, second and third-
rate critics. However, I believe implied in Rorty's statements is
the concept of connoisseurship. It is only as one is able to get
"inside" an experience in all its richness and complexity, the
connoisseur's experience, can she/he engage in criticism which
yields new knowledge.

> A third-rate critic of an original
> philosopher usually attacks him (or her) for
> frivolous irresponsibility, or [for] corrupting the
> youth or for having (by underhand rhetorical
> means) briefly made the worse appear to be the
> better cause. By contrast, a second-rate critic will
> spot lacunae in the philosopher's arguments,
> ambiguities in her use of terms, and vagueness in
> her conclusions. . . .

> A first-rate critic will think his way so
> thoroughly into the hopes and fears of the
> philosopher he is criticizing that he is able to shrug

off, on that philosopher's behalf, the strictures of such lesser critics. First-rate critics delight in the originality of those they criticize, and they criticize them only when they are at their best.

The connoisseur "gets inside" experiences. He/she enjoys the care lavished on an instructional system by a sensitive designer. He/she is thankful for the attention paid to aesthetic details. He/she can sense the intellectual and affective intensity which the instructional medium or system will evoke in the learner.

REFERENCES

Belland, J. C., Duncan, J. K. & Deckman, M. (1986). "Criticism as methodology for research in educational technology." Paper presented at the Presidential Session of the Research and Theory Division, Association for Educational Communications and Technology.

Booth, W. C. (1979). *Critical understanding.* Chicago: University of Chicago Press.

Dewey, J. (1935). *Art as experience.* New York: Minton Balch.

Eagleton, T. (1984). *The function of criticism.* London: Verso.

Eisner, E. W. (1985). *The educational imagination, 2nd ed.* New York: Macmillan.

Gagné, R. M. (1985). *The conditions of learning, 4th ed.* New York: Holt, Rinehart & Winston.

Rorty, R. (1987). "Posties," London Review of Books, (3 September).

2

Applying Semiotic Theory to Educational Technology*

Denis Hlynka
Educational Technology
University of Manitoba

Abstract

When education (teaching and/or learning) is considered to be an art, then it seems obvious that the methods of artistic inquiry would be appropriate analysis techniques. Such analysis seems rare or non-existent in educational technology. Semiotics, the theory of signs, provides one such set of methodologies for examining text. This presentation will explore the products and processes of educational technology as text using a variety of semiotic critical methods.

Semiotics is often divided into syntactics, semantics and pragmatics. Semiotic criticism can be based on just one or two of these divisions or it can include all three. Syntactic criticism focuses on the structures of the work. Semantic criticism stresses meaning manifest in the work. While semantics are normally applied to textual materials, critics have also used semantics as a formal approach to visual literacy concepts. Pragmatics links antecedents (causes), features of the work, and results. Such inquiry can address unintended or unanticipated effects a work might have on its audience.

---

* A version of this paper was presented at the 1989 AECT annual conference and appears in the *11th Annual Selected Proceedings* (ED 308 805).

Introduction

THERE IS AN EXCITING DEBATE which appears to be just peaking within the field of educational technology. Our focus of research questions is broadening out. We are moving from questions of "how?" to questions of "why?" We are moving from a search for a single interpretation of reality and truth, towards multiple and simultaneous interpretations. We are moving from an acceptance of strictly scientific modes of inquiry towards an acceptance of a variety of critical alternatives.

The keyword around which this paper will operate is **semiotics**, the study of signs. While the term has been traced back to 1641, referring specifically to "signs and symbols and the study of their use in conveying meaning" (Barnhart, 1988, p. 982), semiotics itself has only recently and rather quietly entered the vocabulary and the consciousness of educational technologists. Yet its import is reflected in the contemporary literature, albeit still almost unnoticed.

Look at only four of the most recent examples. In the latest issue of *Programmed Learning and Educational Technology* from the United Kingdom, David Smith (1988) examines interactive media and instructional software from a semiotic viewpoint. "New ways of conceptualizing human interaction are evolving which are not predicted on hard engineering models. [One such is] a practical development of semiotic analysis" (p. 342).

In the US, the *Educational Communications and Technology Journal* (Korac, 1988) has recently featured a paper suggesting a semiotic analysis of audiovisual media. And another *ECTJ* paper titled "Good Guys and Bad Guys" (Cunningham, 1986) takes on Richard Clark's meta-analytic research. Noting that the educational technologist's elusive goal is to "discover once and for all which method/medium is best, which is the good guy, and which is the bad guy," Cunningham argues for a constructivist and semiotic approach to educational research, so that knowledge is seen as being constructed rather than discovered. Then, "if we come to understand the constructive nature of our knowledge, we can make more modest, context-dependent claims about 'the truth of the matter' and be less embarrassed when we are wrong. In other words, there are no good guys and bad guys, only guys" (p. 7).

A fourth example is a just released book by Marshall & Eric McLuhan (1988). Titled *Laws of Media*, the study presents four "laws," provides a structural analysis of selected media, and concludes with a suggestion for a focus on media poetics (that is, the systematic study of media as literature):

> As the information which constitutes the environment is perpetually in flux, so the need is not for fixed concepts, but rather for the ancient skill of reading that book, for navigating through an ever uncharted and unchartable milieu. Else we will have no more control of this technology and environment than we have of the wind and the tides. (p. 239)

The above examples should at the very least serve to point out that interest in semiotics is not an isolated one. It seems safe to suggest that semiotics is entering the vocabulary and the modes of inquiry of educational technologists. Yet what is semiotics? The term seems to be not well known and writers seem to run immediately into problems of definition. "Education is a field in which semiotics has had relatively little impact" (Cunningham, 1987).

Before we explicate some of these key concepts, it is useful to look at an example. Most significantly, the anecdote deals ultimately with the question of meaning within the practice of instructional development and educational technology.

The Case of the Limp French Fries

A few years ago, I attended a convention on instructional development. I remember a session in which the speaker was talking about how she had identified a training problem and developed a solution. The problem area was restaurant management. A problem had developed in some of the restaurants which were producing "limp" french fries. This was diagnosed as a training problem. There were, as you can imagine, a variety of potential solutions. Perhaps the potatoes were not kept long enough in the fat. Perhaps they were too thick, so could not crisp properly. Perhaps they were allowed to "drip dry" too long; or perhaps it was not long enough. The ultimate cause is not important here. What is important is that a systematic, positivistic model allows one to identify the problem, examine alternative potential causes, develop an appropriate solution, and presto, the problem is solved. And if it turns out that the solution is not the right one, we merely recycle, that is, start again. Eventually, through trial and error, through test and retest, through constant monitoring, the problem will be solved.

So where's the debate? I like limp french fries. In fact, where I come from, Winnipeg, Manitoba, where the winter wind chill temperature can exceed 40 below, the hot, thick, greasy, and yes, "limp" french fry, is the ONLY french fry. A limp french fry means real potatoes were used, not the re-constituted kind. A limp french fry means freshly cut potatoes; not the kind you buy pre-cut, pre-packaged, pre-formed. A limp french fry implies only potato; no unnecessary and unhealthful additives to guarantee a false and unnatural crust. In short, the only french fry is a limp french fry.

There is more. If by chance the french fries come out crisp (heaven forbid), we have a variety of ways to make them limp again. Americans add ketchup. Canadians add white vinegar. And in Winnipeg, an especially popular solution is to serve french fries with gravy. Then they have to be limp!

What I have just presented you with is a rather simplistic example of **deconstruction**, usually credited to Jacques Derrida (1976). Deconstruction is intended to be an astute and careful reading of a text such that the apparent meaning breaks down, and reverses itself when subjected to close scrutiny. Deconstruction is at the heart of the post-modern enterprise. It is carrying the semiotic project to its limit.

Look what our analysis has done. By identifying a problem, we note a series of binary oppositions: limp/crisp; bad/good; unacceptable/acceptable. Second, we see that the concept "crisp" is unintentionally "valorized" as being the ultimate quality. Once we recognize that, we can reverse the valorization. The result is a displacement, and a re-ordering of values. The original meaning crumbles. (Interestingly, in this process, the new reading itself is equally susceptible to a deconstructionist reading.)

What are the implications for curriculum? What are the implications for educational technology? The basic questions of what to teach and why and how are increasingly subject to deconstructionist readings. Why? Because the "post-modern turn" no longer allows a complacent, linear view of how things work. The post-modern view is an all-at-once view, a discontinuous, intermittent view, a view commensurate with a multi-cultural society. The traditional subject is decentered. And most important, we are allowed to question the very ground on which we stand. We are not only allowed, but encouraged to ask "WHY?"

But, of course, I am getting ahead of myself. What I am describing is more likely post-semiotics, or poststructuralism, or post-modernism. At this point, it is necessary to focus on semiotics *per se*.

What Is Semiotics?

Semiotics is the study of signs and sign systems of all kinds. It involves the production of signs, communication through signs; the systematic structuring of signs into codes; the social function of signs, and finally, the meaning of signs. The first important insight which semiotics provides is that signs and sign systems are arbitrary and culturally bound. The second important insight from semiotics, which follows the first, is that linguistic concepts can be used to analyze far more than merely linguistic texts, but all texts, where a text is anything to be read, in the broadest sense.

Robert Scholes: "Semiotics has in fact become the study of codes: the systems that enable human beings to perceive certain events or entities as signs bearing meaning...As an emerging field or discipline in liberal education, semiotics situates itself on the uneasy border between the humanities and the social sciences...As the study of codes and media, semiotics must take an interest in ideology, in socioeconomic structures, in psychoanalysis, in poetics and in the theory of discourse" (p. ix-x). If semiotics is concerned with signs, then it is equally concerned with meaning. Ultimately, semiotics is the study of meaning,

meaning systems, and the origination and generation of meaning. These meanings are grounded in text and discourse.

David Sless: "Semiotics is above all an intellectual curiosity about the ways we represent our world to ourselves and each other" (p. 1). "Semiotics studies messages and in order to study messages we have to read them. A reader is always a participant, never an observer" (Sless, p. 30).

Umberto Eco: "Semiotics is concerned with everything that can be taken as a sign. A sign is everything which can be taken as significantly substituting for something else" (Eco, 1976, p. 7).

Where Do Semiotic Studies Fit Within the Educational Technology Endeavor?

Educational technology, most often described as a "systematic approach" to teaching and learning, is inevitably involved with communication, signs, codes, and meaning. Therefore, it would seem that semiotics should be a compatible and parallel field from which educational technology might benefit. There is a major tradition in education, ultimately overlapping with educational technology, into which a semiological approach seems especially appropriate, namely curriculum theory. It is this tradition which provides a potential coupling of educational technology and semiotics.

Schubert (1988), borrowing from Habermas (1971), identifies curriculum as falling under three potential paradigms. The dominant curriculum paradigm he calls the technical (Habermas: empirical-analytic). A second paradigm for curriculum inquiry he identifies as the situational interpretive (Habermas: Historical-hermeneutic). A third paradigm is identified as critical theoretic (Habermas: critical theory). Aoki (1986) describes the focus of interest in each: In the technical or means-ends model, "interest is in the ethos of control as reflected in the values of efficiency, effectiveness, certainty and predictability. In the situational-interpretive or practical paradigm, interest focuses on "the meaning structure of intersubjective communication between and among people who dwell within a situation." In the critical-theoretic mode, interest is "emancipation from hidden assumptions or underlying human conditions."

This technical/practical/critical trichotomy is useful in locating what is taking place in educational praxis. Educational technology with a penchant for better task analysis techniques, more precise behavioral objectives statements, not to mention our concentration on the next new medium just around the corner, falls squarely within the technical orientation.

There is also a readily identified "practical" dimension of curriculum exemplified in the writings of Joseph Schwab (1973). Schwab's well known commonplaces are the teacher, the learner, the milieu, and the subject matter. "Defensible educational thought must take account of the four commonplaces of equal rank . . . None of these can be omitted without omitting a vital factor in educational thought and practice" (Schwab, 1973). When one examines the AECT "official" definition of educational technology side by side with these four commonplaces, the similarity becomes apparent:

> Educational technology is a complex, integrated
> process involving people, procedures, ideas, devices,
> and organization for analyzing problems, and
> devising, implementing, evaluating, and
> managing solutions to those problems (AECT, 1977).

The juxtaposition of the two definitions is additionally significant, since it illustrates that educational technology is not locked into the technological paradigm, but indeed has apparently endorsed this second significant alternative paradigm. Such a positioning of educational technology shows that the field is not as one sided and single-minded as some would have us believe.

Semiotic, critical, connoisseurship, and post-modern approaches fall within the third paradigm, the critical. Within this third paradigm "the object of the critic . . . is to seek not the unity of the work, but the multiplicity and diversity of its possible meanings, its incompleteness, the omissions which it displays but cannot describe, and above all, its contradictions" (Belsey, p. 109). It has **not** normally been the concern of educational technology to focus on this domain. The role of the technologist is to implement someone else's objectives. As recent a text as Knirk and

Gustafson (1986) is clear on this point: "Although an instructional technologist may have a voice in creating policy, he or she is primarily responsible for *implementing* policy decisions. . . . If an instructional technologist questions the goals, an interpretion should be provided by a representative of the policy making body" (p. 33) (emphasis mine). Such a statement clearly places educational technology as overlapping the technical and practical dimensions as identified above, but outside the critical dimension. Yet this paper argues for the vitality of and the necessity for this third paradigm in educational technology.

Semiotic Questions in Educational Technology

The final section of this paper will identify some key semiotic concepts which appear to hold particular promise for educational technology. Time and space permit not much more than a mere listing of areas ripe for exploration. We shall therefore select one topic and provide a brief example therein.

1. **The concept of sign**. The nature of the interaction between signifier and signified (from Saussure), and the importance of semiosis and the interpretant (from Peirce) provide starting points for an examination of meaning of and within educational products.

2. **Structure of educational media as constructed "text."** A variety of methodologies exists which has been used to explicate underlying structure in literature, poetry and film. Such techniques need to be applied to educational media and technology.

3. **The role of the reader**. Reader response theory extends semiotics by focusing on the newly rediscovered importance of the reader in the triadic relationship between the author, the text, and the reader.

4. **The Rhizome**. The rhizomatic (rhizome = tuber, plant root which is at once root, stem, bulb, connects all parts of the plant to all other parts) metaphor of Umberto Eco (1984) provides a useful extension and/or alternative to the cognitive view of learning.

5. **Syntagmatic and paradigmatic analyses.** Paradigmatic and syntagmatic analyses require the reader to examine the structure of texts in terms of its horizontal and vertical

dimensions. Sophisticated insights into the nature of media, technology, and mass culture have resulted from such analyses in a variety of fields from literary criticism to sociology.

Let us return to the case of the limp french fries. Our purpose will be to unpack the text and to uncover the structural ambiguity which is inherent in the process of reading, of interpretation, and of understanding. For educational technologists, such a task is paramount. Following the schema of Sless, we begin by recalling the author—text—reader paradigm. In fact, there are two types of texts. The author/text is the text generated by and understood by the author. The reader/text is the text generated by the reader in his search to make sense of the author/text.

We can horizontally represent my role as reader of the story of the limp french fries as R1. This reader is directly linked to the instructional developer who authored the ID report. Let us call this individual A2. Thus we have:

$$R1 \bullet \bullet \bullet \bullet \bullet \bullet A2$$

However, A2, before becoming an author, was a reader, designated R2. It was this reader who was called in by management, A3. Now we have:

$$R1 \bullet \bullet \bullet \bullet \bullet \bullet A2/R2 \bullet \bullet \bullet \bullet \bullet \bullet A3$$

The restaurant management noted the problem as a reader (R3), when examining the product itself (P), and explained it as A3 to the instructional developer.

Returning to the beginning of the scheme, we see a missing step. I am no longer a reader R1 of this story; but in telling it to you, I am an author.

Ro $\bullet\bullet\bullet\bullet\bullet\bullet\bullet$ A1	R1 $\bullet\bullet\bullet\bullet\bullet\bullet\bullet$ A2	R2 $\bullet\bullet\bullet\bullet\bullet\bullet\bullet$ A3	R3 $\bullet\bullet\bullet\bullet\bullet\bullet$ P
This Presentation	Instructional Developer	Management	Product

What we have produced is a schematic representation of the story of the limp french fries from a variety of perspectives and interpretations. The model brings out an intriguing comparison with the cognitivist's penchant to model the human mind on the computer. There is, interestingly, a computer version of this activity which I have just described. Whenever one wishes to copy a file onto a backup disc, one goes through a process as follows. First, place the file to be duplicated into a position such that the computer reads the file, then copies or writes that file onto the new disc. While this is happening, the computer screen presents a message which typically says "reading" during the first phase, then "writing" during the copying phase. These terms, reading/writing alternate until the entire file is copied.

The situation is analogous to the reader/author interaction described above. However the difference is significant. In the computer model, the computer "reads" everything, literally, then "writes" everything. What makes humans special is that we read selectively and individually, then we write, also selectively and individually. That difference may well be a key one in discussions of artificial intelligence, and in models which attempt to model the human brain after the electronic computer. Semiotics brings out clearly the very human characteristic of message analysis.

The case of paradigmatic and syntagmatic analysis provides one example of semiotic methodology used to analyze basic educational technology concepts. While a study of concepts such as "educational technology," "instructional media" or names such as AECT and *ECTJ* may not be especially high on the list of practical research topics, such an analysis is nevertheless useful here to illustrate the structured and cultural dimensions inherent in the names and terms we take for granted.* In brief, a syntagm is a linear statement such as "He saw the cat." A paradigm is a vertical selection. In "He saw the cat," a paradigmatic selection would allow a variety of alternatives for "cat": animal terms such as dog, fish, horse; cat terms such as lynx, leopard, lion; or even object terms such as house, car, or television. The point is that the vertical and horizontal choices

---

* For example, one might want to investigate why the journal *Educational Technology was so named as early as 1961 while Audiovisual Instruction* still was used on the journal now called *Tech Trends for more than a decade thereafter.*

onc makes become clear, and the system's formal structure becomes apparent.

Now consider the term "educational technology" in light of explicit and implicit meanings. The basic syntagm is "educational technology." Taking the second word first, the following paradigmatic alternatives present themselves: educational science, art, or technology. The difference among the three terms becomes readily obvious, and highlights the alternatives. The first term, "educational," is perhaps more problematic. The obvious major contestant is of course "instructional," and the distinction between the two has been the subject of much terminological debate.

Let us move further. A similar syntagmatic analysis would be quite appropriate for the names of the AECT research journals, now changing from *Educational Communications and Technology Journal* to *Educational Technology: Research and Development*. The former title provided a generic focus working within a defining term of "educational communications and technology," a term which, in retrospect, never quite caught on. The new title accepts the shorter and widely used "educational technology" name and adds explicitly what was before implicit, namely "research and development."

Significantly, a similar change is taking place at precisely this same moment in the British counterpart to AECT, namely the AETT, the Association for Educational and Training Technology. The British change in journal titles is a far more telling change, from the current *Programmed Learning and Educational Technology* (PLET) to the newly announced *Educational and Training Technology International*. The original title contained the now dated and even obsolete term "programmed learning." The new British journal designation apparently focuses on two dimensions. First there is a separation of educational technology and training technology, and second is an explicit claim for an international appeal.

Indeed, one can learn much about the history of the field from a careful study of the names of our field. In the US alone, that means moving from the Department of Visual Instruction (DVI), to Department of Audiovisual Instruction (DAVI), to Association

for Educational Communications and Technology, and from the
Audiovisual   Communications   Review to *Educational
Communications   and   Technology   Journal* to *Educational
Technology: Research and Development.* If names reflect what a
field is all about, then name changes must reflect some rationale
as well. Is the meaning of a name more than cosmetic? Is change
itself more than cosmetic? That educational technology and its
names have changed, have changed often, and have changed
differently in different cultures, is only one semiotic concern.

Conclusion

In this paper, I have tried to highlight some dimensions of
applying semiotic techniques to educational technology.
Semiotics produces new techniques for reading texts.   As
educational technology becomes more and more sophisticated, we
need to familiarize ourselves with the complex relation of text to
author to reader. As educational technologists we are all three.

Yet our road to improve communications is a thorny one.
As Douglas Adams in *Hitchhiker's Guide to the Galaxy* has so
carefully pointed out:

> . . . if you stick a Babel fish in your ear you can
> instantly understand anything said to you in any
> form of language . . . the poor Babel fish, by
> effectively removing all barriers to communication
> between different races and cultures, has caused
> more and bloodier wars than anything else in the
> history of creation. (p. 50)

REFERENCES

Adams, D. (1979). *Hitchhiker's guide to the galaxy.* London:
      Pan.
Association for Educational Communications and Technology.
      (1977). *Educational technology: Dictionary and glossary
      of terms.* Washington, DC.
Barnhart, R. (1988). *The Barnhart dictionary of etymology.* New
      York: H. W. Wilson.
Belsey, C. (1980). *Critical Practice.* London: Methuen.
Berger, A. (1982). *Media analysis techniques.* Beverly Hills:
      Sage.

Bullock, A. & Stallybrass, O. (1977). *The Fontana dictionary of modern thought.* Aylesbury: Fontana Collins.

Cunningham, D. (1984). What every teacher should know about semiotics. Paper presented at the Annual Meeting of the American Educational Research Association, New Orleans, LA., ED 250 282.

Cunningham, D. (1986). Good guys and bad guys. *Educational Communications and Technology Journal, 34*(1), 3-7.

Cunningham, D. (n.d.). *Cognition as semiosis.* Unpublished manuscript.

Cunningham, D. (1987). Semiotics and education—strands in the web. *The Semiotic Web,* Approaches to Semiotics Ser. #81, 367-378.

Derrida, J. (1976). *Of grammatology.* Baltimore: Johns Hopkins Press.

Eco, U. (1976). *A theory of semiotics.* Bloomington: Indiana University Press.

Eco, U. (1984). *Semiotics and the philosophy of language.* Bloomington: Indiana University Press.

Fiske, J. (1987). *Television culture.* London: Methuen.

Fowler, R. (1987). *A dictionary of modern critical terms.* London: Routledge and Kegan Paul.

Gibson, R. (1984). *Structuralism and education.* London: Hodder and Stoughton.

Habermas, J. (1971). *Knowledge and human interests.* London: Heinemann.

Hawkes, T., (1977). *Structuralism and semiotics.* Berkeley: University of California Press.

Heller, M.(1982). Semiology: A context for television criticism. *Journal of Broadcasting, 26*(4), 1982, 847- 854).

Hlynka, D & Nelson, B. (1985). Educational technology as metaphor. *Programmed Learning and Educational Technology, 22*(1), 7-15.

Hlynka, D. (1988). Making waves with educational technology: A deconstructionist reading of Ted Aoki. Paper presented at the annual Bergamo Conference, Dayton, Ohio, October 1988.

Innis, R. (1985). *Semiotics: An introductory anthology.*
    Bloomington: Indiana University Press.
Knirk, F. G. & Gustafson, K. L. (1986). *Instructional
    technology.* New York: Holt, Rinehart, & Winston.
Korac, N. (1988). Functional, cognitive, and semiotic factors in
    the development of audiovisual comprehension.
    Educational Communications and Technology Journal,
    36(2), 67-92.
McLuhan, M. & E. (1988). *Laws of media: The new science.*
    Toronto: University of Toronto Press.
Muffoletto, R. (1987). Technology and texts: Breaking the
    window. *Educational Media International, 24* (2), 105-109.
Piaget, J. (1970). *Structuralism.* New York: Harper and Row.
Saussure, F. (1956). *Course in general linguistics.* New York:
    McGraw Hill.
Scholes, R. (1974). *Structuralism in literature.* New Haven: Yale
    University Press.
Scholes, R. (1982). *Semiotics and interpretation.* New Haven:
    Yale University Press.
Schubert, W. (1986). *Curriculum: Perspective, paradigm, and*
    possibility. New York: Macmillan.
Schwab, J. (1973). The practical 3: Translation into curriculum.
    School Review, 81 (4), 501-22.
Sless, D. (1986). *In search of semiotics.* London: Croom Helm.
Smith, D. (1988). Institutional contexts for interactive learning
    media (or semiology meets the 'beeb.') *Programmed*
    Learning and Educational Technology, 25 (4), 340-3.
Suhor, C. (1984). Towards a semiotics-based curriculum. *Journal*
    of Curriculum Studies, 15(3), 247-257.

3

Whose Knowledge?*

William D. Taylor & James D. Swartz
Instructional Design & Technology
The Ohio State University

Knowledge is not value neutral. While the idea that knowledge is not value-neutral has been steadily gaining adherents for over a century, its impact on the field of education has been limited, by and large, to the decade of the 1980s. The dramatic expansion of interest in qualitative research in recent years, for instance, signals a shifting notion of what constitutes knowledge. The emerging view holds that knowledge is created, but it is not created equal; that is to say, knowledge is no longer assumed to have universal status. Knowledge is the result of a way of knowing and is marked as such. Knowing and knowledge are inextricably bound up together.

It has been commonly understood that instructional technology is a value-neutral method of conveying instructional information. We will want to challenge that assumption by showing throughout this paper how instructional technology is value intensive in its support of a particular worldview, what we will call the scientific worldview.

When we use the term instructional technology in this paper we will have in mind the definition of that term as provided by Heinich in his 1984 *ECTJ* paper, "The Proper Study of Instructional Technology." Heinich is concerned with studying instructional technology in a way that makes clear its

---

* Originally published under the title, "Instructional technology and proliferating worldviews," in Shorey, M. & Evans, A. *Preparing educators with essential media competencies.* Columbus, OH: Higher Education Division, Ohio Educational Library/Media Association, copyright © 1988, reprinted with permission.

technological origins. He offers definitions of general technology
then explores how these definitions might help guide the
development of instructional technology. While drawing on the
definitions of general technology offered by John Kenneth
Galbraith and Daniel Bell, Heinich moves beyond these to provide
a definition of general technology that he finds isomorphic with
his vision of instructional technology.   Heinich's definition
emphasizes the elements of replicability, reliability,
communication and control among others (Heinich, 1984).

       We are using Heinich's definition because we agree that a
study of the larger notion of technology adds clarity to our
understanding of instructional technology. His definition also
serves to bring into sharp relief the counter issues we seek to raise
in this paper.

       Within the scientific worldview the assumption seems to
be that systematic processes, scientific methods and scientific
knowledge were not arrived at through political, economic and
cultural decisions. Even if they were, the discussion is now over.
Today, we have a reliable, authoritative and stable store of
knowledge that can be passed on to the next generation. Earlier,
we mentioned that these assumptions are beginning to attract
sustained debate among a number of groups. These groups do not
necessarily repudiate the practice and the tenets of science,
general technology or instructional technology; rather, their
objection appears to be that such entities do not represent their
worldview and attendant knowledge.

       Science, technology and instructional technology, as
traditionally conceived, have influenced the way we view many
ethical issues. One such ethical issue, important in the 1980s, has
been the national debate carried on in the various educational
reform documents over the subject of educational equity vs.
educational excellence. Equity in education may be understood as
extending the available educational resources to all people in the
name of "justice, fairness or even mercy" (Smith and Traver,
1984). Instructional technology seems to be a good choice to
distribute educational resources because it uses replicable, well
documented, reliable techniques to communicate information.
For example, an instructional technology product that involves

mathematics instruction for girls is a public document that can be inspected for potential biases and general appropriateness. This is seen as an advantage over a live teacher whose instruction may not be available for perusal. Also, special provisions can be made for handicapped students to assist them in gaining access to educational resources via instructional technology. On the other hand, instructional technology may be assumed to be equally effective while serving the opposing position of excellence in education. Excellence, in contrast to equity, seeks a higher degree of human perfection and emphasizes higher individual achievement as the goal of reform in American education. The excellence movement "assumes that the only way to produce a good person or a good society is to have high expectations and to demand that these expectations be met through independent, individual effort" (Smith and Traver, 1984).

Equity seems to emphasize maximum access to educational resources for everyone while excellence seems to emphasize increased access to educational resources for those who excel. Here we have an example of how instructional technology becomes perceived as a value-neutral vehicle for the delivery of all knowledge. Within the scientific worldview, equity and excellence seem to be major opposing positions which can be served impartially via instructional technology when, in our view, these issues are primarily disagreements about how to distribute agreed upon, static information. That is, equity and excellence are part of a worldview that includes the notion that the established scientific knowledge base can be subdivided and redirected toward a pre-selected audience. This worldview does not assume a challengeable, fluid knowledge that requires constant review by different social groups with varying views as to what knowledge is pertinent to their world.

We want to provide here a brief sketch of one of the many ways the scientific worldview is being undermined today. It will hardly come as a surprise when we note that something major has happened to the underpinnings of the human sciences during the past decade. Scientifically generated knowledge, once assumed to be unequivocal and atemporal, but open to accretionary growth like the Great Barrier Reef, has come under increasing attack.

The presumed epistemologically privileged position of knowledge that results from rigorous application of the scientific method has been deeply—some would say mortally—challenged. Clifford Geertz (1983) dramatically sums up the situation by saying ". . . agreement on the foundations of scholarly authority . . . has disappeared" (p. 161). Extending this notion to professional practice, including theory and practice in our field, Donald Schon calls attention to "the crisis in confidence in professional knowledge" (Greene, p. 69).

This climate of crisis created by the challenge to a positive science worldview is allowing groups who hold alternative worldviews about the production and justification of knowledge, to take a greater forthrightness in the assertion of their positions. Groups such as the religious fundamentalists, blacks and people of color, and women's groups are, with growing confidence, demanding a fair hearing for their knowledge claims at the public policy level and in the curriculum and instructional programs of the public schools. We think these demands will grow and eventually translate into a significantly altered common education for public school students.

While these groups struggle to occupy a space left open by a retreating scientific worldview, it is not the knowledge claims, *per se*, of these groups that challenges science nor opens the space for the advancement of their claims. For this is the project of yet another group that will concern us here.   The term "group" is perhaps granting too great a measure of coherence for what really amounts to a broad movement with disparate and even contradictory elements.   Currently, there is no label that adequately characterizes the range of work under way. Quentin Skinner (1985) in *The Return of Grand Theory in the Human Sciences,* speaks of the "invading hordes" of "hermeneuticists, structuralists, post-empiricists, deconstructionists, and other(s) . . ." (p. 6). A subset of the invading hordes that intrigues us most goes under the rubric of "new pragmatism" or "social construction."   We will use the terms interchangeably, although we admit to a growing preference for the term "new pragmatism" because it reminds us that elements of this position have been around since the beginning of the twentieth century.   Richard

Rorty, more than anyone else, has carefully articulated the arguments of the new pragmatism; therefore, our discussion, in this section, will take up his major ideas.

As a preface to a discussion of Rorty's new pragmatism, we think it prudent to provide a framework for understanding his ideas. One approach is to begin with the work of Thomas Kuhn. In his book, *The Structure of Scientific Revolutions* (1970), Kuhn lays out a theory of change in scientific knowledge that has been widely discussed. Change in science occurs in a revolutionary rather than an evolutionary way. Scientific knowledge does not gradually grow into ever-larger structures. Rather, current structures or paradigms are replaced by newer paradigms that answer a broader set of questions or interests. This revolutionary process resolves extant anomalies between competing paradigms. This is the familiar part of Kuhn's thesis. Less familiar is Kuhn's conception of the nature of scientific knowledge that undergirds paradigmatic change. "Kuhn's understanding of scientific knowledge assumes that knowledge is, as he puts it on the last page of his book, 'intrinsically the common property of a group or else nothing at all' " (Bruffee, 1986 p. 774). In Lauden's (1977) review of Kuhn's conclusions about scientific decision making and the corpus of knowledge flowing from such decisions, he notes that the process for Kuhn ". . . is basically a political and propagandistic affair, in which prestige, power, age and polemics decisively determine the outcome of the struggle between competing theories and theorists" (p. 4). Kenneth Bruffee writes this about Kuhn's position:

For most of us, the most seriously challenging aspect of Kuhn's work is its social constructionist epistemological assumptions. A social constructionist position in any discipline assumes that entities we normally call reality, knowledge, thought, facts, texts, selves, and so on are constructs generated by communities of like-minded peers. Social construction understands reality, knowledge, thought, facts, texts, selves, and so on as community-generated and community-maintained linguistic entities—or, more broadly speaking, symbolic entities—that define or "constitute" the communities that generate them, much as the language of the *United States Constitution*, the

Declaration of Independence, and the "Gettysburg Address" in part constitutes the political, the legal, and to some extent the cultural community of Americans (p. 774).

For Kuhn, scientific knowledge is a social construct. For Richard Rorty, all knowledge is a social construct. Rorty ". . . assumes that there is no such thing as a universal foundation, ground, framework, or structure of knowledge. There is only an agreement, a consensus arrived at for the time being by communities of knowledgeable peers. Concepts, ideas, theories, the world, reality, and facts are all language constructs generated by knowledge communities and used by them to maintain community coherence" (Bruffee, 1986, p. 177).

At least four ideas important to our discussion can be found above. Knowledge, for Rorty, is socially justified belief. Knowledge does not ground in universal principles. Truth is made, not discovered, and since truth is arrived at "only for the time being," truth is perishable. Therefore, truth is made in a community. It is not discovered, that is, it is not "out there" in the world waiting to be gradually uncovered through rigorous scientific investigation. According to Rorty, no single epistemology can lay claim to immutable truth that a second community is obliged to accept (Rorty, 1979).

For Rorty, truth and knowledge are no more or less than what someone wants them to be. Knowledge is words, metaphors offered by human wordmakers to describe how we might live (Rorty, 1986). Rorty invokes Nietzsche's concept that "Truth is a mobile army of metaphors."

The creation of worldviews or evolutionary change within a worldview results from the metaphors invented by the "strong poet." Strong poets created the two worldviews that have dominated Western culture over the past two millennia, namely the religious worldview and the scientific worldview. Rorty views religion and science as simply competing literatures. Literatures created by strong poets as to how we might obtain truth and use it as a standard to live by (Rorty, 1987). Religion and science are exclusionary literatures: only one way of knowing is to be sanctioned. Nonbelievers of the religious epistemology of divine revelation are considered "heretics"; claims of knowledge not validated by the epistemology of science are dismissed as "nonsense." Religion and science are prescriptive in terms of values. Similarly, technology is the embodiment of values that spring from the chosen literature. Technology, if not value saturated, does not exist at all.

Rorty's ideas, which for the sake of brevity we have admittedly simplified, we think will provide bases for the formation, in the years to come, of a large and powerful social group or coalition. Recruits for this group most likely will be made up of defectors from the scientific camp. It seems probable they will continue to translate their ideas into an educational agenda. At a minimum, the classroom will become a place where knowledge is created and recreated and where received knowledge, stripped of its epistemological authority, is closely criticized. To paraphrase an old line from Ted Rozack, received knowledge is not for the taking, but for the debunking.

Social change, even upheaval, would likely follow such a metamorphosis. As Ira Shor and Paulo Freire (1987) put it, "If teachers and students exercised the power to remake knowledge in the classroom, then they would be asserting their power to remake society. The structure of official knowledge is also the structure of social authority" (p. 10). Shor and Freire also foresee changes in the purpose and methods of instruction. Current instructional models, and we might include standard instructional technology here, are viewed as being compatible with a static and passive curriculum that promotes the current dominant authority in society and disempowers non-dominant groups. "New pragmatism" does not endorse any epistemology, but in its attack on science it creates a void allowing for the empowerment of alternative "knowledge communities." In terms of public schooling, for instance, religious fundamentalists will expect their divinely revealed knowledge to be taken seriously. They will assert that their knowledge allows access to the fundamental nature of the meaning of life—the very purpose of human existence. They claim their knowledge reveals human destiny beyond physical death. Religious fundamentalist knowledge purports to show how to achieve contact with the Divine and to derive tangible benefits from such contacts. If religious fundamentalists are to perceive the public school curriculum to be representative of their knowledge community, then they will expect their knowledge to be woven into the fabric of school knowledge.

People of color are also asserting their own notions about how their knowledge should be represented. Beverly Gordon (1987) foresees the coalescence of a powerful new educational agenda: "In the twenty-first century, the struggle will be for the hearts and minds of people of color within Western societies and the global community. The critical battle will be for control over who educates people of color and over the nature of that education" (p. 442).

Women's groups are another instance of a knowledge community, historically ignored, that is now demanding recognition. The form this recognition will take, in the public school classroom, is still evolving. A major struggle of the past decade was to establish a place for women's work, both past and present, within the knowledge communities of the existing physical and human sciences and the humanities. This amounts to an adjustment in the literary canon of the existing disciplines. More recently there is talk of parallel disciplines, space that encourages women to create knowledge that is consonant with their deeply-felt values.

In the past women and people of color have been typically characterized as gender and ethnic groups rather than knowledge communities with distinct worldviews. This reflects their traditional lack of power. This is likely to change. Women and people of color want students representing their constituencies to be able to *make their own* knowledge in schools instead of simply receiving and digesting knowledge supplied by the dominant worldview. They expect school to be a place where knowledge is produced rather than merely reproduced.

With these converging claims, the classroom is likely to become contested turf. Knowledge from conflicting worldviews will need to be honored. No longer will the knowledge of the scientific worldview be considered sufficient to animate classroom life.

We think that the classroom interplay of competing worldviews will be characterized in ethical terms. Major ethical issues seldom arise when a single monolithic worldview holds sway over what counts as legitimate knowledge. Ethical issues within a single worldview tend to be relatively trivial since they involve matters of style or interpretations of the canon. Ethical questions are more likely to become central when competing worldviews clash over matters of substance and practice. When adherents of one worldview take positions based on perceived foundational principles that are idiosyncratic to their worldview, they are likely to view as unethical those demands for change originating from other worldviews. Overarching agreement on a theory of ethical error seems unlikely since consensus itself might be viewed as unethical.

From this particular ethical perspective, educational equity might be viewed as something other than a simple exercise in altruism. Equity can be offered by members of the dominant worldview to members of other worldviews it deems inferior as a ploy to eliminate competing worldviews. Is equity a device for enforcing conformity? This question in a variety of forms is often raised today as a basic element in the revisionist critique of the Western liberal tradition.

Deconstructionists would raise similar questions. Their work seeks to demonstrate that our most cherished ideas, ideas such as equity, or justice, or even mercy, do not exist "out there" in the universe in some sort of ahistorical limbo waiting to be discovered and pressed into the service of humankind. Ideas, as such, have no existence apart from the individuals and groups who propose them. Michel Foucault constructs histories which describe how such ideas come to be proposed, how they are justified in a knowledge community and what use is made of them. In Foucault's dark formulations, the invention of such ideas—or knowledge—is inseparable from power. Knowledge and power are mutually reinforcing. Ideas are created to extend the power of a group already powerful enough to judge and punish a second group they label as deficient or deviant (Foucault, 1982, 1975).

In the public school classroom, the question is being raised as to whose knowledge is to count. Is it possible that at some future time knowledge from all knowledge communities or worldviews can be equally honored? How would the difficult ethical issues be negotiated? How can we hope to even hold open the conversation? As Richard Bernstein (1983) observes when writing about the work of Rorty: "We must appreciate the extent to which our sense of community is threatened . . . by the faulty epistemological doctrines that fill our heads. The moral task of the philosopher or cultural critic is to defend the openness of human conversation against all those temptations and real threats that seek closure" (p. 205).

     If the common school classroom is to offer a space for the "great human conversation," where values, knowledge and action are guided by ethical negotiations and where knowledge groups are equally empowered, what might this mean for an evolving instructional technology? Instructional technology, as it has been thought of, has supported the delivery of an authoritative and relatively fixed knowledge base across time and space. Heinich holds that ". . . the basic premise of instructional technology is that all instructional contingencies can be managed through space and time . . ." (p. 68). The phrase "through space and time" means that the same static knowledge is delivered to the client group no matter where they reside, Malibu or Harlem, and, because that knowledge is locked into a software "time capsule," it can be opened when needed by the client group, tomorrow, six months or six years from now.

     Replicability, alluded to earlier in Heinich's definition, means *sameness*: the same product once designed can be reproduced endlessly and used repeatedly. *Reliability*, as used in the definition, means the results or outcomes for the groups using the product are the same no matter where or when they use it. From an instructional design point of view, convergent and measurable responses pegged to carefully specified objectives make sense when attempting to transfer a pre-selected, invariant body of knowledge. Instructional designers use formative evaluation procedures to vouchsafe reliability; that is, to ensure the pre-selected knowledge is reproduced by the learner.

     All this has served the field well. But how well will it serve the members of alternative knowledge communities who expect their young people to collectively engage in the creation of knowledge, or people who think knowledge, like bread, is best made at the local level? In the future, how will instructional technology respond to the requirements of fluid, multiple knowledge structures negotiated at the local level?

REFERENCES

Bernstein, Richard J. (1983). *Beyond objectivism and relativism: Science, hermeneutics and praxis.* Philadelphia: University of Pennsylvania Press.

Bruffee, Kenneth A. (1986). Social construction, language, and the authority of knowledge: A bibliographical essay. *College English, 48* (8), 773-790.

Foucault, Michel (1983). The subject and power. In H. L. Dreyfus and P. Rabinow, *Michel Foucault: Beyond structuralism and hermeneutics.* 2nd Ed. Chicago: University of Chicago Press, 208-226.

Foucault, Michel (1972). *The archaeology of knowledge.* New York: Pantheon.

Geertz, Clifford (1983). *Local knowledge.* New York: Basic Books.

Gordon, Beverly M. (1987). [Review of *Multicultural education: Towards good practice* and *The politics of multicultural education*]. *Educational Studies, 18* (3), 434-443.

Greene, Maxine (1986). Reflection and passion in teaching. *Journal of Curriculum and Instruction, 2* (1), 41-81.

Heinich, Robert (1984). The proper study of instructional technology. *Educational Communications and Technology Journal, 32* (2), 67-87.

Laudan, Larry (1977). *Progress and its problems.* Berkeley: University of California Press.

Rorty, Richard (1979). *Philosophy and the mirror of nature.* Princeton: Princeton University Press.

Rorty, Richard (1986). The contingency of language. *London Review of Books, 8* (7), 17 April, 3-6.

Rorty, Richard (1987). *The contingency of selfhood.* Champaign-Urbana: University of Illinois Press.

Shor, Ira and Freire, Paulo (1987). *A pedagogy for liberation.*
    Massachusetts: Bergin & Garvey.
Skinner, Quentin, Ed. (1985). *The return of grand theory in the
    human sciences.* Cambridge: Cambridge University
    Press.
Smith, Philip and Traver, Rob (1984). Classical living and
    classical learning: The search for equity and excellence
    in education. *Proceedings of the Philosophy of Education
    Society.*

Section 2

From Critical Theory to Educational Technology

✽✽✽✽✽

4

Interests, Knowledge and Evaluation: Alternative Approaches to Curriculum Evaluation*

T. Aoki
Curriculum Theory
University of Alberta

In any serious discussion of school improvement, improvement of curriculum is implied. Curriculum improvement, in turn, implies curriculum evaluation.

In spite of the many years of curriculum evaluation activities at local, provincial and national levels, it is only in recent years that the notion of "curriculum evaluation" itself has been made problematic and subjected to rigorous scrutinizing. It is this meta-level concern in curriculum evaluation that is the focus of this paper, guided by an interest in understanding more fully what is meant when we say "curriculum evaluation."

In recent years, some of us have come to question the tendency of educators to reduce the idiom of educational evaluation to the paradigm of scientistic research. In our search flowing from our questioning, we have come to know some Continental European scholars who did not succumb to the persuasions of logical positivism expounded by members of the Vienna Circle as did North American scholars. Among them is Jurgen Habermas, a German scholar affiliated with the

---

*Reprinted with permission from *Journal of Curriculum Theorizing,* 6(4), copyright © Corporation for Curriculum Research, 1986.

Frankfurt School.[1] He, together with others such as Horkheimer, Marcuse and Adorno, announced what they saw as a serious crisis in the Western intellectual world so dominated by instrumental reason based on scientism and technology. Habermas appealed to philosophical anthropology to reveal knowledge constitutive of human interests embedded in basically different paradigms. In our endeavor to transcend the dominant tradition in curriculum evaluation, we appropriated Habermas's paradigms, and re-labeled them for our purposes.

These we have termed:
1. Ends-Means (Technical) Evaluation Orientation.
2. Situational Interpretive Evaluation Orientation.
3. Critical Theoretic Evaluation Orientation.

I wish to discuss these orientations by grounding my discussion in a concrete evaluation experience: the assessment of the British Columbia Social Studies program.

Public school educators in British Columbia are very aware of the many evaluation activities spawned by the office of the Assessment Branch of the Ministry of Education over the past several years in response in part, we sense, to the public clamor for accountability in education.

Our experiences in evaluating the British Columbia Social Studies[2] provides an exemplar of how multiple perspectives can

---

[1] I have been influenced greatly by the writings of Jurgen Habermas, principally, Knowledge and Human Interests (Boston: Beacon Press, 1972). The reader will note the relationship between the title of the book and the title of this paper.

[2] The British Columbia Social Studies Assessment: A Report to the Ministry of Education, 1977, is comprised of six reports in four volumes. The reports are as follows:
- Views of Goals of Social Studies
- Teachers' Views of Social Studies
- Teachers' Views of Prescribed Social Studies Curriculum Resources
- Student Achievement and Views in Social Studies
- Interpretive Studies of Selected School Situations
- British Columbia Social Studies Assessment: Summary Report
The Contract Team consisted of Ted T. Aoki, Chairman, Caroline Langford, David M. Williams, and Donald C. Wilson, and the reports were submitted to the Ministry of Education, Government of British Columbia, Victoria, BC.

guide curriculum evaluation. From the outset, as we ventured into various centers in British Columbia, seeking out and trying to make sense of concerns about Social Studies expressed by teachers, students, parents, school trustees, administrators and professors of Social Studies education, we seriously posed ourselves a question: "What are the evaluation frameworks and approaches we should employ in evaluating the phenomenon called Social Studies in British Columbia?"

We took a cue from what Kenneth Beittel[3] called, appropriately, the "Rashomon effect," a notion borrowed from Kurosawa's acclaimed film in which he disclosed the same event from several perspectives. Simultaneously, we were mindful of the risk of reductionism of evaluation possibilities to the dominant ends-means orientation in evaluation research, a point M. Q. Patton made in the following way:

> The very dominance of the scientific method in evaluation research appears to have cut off the great majority of practitioners from serious consideration of any research paradigm. The label 'research' has come to mean the equivalent of employing the Scientific Method . . . of working within the dominant paradigm.[4]

We approached our evaluation activities mindful of the importance to us of ourselves being open to fresh possibilities. We began our evaluation tasks guided by paper-and-pencil-oriented questionnaires that sought teachers', parents' and students' views of aspects of Social Studies, and also students' views and knowledge of Social Studies content. We extended ourselves to include on-site studies, guided by concerns for meanings people who dwell within classroom and school situations give to Social Studies. Further, we added a critical evaluation dimension,

---

[3]K. R. Beittel, Alternatives for Art Education Research. Dubuque, Iowa: Wm. C. Brown Co. Pub., 1973, p. vii. What Beittel has to say about art education research is applicable to evaluation studies.

[4]M. Q. Patton, *Alternative Evaluation Research Paradigms*. Grand Forks: University of North Dakota Press, 1975 p. 6. This is a monograph in a series developed by the North Dakota Study Group on Evaluation.

seeking out underlying "official" perspectives embedded in the Ministry's official curriculum documents.

These activities led to the formulation of five reports and a special paper as follows:

Report A:	Teacher Views of Social Studies
Report B:	Teacher Views of Prescribed Social Studies Curriculum Resources
Report C:	Views of Goals of Social Studies
Report D:	Student Achievement and Views in Social Studies
Report E:	Interpretive Studies of Selected School Situations
Special Paper:	"An Interpretation of Intents of the Elementary and Secondary Curriculum Guides" in the Summary Report: B.C. Social Studies Assessment

Now, some years after the completion of the evaluation, we are in a position to provide a reconstructed version, possessing to some degree a clarity and tidiness which only a reconstruction can give. In fact, it is through such a reconstruction that we were able to provide a portrayal of our evaluation approaches interpreted within a framework of evaluation paradigms.[5]

We must now turn to an effort to illuminate to some extent these three evaluation orientations.

Ends-Means (Technical) Evaluation Orientation

Evaluators acting within an ends-means orientation reflect their interests by entertaining a set of evaluation concerns.

Ends-Means Concerns:

1.   How efficient are the means in achieving the curricular goals and objectives?
2.   How effective are the means in predicting the desired outcomes?

---

[5]See Ted T. Aoki, "Toward Curriculum Inquiry in a New Key," in Concordia University, *Phenomenological Description: Potential for Research in Art Education.* Montreal, 1978, p. 54.

3. What is the degree of congruency between and among intended outcomes, the content in the instructional materials and the teaching approaches specified?
4. How good is Curriculum A compared with Curriculum B in achieving given ends?
5. Of given curricula, which one is the most cost-effective and time-efficient?
6. What valid generalizations can be made for all schools in a district?
7. How well are inputs organized to achieve organizational goals?
8. What are the principal means used to achieve goals? How do we know that these means are actually enacted, with what frequency, and with what intensity?

These ends-means concerns reflect an orientation to evaluation which can be characterized as technical or instrumental. As such, these concerns reflect the dominant evaluation approach in use, going hand-in-hand with the technically oriented mainstream curriculum development/evaluation rationale, known popularly as the Tyler Rationale. We know it by Tyler's sequentially arranged four-step formulation:[6]

Step 1 -   What educational purposes should the school seek to attain?

Step 2 -   How can learning experiences be selected which are likely to be useful in attaining these objectives?

Step 3 -   How can learning experiences be organized for effective instruction?

Step 4 -   How can the effectiveness of learning experiences be evaluated?

The ends-means evaluation orientation has for the pragmatically oriented a commonsensical ring carrying with it

---

[6]From Ralph W. Tyler, Basic *Principles of Curriculum and Instruction.* Chicago: University of Chicago Press, 1949.

the validity of popular support. Further, its congruency with the mainstream social theory idioms of basically instrumental reason, such as behaviorism, systems thinking, structural functionalism borrowed heavily by educators, lends ends-means evaluation a credibility which assumes the status of consensual validity of legitimated educator "scholars." Such legitimated authenticity has led many evaluators to regard this evaluation orientation as *the* orientation.

But what does this orientation imply in terms of cognitive interests and assumptions held tacitly? I suggest that underneath the avowed interest in efficiency, effectiveness, predictability and certainty, as reflected in the list of concerns we examined, is a more deeply rooted interest—that of *control*. It is saturated with a manipulative ethos that leads evaluators of this orientation to value evaluation questions such as: How well have the ends been achieved? Which is a better program, Curriculum A or Curriculum B?

Within this framework, the form of knowledge that is prized is empirical data; the "harder" they are, the better, and the more objective they are, the better. Data are seen as brute facts. In scientific terms the form of knowledge assumes nomological status, demanding empirical validation and seeking levels of generalizability. Knowledge is objective, carrying with it the false dignity of value-free neutrality, reducing out as humanly as possible contamination by the subjectivity of the knower.

Evaluators who subscribe to the ends-means view are technologically oriented, primarily interested in seeing how well the system is able to control components within the system as it struggles to achieve its goals. In their tasks, these evaluators seek efficient tools and instruments such as tests and questionnaires, and seek rigor by bringing to bear the expertise of psychometricians and statisticians. They tend to resort to measurable quantitative data subjected to sophisticated statistical analyses.

In our B.C. Social Studies Evaluation, we administered achievement tests to classes in grades 4, 8 and 12 randomly selected throughout the province, and we sent questionnaires to randomly selected teachers in order to seek the teachers' assessment of instructional resources. These are illustrations of the instruments we used in the technically oriented dimension of our evaluation.

In summary, we might say that the ends-means evaluation mode just considered is framed within the orienting perspective of the following cognitive interest, form of knowing, and mode of evaluation:

> *Interest* in the ethos of control as reflected in the values of efficiency, effectiveness, certainty and predictability.

> *Form of Knowing* emphasized is that of empirical nomological knowing. Understanding is in terms of facts and generalizations.

> *Mode of Evaluation* is ends-means evaluation which is achievement oriented, goal based, criterion referenced, and cost benefit oriented.

Situational Interpretive Evaluation Orientation

In contrast with the technical interest and concerns reflected in the ends-means approach to evaluation, those evaluators oriented towards the situational interpretive mode of evaluation register interest in the following kinds of concerns:

Situational Interpretive Concerns:

1. How do various groups such as teachers, the Ministry, parents, students and administrators view Curriculum X?
2. In what ways do various groups approve or disapprove the program?
3. How do the various groups see Curriculum X in terms of relevance, meaningfulness and appropriateness?
4. What are the various groups' perceived strengths and weaknesses of the program?
5. What questions do administrators and significant others have about Curriculum X?

The situational concerns expressed in these evaluation concerns reflect an orientation to evaluation which we can characterize as situational interpretive. As such these concerns reflect an approach to evaluation in which evaluators show interest in the meanings those living in the situation give to a given curriculum.

Whereas, the technical evaluator assumes a posture as an outsider external to the situation (*i.e.*, as a disinterested observer or as a stranger), the situational interpretive evaluator attempts to gain insights into human experiences as they are experienced by insiders, as they live within the situation.

For example, at this very moment as I write I find myself situated within my world of teacher educators. In this world of mine, my "I" is at the center. I am experiencing life as I am now living it, guided by my common-sense typified knowledge about educators' writings and about people who read such writings. I define my life now by giving meaning to my paper on evaluation, as I sit at my desk awaiting words to come into view and to on-going events about me as I experience them. I am continuously involved in meaning-giving activities as I am subjectively engaged in constructing my personal world of meanings. The structure of these meanings is my present reality.

I can also picture you seated with the text of this writing before you as you are experiencing the reading of my paper. You are situated with yourself at center, that central point of your being that allows you to say "I." You are experiencing life as you are now living it in your typical "reading" way, giving your own meaning to the text of what you are reading. You, too, are continuously involved in meaning-giving activities as you construct your own personal world of meanings. The structure of these meanings is your present reality.

In a social situation, which a classroom or school significantly is, there are multifold ways in which things, people and events are given meaning by those who are living in the situation. In other words, people are continuously interpreting events that they experience, and these interpretations differ from person to person. Hence, an evaluator oriented towards situational interpretation must keep two significant features in mind: (1) people give personal meanings to each situation experienced, and (2) people interpret the same event in different ways.

Whereas, as we have seen, the human activity of central concern within the ends-means orientation is man's technical productive capacity to achieve ends, the activity of most concern for evaluators in the situational interpretive framework is communication between man and man. Since evaluation guiding interests of the situational interpretive evaluation are insights into human experiences as socially lived, the evaluator needs to direct his efforts toward clarifying, authenticating and bringing into full human awareness the meaning structures of the constructive activities of the social actors in the situation. Thus, the form of knowledge sought by the evaluator within this situation is not nomological statements, but rather structures of meaning as man meaningfully experiences and cognitively appropriates the natural and social world. Hence, when the situational interpretive evaluator comes to know situationally, he knows his world in a different form and in a different way compared with the knowledge gained by the ends-means evaluator.

In seeking out, therefore, the structure of meanings which are not accessible to ends-means evaluators, those in the situational interpretive orientation must attempt to provide explanations of a different kind. That is, whereas "explaining" within the ends-means orientation means giving causal, functional, or hypothetico-deductive statements, within the situational orientation, "explaining" requires the striking of a responsive chord among people in dialogue situations by clarifying motives, authentic experiences and common meanings. The evaluator, hence, cannot stand aloof as an observer as is done in the ends-means evaluation, but must enter into intersubjective dialogue with the people in the valuation situation.

Within the situational interpretive orientation, there are different approaches, each allowing a description of the meaning structure in a situation. There is growing interest among evaluators in studies that fall within the phenomenological attitude. The phenomenology of socially constructed understanding, requiring investigation of meaning-giving activities in the everyday world, is the main interest of sociologists of knowledge such as P. Berger, T. Luckman, and A. Schutz, ethnomethodologists such as H. Garfinkel, I. Goffman, and Cicourel, or hermeneuts such as F. Schleiermacher, H. Palmer and Hans-George Gadamer.

Such interpretations of situations are called phenomenological descriptions, providing first-order experiences people directly experience. Evaluators of this persuasion are interested in the quality of life-as-lived in the classroom or school, life experienced by those who dwell within the situation.

Within the B.C. Social Studies Assessment, we experimented with two situational evaluation approaches: (1) an ethnographic approach in which we sought out views of the curriculum-as-plan and curriculum-in-use as interpreted by parents, students, teachers and administrators, and (2) an approach using conversational analysis of the meaning structures of the existential life of teachers and students. The inclusion of these reports represented our attempt to portray more fully the Social Studies phenomenon as it existed in British Columbia.

We can summarize the situational interpretative framework in terms of its cognitive interests, form of knowledge and mode of evaluation as follows:

- *Interest* in the meaning structure of inter-subjective communication between and among people who dwell within a situation.
- *Form of Knowing* is situational knowing, within which understanding is in terms of the structure of meaning. Within this orientation, to explain is to strike a resonant chord by clarifying motives and common meanings.
- *Mode of Evaluation* is situational evaluation, which seeks the quality of meanings people living in a situation give to their lived situations.

Critical Evaluation Mode Orientation

Evaluators thinking and acting within the critical mode reflect their interests by committing themselves to a set of evaluation concerns which differ markedly from either the technically or the situationally oriented evaluators. The following concerns illustrate the interest of critical evaluators:

Critical Evaluation Concerns

1. What are the perspectives underlying Curriculum X? (What are underlying root interests, root assumptions, root approaches?)

2. What is the implied view of the student or the teacher held by the curriculum planner?

3. At the root level, whose interests does Curriculum X serve?

4. What are the root metaphors that guide the curriculum developer, the curriculum implementor, or curriculum evaluator?

5. What is the basic bias of the publisher/author/developer of prescribed or recommended resource materials?

6. What is the curriculum's supporting world view?

The evaluation concerns illustrated above reflect an orientation to evaluation which we can characterize as critical or critical theoretic, rooted in critical social theory, an emerging discipline area. These concerns reflect an approach to evaluation in which the evaluators are interested in bringing into full view underlying perspectives of programs that are typically taken-for-granted and therefore, hidden from view. Implied within a "perspective" are root metaphors, deep-seated human interests, assumptions about man, world view and knowledge, as well as stances that man takes in approaching himself or his world. Critical evaluators are interested in making these visible. But they do not stop here.

As we have noted, whereas evaluation is seen in ends-means evaluation within the framework of instrumental or technical action, and in situational evaluation within the framework of communicative action, in critical theoretic evaluation, it is seen within the dialectical framework of practical action and critical reflection, what Paulo Freire refers to as praxis. In critical reflection, the actor, through the critical analytic process, discovers and makes explicit the tacit and hidden assumptions and intentions held. Such reflective activity is guided by interest in revealing the root condition that makes knowing possible, or in revealing the underlying human and social conditions that distort human existence, distortions that tend to alienate man. Thus, critical evaluators attempt to determine when theoretical statements grasp invariant regularities of human and social action or when they express ideologically frozen relations of dependence that can, in principle, be transformed. Richard Schaull captures aptly this critical orientation in the following way:

> There is no such thing as a neutral educational process. Education either functions as an instrument which is used to facilitate the integration of the younger generation into the logic of the present system and bring about conformity to it, or it becomes "the practice of freedom" the means by which men and women deal critically and creatively with reality and discover how to participate in the transformation of their world.[7]

Thus, a critically oriented evaluator, himself, becomes a part of the object of the evaluation research. The evaluator, in becoming involved with his subjects, enters into their world and attempts to engage them mutually in reflective activity. He questions his subjects and himself, and encourages his subjects to question him and themselves. Reflection by himself and by participants allows new questions to emerge from the situation, which, in turn, leads to further reflective activity. Reflection, however, is not only oriented toward making conscious the unconscious by discovering underlying interests, assumptions and intentions, but it is also oriented towards action guided by the newly gained conscious, critical knowledge. Hence, in the ongoing process, which is dialectical and transformative, both evaluator and subjects become participants in an open dialogue.

Reflection in the foregoing sense is not the kind of activity school people, as actors, engage in in their ongoing lives. For in

---

[7]Richard Schaull, "Foreword," in Paulo Freire, *Pedagogy of the Oppressed.* New York: Herder and Herder, 1968.

their everyday existence actors deal with their concerns in routine ways, guided by the commonplace recipes that sustain them in good stead. What is missing is a conscious effort to examine critically the assumptions and intentions underlying their practical thoughts and acts. They may be reflective but not critically reflective. Critical reflection leads to an understanding of what is beyond the actor's ordinary view, by making the familiar unfamiliar, by making the invisible visible. Such reflective activity not only allows liberation from the unconsciously held assumptions and intentions that lie buried and hidden. For example, at the personal level the content of reflection may be the "rationalization" an actor uses to hide underlying motives for his actions. Or at the societal level, the content may be the "ideology" used to support social practices and policies, rendering obscure society's manipulative ethos and interests that lie beneath. Critical interest thus sees interest in uncovering the "true" interests embedded in some given personal or social condition.

But more than that, it is interested in bringing about reorientation through transformative action of the assumptions and intentions upon which reflection and action rest. Critical orientation, then, with its evaluation-guiding interest to liberate men from hidden assumptions and intentions, promotes a theory of man and society that is grounded in the moral attitude of emancipation.

Curriculum evaluation within this orientation would ask that focus be given to the dynamic of the dialectic between the knowledge structure of life experiences and the normative structure as well. Within this critical framework, phenomenological description of educational phenomena will be regarded as incomplete, but significant in making possible critical reflection and action. Within such a framework of interest the pioneer work of Langeveld, associated with the School of Utrecht, makes sense. He has argued that phenomenological disciplines are conducted within the dialogical context of an ongoing situational interpretive activity but guided by some normative purpose of what it means to educate and to be educated within the critically reflective orientation. As van Manen states, referring to Langeveld's pedagogical position:

> Educational activities must always be structured pedagogically; that is, they should be grounded reflectively in the emancipatory norms toward which all education is oriented.[8]

Within the British Columbia Social Studies Assessment, critical evaluation was included under the innocuous title, "An Interpretation of Intents of the Elementary and Secondary Curriculum Guides," and exists as an afterthought, an addendum to the Summary Report. In it we examined the official text of the Social Studies curriculum-as-plan and gave it a critical look.

To get a sense of the flavor of this evaluation, read the concluding statement of the critical analysis:

> The B.C. Social Studies program approaches the study of man-in-his-world from three different perspectives: scientific, situational and critically reflective knowing. Through each of these, students are exposed to various interpretations of how the social world has been constructed. The program, however, does not provide a balance among these perspectives: rather, it emphasizes scientific knowledge. Through such an emphasis teachers and students are made dependent on one particular way of viewing the social world. Such dependence limits the possibilities which the participants have available for exploring their social environment. The extent to which the perspectives influence classroom presentations (passive vs. active, non-committal vs. committal) stresses the importance

---

[8]An account of Langeveld's conception of phenomenological pedagogy is described by Max van Manen, "A Phenomenological Experiment in Educational Theory: The Utrecht School." Paper presented at the Annual Conference of the American Educational Research Association, Toronto, Ontario, March, 1978. p. 5.

of providing a balance of knowledge perspectives in the program.[9]

What we have done is to bring the official B.C. Social Studies Program into fuller view by revealing the tacitly held assumptions and intentions. Following the comment we added, as a recommendation to the Ministry, the following:

To aid teachers in moving towards consideration of perspectives, it is recommended that a full description of the perspectives incorporated into the B.C. Social Studies program be carefully described in the Curriculum Guides. Students and teachers are entitled to a full explanation of the curriculum developers' knowing stance. The curriculum developers' perspective toward the social world should not, in other words, be hidden from users of the curriculum.[10]

We might summarize the third evaluation mode discussed above as follows:

Critical Evaluation: A Summary

- *Interest* in emancipation from hidden assumptions or underlying human conditions.
- *Form of Knowing* is critical knowing in the sense of understanding hidden assumptions, perspectives, motives, rationalizations, and ideologies. To explain within critical knowing is to trace down and bring into fuller view underlying unreflected aspects.
- *Mode of Evaluation* is critical theoretic evaluation which involves (1) discovering through critical reflection, underlying human conditions, assumptions and intentions, and (2) acting upon self and world to improve the human conditions or to transform the underlying assumptions and intentions.

In this paper I have attempted to trace out a post-hoc reconstruction of three orientations that undergirded the

---

[9]T. Aoki and E. Harrison, "The Intents of the B.C. Social Studies Curriculum Guides: An Interpretation." In T. Aoki, et al., The British Columbia Social Studies Assessment: A Summary Report, 1977. p. 1962.
[10]*ibid.*

evaluation we conducted. By embracing these perspectives we acknowledged multiple human interests, each associated with a form of knowledge. We stated that within the ends-means evaluation approach, the implied interest is intellectual and technical control and the implied form of knowledge, generalizable objective knowledge. Within the situational interpretive approach, the implied interest is authentic communicative consensus, and the form of knowledge, situational knowledge in terms of meanings. Within the critical orientation, the implied interest is emancipatory, based on action which brings into fuller view the taken-for-granted assumptions and intentions. The knowledge flowing from this activity is critical knowledge.

It has been said that an educator's understanding of his task as educator is most clearly demonstrated by his method of evaluation. If that be so, the evaluation approaches we used disclose our understanding of possible ways of understanding what it means to be an educator and what it means to be educated. In our efforts we employed evaluation orientations that reflect to some extent our commitment to our understanding of evaluation as human intentional activities grounded in multiple human interests. So committed, we directed our efforts to go beyond technical instrumentalism, to which we educators in North America have been so prone.

We feel that we have gained a fuller and richer understanding of curriculum evaluation and a sense of how this understanding might help in efforts toward school improvement. And yet, in reaching out for a fuller understanding, we have a gnawing sense flowing from having experienced a reaching out that never fully reaches.

We acknowledge that our effort in conducting this evaluation was a human effort and, as such, subject to the weaknesses and blindness to limit situations that all humans, being human, suffer.

And so, when we felt the task was done, we asked ourselves these questions: "Has the job been done? Has the picture of Social Studies in British Columbia been adequately drawn?"

We replied:

Certainly in our efforts to give an accurate portrayal, we have employed not only traditionally accepted techniques, but also more personalized ones aimed at seriously attempting to 'hear' what the people of the province are saying about the subject.

There may be dissatisfactions. Some may feel that this is 'just another assessment' and thereby dismiss it. Others may argue quite rightly that the findings do not represent the true picture as they see it. But all this is as it should be.

Whenever we see a picture of ourselves taken by someone else, we are anxious that justice be done to the 'real me.' If there is disappointment, it is because we know that there is so much more to the 'real me' than has been momentarily captured by the photographer's click. So too with this assessment: there are deeper and wider dimensions to the total subject than can be justly dealt with from such a hasty glance. Any ensuing dissatisfaction should not be simply taken as a measure of the assessment's failing but as testimony to that crucial vitality of the subject that eludes captivity on paper. We know that the true magic of the educating act is so much more than a simple, albeit justifiable, concern for improved resources, more sensitively stated objectives, better pre-service and in-service training for teachers, or improved bureaucratic efficiency. Rather it has to do with the whole meaning of a society's search for true maturity and responsible freedom through its young people.[11]

---

[11]T. Aoki, et al., *The British Columbia Social Studies Assessment: A Summary Report*, 1977. This was written for the project by David Smith, currently Professor of Education at the University of Lethbridge, Canada.

5

Emancipative Educational Technology*

Gary M. Boyd
Educational Technology
Concordia University, Montreal

Introduction

Almost any technology can be liberative or dominative; indeed most technologies are both, but to/for different people. What I mean by liberation or emancipation is increasing a person's abilities and opportunities to make rational choices about matters important to that person. Both 'advertainment' and peer or colleague pressure are terribly dominating influences, the former largely mediated by technology. The main form of educational communications technology is TV/Video in society at large, while in schools it is the paper copier. There is a vast difference between those two technologies; TV is mostly a few well endowed interest groups influencing vast numbers of people, whereas copiers usually involve many to many influence, or few to few many times repeated.

Emancipation or liberation is not simply freedom from involvement with other people concerning one's decisions but rather requires discussion with others where the outcome is determined by the best argument, not by promises or threats or captivating art or music. This notion of discursive emancipation is due to Jurgen Habermas (1981/1984). I find his perspectives very helpful in considering technological options, as opposed to the non-option of total rejection of technology. It seems to me that the

---

* Reprinted with permission from the *Canadian Journal of Educational Communication, 16*(2), copyright © Association for Media and Technology in Education in Canada, 1987.

ideal conditions for non-dominative, or liberative discourse which he puts forward can more easily be achieved through computer-telecommunications-mediated communications than in any other manner. In this paper I am concerned to demonstrate why I believe computer conferencing in particular is best suited to provide emancipative educational learning situations.

Problem Area

People in our society are constrained by a double yoke: mechanical bureaucratic administrations on the one hand; and time-consumptive 'advertainment' on the other. Both seriously constrict our opportunities to make autonomous and responsible choices about the propagation of culture and the conduct of education as cultural propagation. For example in Quebec, Law 101 and its language police are an attempt to publicly control cultural propagation, but one which is not legitimate if all the people involved have not been able to participate in debates about the means and ends concerned. This is an unusual case, though, because there actually have been public debates about the issues. In other crucial areas such as class size, and timetable hours, decisions have been made by administrators on technical and financial grounds without any debate among those affected.

The other side of the yoke—the advertainment which gobbles up people's quality attention-time so that very little is left for debating educational questions—is all too easily exemplified by Coke™ commercials, and *Dallas,* etc. Concerned teachers, learners and citizens have no efficacious forum for debating key educational issues such as the relative place of fundamental intellectual skills versus peculiar vocational skills in curriculum and instruction. Even at the (micro-) instructional level there is very little opportunity for rational discourse to negotiate and validate instructional objectives, criterion measurement methods, or choice of media and materials. Some teachers do hold discussions on the responsibilities and rights of both learners and teachers, but it is an uphill struggle to do so. "Historically legitimated" bureaucratic norms prevail over the classroom, while tired learners with poor attention skills have had their best time leeched-up by advertainment to which they are addicted. Actual formal education has to make do with what little functional time and discretion is left between the pressures of the administrative, and the advertainment pincers.

Jurgen Habermas (1973/75) envisions a possible way beyond the double impasse of modern society (which incidentally he refers to as our legitimation crisis). This way lies through the widespread practice of life-world validating discourse. So called "practical discourse" is discussion of a fully rational kind about the validity of norms and rights, and rules, and factual propositions, where the only determinants of the outcome of the discussion are the solidity of facts and the logicality and comprehensiveness of the arguments (Habermas, 1981/1984). This contrasts with ordinary debate where rhetorical tricks, and threats or promises often determine the outcome. For discourse to provide genuine legitimation for norms and procedures it must be undominated; that is to say, threats and promises must be censored out, and so must aesthetic enticements or repulsions (Boyd, 1984). Free speech should mean freedom to state arguments and ground them in facts, not license to seduce or frighten people. If there can be some way for us to conduct liberative discussions about curriculum goals, instructional system configurations and individualization, expeditiously and freely, then we may be on our way to orienting activities toward our highest-level educational goals (such as promoting culturally rooted autonomy and potency) rather than making such a fetish out of tiny fact/skill low-level objectives.

Face-to-face discussion has two grave disadvantages when viewed in terms of Habermas' desiderata for life-world validating discourse: (1) it is difficult in ordinary meetings to arrange for each person to have a full and equal chance to contribute, and to digest the contributions of others (especially if there are many vociferous people); and (2) unfair dominative speech acts cannot be ruled out of order until they have taken place if the actor insists on uttering them. By the time that the chair can rule a remark to be out of order it has already done its damage. "Ignore that!" is a weak command. For these reasons and some others, critics have considered Habermas' option of legitimative discourse to be merely an impractical ideal. However, it occurred to me when I came across Habermas, that perhaps computer-mediated teleconferencing is a medium through which his ideal discourse conditions can (very nearly) be met.

This is so because everyone can be given equal opportunity to enter arguments in the conference, and also because a moderator system can hide illegal entries from view. Threats and promises and rhetorical tricks can be archived, and dragged up after the main decisions have been taken if there is a challenge, but they can be kept out of immediate effect. It is crucial for liberative, life-world legitimating discourse that a centralized computer-mediating moderating conferencing system be used and not just exchanges of electronic mail. This is so, not only because illegal statements can be kept from influencing judgments, but in order that a permanent time-stamped archive of all transactions can exist and be publicly accessible. It may also be important to hold frequent anonymous discussions, with the moderator system archiving those who actually made which inputs, in case a serious *post hoc* challenge arises (or in cases like that reported by Karl Zinn [personal communication] where some participants masquerade as others, and try to play the pathological game "let's you and him fight!").

That computer-mediated conferencing can function to support and promote liberative discourse has been demonstrated by David Stodolsky's experiments at Irvine (1976) and in Sweden (1986). However, many questions remain open concerning appropriate system configurations and protocols for educational life-world building.

There are other technologies such as video-playback (Ryan, 1974), which can be liberative and should be combined with computer-mediated conferencing when possible (Boyd and Jaworski, 1985).

Theory

The relevant theory for research on liberative educational computer-mediated conferencing has to be assembled from several sources. The whole system consists of participants (Paskian "p" individuals), personal interfaces, the communications network, the mediating and archiving host computer system, software, and protocols. Another way of characterizing and modelling it is by using Helmar Frank's six dimensions of the pedagogic space (Frank, 1969). These are:

1) *goal*—the learning objectives and meta-objectives agreed upon;
2) *content*—facts, skills, and their organization meshes;
3) *psychostructure*—the cognitive styles, schema and identity traits, entry level skills, etc. of participants;
4) *media*—the communications and control media and environment;
5) *sociostructure*—the grouping of "p" individual into coalitions, or dialog partners, or their separation as teacher, moderator, etc.; and
6) *procedure*—the algorithms, or heuristics, and rules of order, etc.

These dimensions are, in order, answers to the questions: (1) To what end? (2) What? (3) Who? (4) Through what? (5) With whom? (6) How? Answers to these questions in the form of both structures and processes are required to model any learning system. Habermas' desiderata for legitimating discourse largely fall within the sixth dimension *procedure,* but they implicate aspects of all the others. Pask's conversation theory mainly relates to the first three dimensions and a little with the sixth (Pask, 1976). To tie all of the above together into a probabilistic causal model, or at least a good heuristic model which can successfully promote understanding, is a big job. All I can do here is sketch how I think it might be done.

There is one more essential piece, which falls into Frank's third dimension *psychostructure,* and that is a model of the participant's higher level aspirations and fears insofar as they are relevant to participation in the system. In any real system it is necessary to live and work together with people in order to grasp aspirations and fears, before intervening—even then the intervention becomes a conjugation with the others also intervening in the teacher's own life world. If one cares for real education there must be *reciprocity* of communicative control.

The actual goals for any educational teleconference will depend on many situational factors and the goals of each

participant.   My conjectural model of the functioning of "p"
individuals is that at any given time a "p" individual
(participating entity—see Pask, 1982) can operate or interact at one
or more of three levels:

1) *Receptive-Acquisitive level* of merely attending to
    and capturing pattern-forms and adding some of
    them to one's active schema;

2) *Transmissive level* functioning as a conduit by
    repeating received forms (e.g., memes) and
    outputting them or imposing them upon any thing, or
    anybody—any other "p" individual who seems
    likely to pay attention; and

3) *Conjugative-Propagative level* where the "p" in-
    dividual connects part of its own core identity form to
    some transmissible symbolic "child" meme in such
    a way that some further "p" individuals are likely to
    take up the form, and connect parts of their identities
    to it, and "pass-it-on" indefinitely.

In short, each player at each "play" can either: (1) accept or reject;
(2) just pass-it-on; or (3) conjugate some "self-pattern" with it and
pass the changeling on.

This is a very rudimentary model, but I think it captures
the most important communicative activities (actually there may
be a sort of continuum between these possibilities).   The above
seems to belong more to Frank's *procedural* dimension than to the
goal dimension; they are closely linked.   As I see it, human
beings have a wired-in "ought-that-is" or highest-level imperative
to propagate portions of their identity.   One might call them
"identi-memes," or even "soul-memes."   This instinctual
imperative is satisfied when I see some aspect of my own way of
doing things being performed by others. That is the goal of the
game. The highest payoff is to see such propagation when it has the
appearance of being able to go on forever.   The next best pay-off is
to have someone copy something that you have taught them, even if
it doesn't carry your own characteristic style.

Those are the desirable goals of the game in this model.
They have their converse: at Level 1 a negative payoff occurs
when one accepts and keeps "garbage-forms" which are no use for

helping make new messages; at Level 2 of operation one may be infected by and propagate parasitic memes which one doesn't own at all, but which use up one's attention time and communicative opportunities; at Level 3 one may be infected by a virulent parasitic meme which does couple to one's identity so that one is now a gambler, or an alcoholic, or some other kind of self-destructive contagious addict (pay-off minus infinity) (see Hofstadter [1985] for examples).

At the procedure level and also at the goal level it seems to be necessary to have a mediating variable, which is used to help allocate resources. This is "status" or reputation (or in life off-line it may be money). In particular I have argued (Boyd, 1977) that relevant-credibility status is the most important moderator variable in knowledge development games. Normally, status increases if high-status persons pay attention to your transmissions, and that in turn draws the attention of others. A deviation-amplifying feedback loop exists so that those whose status starts to increase tend to get propelled to the top, while those who are initially ignored lose heart, do less, get fed less, get less support, and eventually drop out. Elaine McCreary's recent results (1987) tend to indicate a much more complicated role for status. There is also the difficulty that status in the computer-mediated conference may not correlate directly with status otherwise assigned.

This issue of status in the conference brings one back to Habermas (1984); for a message to be properly received and for the sender to be accorded full-participant status four essential conditions must be met: (1) truth of factual propositions; (2) rightness of collective norm assertion; (3) truthfulness of commitment; and (4) honesty of expressive parts of a communication. Failing on any of these weakens both the validity of the message, and the credibility status of the sender. These conditions seem to hold for any communicative act which is intended to promote *understanding* first and foremost. "Understanding" is knowledge that has an open-ended, on-going or heuristic property. This is defined in opposition to mere "instrumental" knowledge that only allows one to extrapolate, or interpolate correctly, but has no leading-on quality (an operational test for understanding is whether the learner can *extend* the concept in an interesting and *valid* way).

The above is a gross over-simplification of the process of life-world building through message exchange, but I think it has the essential entities, goals and procedures. Therefore, it should be possible to use it to understand computer-mediated conferencing and to situate research work, most of which lies ahead of us, notwithstanding the nice work of others in The *Canadian Journal of Educational Communication, 16*(2), and of still others like Hiltz, Johnson and Turoff (1986) and Stefik, Foster, Bobrow, Kahn, Lannry and Suchman (1987).

Envoi

The foregoing may have given the impression that rational discourse for positing and criticizing validity claims lies at the heart of educational practise; it does, if the education has an emancipative meta-objective. But it is not all that lies at the heart of education. If we go back to Alfred North Whitehead's (1955) characterization of learning as a three phased cyclic process with an initial phase of *romance,* followed by a phase of *precision* and completed by the *generalization* phase, then it would seem that text-based computer-mediated conferencing (notwithstanding Ferrarini, 1984) is best suited as the vehicle for the latter two phases.

It is fairly easy to see how precision, the clear definition of one's thoughts and procedures, can be facilitated by interaction via computer, and even clearer how multiple dialogues can aid with generalizations. Perhaps the *romance phase* needs solitude or museums, theatres and wilderness parks. It is more directly appropriate to employ aesthetic techniques (Boyd, 1984) to support the *romance phase,* and possibly also ritual (See the chapter on Mary Douglas in Wuthrow, Bergesen, & Kurzweil, 1984). Habermas' ideal discourse desiderata are to life-world construction what Karl Popper's *Conjectures and Refutations* desiderata are to doing science; necessary but not sufficient. What is left out in both cases is both the creative imaginative synthesis which enlarges our cultural worlds, and also the ritual observances through which we re-enact our affiliation with these worlds, through which we re-create our collective identities.

REFERENCES

Boyd, G. M. (1977). Towards a formalization of educational cybernetics. In Rose, J. & Biliciu, C. (Eds.), *Modern trends in cybernetics and systems, Vol. III* (pp. 15-21). New York, NY: Springer.

Boyd, G. M. (1984). Cybernetic aesthetics. In Trappl, R. (Ed.), *Cybernetics and systems research 2* (pp. 677-682). Amsterdam: North Holland.

Boyd, G. M. & Jaworski, W. M. (1985). *PALS, PATHS, PLACES, and PRODUCERS: Four more appropriate forms of computer aided education.* In *IEEE/ACM, Proceedings of COMPINT85* (pp. 614-616). Washington, DC: IEEE.

Dawkins, R. (1982). *The extended phenotype.* Oxford: Oxford University Press.

Ferrarini, E. M. (1984). *Confessions of an infomaniac.* Berkeley: Sybex Computer Books.

Frank, H. (1969). *Kybernetische grundlagen der padagogik.* Baden Baden: Agis Verlag.

Habermas, J. (1975). *Legitimation crisis* (T. McCarthy, Trans.). Boston, MA: Beacon Press. (Original work published 1973).

Habermas, J. (1984). *The theory of communicative action* (T. McCarthy, Trans.). Boston, MA: Beacon Press. (Original work published 1981).

Hiltz, R. S., Johnson, K., & Turoff, M. (1986). Experiments in group decision making. *Human Communication Research, 13*(2), 225-25.

Hofstadter, D. R. (1985). *Metamagical themas.* New York, NY: Basic Books.

McCreary, E. K., & Van Duren, J. (1987). Educational applications of computer conferencing. *Canadian Journal of Educational Communication, 16*(2), 107-115.

Pask, G. (1976). *Conversation theory.* Amsterdam: Elsevier.

Pask, G. (1984). The architecture of knowledge and the knowledge of architecture. In Trappl, R. (Ed.), *Cybernetics and systems research 2* (pp. 641-645). Amsterdam: Elsevier.

Ryan, P. (1974). *Cybernetics of the sacred.* New York, NY: Doubleday.

Stefik, M., Foster, G., Bobrow, D. G., Kahn, K., Lannry, S., & Suchman, L. (1987). Beyond the chalkboard: Computer support for collaboration and problem-solving in meetings. *Communications of the ACM, 30*(1), 32-47.

Stodolsky, D. (1976). *Machine mediated group problem solving.* Unpublished doctoral dissertation, University of California, Irvine, CA.

Stodolsky, D. (1987, May). *Computer-based support of rational debates.* Paper presented at the meeting of the IFIP 8.2 Conference on Information Systems, Atlanta, GA.

Whitehead, A. N. (1955). *The aims of education.* London: William and Norgate.

Wuthrow, R., Bergesen, J. D., & Kurzweil, E. (1984). *Cultural analysis.* London: Routledge.

6

Instructional Development as an Art:

One of the Three Faces of ID*

Ivor K. Davies,
Instructional Systems Design
Indiana University

Effectiveness, not efficiency, converts action into results.

Some years ago Francis Crick, who shared the Nobel prize for work on DNA, was at a dinner party in New York. During the course of the meal, his neighbor asked him why so few people made really significant contributions to knowledge. Professor Crick thought for a few moments, and—playing for time—said there were many reasons.

Sometimes, he explained, the necessary resources were not available; sometimes, people were in the right place at the wrong time. A key piece of information was lacking, or methodology had not been developed. Rarely, he went on, was the failure due to the absence of the necessary facts. Usually, they were there all the time. Then, pausing, he said that on reflection he thought that the reason so few people made important contributions was that they were not aware of the assumptions that they were making.

---

*Reprinted with permission from *Performance & Instruction*, Vol. 20(7), copyright © National Society for Performance and Instruction, 1981.

The Nature of Instructional Development

So it is with instructional development. All developers make assumptions in the course of their work. Often the assumptions are made unconsciously and unthinkingly. Rarely are assumptions questioned. Yet out of every assumption flows a set of consequences. These serve to limit not only what is seen and done, but also what can be achieved. Nowhere is this more apparent than in some of the current views of the nature of instructional development itself. It is a truism to say that instructional development represents the application of behavioral science to the problems of instruction. Like all definitions, the statement is fine as far as it goes. Unfortunately, it does not go far enough. The definition has a certain clinical charm about it, but it hardly seems revolutionary in its orientation.

Instruction has always been set with problems, and education and training are rich in ways of dealing with most of them. The idea that there is a new one best way, based upon science, seems to argue a certain pride of spirit that is obviously out of place. Art and craft run deep in the very idea of instruction, just as much as they are basic to the strategies and tactics of training and education.

There is no one best way of developing instruction. If there is no one best recipe for making tomato soup, it is absurd to argue that there is a best way of teaching someone to acquire worthy performance (see Gilbert, 1978). Science will most likely contribute, but so will art and craft. Imagination, creativity, cunning and human wit all have their place, as do hard work, rigor, disappointment and ceaseless questioning of results.

Towards a Theory of Human Performance

Education and training, by their very nature, contribute to human performance. Industry, government, military and business employ people to perform particular tasks, each with its own duties and responsibilities. Schools, colleges and universities, similarly, prepare people for living and being by initiating them into worthwhile activities (see Peters, 1974).

Anything that can be done to help people acquire desired performance, or to improve upon it, is an important matter. In this way, not only will competence be obtained, but also morale and satisfaction with the matter in hand. Not only will productivity be improved, but also safety and protection of the environment. The overall quality of human performance, in other words, is key in both education and training programs. Eroding human performance of all kinds, however, is error or faulty judgment.

Published data indicate that almost 50 percent of all interruptions that directly affect industrial production are due to failings in human performance. It has been calculated that the cost of training in the hotel and restaurant business can be recouped ten times over from the resulting reduction in inefficiencies. Similarly, the discouragement and overwhelming feelings of incompetence that can occur when all learners (children, students and trainees) fall into error offers similar evidence of the enormity of the problem. Not only are resources wasted and opportunities lost, but human potential is short-changed.

Instructional development offers something much more than a set of procedures for solving the problems of instruction. Instructional development is intimately concerned with worthy performance. It offers an opportunity of setting up conditions so as to:

significantly reduce the probabilities of error both in the acquisition and execution of human performance.

Since errors can arise from the way that tasks are designed, as much as from deficiencies in knowledge, skill and attitudes, instructional development involves much more than lesson planning or module design (Davies, 1981). Tasks can be fitted to people just as people can be fitted to tasks.

Such a view of instructional development places it in a central role as far as human reliability is concerned. The overall aim is the availability of performance, not just the solution of problems after they have occurred. ID represents a striving for excellence through enhanced opportunities, by eliminating the need for unnecessary work and resources. When viewed from such a perspective, instructional development has both a strong analytical and synthesis role, as well as a reflective and evaluative one. Prevention, however, is more highly prized than cure.

The Three Faces of Instructional Development

Significantly reducing the probabilities of human error is a demanding goal. As such, art, craft, and science all have a role to play in the strategies and tactics of instructional development. There are many ways to go, and developers have to make decisions on the issue of appropriateness at every turn. Inevitably, effective instructional development involves a subtle and sensitive blend of all three according to the needs of the task and the people involved in that task.

Admitting the role of art, craft, and science in instructional development, however, is not the same as suggesting that ID, itself, is a craft or science. Indeed, instructional development is very definitely an art. There have been, however, many attempts to make it a craft, while arguing that it is a science. It is ironic that when developers highlight the design, development, implementation and evaluation stages—in the belief that these somehow confer the status of scientific endeavor— they are, in fact, reinforcing the craft side of what is essentially a creative act of inquiry.

Attempts to make instructional development a craft or a science have supplied in the first case a heuristic, and in the latter case a recipe or algorithm, that has largely failed to realize the potential of ID. To a certain extent, the problem arises from a misunderstanding of the nature of art, craft, and science. Over- valuing the concept of science has also played its part. So has the equation of science with technology. A final difficulty has also arisen, as we have just seen, through confusing art, science and craft in instructional development with instructional development itself.

Art and craft are often confused. They are usually seen as somewhat similar, the one shading into the other. Science, on the other hand, is perceived as an entirely different process, probably because of its strong empirical basis. The distinctions, however, in reality are much more subtle than they appear. It is easier to distinguish between art and craft. It is much more difficult to distinguish between either art and science, or craft and science. The values of one are to be found in the other.

Values are essentially a human affair. Indeed, the achievements of truth, honesty, and originality, as well as tolerance, flexibility, and independence, are ranked amongst the greatest of human accomplishments. Not only are these accomplishments the values of civilized people, they are also the values of art and science.

Jacob Bronowski (1977) put the point nicely in his essay *A Sense of the Future* when he wrote:

To listen to everyone; to silence no one; to honour and
promote those who are right—these have given science
its power in our world and its humanity . . . Science
has filled our world because it has been tolerant and
flexible and endlessly open to new ideas.

Science, like art, cannot be value free. Art and science, as processes, are not neutral. While the products of art and science should describe rather than exhort, the processes involved must necessarily reflect a concern for truth, tolerance, originality, and flexibility.

The aesthetic nuance attaching to the word "art" is of recent origin. From ancient times to the seventeenth century, art meant but one thing. It implied a specialized skill or craft, like the craft of printing or the craft of tanning. Poetry, music, instruction were also seen as crafts. They differed from each other in much the same way as the craft of carpentry differed from the craft of surgery. The art, in all cases, came from the learning that was involved, not from the practice.

Modern distinctions between art and craft have particular meaning for instructional development. Far from being of only academic interest, the difference defines the field of ID. The distinction has meaning not only in terms of its past accomplishments, but also in terms of its future ones. In defining one, the other is illuminated.

Basic Characteristics of Art and Craft. The distinctions between art and craft Collingwood (1938) argues in his now classic *The Principles of Art* are best seen from the perspective of certain key characteristics. These include:

- Distinctions between means and ends.
- Distinctions between planning and implementation.
- Distinctions between raw material and the finished product.
- Distinctions between form and matter.

In essence, if the distinctions are maintained in an activity, Collingwood argues that a craft is involved. If the distinctions are largely absent, blur, or coexist one with the other, then an art is at work. What is important is what is done, not what is said.

Although Collingwood did not have instructional development in mind when he drew the four distinctions, his work has considerable meaning for ID. Indeed, the very terms used carry over into the field, for the literature of ID is replete with discussions of ends and means, planning and implementation. Getting one's objectives clear before any other activity is undertaken has, in fact, become a caricature of instructional development. Fortunately, the nostrum is more advised than practiced. As in most human affairs, there is a healthy gap between what people say and what people do.

Ends involve the goals or objectives to be achieved. Means involve the things that have to be done in order to achieve them. The relationship between part and whole is very similar. A part represents a tactic for realizing some desired outcome. In instructional development the distinction between means and ends is an important one, and represents the essence of the systematic approach towards improving instruction (Davies, 1976).

An alternative is first to identify the means or resources available, and, only then, to define the ends that realistically can be achieved. In other words, to look around at what you have to hand, and then to decide on what is possible—within the limited resources at your command. Such an approach, of course, is expedient. It recognizes that constraints are usually present in the real world, and are better recognized rather than ignored.

While a systematic approach to planning is idealistic, an expedient one is politic. A third option, however, exists, which is both realistic and prudent. In this approach the means are seen as existing within the ends. Rather than defining first one then the other, ends and means are seen as heads and tails of the same situation. The one defines the other.

Such a view of planning involves a piecemeal approach. When no master plan or blueprint is available, successive approximations to some desired state are essential. First, one gets a rough idea of what is needed, and then looks around at what resources are to hand. Once this has been done, the ends can be redefined. Additional resources might then become available as the project begins to take shape, so that the objectives can again be sharpened. And so it goes on. Art, not craft, is involved. For, as a result of the recycling, ideas change, coalesce, and develop. When the ends pre-exist in the means creativity is possible. When the ends exist outside the means, the one can become a straightjacket for the other.

Planning involves foreknowledge. It is concerned with anticipatory decision making. It involves deciding, after due consideration, the nature of the relationship between the ends to be accomplished and the means available. Implementation, on the other hand, involves executing the plan once it has been made, and the resources are available.

Planning in instructional development is often viewed as a discrete activity separate from implementation. Both activities typically occupy separate boxes in the PERT networks usually used to represent the development process. Such separation highlights the attempts that have been made to craft out of ID, as part of the overriding need for efficiency at the expense of effectiveness. In a craft, planning is separated from implementation; in an art, the separation does not necessarily occur. Planning can be separated from implementation in the art of instructional development, but usually they go on together. The one feeds and sustains the other.

A final product is directly related to a desired end. It represents, in a craft, the successful implementation of a plan. In order to obtain such a product, certain raw materials have had to be used in a particular manner. Maintaining such a distinction in instructional development, however, has little meaning. Words,

ideas and feelings hardly form the raw material of ID.
Something much more is involved, and involved in a unique and
creative way. Instructional developers don't make products, they
create experiences likely to lead to worthy performance.

In drawing the distinction between form and matter,
matter refers to what is common to both the raw materials and the
finished product. The same content can be found in both the raw
and the finished state. Only the form has been changed. As such,
it is to be found in the design, organization, variety, structure and
rhythm of the end result. Such a distinction, like the one between
materials and product, has little meaning in the context of
instructional development. The distinction, however, is essential
if it is to be maintained that ID is a craft rather than an art.
Exercising craft changes form. Exercising art creates, rather
than transforms. There is no magic.

The Role of Technique or Method. Technique implies
some mechanical skill. As such, it is important to any craft.
There are important specialized skills, often science based, which
are essential if mastery is to be obtained. Technique can make a
craftsperson, but not an artist. In instructional development as an
art, people can work effectively even though their technique is
flawed. Technique married to the art, however, can produce an
outstanding result.

Knowing how to write objectives, select media, choose
appropriate learning experiences, select content, organize and
integrate these, and then evaluate the end results are essential
things to know and do. They guarantee the craft, however, but not
the art of instructional development. In the art, there is a certain
spontaneity. Certain emotions and attitudes demand release,
certain ideas demand realization. What has to be done becomes
clearer, and takes shape, as the development proceeds. Technique
is not identified with the art of instructional development, but is
used in the service of that art.

When instructional development is viewed as a craft,
learners are cast in the role of consumers or users. Although they
are hopefully borne in mind during the whole process of
development, they usually have little or no share in the process as
a whole. When students and trainers become collaborators in the

process of instructional development, the art takes over and becomes paramount.

The experience of the learner should not be a by-product of the development experience. Instead, it should be an integral part of it. This is why the skills or techniques of instructional development should be taught to students and trainees. Needs analysis, defining objectives, task analysis, audience analysis, evaluation, etc., are significant skills. Indeed, mastery of such skills will enhance performance, whether at home or work. They represent valuable everyday skills for living, and so need to be communicated to everyone.

Instructional Development as an Art

All too often, instructional development is represented by a diagram in which boxes and arrows predominate. The process is seen as a series of steps or activities carried out in some predetermined sequence. Such a systematic set of procedures captures the craft of instructional development, but not the art. As a portrayal of the techniques involved, and perhaps of the sequencing of the techniques, such diagrams are inadequate, but serve a purpose.

It is much easier to talk to the uninitiated about ends and means separately, than to describe them co-existing one within the other. It is simpler to distinguish planning from execution, raw materials from finished product, and form from matter than to portray them as a whole or "system."

The two words systematic and systemic are often used interchangeably in instructional development. Yet, there is a very important difference between them. Not only do they come from different roots (the one Latin with the nuance of order or interval, the other Greek with the meaning of organized whole), but they imply different orientations. Systematic emphasizes craft; systemic emphasizes art. Indeed, the phrase "systems thinking" is rich in meaning, within the context of the art of instructional development.

When instructional development is viewed as art, two concerns become paramount. They revolve around two questions, both of which emphasize and reinforce each other. The concerns are:

- How can instructional development as a concept be
  communicated?
- What dimensions of knowing does it recognize?

     The answers to these two questions each contain within themselves the principle of instructional development's integrity.

     Instructional Development Is Not Itself a Process. As the literature of instructional development makes clear, ID is not a concept that is near the ground. It is not an easy thing to describe or explain, without someone exclaiming that it all sounds rather like common sense. The simpler it is made, the more obvious the concept becomes; the more complex it is made, the more bewildering it becomes. Instructional development is not a concept like mechanics, it is more like liberty to which, in fact, it is related.

     As an art, instructional development refers to no particular process. Needs analysis, learner analysis, task analysis and all the rest are techniques or processes within instructional development. They don't define ID. Instructional development refers not to a process. Instead, instructional development as an art:

     encapsulates criteria to which each one of the processes
     must contribute and the final product must conform in
     some meaningful way.

     Instructional development has certain standards to maintain. There is an expectation that they will be achieved in each development project.

     Although projects vary, the criteria are unchanging and demanding. They ask, both in terms of the short-term as well as long-term, a series of questions. These include:

- Are the end results (sensitivities, values, attitudes, skills, knowledge) worthwhile? The experience should be relevant, and capable of justification.
- Have the understandings, attitudes and skills essential to mastery been acquired? Knack, simple technique, and basic knowledge are insufficient to worthy performance.

- Have the learnings been integrated into people's lives, so that reliable performance is achieved? Learners should actively portray the standards, skills and thoughts.
- Has the experience been a motivating and joyous one for everyone taking part? Learners and developers should both feel a sense of achievement, and personal involvement.

Instructional development can be correct and sterile, cold and clinical. It can also be relevant and exciting, warm and imaginative. ID should result in a total experience demanding expression, reflection and spontaneity from everyone. Art creates experiences, it does not make them.

Dimensions of Knowing. "The goal of art," says Aristotle, "is to suggest the hidden meaning of things and not their appearance. This profound truth contains the true reality of things not conveyed by their appearance" (see Chiari, 1977). Art in other words is concerned less with appearance, and more with meaning. Instructional development, too, has similar concerns, and the quality of experience is a matter of deep concern for developers and learners alike.

In his essay "A Defense of Poetry," Shelley (1821) distinguishes two ways of thinking—reason and imagination. Reason, he argues, involves thinking about the relationship between one thought and another. Imagination, on the other hand, involves the "mind acting upon those thoughts so as to colour them with its own light, and composing from them . . . other thoughts." Put more directly, reason involves the still greater skill of synthesis. Reason respects differences, and imagination similarities.

A similar distinction has been drawn by De Quincy (1848). Discussions of the same point will be found in Polanyi (1958 and 1967), and Davies (1976 and 1981). In effect, it is possible to distinguish between two broad classes of knowing:

- *An explicit dimension whose:*
  - Objective is knowledge;
  - Strategy is clarity or good communication;
  - Function is to teach; and

- • Skills are cognitive and motor.
- • *A tacit dimension whose:*
  - • Objective is understanding heart;
  - • Strategy is to go beyond words;
  - • Function is to move; and
  - • Skills are values, emotions and attitudes.

The explicit dimension yields knowledge. The tacit one yields power, with all its rich connotations of influence, energy and mercy. Explicitness is a rudder for knowing; tacitness an oar or sail (De Quincy, 1848).

The distinction between explicit and tacit dimensions is critical for instructional development. Replication and clarity are highly valued in ID as a craft and science.

Interpretation and an ability to go beyond what is known (to know more than can be said), however, lie at the very heart of what instructional development is able to achieve. Clarity is certainly important, but so is abstraction. Discipline and habit are essential, but so are contrary imaginings and creativity. Only instructional development, perceived as an art, is capable of realizing the potential of the two dimensions in their richest and fullest form.

Conclusion

Art, craft and science can and do exist in instructional development. As a contribution towards preventing and solving the problems of human performance, however, instructional development is more art than craft and science. As an art, it is characterized by a perspective in which the ends largely pre-exist in the means. Similarly, implementation pre-exists in the planning; the finished product in the raw material; and matter in the form. The parts are indispensable to the whole.

Instructional development is not a process. Its integrity cannot be captured by a family of techniques or activities. Rather, ID enshrines a set of criteria to which the activities and final products must conform. The end results of development must be worthwhile, relevant and capable of justification. More than knack and basic technique should be achieved. Learnings should be internalized, and the experience a joyous one for developers and learners alike.   Only if these four criteria are met will mastery have meaning, and even more important, integrity.

Effectiveness and competence are the name of the game. Developers, with teachers and instructors, are a bridge between experience and inexperience. As a bridge, they serve learners on the one hand, and society or an organization on the other. In this sense, instructional development is orientated more to the future than to the past. It is concerned with human reliability. Such an orientation is both challenging and humbling. Change, through rich experiences, is the essence of the art. But behind all of it, despite the impression of un-labored force, is a great deal of dedication and hard work. *Labore et ingenio,* by work and by wit, is a motto for instructional developers for all seasons.

REFERENCES

Bronowski, J. (1977). *A sense of the future.*   Cambridge, MA: MIT Press.

Chiara, J. (1977). *Art and knowledge.* London: Paul Elek.

Collingwood, R. G. (1938). *The principles of art.* Oxford: The Clarendon Press.

Davies, I. K. (1972). *Competency based learning: Technology, management and design.* New York: McGraw-Hill.

Davies, I. K. (1976). *The organization of training.* London & New York: McGraw-Hill.

Davies, I. K. *Objectives in curriculum design.* London & New York: McGraw-Hill, 1976.

Davies, I. K. (1981). *Instructional technique.* New York: McGraw-Hill.

De Quincy, T. (1848). *An essay on Pope. The collected works.* D. Masson (ed.). London: Black.

Gilbert, T. F. (1978). *Human competence: Engineering worthy performance.* New York: McGraw-Hill.

Kaiser, C. H. (1952). *An essay on method.* New Brunswick, NJ.

Lerner, D. (1963). On parts and wholes. In D. Lerner (ed.). *Parts and wholes.* New York: Free Press.

Peters, R. S. (1974). *Ethics in education.* London: George Allen.

Polanyi, M. (1958). *Personal knowledge*. New York: Harper &
 Row.
Polanyi, M. (1967). *The tacit dimension*. New York: Doubleday.
Shelley, P. B. (1821). *In defense of poetry*. Complete works. R.
 Ingpen & W. E. Peck (eds.). New York: Scribner.
Whitehead, A. N. (1938). *Modes of thought*. New York:
 Macmillan.

7

Educational Technology as Metaphor*

Denis Hlynka and Barbara Nelson
Educational Technology/Curriculum Theory
University of Manitoba

"A world ends when its metaphor has died."
(Archibald MacLeish)

"We so love work we make it a creative thing,
Love music, too, that moves our very hearts.
Man's happiness is formed of two equated wings:
  The grapes and roses, use and beauty—both are arts."
(Maxim Rylsky)

"Even if the sockets were to be filled in and the secret of electricity lost forever, we should still need educational technology."
(Derek Rowntree)

Introduction: A Tale of Two Metaphors

The concept "educational technology" is at once rich, multifaceted and ambiguous. It is rich in that it encompasses many aspects of teaching and learning; it is multifaceted in that there is more than one possible stipulative meaning of the concept; and it is ambiguous in its lack of a precise definition. This paper will explore educational technology as metaphor, that is, in terms of implicit structures which help to define its nature. In so doing,

---

*Reprinted with permission from *Programmed Learning and Educational Technology*, 22(1), copyright © Kogan Page Ltd., 1985.

we shall examine the ways in which we order our thoughts, and express the meanings which direct our educational activities. The metaphor is a way to give substance to thoughts and feelings, and to share insights about ourselves and our world.

The field of educational technology has been concerned about the "practical" in education, trying to provide methods and materials to engage people in educational experiences. In this role, it has suffered from a lack of a coherent conceptual framework.

As we write this, in front of us are two metaphorical examples of educational technology. The first is provided by a pamphlet entitled "What is an IDI?" (National Special Media Institute, no date); the second is within the table of contents of a book entitled *Preparing Educational Materials* (Harris, 1979).

The pamphlet is an advertisement for an instructional development workshop. The content of the workshop is summarized by a visual which identifies the basic steps of a typical model of instructional development, based on a define-develop-evaluate paradigm (see Figure 1). What is significant is the visual metaphor which accompanies the nine steps of the model. The metaphor is, quite obviously, an engineering or systematic metaphor. Two key questions are raised at this point:

What assumptions are imposed by looking at instructional development in this way?

How does the engineering metaphor structure our thinking about the nature of educational technology?

Our second metaphor is found within the table of contents of *Preparing Educational Materials*. In particular, the titles of the four concluding chapters use a musical metaphor:

Chapter 9:   The management of learning—the performer
Chapter 10: The management of learning—the conductor
Chapter 11: The management of learning—the composer
Chapter 12: The management of learning—the critic

The questions posed earlier may be repeated. What assumptions are imposed by looking at educational technology in this way?

Figure 1. The engineering metaphor applied to educational technology

And how does the music metaphor structure our thinking about the nature of educational technology?

More will be said about these examples later. For the assumption to be tested is precisely that educational technology is indeed an art form, a practical art, and very susceptible to the device of metaphor.

But, in order to pursue those claims further, it is necessary to digress somewhat and to explore first the nature of metaphor itself. A metaphor, by schoolbook definition, is a particular comparison which omits the use of the words "like" or "as." While the schoolbook typically stops at about that point, art on the other hand takes over. Thus a metaphor is an implicit or implied comparison. But, because of its implied nature, it conceals its nature and controls our thought both intuitively and subliminally. For example, an early metaphoric model of viewing human communication is known popularly as "the bucket theory." One person, the teacher or instructor, poured information from one mind (his own) to another (his student). But communication is more complex than that. Nevertheless, contemporary language is full of the bucket or container metaphor. Lakoff and Johnson (1980) list some dozen common expressions which, put together, provide powerful support for continued acceptance of the bucket metaphor. Some of their examples include:

It's hard to GET that idea ACROSS to him.

I GAVE you that idea.

It's difficult to PUT my ideas INTO words.

His words CARRY little meaning.

The idea is BURIED in the paragraph.

The meaning is IN the words.

You can't STUFF your ideas into a few lines.

And so on. The point is that metaphor is a powerful tool for constructing our thoughts. One may not believe that communication is like pouring water from a bucket, but we talk that way. And, as has been said so often: we shape our tools, and thereafter our tools shape us.

In a sense, metaphor is close to the device of analogy. Analogy explicitly moves our thinking from observed resemblances to inferred resemblances. Thus, if A has characteristics 1, 2, and 3, and B has characteristics 1, 2, and 3, then analogy allows us to suggest that since A and B are alike in those respects, they are probably alike in 4, 5, and 6. Metaphor, on the other hand, does not ask the question; it implicitly assumes such comparison.

Green (1971) suggests that the value of metaphor is twofold. First, he says, metaphors allow us to describe, explain and illustrate more clearly. In the example above, the bucket metaphor becomes clearer in the expression "I gave you that idea." Second, and more important, says Green, metaphor allows us to "carry over" from the familiar to the unfamiliar. Thus the appropriate metaphoric activity is to formulate statements which enable us to explore the unfamiliar. The construction of such a metaphor is called, appropriately, a constructive metaphor.

Metaphors may be dead or alive. Fowler (1965) distinguishes between the two, pointing out that a dead metaphor is one which has been used so often that "speaker and hearer have ceased to be aware that the words used are not literal." Thus "the sun rises" is a dead metaphor. Living metaphors are, according to Fowler, "offered and accepted with a consciousness of their nature as substitutes for their literal equivalents."

Gowin (1981b), deriving his thoughts on metaphor from Black, identifies three kinds of metaphor. A substitution metaphor is one which substitutes for some literal sense. At a different level is a comparison metaphor which does more than substitute, but provides an implied comparison. Third is the interaction metaphor, best described by Pratte (1981), in which "one context is deliberately replaced with two, the second functioning as the cognitive ground for considering the first." Thus, he continues, "two heretofore unrelated contexts are now collapsed into a single, larger field of perception, but whose specific distinctions are obscured by the interaction."

Pratte also makes an important distinction between metaphoric statements ("statements that may make some point clear or understood by way of illustration") and metaphoric models ("models constructed as ways of dismembering and picturing phenomena and presenting them via a simplification").

Since models are so predominant in educational technology (indeed in all of education), it is important to recognize their metaphoric nature. In particular, Belth (1977) notes that hard models are those like a road map which symbolize actual features of the real event; and soft models are those "in which there are symbols of purely theoretical or hypothetical or conceptual matters, of imagined characteristics of some event." Educational technology, it can be suggested, is replete with soft, not hard, models. If this is so, then it may well be inappropriate to test the model via empirical methods.

Finally, Gowin suggests, education requires a concentrated search for "telling metaphors," those metaphors which can tell about, or best represent the way education works. Educational technology, too, is in desperate need to discover its "telling metaphor," if such there be.

Educational Technology as Metaphor

Having considered some of the focuses of study, it is necessary to consider the thinking that directs different perspectives of educational technology and provides the conceptual goggles for the various approaches. Our goal is to find that "telling metaphor" which can encapsulate the important facets and the richness, but does not structure the meaning in a limiting manner. At the same time, we search for a "living" metaphor, one which is related to the times and is meaningful because it reveals and explains events which occur around us.

In the history of educational technology, there are a number of views that have "made sense" and provided the driving force that affects practice. A study of these metaphors used by educational technologists should reveal the principles by which they sort out their perceptions, and control and justify their actions. Thus, in the words of Embler (1966), "We do not use metaphor, so much as metaphors use us."

Most amenable for metaphoric analysis are the three categories explicated by Davies (1971, 1978, 1981) as Educational Technology One, Two and Three, or the tools approach, the systematic approach and the systemic approach. Sometimes Davies has expressed these more concretely as archetypes or root metaphors: a hardware metaphor, an engineering metaphor, and a chess metaphor. While it is unnecessary to recapitulate Davies' views in full here, a brief commentary is nevertheless in order.

The tools metaphor

In search of ways to meet the problems of education in the 1950s and 1960s, the industrial metaphor was one which carried much meaning for educators. The teacher needed good "tools" to do a good job. And the new "tools" of good teaching were the audio-visual media—film, radio, overhead projectors, and television. To think of educational technology as a tool requires examination of several underlying questions. Is a tool always to be used for a specific purpose? Does the tool make the job of teaching easier, faster, and more interesting to accomplish? Is, indeed, the medium the message? How is the learner perceived in this view of educational technology?

Educational technology as tool makes sense if teaching is thought of as crafting a product. By this metaphor, the teacher is perceived as a potter at the wheel, moulding and shaping the thinking of students. To improve upon the tools should obviously improve upon the product. Educational technology, not unexpectedly, began its search for better tools, then its elusive search for the ultimate tool, the master medium. Of course, like the Raintree, the master medium was only mythical.

It is interesting to speculate along a different line within the "tools metaphor." Is a tool, in fact, an instrument? The word instrument derives from "instruct," something which contributes to the accomplishment of a purpose. The "tool" meaning is still here, but a new meaning appears. A musical instrument is a tool of the arts. An instrument placed in the hands of a master violinist reveals not just notes, but qualities, feelings, expressions, and new kinds of meaning.

Thus a paradox arises. Educational technology as tool, in the first sense, is not the service of applied science. But when educational technology is considered as an instrument, then the purposes of both art and science are served. What then is educational technology? Is it an art, science, or craft?

The systematic/engineering metaphor

In the 1960s and 1970s, a growing faith in the relationship between increasing production and "the good life" expanded the focus of education from "better tools" to an organized plan for production, requiring minimal expenditure of time, labor, and materials. Good teaching was seen to be efficient teaching, using strategies to develop identified competencies in learners. The metaphor of engineering is more than a substitute; it implies a comparison between industry and education. This engineering metaphor implies many procedures which raise questions about its application to education. Is there a blueprint for educating? Which product, in human terms, is most desirable? Is there a profit? Who profits? Who controls? Is product control desirable? Is efficiency in education a prime goal? Those who can answer these questions positively will find themselves in the camp of the instructional engineers. On the other hand, those who react with some doubt belong elsewhere.

Educational technology as engineering is appealing in as much as educators are concerned about the vast expenditures in education, and the undetermined range of outcomes. To be able to plan for and manage the activities of a classroom with a "guaranteed product," even a "teacher proof" guaranteed product, is still a goal which has a certain appeal. But the system in many cases may become the heart of the process, rather than the learner. For many teachers, the engineering metaphor, with the acceptance of predetermined objectives and the carrying out of a series of activities to achieve those objectives, has become accepted as "the way" to teach. Paradoxically, to the extent that such a response is automatic, this approach becomes "lifeless," and indeed a dead metaphor.

The systemic metaphor

The above analysis raises the question of a need for metaphors which are interactive and alive, promoting creative thinking about the practice of educational technology. In chess, there is no one best strategy, no one best opening move, no one best procedure. Rather, a good game requires a holistic or systemic view. If the chess metaphor implies, however, "playing the game," then perhaps a music metaphor is more appropriate. The systematic metaphor of a musical performance (Harris, 1979) indeed makes us stop and think. Teaching is the orchestration of many simultaneous performances. Students do participate in the creation of the "music." A teacher does act like a conductor in choosing the "music," setting the tempo, and arranging the order of the pieces for performance. What is a developer of curriculum materials, other than one who sets out the order of performance and also makes interesting and stimulating "music"? And, a new key focus, who serves as the critic?

The music metaphor captures the perception of educational technology as a human enterprise, concerned with relationships between human beings. The goal is a holistic outcome, evidence as students become expressive human beings, creative thinkers, and compassionate citizens. This process is facilitated by a teacher with expert knowledge in a field of study, who is able to mesh content with teacher and with student in diverse daily practices which draw upon a firm set of underlying assumptions, intentions, and principles. The teacher must be able to "read the meanings" of students as they affect the system, if it is to be operated in a way that individuals may be liberated by their knowledge. This is in contrast with the applied science concept of a system which is well regulated by rules and routines, which is methodical and requires uniformity of behavior. There are some more questions about the assumptions of the metaphor. Who creates the system? Is the system in equilibrium? Can people transform the system? Do teachers and students share a common purpose?

Our position is that each of the three metaphors—tools, engineering, systemic—has its legitimate place in the practical day-to-day operation of education and educational technology. Indeed, educational technology should be considered through a "polyfocal conspectus," in which each of the three metaphors is constantly shifting. At one point, teachers as technologists function within the tools metaphor. At another time the same teachers may function systematically while, at a third point, the systemic, gestaltic, and aesthetic metaphor gains control.

In examining the value of the metaphors described, it is obvious that tools or instruments (the first metaphor) are important to the artist, the scientist and the practical professional. But those tools must be chosen and used well, in order to create the desirable outcome. That outcome may be assessed as "good" or "bad" by use of specific criteria. If those criteria are the tools of science, then we slide into the systematic, engineering metaphor. On the other hand, if those criteria are the methods of art criticism, we move into the systemic metaphor. The contemporary view of education would appear to be compatible with evaluation techniques and the accompanying engineering model, as opposed to criticism and its aesthetic implications. Evaluation, we suggest, is not in keeping with the spirit or meaning of the "systemic" metaphor. Of course, by this statement we use the word "evaluation" as it is most often used in systematic thinking, that is, in its most narrow sense, and in opposition to terms such as Eisner's "criticism" (1983) or Kosloff's "renderings" (1969). Educational criticism is only beginning to make inroads in the contemporary educational scene and is not yet an integral component of educational technology.

Conclusion

It has been the purpose of this paper to explore the metaphoric assumptions made when we talk about educational technology. It was suggested that some people think of educational technology in terms of tools and hardware. Others see educational technology as a systematic approach which, at its extreme position, might not even need "tools" at all. Our third quotation which prefaces this paper reflects that viewpoint. Others view educational technology systematically.

Our view is that all three serve equally, and validly. Unfortunately, the three metaphors of educational technology are in danger of dying, or of being dead metaphors through thoughtless application of institutionalized values. But they need not be dead. We want to believe that they are very much alive, and indeed it is in the synergistic combination of all three that one finds the telling metaphor of what educational technology is all about.

Is there a metaphor which can "tell on" the field of educational technology, invoke creative discussions and reflections on its meaning, and combine each of the three metaphors discussed in this paper? Such a metaphor might be found in the concept of design. A potter designing a beautiful vase expresses the values of art. He chooses instruments and tools, as well as his bare hands to mould the clay sensitively, and to push and pull on the material. The process is not haphazard, but carefully developed, nurtured, and perfected over years of experience. The material affects the artist, and the artist affects the material. The potter uses craft in his adaptation of methods. He bases his craft on art. He knows how his clay functions, based on laws of science, and he applies those laws, producing his artistic product via the best that his technology can offer him. Art, craft, science and technology are all present in a synergistic combination. All domains provide input and relevance.

And to those who say that educational technology is not a scientific field, not open to metaphoric and aesthetic analyses, we return full circle to Archibald MacLeish, who aptly reminds us that: "A world ends when its metaphor has died."

REFERENCES

Association for Educational Communications and Technology (1977). *Educational technology: Definition and glossary of terms.* Washington, DC.

Belth, M. (1977). *The process of thinking.* New York: David McKay.

Carnegie Commission on Higher Education (1972). *The fourth revolution: Instructional technology in higher education.* New York: McGraw-Hill.

Davies, I. (1971). *The management of learning.* London: McGraw-Hill.

Davies, I. (1978). Prologue: Educational technology: Archetypes, paradigms, and models. In Hartley, J. and Davies, I. (eds.) *Contributions to an educational technology.* London: Butterworths.

Davies, I. (1981) Instructional development as an art: One of the three faces of ID. *Performance and Instruction 20(7)*, 4-7.

Ebel, R. (ed.) (1969). *Encyclopedia of research in education (4th edition).* New York: Macmillan.

Eisner, E. (1983). Educational connoisseurship and criticism:
    Their form and functions in educational evaluation. In
    Maddaus, G. et al.(Eds.), *Evaluation models.* Boston:
    Kluwer-Nihjoff.
Embler, W. (1966). *Metaphor and meaning.* DeLand, Florida:
    Evrett/Edwards Inc.
Fowler, H. W. (1965). *A dictionary of modern English usage (2nd
    edition).* Oxford: Oxford University Press.
Gowin, D. B. (1981a). *Educating.* Ithaca: Cornell University
    Press.
Gowin, D. B. (1981b). "Criticising." Unpublished manuscript.
Green, Thomas (1971). *The activities of teaching.* New York:
    McGraw-Hill.
Greene, M. (1978). *Landscapes of learning.* Teachers College
    Press, Teachers College, New York: Columbia
    University.
Harris, C. (ed.) (1960). *Encyclopedia of research (3rd edition).*
    New York: Macmillan.
Harris, N. D. C. (1979). *Preparing educational materials.*
    London: Croom Helm.
Hlynka, D. (1982).   Towards a definition of educational
    technology.   *Canadian Journal of Educational
    Communication 11*(3), 2-4.
Hlynka, D. (1984). Defining educational technology. *New
    Technologies in Education in Canada: Issues and
    Concerns. New Technologies in Canadian Education.*
    Canadian Commission for UNESCO, TV Ontario,
    Toronto.
Hlynka, D. (1984). Educational technology: Art or science?
    Proceedings of the Conference of the Association of Media
    and Technology in Education in Canada Annual
    Conference, London, Ontario.
Kozloff, M. (1969). *Renderings.* New York: Simon and Schuster.
Kuhn, T. (1962). *The structure of scientific revolutions.* Chicago:
    The University of Chicago Press.
Lakoff, G. and Johnson, M. (1980). *Metaphors we live by.*
    Chicago: The University of Chicago Press.

Lockridge, R. (1948). *Raintree county*. Boston: Houghton Mifflin.

Mitzel, H. (ed.) (1982). *Encyclopedia of research in education (5th edition)*. New York: Macmillan.

Munroe, W. (ed.) (1941). *Encyclopedia of educational research (1st edition)*. New York: Macmillan.

National Special Media Institute's Project of the National Center for Educational Technology (no date). "What is an IDI?" US Office of Education.

Pratte, R. (1981). *Metaphorical models and curriculum theory*. In *Curriculum Inquiry*, 11, 4, 307-20.

Rowntree, D. (1974). *Educational technology in curriculum development*. London: Harper and Row.

Rylsky, M. (1980). *Maxim Rylsky: Selected poems*. Kiev: Dnipro Publishers.

Saettler, P. (1967). *A history of instructional technology*. New York: McGraw-Hill.

Schwab, J. (1971). The practical: Arts of the eclectic. *School Review 79*, 493-542.

Tickton, S. G. (ed.) (1970). *To improve learning*. New York: R. R. Bowker for Commission on Instructional Technology.

Toeffler, A. (1980). *The third wave*. New York: William Morrow.

8

Toward a Conscience: Negative Aspects of Educational Technology*

Randall G. Nichols
Educational Technology
University of Cincinnati

Abstract

General and educational technology are largely alike in their philosophic positions. And just as general technology has negative aspects so, too, does educational technology. This article explores negative aspects of educational technology in relation to philosophy, education and society.

General technology often is recognized as having decidedly negative outcomes. For example, holes in the earth's ozone and resultant skin cancers are associated with technologies that produce pollutants. Surely, if educational technology is a subset of general technology (Heinich, 1984, p. 67), then one must expect that educational technology also has negative consequences. This article explores ways in which educational and general technology share a common conceptual framework associated with negative results of those technologies. As well, I attempt to show that the framework itself has negative aspects.

The exploring is based on two premises. First, educational technology and technologists are of a philosophic nature, at least insofar as our beliefs about technology are based in empiricism and rationalism. Similarly, I submit that our beliefs also arise from beyond the empirical and rational, that is, from beyond consciousness. In other words, what we believe also is

---

*Reprinted with permission from the *Journal of Visual/Verbal Languaging*, 7(1), © 1987.

based on our intuition and tacit knowledge which may not necessarily be rational and empirical.

Let me add that I am aware of most of the positive potentials of educational technology. However, primarily because of my ethical sense, I have chosen to focus here on the negative possibilities. If educational technology has nearly the same negative aspects as technology in general, then I would be remiss in not exploring those aspects.

Philosophic Background

I believe it is from a brief look at a long history of philosophic concepts that we might best begin to characterize educational technology with respect to any negative aspects it might have.

Educational technologists and technology portray a mostly traditional Western philosophic stance. The stance has it origins in Greek thought. For Plato, knowledge of reality comes through rationalism, unaided inner reason. For Aristotle, knowledge also comes through empiricism, conclusions reached through information about the "outside" world. From Aristotle we begin to think in terms of cause and effect, and the world outside the mind begins to be the object of observation. However, both these Greeks remain largely metaphysical. That is, both believe that existence is of a nonmaterial essence that can be described in basic, unifying principles; the world of people and nature is whole.

Berman (1981) has shown that at the end of the Middle Ages, a drastic shift of thinking and belief begins. In *New Organon,* Bacon argues for a marriage of reason and empiricism in which data about nature should be manipulated and agitated to reveal truth. About the same time, Descartes, in *Discourse on Method,* expresses the belief that existence outside the mind is too unsure. He exists only to the degree that his mind can clearly and distinctly apply the Cartesian method. In time, Descartes' mathematics, so-called pure reason, becomes the instrument for Bacon's empiricism.

As Berman (1981) puts it:

Finally, atomism, quantifiability, and the deliberate act of viewing nature as an abstraction from which one can distance oneself—all open the possibility that Bacon proclaimed as the true goal of science: control.

> The Cartesian or technological paradigm is . . . the
> equation of truth with utility, with the purposive
> manipulation of the environment. The holistic view of
> man as part of nature, as being at home in the cosmos,
> is so much romantic claptrap. Not holism, but
> domination of nature; not the ageless rhythm of
> ecology, but the conscious management of the world . . .
> (p. 46).

As part of this conscious management, or "mental model,"
Archimedes, Copernicus, Kepler, Galileo, Newton and many
others develop formal conceptions of science and, in conjunction
with technology, extend the belief in the mental model. Galileo,
for instance, outlines the new science of mechanics, and invents
the concepts of perfectly frictionless surfaces and planes of
infinite extension. He rolls ball after ball down inclined planes
and begins developing the concept of inertia. To him it does not
matter that perfectly frictionless surfaces or infinite planes exist
only in his mind. The mental conception dominates.

In one view, the mental model and technology first emerge
so that people can explain their universe. They are tools for
humans. But they quickly become the explanations to which the
world conforms; they create a world view. As Kant said, reason
becomes "legislative of experience," or as Berman observes,
"Bacon leaves no doubt that he regards technology as the source of
a new epistemology" (Berman, 1981, p. 30). In another view, in
The Illusion of Technique, William Barrett states that technology
is simply the manifestation of this thinking: "Every technique is
put to use for some end, and this end is decided in the light of some
philosophic outlook. The technique cannot produce the philosophy
that directs it" (Barrett, 1979, p. 117). He might argue that
technology cannot legislate experience. Technology is the
manifestation of the mental model.

The correctness of one view or another is not the point at the
moment. It is that technology is very closely related to a belief in a
mentalistic conception, whereby the mind is encouraged to split
from the rest of existence, so that it can explain existence by
controlling it.

With the advent of technologies capable of mass
production, technologies such as movable type, interchangeable
parts, and the telegraph, the mental model of the world and

technology are able to predominate on a massive scale. There is a spiraling effect. Technology encourages the mental conception of existence, so the conception grows in pervasiveness. So technology grows, and so on.

Over time, and in conjunction with politics, social changes, economic views, and various forms of rational and empirical philosophies, what emerges, predominantly in the West, is the belief in a new reality in which knowledge, truth, and existence itself are more or less equivalent to logic, science, and technology. It is a belief in which existence is controlled for material gain, mind is believed to be separate from the rest of nature and even from aspects of itself and in which technology even may be the model by which we judge existence.

Negative Aspects of the Mental Model and Technology

Our attempts at controlling nature have led to some current and obvious threats to human existence. For instance, general technology is helping to create a degenerating earth environment of amazing proportions. Our technologies have enabled us to begin deforestation of the Amazon River Basin, which provides one third of the earth's oxygen.

Beyond ecology, the presence of the mental-technical belief and harmful effects associated with it are exhibited in two currently pervasive concepts: the technological fix and autonomous technology. The "technological fix" is the notion that technology is *the* answer to our problems, especially those problems caused by our technology. The technological fix, however, very often does not work as we expect. For example, two hundred years ago, flooding on the Mississippi River caused relatively few lives and livelihoods to be threatened. Early attempts at flood control on parts of the Mississippi created slightly greater flooding and human distress elsewhere along the river. More recently, large-scale technologies have been used to control nearly the entire length of the river. Consequently, changed hydrology and silting are causing New Orleans to sink. At the same time, the Mississippi flows more powerfully through its channel, and a dam above New Orleans is in constant danger of bursting because of erosion. If it bursts, millions of lives will be threatened, both from the deluge of water and from a wrecked economy across the United States and the world (WTTW and

BBC, 1986). The belief in technology and the power of the spiraling effects of it are obvious in the notion of a technological fix. The belief in the "fix" is so great that it can even be considered a fix in the sense of an addiction.

The second concept is related to Kant's notion that "reason becomes legislative of experience." It can be seen in the ironic way in which first humans create technological tools, then the tools "create" altered humans or altered human consciousness. People actually lose control when they use the mental model of existence and technology. This notice has been called "autonomous technology" (Ellul, 1964).

One of the clearest examples of loss of control may lie in the current notion of "lifelong education" in which people must continually learn new skills to order to keep up with technological innovations, in order to stay employed, so that economic institutions can stay on "the cutting edge." In effect, people are conforming to the requisites of the mental-technical model. This may be a profound and even cruel twist in human existence. Whereas technology is thought to serve people, people serve technology.

Instructional Technology and the Mental Model

The mental model exists clearly in many forms of educational technology. Examine Heinich's (1984) characterization of instructional technology, for example. Technology, he notes, is the systematic application of scientific and other organized knowledge to practical tasks. And it is the instrumental ordering of human experience within a logic of efficient means. Of further characteristics that fit instructional technology well, Heinich (1984) adds:

1. Replicability, with which the goal becomes mass production of necessities for all, and the control shifts from artisans to skilled designers and producers;
2. Reliability, where outcomes are predictable;
3. Algorithmic decision making, wherein technology is decision theory, and decision rules substitute for human judgment. (Bell describes this as the dream in which technologists seek reliable replication through "stochastic,

probabilistic, and deterministic methods" [Bell, 1973, pp. 52-53]);

4. Communication and Control, in which instruction is delivered any time, any place, to any one;

5. The Effect of Scale, wherein "sufficient quantitative change causes a qualitative change" (Heinich, 1984, p. 76).

These characteristics indicate that instructional technology is a mentalistic perspective of the world. Logic, science, and technology are used to try to control learning for material and practical purposes. Human learning is believed to be ultimately explainable and predictable via science and technology. The world of learning is that of mind over experience, including "qualitative" experience. And fueled by technology, we find the spiraling, where the belief and the educational technology feed one another and tend toward more and more dominance in education.

Negative Aspects of Educational Technology

As with general technology, the philosophic view associated with educational technology is related to various negative outcomes. I will now examine its negative aspects in educational research and in the meaning of an educated person.

First, our research, one form of the mental model, often leads to negative consequences. For instance, Clark and Salomon conclude that some symbolic features of media "may actually inhibit learning by preventing the use of previously acquired but more efficient skills that serve the same ends" (Clark & Salomon, 1986, p. 469). About this inhibition, they suggest that, "it should be remembered that Salomon's (Salomon, 1974a) research demonstrates that symbolic features of media *can be made* to cultivate cognitive effects . . . [but] the occurrence of cognitive effects depends on a number of factors including the effort invested, depth of processing, and special aptitudes of individual learners" (Clark & Salomon, 1986, p. 469). They recommend, in part, the application of more research techniques to address the effects of such factors. It is noteworthy that media may prevent the use of cognitive skills and inhibit learning and that media *can be made*, in effect, to do so. From my point of view, though, it is most important to suggest that the inhibition of learning and cognitive skills is more closely associated with a philosophic view. A belief in the mental model may lead unavoidably to a separation, or fragmentation, such that even cognitive aspects of humans are isolated from one another by research and, so, negatively affected. Therefore, applying the power and control of more science and technology is not likely to stop the inhibition of cognitive skills, but to exacerbate it.

Educational technology also runs contrary to some meanings of an educated person. A belief in and an ability to control nature and existence accompany educational technology. One result of the belief and power is that it tends to concentrate power within few people. Heinich acknowledges this, at least implicitly, when he says, "as technology becomes more powerful and more pervasive in effect, consideration of its use must be raised to higher and higher levels of decision making" (Heinich, 1984, p. 77). This kind of control exists especially in the instructional development process, where instructional means and methods are determined by a team of experts. Students do not typically choose the instructional strategies or media, and rarely do students decide if the goals and objectives meet their own, self-determined purposes. And learning is usually judged by everyone but the student.

Now, if education is construed as student willingness and voluntariness about means and ends (Peters, 1967), the higher and higher levels of decision making in much educational technology tend to discourage education. Therefore, the power and control afforded by educational technology can be called negative.

Negative Social Aspects of Educational Technology

If Taylor and Johnsen (1986) are correct about illiteracy in the face of the "technological momentum" prevalent in society, and if Heinich (1984) is correct about needing to look at general technology, and if the more overtly philosophic view presented here has merit, then any negative societal aspects of our technology must begin to be examined more assiduously.

The relationship between educational technology and society exists especially in that educational technologists very often *react* to social imperatives of various sorts, especially the imperative to buy hardware. Holloway (1984), argues that we adopt rather than adapt or create educational technology. I must wonder, therefore, how "witting and voluntary" educational technologists are about purchases. To the degree that our purchases are less a professionally conceived activity attending primarily to education, and more a social imperative connected to economic, political, or military gain, our buying hardware can be called negative.

Social entities, including education and educational technology, combine to form a complex web of interactions in which determining motives, responsibility, and the exact nature of the interactions is very difficult. We know, however, that technology and the people who use it have combined to put the world and its people in peril. Educational technologists and technology are, in some measure, culpable for this peril.

The Future

Of the many possible future forms of educational technology, one in particular leads me to believe that the future may be more perilous. I conceive of this form as educational biotechnology (EBT). EBT is the study and application of scientific and other organized knowledge, processes and products to the physical state of humans for the purpose of creating changes in learning. The key characteristic is physical invasion of the body, though psychological changes certainly occur also. Educational biotechnologies could consist of implanting microprocessors in people or giving food and drugs to people to change some aspect of their education. For example, Knirk and Gustafson (1986) report on the use of computers and EEGs and speculate that, "Perhaps in the future this could be monitored so that when a learner's attention begins to wander, a switch could be triggered and the student's attention brought back to instruction" (Knirk & Gustafson, 1986, p. 242).

With EBT, ethical issues glare. When the body is invaded for health purposes, technology *may* be ethical. But invasion for the purpose of creating an "educated" person might be called "cosmetic surgery." I would add that when biotechnologists get more whole-heartedly into education, the comparative achievements of educational technology will pale. Human physical manipulation for learning is probably more "reliable" than the psychological manipulation that underpins instructional design, for instance. And educational technologists' jobs may begin disappearing, or they may be reconfigured along biological lines.

Educational Technology and Freedom

Some of the literature in our field has attended, more or less explicitly, to philosophic aspects of educational technology, and selected examples of that literature bear mentioning.

James D. Finn, perhaps more than any other person, guided the profession of educational technology in the 1950s and 1960s, and for Finn, philosophizing was essential. Perhaps Finn's statement from "The Tradition in the Iron Mask" (1961) best indicates his beliefs about educational technology. In defending educational technology against attacks from the literati of the day, Finn wrote that:

"words alone and the literary sensibility will never solve our serious educational problems. They can help, but our culture is turning—must turn—to technology for this job. Thus, the demands on the audio-visual tradition are great. Realizing this, we certainly do not wish to turn people or schools into automatons and factories. Yet we must wield the technology we are developing to solve the problems of education" (Finn, 1961, pp. 238-243).

Finn's great belief in technology helped the field to move toward a professional status.

Charles Hoban also had a great influence on our field. In his last published piece (1977), Hoban warned that without serious consideration of educational technology and values, "unity of purpose in common concerns and broad educational philosophy will remain obscured in rushes of activity without significant action" (Hoban, 1977, p. 239). He deeply sensed that our field needed to consider the values we imply. I wonder if the "rushes of activity" referred to computers in education?

Mansfield and Nunan (1978) argue that educational technology represents an ideological position concerned with "knowledge production, transmission, and receival [*sic*], the basis of which is contained in a belief of the application of explicit and 'rational' processes to problems of human learning" (Mansfield & Nunan, 1978, p. 171). They suggest that the weaknesses in such an ideology include,

"the dangers of attempting to reduce all learning to
behaviors, the difficulties of achieving precise
specification, the unreliability of observation, the
distortion of knowledge, the repression of potentially valuable outcomes, the confusion between
education and training, the equation of education
with evaluation, excessive expenditure of time and
resources, and the impossibility of controlling all
system variables" (Mansfield & Nunan, 1978, p.
171).

They urge the inclusion of philosophy in our instructional
development process as a way of ameliorating the danger.

Jonassen (1984) presents a philosophic analysis and draws
conclusions about media and reality, feedback, and intellectual
liberation. He points out that, "Since experiencing the mediated
event is substantially different from direct experience of an event,
the resulting phenomena or conscious perceptions must be
substantively different. That is not necessarily bad. In fact, those
perceptions are increasingly favored" (Jonassen, 1984, p. 166). He
goes on to ask, rhetorically, what impact the standardized
experiences of mediation might have. These are the kinds of
questions I am addressing here, and I would counter that the
impact is bad. Mediating reality emphasizes the separation
between mind and the rest of existence.

Bork (1986) identifies ethical concerns such as piracy,
privacy, quality, and socialization, at least implying that each is
threatened by educational computing. As Bork says, though, there
appears to be little professional discussion about the ethics of
educational computing.

Taylor and Johnsen (1986) analyze educational
technology in light of its socio-economic, political, and somewhat
philosophical characteristics in order to "suggest that the swelling
momentum that attends the creation of a new technology in our
society in fact works to diminish the potential for human choice
and action" (Taylor & Johnsen, 1986, p. 38). In this very
thoughtful and original piece, the authors seriously examine the
possibility that our educational technology threatens freedom.

The preceding not withstanding, it seems to me that, on the
whole, educational technologists have taken a predominantly
narrow and uncritical view about the effects of our technology.

Some of us tend to focus only on media. Also, as Heinich (1984) says, "We have emulated science in our research for too long" (Heinich, 1984, p. 84). We are "obsessed" with learning gains. And quite naturally, we tend to focus only on the positive potentials of our technology.

The narrowness of our world view may be indicated by the theme issue of *ECTJ* (Kerr & Taylor, 1985) about social aspects of educational technology. In one article, for instance, Stewart (1985) discusses American educational technology and suggests that the cultural bias in that technology is contributing to "social dislocation" in developing countries. He gives us a conscientious and necessary description of negative societal aspects of our technology. However, he recommends primarily that we adjust our theory and research so that we simply add cultural considerations. In fact, most of the articles in the theme issue seem to argue for more science and technology. Evidently, it is difficult for us to consider that our belief in the mental model and technology may be fundamentally misguided and that more of the belief will only prompt more social dislocation.

The narrowness of our view is indicated also by the fact that of the 941 faculty who describe their primary interests in *Masters Curricula in Educational Communications and Technology: A Descriptive Directory* (Johnson, 1985), only five faculty are interested in social issues, and only two are interested in cultural issues. Further, as of October 1986, only 188 of 7242 ERIC documents (.025%) about educational philosophy addressed educational technology.

Freedom

We may ultimately view the foregoing issues as issues of freedom. As Barrett (1979) says with respect to technology, "The question of our generation . . . is whether or not mankind will decide for liberty or sink under some modern form of tyranny" (Barrett, 1979, p. 246). To the degree that our use of technology controls rather than frees student choices, and to the degree that students are illiterate about technology, as is indicated by The Carnegie Commission on Education (Boyer, 1983), educational technology may be construed as tyrannical. And to the extent that educational technologists do not deal with the sorts of issues I've raised, we may contribute to any tyranny.

Educational Technology Need Not Be Deterministic

Admittedly, I have taken a rather one-sided position: educational technology is really and potentially harmful. I have done this primarily because of an ethical sense. There comes a time when pointing almost wholly to the positive potentials of technology may be morally indefensible. But I do not think all is hopeless. Technology need not be deterministic. Alternatives are possible. For instance, Fosnot's (1984) constructivist view not only reminds us of our connections to philosophy, but encourages us to consider specifically the notion of controlling students. She concludes that, "If learning is understood as a series of constructions that depend on the learner's structures and schemes, then the educator must be willing to give up control and allow self-regulation to occur" (Fosnot, 1984, p. 203).

Ironically, there is hope also, because a few people in the scientific community at large have shifted their perspective about the purpose of science. Physicist Fritjof Capra (1982), for instance, urges working in harmony with nature and seeing that we must live *with* our world rather than controlling it and using it up. The most important question of our time may be whether or not scientists will develop fully such a perspective. Will educational technologists?

I am somewhat hopeful primarily because of my faith in the survivability of those human aspects that tend to be denied by educational technology, for no matter how we might try to ignore them, they are with us. In "The Question Concerning Technology," philosopher Martin Heidegger (1977) has said,

"It is precisely in this extreme danger that the innermost indestructible belongingness of man . . . may come to light, provided that we, for our part, begin to pay heed to the coming of presence of technology" (Heidegger, 1977, p. 32)

". . . Because the essence of technology is nothing technological, essential reflection upon technology and decisive confrontation with it must happen in a realm that is, on one hand, akin to the essence of technology and, on the other, fundamentally different from it" (Heidegger, 1977, p. 35).

He suggests that difference lies in something like art.

Recommendations

In preparing this chapter, I called the Association for Educational Communications and Technology (AECT) headquarters to ask if a written philosophy of our field exists. I was referred to the *Human Resource Directory* (1985), which states that AECT is dedicated to the development and use of technology and media; campaigns at state and federal levels for resources; provides a clearinghouse for ideas; and has members who pioneer in the use of technology for improved education and who recognize the "importance of the technological revolution in education and training" (1985, p. 3). We can glean from these statements the philosophy that pervades our profession, at least as one of our professional associations sees it. The zeal implied by the use of "revolution" may be particularly indicative of our beliefs about technology. But in an academic sense, it seems to me that this association does not have a well-stated philosophy. First, there is no extended analytical *statement* of a belief about the relation of technology to a meaningful and significant life. Secondly, there is no extended analytical discussion of the philosophical *processes* we employ. Accordingly, I recommend that we study and make explicit the current philosophy under which our research, theory, and practice operate. I recommend the same for a philosophy under which we *might* operate.

Though I have intended to show a need to investigate philosophic matters, I have not intended, necessarily, to offer a philosophic alternative. However, I suggest that a more purely mental-technical philosophy is not likely to suffice and that, instead, we could investigate relativism or constructivism more closely. Metaphysical and Eastern philosophies offer viable possibilities. Attention to Bateson's notion of Learning III (see Berman, 1981, for a discussion of this topic) could prove extremely valuable to us. Put most generally, I believe we need to find a way to bring together the conscious and unconscious in us before we destroy both.

Given the impending proliferation of educational bio-technology, I recommend that consideration of ethics be given highest priority. When biological and educational technologies meet as they can, the ethical questions are at least as dramatic as those currently seen in medicine. Beyond most conceptions of ethics in our field, which deal predominantly with *how* to insure privacy, ownership, or equality, we should be asking *if* our current conceptions of educational technology are ethical at all. Likewise, we should examine our ethics with respect to socio-ecological issues.

Our research might begin tracking negative aspects of educational technology just as the American government has done with the Office of Technology Assessment. We might have an Office of Educational Technology Assessment (OETA), though I would caution that OETA not be wholly technological in terms of its philosophy and procedures. At the very least, our journals ought to report more fully the kinds of negative aspects I have tried to address here.

If, as Barrett (1979, p. 117) says, "every technique is put to use for some end," we should make assessments that ask about ultimate purposes. These are purposes beyond instructional objectives. We (we especially includes students) must observe an instance of educational technology and ask why it exists. If we find that it is primarily for economic, political, or military purposes, we must judge these purposes against a conception of an educated person. If we find educational technology is more in response to a "technological imperative" than to education, judge this response. If we find that educational technology opens us to holistic conceptions of the world, judge this. Then ask again about purposes. I believe that inquiry about the ultimate purposes of technology fosters learners and education professionals who are more wholly literate about technology.

Conclusion

I am certain that reactions to what I have presented are mixed. My view may run contrary to predominant conceptions and aspirations of the field of educational technology. I have not always presented "hard data," but philosophic analysis and speculation. Regardless, I hope I have made a case that educational technology is dangerous. I hope that I have shown that our field needs to develop a philosophic and social conscience. I hope that what may be a distant chord has been struck in some of you—a chord that helps you to wonder about the nature of educational technology and its meaning to human existence beyond the hardware, the classroom, and even the mind.

As Heidegger has said, "For questioning is the piety of thought" (Heidegger, 1977, p. 35).

REFERENCES

Bacon, F. *New organon*, Book I. In Hugh G. Dick (Ed.), *Selected writings of Francis Bacon*. New York: The Modern Library. (1985)

Barrett, W. (1979). *The illusion of technique*. Garden City, NY: Anchor Books.

Bell, D. (1973). Technology, nature and society. In *Technology and the frontier of knowledge*. Garden City, NY: Doubleday.

Berman, M. (1981). *The reenchantment of the world*. Ithaca, NY: Cornell University Press.

Bork, A. (1986). Ethical issues associated with the use of computers in learning environments. Unpublished manuscript.

Boyer, E. L. (1983). *High school: A report on secondary education in America*. (The Carnegie Foundation for the Advancement of Teaching) New York: Harper & Row.

Capra, F. (1982). *The turning point. Science, society, and the rising culture*. New York: Simon and Schuster.

Clark, R. E. & Salomon, G. (1986). Media in teaching. In M. C. Wittrock (Ed.), *Handbook of research on teaching* (pp. 464-478). New York: Macmillan.

Descartes, R. (1950). *Discourse on method*. (L. J. Lafleur, Trans.). Indianapolis: The Liberal Arts Press. (Original French edition, 1637).

Ellul, Jacques. (1964). *The technological society*. New York: Vintage Books.

Finn, J. D. (1961). The tradition in the iron mask. *Audiovisual Instruction, 6*, 238-243.

Fosnot, C. T. (1984). Media and technology in education: A constructivist view. *Educational Communications and Technology Journal, 32*, 195-205.

Harrington, M. (1984). *The new American poverty*. New York: Penguin Books.

Heidegger, M. (1977). The question concerning technology. In *The question concerning technology and other essays*. New York: Harper and Row.

Heinich, R. (1984). The proper study of instructional technology. *Educational Communications and Technology Journal, 32*, 67-88.

Hoban, C. F. (1977). Educational technology and human values. *Audio Visual Communications Review, 25*, 221-241.

Holloway, R. E. (1984). *Educational technology: A critical perspective*. Syracuse University: ERIC Clearinghouse on Information Resources.

Holloway, R. E. (1985-1986). *Human resources director to AEC membership directory*. Washington, D.C.

Johnson, J. K. (Ed.). (1985). *Masters curricula in educational communications and technology: A descriptive directory*. Washington, D.C.: Association for Educational Communications and Technology.

Jonassen, D. H. (1984). The mediation of experience and educational technology: A philosophical analysis. *Educational Communications and Technology Journal, 33*(1).

Knirk, F. G. & Gustafson, K. L. (1986). *Instructional technology*. New York: Holt, Rinehart, & Winston.

Mansfield, R. & Nunan, E. E. (1978). Towards an alternative educational technology. *British Journal of Educational Technology: Journal of the Council for Educational Technology, 9*, 170-6.

McBeath, R. J. (Ed.). (1972). *Extending education through technology, selected writings by James D. Finn on instructional technology*. Washington, D.C.: Association for Educational Communications and Technology.

Peters, R. S. (1967). *Ethics and education*. Atlanta: Scott, Foresman and Company.

Salomon, G. (1974a). Internalization of filmic schematic operations in interaction with learners' aptitudes. *Journal of Educational Psychology, 66*, 499-511.

Stewart, A. (1985). Appropriate educational technology: Does 'appropriate-ness' have implications for the theoretical framework of educational technology? *Educational Communications and Technology Journal, 33*, 58-65.

Taylor, W. D. & Johnsen, J. B. (1986). Resisting technological momentum. In J. A. Culbertson & L. L. Cunningham (Eds.), *Technology and education* (85th Yearbook of the National Society for the Study of Education). Chicago: University of Chicago Press.

WTTW & BBC. (Producers). (1986). *The great river* (film). Chicago: WTTW & BBC.

Section 3

Case Studies

✳✳✳✳✳

9

Technology and Texts: Breaking the Window*

Robert Muffoletto
Teacher Preparation Center
California State Polytechnic University

As systems and hardware move to more complex and interdependent structures, the gap between producers and users widens. Educational television provides an interesting point of analysis for this relationship. The general purpose of educational and instructional television is to deliver to the learner an experience that was designed to instruct or inform (both are apples off the same tree). The educational programme, especially in the areas of mathematics, science and social studies, assumes a form that suggests an objective scientific base, presented through the eyes of an assumed neutral observer (the camera) and the voice of an informed observer (the narrator). The image and sound then become the learner's window to that world. Not until the programme is analyzed from either a cognitive or social perspective, such analysis including its form of production, are the ideological, nonscientific, social meanings revealed. The programme is then seen as presenting only one point of view about what it means us to know—the window is broken.

What I have attempted to stake out with this brief introduction is first, the concern for the relationship between media producers and media receivers of what has been referred to elsewhere as product, effect or text;[1] and second, a consideration of

---

* Reprinted with permission of Kogan Page Ltd., London. This chapter was originally published in *Educational Media International, 24*(2), 105-109.
[1]A text may be considered to be anything that is read. There are social texts, visual texts and written texts. Each draws upon its own forms of encoded

distancing of the readers of media texts from their forms of production.[2] The rest of this paper will discuss producers, readers and texts in relation to the development of complex media technologies and the question of meaning.

Producer-user gap

As media technology (the hardware, the software and consciousness that drives them) become more complex, the relationship between producers and users or readers of the technology texts (or products) widens in one important way. The reader of the text understands, and continues to understand, the text as a given object and not as a constructed text. Too often the designed computer program is referred to as 'the software' or as 'the technology.' It is embedded in the notion of common sense and language as representation; seeing technology as an existing 'thing' with no history or social context, is seeing it from an empirical idealist perspective (Belsey, 1980). For example, in a recent essay on educational technology the following was written: "When technology helps make such learning to be not only possible but universally available and achievable, our hoped-for vision of the educational system of the future will be within reach" (Gubser, 1986, p. 14). If the word 'technology' is changed to 'designers' or 'producers', the meaning of that section changes. No longer would technology be seen as an objective helper, but only as the product of different social and political forces. The future of 'educational systems' will not be understood as a result of

---

presentation and dissemination. For more discussion see Becker, 1986; Fish, 1980; Metz, 1977; Nicholas, 1981.

[2]An example of this concern is found in curriculum focusing on critical viewing and critical thinking skills. In both cases, the critical thinker/viewer is to consider the productive nature of the phenomenon experienced. In teaching television production to students and by providing public access channels for local production, the viewers of texts are transformed into producers of texts. The readers of history become historians. Through this process it is hoped that readers may become aware of the constructive nature of perceived reality.

a technology, but as the result of a system of production—a system that encompasses ideology and science.

> Technology is a social construct and serves the prevailing system of social power. . . . To accept technology as a universal tendency . . . inevitably leads people to regard technology as something that is happening without their consent, awareness or the possibility of controlling it . . . . Inability to recognize the social origins of technology explains, in large part, the sense of individual helplessness that pervades most advanced industrialized states today. (Schiller, 1967, p. 51).

As suggested above, the users of products (technology and its systems) do not need to know where the product comes from, or anything about the nature of its production. They just need to know how to 'turn it on.' From this perspective, the gap widens between users and producers, between the modes of production and the product, between knowledge and its form of production. What is of danger here is the possibility that the readers of text are not aware they are reading a text at all, but see it as real and not constructed.[3] From a realist perspective, the responsibility of media producers is to employ devises that aid the viewer/reader in suspending disbelief—that is, to read the text as a window to the world, as a presentation of reality (Eagleton, 1983). To accomplish this, both the producer and the reader of media texts must draw from similar structures of meaning.

Semiotics

Semiotics offers to this discussion a model for understanding message construction by both producers and readers. Semiotics presents the notion of signs as representations. A sign stands in place of the material it

---

[3]I would also suggest that the guiding forces of education throughout this century have been based upon a product conception of learning, with little, if any, concern for the process of production and the meaning of what is learned. In reference to this text, you do not need to know the nature of the knowledge you live by, just where to get 'it' when you want it.

represents. Signs within this model are formed between the association constructed between a material thing, a signifier, and a concept (non-material)—the signified. This association formed between material and non-material, between signifier and signified, is meaning. How producers and readers of texts 'make meaning' is based upon the associations made between objects and concepts—the sign.[4] This association is both social and historical. Meaning is social in that it evolves out of interpretive communities existing within social situations. It is historical in the sense that the association has developed and existed over time. The nature of meaning is that it is never static: it is always in flux. Meaning from this perspective is historical and dialectical (Habermas, 1968).[5]

Organizing signs into systems of representation, or meanings, is called codification. The task of media text producers is to encode, from existing sets of social codes, in both a paradigmatic and syntagmatic manner, a meaningful text.[6] The

---

[4]An example would be the letters 'CAT.' At one level they are nothing more than ink spots on this paper. As readers we have taken the spots (signifiers) and have associated them with a concept (signified)–an animal with certain characteristics. This association is the sign. Its meaning, what it stands for, is a social construction. We agree what 'this' stands for, it means, 'this.' In understanding what things mean, what they stand for, the readers of texts are always associating materials–the signifier–with a concept–the signified. It is only through a social agreement that we understand each other.

[5]The reader may wish to consider the use of the sign for peace, victory, and the number two, as an example of the historical meaning of material. The sign used to denote victory in the 1940s had a different meaning in the United States during the late 1960s and early 1970s. The same sign (gesture) may be used in a mathematics class or in a doughnut shop. The point here is that the material has remained the same–the meaning has changed in context and time.

[6]Paradigmatic refers here to the levels of meaning or associations. A flag may be a marker or it may be read as having broader social and historical implications (meanings and interpretations). Syntagmatic refers to the organization of signs, the structure by which we experience them. Film demonstrates this clearly. It is the relationship between shots, between

term 'text' is being used here to designate something that is read (Becker, 1986). Producers select from existing production devices to organize the codes through which intended meaning is created—the intended text, the created effect. The reader takes the intended texts and reconstructs or decodes and recodes them, to create meaning. Whether or not the created meanings are the same depend upon the reading of the codes and their organization within the text by both producers and readers. Meaning from this perspective is relative to the frame of reference held by both (Goffman, 1974).

Developing meaning

In the traditional (and dated) communication model, messages are transmitted to a receiver via some transport form. In this model it is the role of the receiver to re-create the intended message. It would appear from this simplistic model that the producer and receiver are entities that exist and work independently from each other. Rarely are the social, political and economic codes from which both draw their productions, their texts and their interpretations discussed (Boddy, 1983). In referring to the work of Raymond Williams, one writer makes this point on television programme production in suggesting that television "is at once an intention and an effect of a particular social order" (Feuer, 1983, p. 12).

Producers of texts draw their meanings from a number of different code domains (intertextual), thus producing an effect, different from the effect of the individual codes or texts by themselves. These texts are not neutral or independent, but are the results of a social order. For example, the producers of a documentary television programme may draw from various code domains to construct their presentation. These would include codes from science, news and journalism, and social and political institutions. The producers of the programme would also

---

frames that form the structure of the film, forming the experience of the film. Meaning may be considered to fall between the dynamics of the paradigmatic and syntagmatic structure of the film. You cannot have one without the other.

draw upon various production codes including sequencing (editing), lighting, colour or lack of it, camera use (angles, movement), pacing, lens selection, and sound (Feuer, 1983). Producers, in combining and organizing (the syntagmatic development of the message) the various codes, work within an established framework of meaning. The more domains they draw from in the construction of the documentary, the more elaborate and complex its effect and its eventual reading. As technology changes and expands the range of possibilities for producers (as demonstrated by the shift from fixed camera, taped studio productions to handheld cameras and remote live on-location productions), the intended effect also demands from the reader a greater ability to decode the received text. With the increase in complexity, resulting from the available technology accessing a wider range of code domains, the constructed programme may appear to be more of a documentary than previous documentaries. Other examples can be cited in various media forms where, because of the elaborate coding system drawn upon, the reader/receiver of the programme understands it as real and not as a construction.

Influence of technology

Technology, as a determining factor in the construction of intended texts and resulting effects, allows the producers to draw upon various production devices that affect the reading of the social, political, economic and institutional codes drawn upon for the production of the text. ABC's Night Line, Video Rock, and the 1984 Olympics, draw a great part of their meaning from the technologies employed in their production. Whether it is simultaneous live interviews from distant political and geographical locations, musical-visual stories, or a packaged-for-television sporting event (Feuer, 1983), the use of elaborate and complex technological devices exploit, and at times create, new codes for the construction of intended texts for intended readers. In using various technological devices the producer may elect to reveal the device (as in slow motion, wipes, dissolves) or to hide it through other devices (chroma-key, voice overlay, multiple images and perspectives). The reason for revealing or not the devices of production returns to the intent of the producer

(Eagleton, 1983). The producer through selection and organization of various codes intends, for whatever reason, to remind you that you are watching a programme, as demonstrated in a current trend found in some news programmes, to pull back and display the studio, its cameras and personnel.

On the other hand, through a different organization and selection of codes, the intent may not be to bring your attention to the production qualities, in an attempt to construct a realistic impression—this is reality as it is found, brought to you through the objective eye of the camera and the voice of the reporter. After all, it is a report. The producers of narrative feature films do not want their audiences to pull back from the image with the knowledge that there are at least 50 people on the fifth take of a very demanding and emotional death scene. With television, the technology, as a devise of selection and transmission of intended texts, is itself hidden from the reader who has become conditioned to seeing only the image and not the screen—to seeing the programme and not its authors.

The producer, in the production of text for intended readers, may select to reveal the programme's nature of production, but never selects to reveal the selection of codes for an effect leading to the packaging of a social order. As one writer states it, "Technology is a social construct and serves the prevailing system of social power . . ."(Schiller, 1976, p. 51). Out of the call for effectiveness—in educational technology you would add accountability and efficiency—producers will utilize various technologies and forms of production for the creation of messages or texts. To do so they must draw upon existing social and production codes. Whether or not the text reveals itself as a carrier of social order is left up to the readers of the text and their position in relationship to the constructed text and their sense of reality.

Reader-text relationship

Readers are more than passive receivers of texts. Through the course of reading a text, readers create its meaning. Meaning, then, from a reader's perspective, is not in the text, but is found in the relationship between the text and the reader. As suggested earlier with producers, the meaning they create, as they draw from different code domains, is located in the relationship between them and their created text. It is important to note that the text may mean different things for producers from what it will for readers. As Stewart Hall (1980) suggests, producers work within a certain framework from which they construct texts for some perceived receiver (the first being themselves). Producers, like readers, are directed by their experiences with other texts, their social/cultural histories and their economic, gender and religious positions—in other words, the mental set through which they view and understand the world (Holub, 1984).

The first act of receivers of texts is to understand or recognize that there is a message to be received, and their second act is to understand it. In the process of producing a text, the authors draw upon different systems of codes; the receivers of the text, in order to understand it, must also draw their own experiences with codes in order to give meaning to it. The meaning, then, of any text is relative to the decoding and recoding abilities of the receiver. In this sense, the receiver creates the text (Hall, 1980). As one writer suggests: there is no meaning until the receiver says there is (Fish, 1980).

Cultural context

Readers have a social cultural history which includes the reading of other texts, or inter-textual relationships. In the process of decoding, the reader employs inter-textual relationships with what Gadner (in Holub, 1984) refers to as a "horizon of expectation." Readers in the process of creating meaning, draw upon their historical inter-textual experiences forming their expectations for a particular textual experience.

To modify the idea of all meaning being individually relative, Stanley Fish (1980) refers to the notion of subjective communities. According to Fish, communities are made up of readers with similar histories and expectations, and share similar encoding and decoding systems for the reading of texts. Individuals also hold membership in different communities, which at times brings about a conflict of interpretive strategies. Depending upon which community a text is read from will determine its meaning. With that in mind it is possible to say that at any one historical moment an individual, or community, will read a text from different positions, generating different meanings, different texts. What different communities offer to the process of interpretation is their access to different coding systems or domains. What domains a community will draw upon and legitimate as valid will determine the range of meanings possible—paradigmatic structure of texts.

As the devices for the encoding of texts become more complex, readers without access to their coding systems may come to understand the text as a reflection or window to reality. Not knowing the codes from which texts are drawn limits the interpretive ability of readers. They do not come to an understanding of the text for what it is—a construction which utilizes various coding systems for intended purposes. Readers who hold a 'common sense' vision of messages and texts see the world as given and not constructed.

REFERENCES

Becker, A. (1986). A teaching model for the grammar of television. *Journal of Visual Verbal Languaging, 6*, 1, Spring, 41-48.

Balsey, C. (1980). *Critical practice.* New York: Methuen.

Berger, A. (1982). *Media analysis techniques.* Beverly Hills: Sage Publications.

Boddy, W. (1983). Loving a nineteen-inch motorola: American writing on television. In A. Kaplin (ed.) *Regarding television.* Los Angeles : American Film Institute.

Eagleton, T. (1984). *The function of criticism: From the spectator to post-structuralism.* London: Verso Editions and NLB.

Feuer, J. (1983). The concept of live television: Ontology as ideology. In A. Kaplin (ed.) *Regarding television.* Los Angeles: American Film Institute.

Fish, S. (1980). *Is there a text in this class? The authority of interpretive communities.* Cambridge: Harvard University Press.

Goddman, N. (1978). *Ways of worldmaking.* Cambridge: Hackett Publishing Co..

Goffman, I. (1974). *Frame analysis.* New York: Harper and Row.

Gubser, L. (1986). National task force on technology. *Tech Trends*, May-June.

Habermas, J. (1968) *Knowledge and human interest.* Boston: Beacon Press.

Holub, R. (1984). *Reception theory: A critical introduction.* London: Methuen.

Metz, C. (1977). *The imaginary signifier.* Bloomington: Indiana University Press.

Schiller, H. (1973). *The mind managers.* Boston: Beacon Press.

Schiller, H. (1976). *Communication and cultural domination.* White Plains: M.E. Sharpe.

Williams, R. (1975). *Television: Technology and cultural form.* New York: Schocken Books.

10

Criticism as Methodology for Research in Educational Technology

John C. Belland, James K. Duncan, & Michael Deckman
Department of Educational Policy & Leadership
The Ohio State University

As a field which draws knowledge and practice from a wide range of arts and sciences, educational technology should be able to use a variety of ways of investigating and knowing in order to guide inquiry and practice. The purpose of this paper is to look at the nature of criticism, primarily literary criticism and art criticism in order to suggest some of the opportunities criticism would present to the educational technology researcher. It will then posit some of the essential attributes of criticism in general and those of literary criticism and art criticism specifically because literary and art criticism are concerned with things produced by human creation. Lastly, it will introduce an example of a scenario about a possible technological future of education and one critical essay related to it.

Suggesting that criticism is an appropriate method for inquiry in educational technology is by no means a suggestion that criticism should become an exclusive method. This suggestion is not even intended to imply that there should be any less effort in conducting formal experiments or in pursuing naturalistic investigations or inquiry using any other paradigm. Criticism links with all other paradigms for inquiry being informed by results from other methods and in turn informing other methods with different theoretical perspectives.[1] Criticism has several unique characteristics which would enable educational technologists to investigate different kinds of questions. Among those unique characteristics are the capability of the sophisticated observer to recognize the salient information in a morass of data, the power of the human intellect to make sense out of anomaly or paradox and the transcendence of the creative spirit to link the real and the ideal. Criticism is the process through which an understanding moves from a focus on the trees to a focus on the forest. Disciplined, sophisticated criticism represents: "the liberation of human imagination from domination by the close-at-hand" (Frankel, 1959, p. 163).

Criticism begins simplemindedly. As Papert said (1985, p. 53), "Do I like it [the object]? My judgment is personal and intuitive. I answer to myself alone, and consider only the immediate object of my attention. Soon, however, something more is needed; taste must be justified. Others challenge our opinions and counter with their own, and even personal development eventually requires us to grapple with our reasons." Eventually

---

[1]In the social and behavioral sciences, the field of mental measurements has made effective use of criticism as a paradigm for inquiry. In the seven *Mental Measurement Yearbooks* edited and published by O. K. Buros over the past forty and more years, criticism has been linked effectively with other paradigms of inquiry both by being informed by results of other methods and in turn informing those other methods. Two of the five central objectives of the *Yearbooks* have focused on presenting critical test reviews written by testing and subject specialists representing various viewpoints. Concomitantly the publication staff has seen the *Yearbooks* as a means for improving the quality of texts and their supporting materials; increasing the understanding and sophistication of test users and improving the quality of the critical appraisal of tests used in the mental measurements field. On the whole the *Mental Measurement Yearbooks* have been accepted in the social and behavioral science community even though criticism was used as the fundamental method of inquiry. The most recent edition (seventh) contains 798 critical reviews written specifically for the *Seventh Yearbook* plus excerpts from 181 critical reviews originally published in professional journals.

the critic develops the capacity to focus observation and select criteria for judgment as a connoisseur would.

Criticism is judgment. Whether the objects of criticism be scientific findings, aesthetic works, or technological gadgets or processes, sound criticism is the exercise of intimate, informed judgment. Such judgments are grounded in the organized perceptions of meaning (concepts) that the critic has derived from past experiences with things similar in character and purpose. A competent critic brings to this endeavor a liking, an affection, for the subject-matter that is "informed with the insight that is a product of a rich and full experience" (Dewey, 1934, p. 310). Good judgment, then, with respect to technological objects and processes requires an intimate, well-informed, and insightful understanding of the technological medium itself and the effects it may have in human experience. In John Dewey's words: "A judgment as an act of controlled inquiry demands a rich background and a disciplined insight" (1934, p. 300). And judgments perform the inseparable functions of discrimination and unification or, more theoretically speaking, the interrelated functions of analysis and synthesis.[2]

It is important to note, however, that criticism as a paradigm for inquiry does not provide adjudication. The exercise of judgment is limited by the ascertainment of the qualities of the work being studied. Criticism is thus distinguished from the necessary practices of judging whether a research report should be published or whether a film should receive an award. Criticism may (and probably should) illuminate the adjudication process, but should not be confused with it (Dewey, 1934). Given, for example, a technological product or a documented technological process, the experience that makes such analysis-synthesis

---

[2]Although the critic's subject matter is normally qualitative rather than quantitative, for those who are quantitatively minded, the analysis of variance may be illustrative of the intimate interrelationship between analysis and synthesis. Here measures of variation (analyses) are arrayed around measures of central tendency (syntheses) to provide grounds for making quantitative judgments.

possible is the product or process itself "as it enters into the experience of the critic by interaction with his own sensitivity and his knowledge" (Dewey, 1934, pp. 309-310), the store of meanings from his/her past experience, and the discipline of the concepts or theories of the scholarly community of critics. The ensuing judgments of the critic perform the functions of helping to reeducate our perceptions, deepen our experience through using the product from a more meaningful point of view (Dewey, 1934, p. 304).

While the structuralist critics count elements in literary discourse as a means to ascertain quality, criticism as generally practiced makes judgments possible in a qualitative realm, a realm presently fraught with difficulty for modern science (Smith, 1980). In the qualitative realm, as distinct from the quantitative realm, no set of steps can be specified "for the performance of so delicate an act as determination of the significant parts of a whole, and of their respective places and weights in the whole" (Dewey, 1934, p. 310). And even more intensely, Dewey, philosopher of science, writes: "There is a unifying as well as discriminating phase of judgment—technically known as synthesis in distinction from analysis. This unifying phase, even more than the analytic, is a function of the creative response of the individual who judges. It is insight. There are no rules that can be laid down for its performance" (1934, p. 313).

Eisner (1980, 1985) uses the word connoisseurship to express the complex, sensitive sophistication of the critic in the process of criticism. Such a critic has developed a capability for observation and cerebration which is almost beyond the comprehension of the unsophisticated. Criticism requires the intensive and extensive development of the connoisseur. Criticism relies on the give and take among several persons each of whom may be at a different stage in the development of connoisseurship. Each critic may also approach the critical task from a different theoretical perspective.

It is tempting to reject criticism as a method because of the dependence on the integrity and sophistication of the critic, but scientific inquiry is perhaps even more vulnerable to fraud. In criticism both the object or phenomenon being studied and the criticism are public and the critic approaches the critical study as an enlightened skeptic. In scientific inquiry, the data are seldom public, the instruments used to gather those data are often poorly calibrated, and the statistical analysis used to infer from the data may be either misappropriated or inaccurately calculated. All of these things can be hidden from scrutiny by the scientific community. A study can be replicated by another scientist, but differences between the original study and the replication are usually explained by presumed differences in the sample or in the context of the experiment. In addition, reports of scientific inquiry rarely discriminate between inferences which are statistically significant but unimportant and those inferences which can guide both theory and practice.

Although the social and behavioral sciences appear to be increasingly responsive to research methods focused on qualitative characteristics of phenomena, this emphasis appears to be far from mature. Being sciences, it is reasonable that scientific canons would be used to formulate the canons of qualitative research. Thus qualitative or naturalistic research asserts the relevance of qualitative measures and elaborates rigorous procedures for assuring that such research will be respectable (Guba and Lincoln, 1982). Actual studies seem to be idiosyncratic in method and ungeneralizable in implications, a situation which would suggest an even greater need for critical review.

Gagné (1985) has stated that research has provided considerable information about the learnings which intentionally result from media use. He then suggests that researchers should study all the other effects (he calls them incidental learnings). While research to study incidental learnings will undoubtedly involve gathering quantitative and qualitative data, critical inquiry might stimulate and guide such data gathering and surely would expand the interpretability of the results. Only a sophisticated observer is likely to be able to suggest what the significant incidental effects might be.

Contributions of Criticism

What is the nature of the contributions criticism might
make to the understanding of technological objects and their
educational effects? Such contributions lead to consideration of
what Dewey (1934, p. 415) calls the most far-reaching question,
"the relationship between existence and value, or as the problem is
often put, between the real and the ideal." There seem to be six
broadly conceived fundamental areas where criticism could
enrich our understanding of educational products and processes
that are technological in character. The substantive range of the
contributions that such criticism might make will be more
apparent if one realizes that the subjects of criticism not only have
aesthetic properties but also can have educational and
technological properties among the complex of properties inherent
in any object or process. The six areas within which criticism
could focus attention and enhance understanding are the
following.

1.   *Criticism could help explain a technological
       object or process in terms of the quality of the
       relationship between its content and its form.*
       Aesthetic objects *express* meaning through
       unique integrations of substance and form in
       human experience. The competent critic has a
       deep understanding of *what* is being expressed,
       how it is being expressed, and the *relations*
       between them. Although the substance (what)
       and the form (how) are inextricably linked
       together in actuality, the critic, through
       intelligent and sensitive reflection, can
       discover the most essential character of both
       substance and form, their interrelationships,
       and their likely impacts on human experience.

2.   *Criticism could help explain a technological
       object or process in terms of the relationship
       among the constituent parts and the whole.* In
       works of some aesthetic distinction many
       significant elements and details are brought
       together to form an aesthetically pleasing

whole. In literature, for example, the creator draws upon elements of literary structure, literary style, literary devices and conventions of literary aesthetics. Similarly, in the visual arts, the creator draws on conventions for visual expression, the artistic media, and media tools and techniques. The critic can explain how such elements and details do or do not coalesce and help us to understand the deeper meanings being expressed by these relationships.

3. *Criticism may provide insight into the unifying theme(s) and design(s) which help to hold the technological object or process together in all its richness and complexity.* "It is significant that the word 'design' has a double meaning. It signifies purpose and it signifies arrangement, mode of composition" (Dewey, 1934, p. 116). Both purpose and mode of composition help bring unity to educational products and/or processes that are aesthetic in character. In addition, there are at least one and often more themes that give coherent meanings to the human experience entailed in their use in educational settings. The competent critic is capable of illuminating not only the nature of the purposes and the meanings intrinsic to our educational technological endeavors but also the means by which they were achieved. The insight of the connoisseur is indispensable here.

4. *Criticism may reveal the nature of the intimate experience a well-informed, sensitive, and reflective individual has with the process or product of educational technology.* Criticism is a form of disciplined inquiry. As such it draws upon the complex and specialized understandings and the disciplined insight

possessed by individuals having rich and extensive experience in a particular realm of human endeavor. Although critics may differ significantly in their theoretical beliefs, interpretations, and judgments because of the idiosyncratic nature of their understandings and their capacity for insight, good criticism is thoroughly and robustly constrained by the nature of the products and/or processes within human aesthetic and educational experience which nevertheless are embedded in a community of meanings and values (Booth, 1979, p. 31-3).

5.   *Criticism may reveal the grounds upon which interpretations and judgments of the processes and objects of educational technology may rest as well as the consequences the object and/or process may entail in human experience.* In order to arrive at some defensible interpretations and judgments, the critic must explore in some detail the grounds which led him/her to those interpretations and judgments. In this sense the critic is bound very much as the scientist is when the latter discusses the results of his/her investigation. In the process of exploring in detail the grounds for his/ her judgments, the competent critic experiences the product of educational technology in most of its richness and complexity. He/she experiences the consequences of intimate interaction with the product and, if he/she is knowledgeable about education, can say much about the consequences of its use in a variety of educational settings.

6.   *Criticism may serve to synthesize the knowledge derived from disparate research processes into more comprehensive theory.* The

products and processes with which educational technologists work are simultaneously educational, technological and often aesthetic in nature. Sometimes those products and/or processes have been subjected to formal scientific investigations yielding verifiable results. Often they have been evaluated through formal and/or informal field trials yielding a body of data about their use in a variety of educational contexts. Rarely are the results of these different kinds of inquiry brought together (see note 1 above) into some more comprehensive view of the product and/or process. Criticism might help in bringing the results of such inquiries together while adding rich, aesthetic dimensions of understanding to our predominantly scientific-professional explanations.

Educational technology products are media, instructional systems and the reports of the processes used to develop both. All can be studied using critical methodology. Since language is involved in both auditory and visual form, literary criticism would appear to be applicable. An outline of the scope of literary criticism will suggest some of the foci for inquiry. Iconic representation of visual phenomena are also present in educational media. An outline of dimensions of art criticism will suggest additional research possibilities.

Literary Criticism

Literary criticism like any field of inquiry is not monolithic. It has developed through many different phases and includes many different theories and metatheories which deal with all parts and processes of the general communication model—universe, work, encoder and decoder. While the different theoretical perspectives are sometimes viewed as chaotic, they actually provide a rich complex of ideas to challenge and stimulate thinking. Literary criticism thus can study all aspects of a technological object or process, focusing on one or more of those aspects. In addition, literary criticism can study technological objects and processes from a single theoretical viewpoint or from several. The outline of possible foci below is organized by the general communications model concepts.

From a *universal* standpoint, literary criticism can address the particular object or process in relation to all other common objects or processes, past and present, in both content and form. Instead of merely comparing those objects and processes by medium alone, one can analyze genres, archetypes, myths, metaphor, irony and paradox, trope, narrative structure, allegory, character development, plot, revelation as well as many others. One can ask whether a technological object or process has "broken new ground," refined or extended, or merely replicated past work on any number of universal dimensions.

From a *work* standpoint, the particular object or process could be examined as to its linguistic and literary structure—*e.g.*, narrative movement, plot devices, dialogue, character interaction; its literary style—*e.g.*, rhythm, tone, texture; or its use of literary device—*e.g.*, metaphor, symbol, synecdoche, metonymy, irony, paradox, ambiguity, onomatopoeia, alliteration, and so on. One can examine the internal consistence of literary structure within an object or process or examine how the literary structure relates to explicit or implicit purpose.

From an *encoder* perspective, one can examine the producers and developers of the objects and processes. A variety of people are involved in the conception and production of instructional media or instructional systems. Such persons can be studied for aesthetic tendencies—*e.g.*, character or narrative similarities, stylistic similarities, common tropes; and expressive tendencies—*e.g.*, emotional tone, philosophic base, political viewpoint, didactic revelation. These can be studied across all the works created by an individual, a group, an institution, or a funding agency.

From a *decoder* viewpoint, the effects of different literary techniques—*e.g.*, narrative reversal, melodrama, character development; literary forms—*e.g.*, tragedy, comedy, farce, satire, allegory; and literary devices—*e.g.*, metaphor, synecdoche, rhyme, rhythm—could be studied across various media and with various learners. In the context of the learner, criticism would serve to help define questions for scientific inquiry.

Finally, one could approach the entire field of educational technology from a literary perspective. A metacriticism could center on this technology as classical rhetoric—*e.g.*, didactic aim, tropes, persuasive devices (examples, maxims); as allegory—*e.g.*, stock characters, standard plots; as informative discourse; or as a cultural object. One could explore how the products of educational technology relate to other classified "literatures"—*e.g.*, canonical works, popular works; or how they function in expressive discourse—*e.g.*, prevailing emotion, change of expression over time, intrinsic and extrinsic expression regarding work, culture, teachers, learners and the educational process itself.

Art Criticism

Art is intended to stretch and thus to extend the capacities of a person's perceiving, thinking and feeling self. Art criticism tends to focus on aesthetic attributes of an object—*e.g.*, medium, form, style, composition, harmony, balance. It also examines whether an object should be classed as an artistic work—a controversial determination at best. Art criticism can be discussed in parallel with the way literary criticism was discussed above (most of the ideas expressed apply to art criticism as well), but it will not be since communicability is not regarded as an important criterion for art. Similarly, most of the ideas outlined below as aspects of art criticism could be applied to literary criticism.

Using art criticism in the study of educational media would allow the researcher to explore a range of questions not ordinarily explored. Even though it can often be demonstrated that desired learning is taking place as a result of using educational media, would it not also be appropriate to examine whether the aesthetic properties of the medium were being used to extend the learner's appreciation of artfulness? Are learners being exposed to the slick and ephemeral or to the creative and enduring? Are students stimulated by shallowly conceived illusion or by uniquely creative expression? Are the conventions of the producers of educational media in harmony with the conventions of artists in other creative media? Should those conventions be the same or different?

Art criticism is disciplined by the rich tradition or art itself. There have been so many artists whose work has been preserved for continuing criticism by critics from those contemporary with the artist to those of the present day. In addition, some of the work of the critics has been preserved. Such a heritage keeps both the art and its criticism in a public community of scholarship. Such a community of scholarship contrasts sharply from that of science in which the sources of data and the actual data are not public. Public critical scholarship is on constant guard against what Dewey (1934) called the two great fallacies of criticism (although they are certainly fallacies of the other paradigms of inquiry as well)—reductionism and confusion of categories.

Reductionism results from oversimplification. It occurs when a critic isolates some particular aspect of the work, ignores its relationships to the other aspects, and reduces the art to the terms of the single element. For example, if art is discussed in terms of sensory quality like color or texture without exploring how such properties relate to a formal element such as composition or perspective, the work of art is not likely to be understood as art. Reductionism also results from analyzing a work of art from the point of view of a single aesthetic tradition or of the specific cultural milieu in which the art was created.

Confusion of categories springs from the fallacious notion that "the artist begins with material that has already a recognized status, moral, philosophic, historical or whatever, and then renders it more palatable by emotional seasoning and imaginative dressing" (Dewey, 1934, p. 318). Almost all fields of human inquiry have impacted on art. To select just one example, science has had great influence on art. DaVinci studied anatomy and applied anatomical principles in his drawings and paintings. Yet artists who have not been privy to formal anatomic inquiry have provided rich aesthetic expression of the form and movement of living creatures. If one criticizes the art using the criteria of anatomy, the critic is contributing to an understanding of anatomy not to the understanding of art. In general, confusion of categories results from the neglect of the intrinsic characteristics of the artistic medium, a problem which can be found explicitly in educational technology as well when educational technologists confuse the process of extracting of subtle meaning from a mediated experience with the characteristics of the medium itself.

The relationship between permanence and change also disciplines criticism. Critical categories can become as hardened as scientific ones. When the critic's perceptions are hardened into a fixed system of categories and his/her criticism becomes characterized by invariate predictability, the extension of sensitivity is ended. Such a critic cannot be inspired by the possibilities of innovative creativity. "The function of criticism is the reeducation of perception of works of art; it is an auxiliary in the process, a difficult process, of learning to see and hear" (Dewey, 1934, p. 324).

An Example

The scenario "Kelly's Education," which follows this chapter, was developed to enable multifaceted criticism of a possible technological future of education. Scholars from various disciplines were invited to respond to it from the vantage point of his/her own discipline. Chadwick Alger's response, which is appended following the scenario, is an example of the power of criticism to expand the ways one might think about the future expressed in the scenario. As Dewey (1934) has reminded us, "the critic shall seize upon some strain or strand that is actually there, and bring it forth with such clearness that the reader has a new clue and guide in his own experience" (p. 314). The ideas out of which Alger's judgment grew are the synthesis of the document from the scenario writers and the lifetime of study Alger has put into political insight. The authors of this paper hope that the example serves both to raise consciousness about criticism and to stimulate reflection on technological futures as well.

REFERENCES

Booth, W. C. (1979). *Critical understanding*. Chicago: University of Chicago Press.

Dewey, J. (1934). *Art as experience.* New York: Minton, Balch & Co. 298-325.

Dewey, J. (1925). *Experience and nature.* Chicago: Open Court.

Eagleton, T. (1984). *The function of criticism.* London: Verso Press.

Eisner, E. W. (1976). Educational connoisseurship and criticism: Their form and functions in educational evaluation. *Journal of Aesthetic Education, 10(1),* 135-50.

Eisner, E. W. (1985). Aesthetic modes of knowing, *National Society for the Study of Education Yearbook, Pt. 2.* Chicago: University of Chicago Press. 25-36.

Frankel, C. (1959). *The case for modern man.* Boston: Beacon Press.

Guba, E. G. & Lincoln, Y. S. (1982). *Effective evaluation.* San Francisco: Jossey-Bass. 103-27.

Papert, S. (1985). Computer criticism vs. technocratic thinking. *Logo 85 theoretical papers.* Cambridge, MA: Massachusetts Institute of Technology Press. 53-61.

Said, E. W. (1983). *The world, the text and the critic.* Cambridge, MA: Harvard University Press.

Smith, P. L. (1980). On the distinction between quantitative and qualitative research. *CEDR Quarterly, 13(3),* 3-6.

11

Kelly's Education
A Scenario

John C. Belland & William D. Taylor
Instructional Design & Technology
The Ohio State University

Accompanied by a soft breeze and the sounds of bird calls, Kelly sits on a rock in a meadow, the LINC presenting the day's learning. Kelly's continuing education is dependent on LINC, the Learning-Information-Network-Console. Soon after the removal of the fetal monitor, Kelly was fitted to LINC I, which began immediately monitoring vital life processes and presenting infant stimulation for learning. Changes both in Kelly's development and knowledge of LINC technology are so rapid that Kelly now has a LINC XVI, but Kelly's entire learning and information input history has been transferred LINC to LINC so that the system can present the world to Kelly arranged to match Kelly's previous learning attainment and preferred learning style. In fact, LINC monitors and gently controls all of Kelly's communication.

LINC is a portable, battery-operated system the size of a briefcase, consisting of a voice-activated computer with high resolution video and audio outputs, and array of physiological sensors and sending/receiving communication devices. LINC also includes a two-way satellite transponder connecting Kelly and LINC to data bases, tutorial and simulation-based instruction, and to any other person or organization in the inhabited portions of the solar system.

LINC interacts with Kelly's personality, optimizing Kelly's use of learning and leisure resources, including access to live people as well as to the recorded social memory. Kelly is free to choose whether or not to interact face-to-face with other humans.

There is a high probability Kelly can comprehend and use incoming communications, regardless of their origins, because LINC has been programmed to monitor and adjust the content and code of a received message to Kelly's presumed physiological response to that message. Thus, a productive match of the external and internal is assured while Kelly's learning, thinking, feeling and response systems are used to their fullest capacity.

LINC also creates an environment wherein Kelly's best talents are focused on the advancement of society through technological development. Kelly finds this environment and life very satisfying. There is purpose, physical freedom and widespread communication in everyone's life. Educational, political, and economic institutions continue to change in Kelly's world. For example, typical employees give little time to their jobs and even less thought, thereby reserving these resources for individual pursuits in the arts and humanities. As soon as LINC determined him or herself—a true electronic democracy.

In retrospect it is remarkable how quickly the groundwork for completely changing education and society was laid during the last two decades of the twentieth century. Technology had finally become the principal force for human fulfillment.

12

Kelly and His/Her World: Where Did We Go Wrong?

A Response to "Kelly's Education"

Chadwick F. Alger[*]
Political Science
The Ohio State University

Questions After Initial Reading

"Kelly's continuing education is dependent on LINC." Who programs LINC? What are their goals? In what ways has Kelly shaped his present LINC program? How different is Kelly's program from that of others? Who is making money off the system? How does this affect the system and its programs? Does Kelly have the option of choosing an alternative educational system?

"The system can present the world to Kelly arranged to match Kelly's previous learning attainment and preferred learning style." What does Kelly lose by not being educated in an environment with people of different attainment and learning styles? Is Kelly able to relate to such people? Is Kelly avoiding them by sitting on a rock in a meadow?

"LINC monitors and gently controls all of Kelly's communication." Again, toward what end, for what purposes? Is control so "gentle" that Kelly is not aware of this control? Does Kelly resent it? Does Kelly give truthful responses to LINC? Who has access to the information on Kelly's interests, activities, goals and intentions? What uses are made of this information?

Kelly is connected "to any other person or organization in the inhabited portions of the solar system." This seems to be exceedingly unlikely. How might it have come about? How did it

[*]For reasons that will become clear to the reader, Chadwick F. Alger is the pen name of a social scientist at a university in Ohio. He is grateful to those who provided information for this report, often at great personal risk.

come to pass that all could afford it? Was it forced on many? How? Were many required to take their LINC in return for bread, medical care, shelter, clothing?

"There is a high probability Kelly can comprehend and use incoming communications, regardless of their origin." This seems to be even more unlikely. Certainly Kelly does not know the thousands of languages of the peoples of the world. Are these communications all translated into LINCese, or into some other common language? Have people learned these languages willingly? If achieved, what are the costs in terms of the impact on cultural variation? What is Kelly losing by avoidance of the need to communicate with other cultures through the language of their culture?

"Kelly's best talents are focused on the advancement of society through technological development." What is happening to other means for "advancing society"—philosophy, religion, music, drama, painting, sculpture, etc.? What is meant by "advancing society"? How has the primacy of "technological development" affected Kelly's "individual pursuits in the arts and humanities"?

"As soon as LINC determines capability, everyone participates in government, representing him or herself—a true electronic democracy." What are the criteria for capability? Who developed the criteria? How do these criteria shape the kind of participation permitted? May all participate, or only those considered to be capable by LINC? Can Kelly create an organization to change the criteria? The quote suggests that the system may only deal with atomized individuals. Is Kelly permitted to opt out of this system of governance? Is Kelly permitted, or is it feasible, to organize an alternative system of governance?

"Technology has finally become the principal force for human fulfillment." What is meant by human fulfillment? What is meant by technology? What is meant by principal force? Why is this piece so vague on such important questions?

Reflections on Second Reading

Why did I take this piece seriously? It is simply an anti-technology hatchet job, intended to generate the very responses I have given.   Belland and Taylor have programmed me as effectively as LINC XVI has programmed Kelly. Now they want me to write the paper they should have written because they have avoided the really difficult questions by this one page polemic. Why didn't I see through this before I agreed to write a response? But it is too late now, so I must write on.

Actually the scenario is so ridiculous that it cannot be taken as a serious description of a remotely feasible future world. The most plausible scenario for me would be that Kelly is a bright communications engineer who is in a mental hospital. Perhaps Kelly wrote the scenario while sitting in a meadow on hospital grounds with a "LINC XVI." Are we being given an insight into a special kind of 21st Century mental hospital—one for all those highly trained technology ideologues who believed in the late 20th Century that "technology had finally become the principal force for human fulfillment"? As thousands of the most extreme found themselves unable to confront the failure of their ideology, they totally lost contact with reality and had to be confined to institutions able to deal with their special malady. The LINC scenario, and LINC XVI, was developed to pacify them as they roam the rocks and meadows of these institutions, believing they are in contact with all the solar system and governing the world through their dialogue with LINC XVI. Of course, they are unaware that all of their interactions through LINC XVI are actually mediated by a team of psychiatrists in a special government bureau in Washington.

Upon a Third Reading

Perhaps I am being too harsh, actually there is imbedded in this scenario an array of admirable educational goals. Are not Belland and Taylor trying to incite people from different disciplines to deal creatively with the possibilities and strategies for implementing these goals? Imbedding them in a scenario with excessive application of one kind of technology is simply a way to make the task challenging and interesting.

Listing these goals in the order they are presented, we come first to the fact that the LINC system will "present the world." This is extraordinarily important in a time in which we are all connected to the whole world in a diversity of ways—as consumers, workers, investors, communicators, potential nuclear victims, etc. Yet education, at all levels, in all disciplines and in all parts of the world, has not yet begun to creatively confront the kind of education about the whole world that is needed for a fulfilling life under these conditions.

Second, there is the aspiration that Kelly be able to communicate with any other person or organization in the solar system. This would go a long way toward diminishing the self-centeredness of a giant country, as reflected in our schools and our press, radio and TV. Might the capacity of organizations now employing terrorism to get the attention of the Kellys of all the world diminish their need to communicate their message through terrorism?

Third, it is desired that Kelly comprehend and use incoming communications regardless of their origins—virtually unachievable, but an indispensable goal on a shrinking globe. It presupposes competency in a variety of languages, knowledge of a diversity of cultures, and skills in cross-cultural communication.

Fourth, Kelly's best talents are to be focused on the advancement of society, not simply in pursuit of personal comfort or amassing of wealth. Since the other goals have no territorial boundary, one would guess, although it is not made explicit, that the society referred to is humanity as a whole.

Fifth, individual fulfillment is given a significant place as Kelly's life is to have purpose, physical freedom and widespread communication. This is closely tied to the sixth, the expectation that everyone participate in government.

Seventh, although the authors are not explicit on this point, we can only assume that the Kelly in the scenario actually represents all people in the solar system. This would plausibly follow from the lack of territorial boundaries in "Kelly's Education." Since all are linked to Kelly, by a LINC XVI or something compatible with it, we assume that all have the same educational opportunities as Kelly.

In reflecting on this rather exciting array of educational goals, one discovers that very significant values are implied but not made explicit.

Indirectly the authors celebrate cultural diversity. Otherwise, why would they wish Kelly to communicate with people in distant places and to comprehend their communications regardless of origins? Obviously, they are bringing this diversity into Kelly's experience as a learning tool. It follows that it must be preserved, otherwise the quality of Kelly's education would diminish.

Also, the authors seem to desire that the Kellys who live in a variety of cultural circumstances be enabled to develop their own purposeful participation, through physical freedom, widespread communication and participation in government. Obviously, the modes for purposeful participation in different cultural circumstances would vary considerably. It is at this point that contradictions in the scenario begin to emerge. Under conditions of cultural diversity, only possible with widespread autonomy, would it be possible for LINC to spread to the entire world? Is LINC not actually but one kind of educational culture? This being the case, is there not a contradiction between the educational goals expounded in the scenario and the educational technology through which it is carried out? It will be helpful to speculate on how LINC might have spread to the solar system.

Scenario for the Worldwide Spread of LINC

The LINC system was likely produced by a worldwide communications conglomerate, LINC Incorporated. Perhaps it was the creation of a late Twentieth Century Henry Ford who was determined to attach a LINC to every brain rather than put a car in every household. Or, it might have been the creation of a consortium of home computer firms in the United States, Europe and Japan. Perhaps extreme competition among firms had driven prices so low that the high profits of the late Twentieth Century had dropped rapidly. Also, users of incompatible systems were frustrated as they tried to communicate with each other. In response, LINC Inc. developed a new consortium for building "one world through LINC." In its efforts to sell LINC as a peace strategy, the firm was first incorporated as "Peace LINCS." But the US organization "Peace-Links—Women Against Nuclear War," quickly brought a successful lawsuit against the use of a title almost identical to their trademark. LINC Inc. responded by changing their name to PAX LINC.

PAX LINC rapidly overcame all competitors in Europe, Japan and the United States. Critical to their worldwide program was access to the Soviet Union. Many were surprised when PAX

LINC made the largest sale in its history, 300-million LINC XVIs, one for every Soviet citizen. Actually this was a contract for the construction and operation of ten regional LINC production and service centers in the Soviet Union. Many interpret this surprising coup of PAX LINC as a bold strategy by the Soviet government to catch up with Western/Japanese electronic technology. Others say the Soviet government saw LINC as a phenomenal improvement over more antiquated and costly ways of controlling the Soviet people.

Unconfirmed rumors still circulate that PAX LINC also developed, in a secret plan in the Urals, a special center for government monitoring of all LINC communications in the Soviet Union. It is also rumored that LINC Urals has the capacity to create its own world for LINC users in the USSR. It is rumored that LINC Urals has created thousands—or even millions—of bogus people with whom Soviet citizens communicate. These bogus people satisfy the desire of Soviet citizens to interact with people from other parts of the world without the negative consequences that the Soviet government perceives would be produced by free communication with the rest of the world.

LINC Urals has, quite naturally, caused great concern in the United States because it would have the capacity to monitor LINC XVI users in the United States and to respond to US LINC users with bogus messages. It has been rumored, but not confirmed, that PAX LINC has secretly built an anti-LINC Urals center in the Rockies for the United States government. Indeed, it is reported that this was a secret US government condition for the export of LINC technology to the Soviet Union, particularly that technology incorporated in LINC Urals.

But the rumors do not stop here. Some are even saying, although few seem to accept this rumor, that the whole LINC effort was a joint effort of the United States and Soviet governments, most specifically of the KGB and CIA. In the closing years of the Twentieth Century both the United States and the Soviet Union faced a variety of internal and foreign disruptions that made US-Soviet collaboration in preserving the status quo preferable to the risk of global turmoil in which the two superpowers might lose their hegemony over the rest of the world and perhaps even their control over their own populations. Evidence for this theory is the rapidity with which the closest allies of the US and the Soviet Union joined the LINC system. Very quickly all members of NATO and the Warsaw pact joined LINC, as well as all other countries in which the US and the USSR stationed troops, had bases, or provided some form of military assistance.

It should not be surprising that China, and other more independently minded countries, were the longest holdouts against LINC, including Libya, Tanzania, Albania, Iran and Burma. Also joining the resistance were groups striving against their government for greater autonomy, such as Native Americans (throughout the Americas), Quebecois, Basques, Kurds, Polisarios, Sikhs, Assams and Estonians, to name only a few of the nations who had been denied entry into the worldwide system of states. At a remarkable conference in Beijing, the Chinese government proposed a counter-LINC strategy based on China's rapidly developing electronic technology that was already challenging PAX LINC in many parts of the world. But many attending opposed this for the same reason they opposed PAX LINC. They feared any communications systems that reached from centers of world economic and political power to individuals in cultural groups without the economic and political power to exert influence on these systems equal to that exerted from the outside. They believed this would inevitably lead to cultural genocide and external domination.

Not many years after the second conference (held in Tripoli) broke up China found it necessary to make its peace with PAX LINC and join the conglomerate. Facing food riots after a long drought, strong pressure was brought on China to join PAX LINC in return for food aid. No doubt of equal significance was the fact that LINC XVIs were finding their way to China anyway, presumably through a joint KGB-CIA program of smuggling across borders and airdrops. So the Chinese government faced two dilemmas: Sell the units for a profit or permit their citizens to get them free; make a contract with PAX LINC that would permit some Chinese control of LINCs in China, or stand idly by while their citizens secretly used units controlled from the USSR or the USA. They had no choice but to fight US and Soviet control of LINC from inside the system.

The Opposition

By 2010 it was widely believed that LINC had spread to all the peoples of the world. But it was virtually impossible to confirm whether this was true or not. Because the people of the world were almost totally dependent on LINC for knowledge about the world, they had no way of knowing whether there were peoples outside the LINC system. Nevertheless, there were persistent rumors that peoples in remote areas such as inner Asia, the Sahel, the Andes and the Himalayas had refused to join the system and even had conducted raiding parties destroying LINC units. Some said the proof of the truth of the rumors, necessarily passed by word of mouth, was the fact that any effort to discuss them through LINC resulted in temporary deactivation of the LINC unit involved.

By 2020 travellers reported seeing NIX LINC graffiti in Buenos Aires, Mexico City, Lagos, Paris, Leningrad, Shanghai, Tokyo, New York and other large urban areas. NIX LINC is demanding the convening of a World congress of Peoples in which representatives of some three thousand states, nations, ethnic groups and linguistic groups would draft a treaty that would guarantee basic communications rights for all peoples. It would be based on the Declaration on Communications Rights of Peoples, already disseminated by NIX LINC.

The Declaration was first published through graffiti in many urban areas around the world, one clause at a time. As each clause appeared simultaneously in many cities, the visible threat of NIX LINC to PAX LINC grew. It became obvious that NIX LINC had established its own worldwide communications network. It is rumored that the declaration itself was the product of months of negotiation by participants in the NIX LINC communications system. Graffiti also reports that clandestine NIX LINC communications centers have been raided by PAX LINC security agents. While NIX LINC has not responded with violence, PAX LINC has noticeably tightened security at their communications centers. There is increasing evidence of the technological sophistication of NIX LINC as PAX LINC users increasingly receive news of NIX LINC activities and goals through NIX LINC penetration of the PAX LINC system.

Now, in 2025, many find it difficult to understand how technological breakthroughs in education with such promise have caused such widespread civic unrest around the world. As computer-based learning spread like wildfire there was the expectation that it would make education possible for everybody, anywhere, around the clock, and throughout life. Advocates promised that societies would become more democratic as more and more acquired access to knowledge at decreasing cost. But more and more educators are now arguing that widespread use of LINC is producing a more sedentary culture of people with declining oral skills, growing inability to deal with face-to-face encounters, particularly those involving stress, decreasing ability to establish enduring friendships and decline in empathy for others. Some say that these criticisms are supported by classified PAX LINC research that demonstrates a high correlation between intensity of LINC XVI usage and cardiovascular and mental illness. A report attributed to NIX LINC reports a high increase in suicides and crimes of violence in inner cities when the PAX LINC system is down. Although they could be apocryphal, a number of stories have circulated about children who have burned to death while unable to rouse the fire department on their LINC XVI. As the stories go, they were either unable to get permission from LINC headquarters to leave the building or were so dependent on LINC that they were psychologically unable to open the window and yell for help from other people. Whether or not these stories are true, they do reflect the growing criticism of LINC-dependent education.

   While admitting that PAX LINC is not perfect, and acknowledging that the system needs some "fine tuning," the United States government strongly defends the system as the most significant achievement of free enterprise in human history. At a recent White House conference on "Communications for All" the President said that the Declaration of Communications Rights of Peoples, and the proposal for a World Congress of Peoples, are a throwback to the proposals for a New World Information and Communication Order (NWICO) in the 1980s. She said that the successful U.S. campaign against NWICO had prevented state control of communication throughout the world. The President cited as a turning point in this campaign the withdrawal of the United States from UNESCO in the 1980s. At this point, she said, the United States made it clear in unmistakable terms that "the free flow of information" is an issue that is non-negotiable for the United States.

One questioner asked the President whether the term "free flow of information" was appropriate for describing a communications system which was largely one-way despite its highly advertised interactive qualities. The questioner emphasized that PAX LINC was exceedingly one-way in the sense that it was the creation of the culture of one part of the world and was controlled from centers in that part of the world. How could there be said to be worldwide "freedom of information" when this culture had overwhelmed other cultures, indeed it has been accused of "cultural genocide," in many parts of the world. The President replied that she was somewhat astounded that the questioner was mouthing the meaningless platitudes of NIX LINC and the long discredited NWICO campaign. She said that the United States led the world in its concern for the masses of the world. Indeed, she was proud that, through PAX LINC, U.S. technology and the free enterprise system, with the cooperation of like-minded leaders around the world, had brought education, and thereby the chance for a better life, to people in all parts of the world. Perhaps this had meant the disappearance of a few "marginal cultures" that could not compete. But this, she said, is always the price of human progress.

Questioning then turned to the increasing resistance to PAX LINC and its potential for disrupting worldwide communication. The President was asked whether this resistance did not suggest that the rejection of NWICO, and the unwillingness of the United States to take part in the exchange of views on communication policy in UNESCO, had contributed to growing conflict over the now dominant worldwide communications system. The President said that the United States was always prepared to discuss any issue but that there was an appropriate time and place for any discussions between states. It was very clear to her that most members of UNESCO in the 1980s were not truly interested in "communication for all," the purpose of this White House conference. Instead, many UNESCO members preferred state control and others were simply interested in disrupting world order.

Presidential aides abruptly ended the press conference when a follow-up question asked about a report circulating at the White House Conference that described NIX LINC plans to render PAX LINC ineffective through a strategy of jamming, false messages and sabotage of communications centers. The report noted that banking, trade, the management of corporations, government and voluntary associations, and the production and acquisition of the necessities of life, had become so dependent on PAX LINC that normal life could not continue without it. Many experts at the conference agreed with the assertion in the report that the abrupt collapse of PAX LINC would lead to world chaos and the death of billions of people. Reporters have been unable to get confirmation that PAX LINC officials and government leaders recognize this possibility and have been quietly stockpiling the necessities of life at key underground centers in order to insure the survival of leaders should PAX LINC be seriously incapacitated.

Some critics of this report claim it is either the product of reckless humor or suicidal madness. They observe that LINC has guaranteed the peace for over a decade. It is the genius of the system that it maximizes interdependence and cannot be destroyed without everybody suffering. Furthermore, why should any sane person want to destroy PAX LINC when the world has made greater material progress in the past decade than at any time in the history of the world? To these arguments NIX LINC communications respond that the inbuilt cultural bias of PAX LINC has prevented broad understanding of the resentment of the intrusion of this material progress on local cultures. Also, progress in wellbeing has not been shared equitably. The differentiation between rich and poor regions of the world that began when Europe colonized the world, and continued throughout the Twentieth Century, has continued to grow in the Twenty-First Century. The same is true of the gap between the rich and the poor within both wealthy and poor countries. For this reason the leaders of NIX LINC have been arguing that they have less to lose. The richer you are the more vulnerable you will be to the collapse of PAX LINC. Hence, the victors in the struggle between PAX LINX and NIX LINC will be people in the peripheries of the world. They say that the destruction of PAX LINX is far from madness.

Rather, it is the only rational strategy for "freeing humanity from the most vicious form of imperialism ever devised."

Where Did We Go Wrong?

While Washington's attention is focused on strategies to "win the battle with NIX LINC, the greatest evil the world has ever witnessed," in the words of the President, some people in other parts of the country are increasingly asking, "Where did we go wrong?" This has led to a lot of finger pointing. Naturally the prime targets are those who produced and marketed LINC. But increasingly the blame is being placed on "educators who rushed to accept LINC in the schools, as an unquestioned progression from the mindless rush to employ mini computers in the schools beginning in the 1980s." Educators reply, "How could the school alone resist the spread of computers throughout society—in business, recreation, churches and homes? After all, the school culture is but a reflection of the society. Parents, and employers, insisted that we computerize our curriculum. How could we prepare young people for a world dominated by LINC without training them for participation in LINC?"

Most who speak out attack critics as unpatriotic and say that they are destroying the unity required in confronting the challenge of NIX LINC. Many of these people are part of a campaign to get government support for the dissemination of LINC XVII and for research and development funds for LINC XVIII. Their view is that their only security is through the technological superiority of the LINC system. Given the promise of some anti-NIX LINC features in LINC XVII (already in use in many government offices), and the possibilities of the END NIX component being designed for LINC XVIII, they believe that "the greatest evil the world has witnessed" can be eliminated by keeping a jump ahead in the technology race.

There are a few scholars engaged in more probing efforts to respond to the question: "Where did we go wrong?" Most of this handful of scholars do not expect to prevent an electronic Armageddon and the consequent death of billions. But they do hope to leave behind for the survivors understanding of what happened so that it might be avoided in the future. Perhaps the best known group in the United States is the Committee of Correspondence, named after the network of Committees of

Correspondence founded by Samuel Adams in Boston in 1772. The modern group shares the revolutionary spirit of the Eighteenth Century groups, and they too communicate in hand written messages, an act of resistance. Because the papers of these critical scholars are passed by hand, journalists have called them *samizdat*, after the documents circulated by Soviet dissidents in the late Twentieth Century.

Those who have read some of this Twenty-First Century *samizdat* say that it includes far ranging criticism of late Twentieth Century trends that pointed toward present world conditions. The value of this *samizdat* is not that it offers solutions to the world crisis, but that repressed questions are being asked, and that untraditional perspectives are being expressed. Some writers look back with great longing to the last several decades of the Twentieth Century. In retrospect they see it as a great time of hope. European colonial systems had just crumbled. There was a surge of independence and autonomy movements on the part of many nationality groups: Sikhs, Kurds, Basques, Palestinians, etc. There were successful challenges to military dictatorships in Argentina, Chile, Nicaragua, El Salvador, the Philippines, etc. Third World development programs were being strongly affected by advocates of local self-reliance. In the industrialized countries there was a resurgence of grassroots, "backyard," or "Green" movements on a variety of issues: environment, utility rates, toxic pollution, flight of corporations, conversion to civilian production, freezing the production of nuclear weapons, etc.

In retrospect this is viewed as a high point in world history with respect to the spread of the spirit of self-determination, or of participation. Certainly, self-determination for individuals, groups and nations was far from complete. One only had to recall that there were many remaining military dictatorships, that many repressed groups found it necessary to use "terrorism" to get the attention of the world, and that millions were unemployed. Yet, some believe that the widespread spirit of self-determination was very near a fundamental breakthrough. *Why, they wonder, did the world pull back from this surge in self-determination?*

Another hopeful sign in the late Twentieth Century was the global education movement, particularly significant in the West.

This movement was beginning to overcome the worldview created by years of Western domination of Africa, Asia and Latin America in which "world history" had become either Western history or a Western view of the spread of Western culture to the entire world. While all parts of the world still had a predilection for a self-centered view of the world, there was growing competence, and desire, to present humanity as consisting of a great diversity of separate experiments in human fulfillment, all having something to contribute and learn from the others, and recognizing that, at least to some degree, they share a common fate. *What happened to the great spirit of cultural equity embodied in the global education movement?*

The late Twentieth Century is also remembered as the first time that humankind assembled, particularly in the various organizations of the UN system, began to approach common problems such as social justice, human rights, disarmament, population, environment, resources, water, food, the global economy, global communications, outer space, the atmosphere, and the oceans. Few problems were really solved: nevertheless, scholars say this too was fundamentally a global education process, as people in different parts of the world learned about the perspectives of people in other countries on significant issues and also became aware of extreme variation in priorities. Fundamentally important, they say, is that this dialogue was reaching toward common standards for life on a planet that technology was making smaller and smaller. Examples are declarations for a New International Economic Order, for the Economic Rights and Duties of States, for a New International Information and Communication Order, and treaties, on Economic, Social and Cultural Rights; Civil and Political Rights; Racial Discrimination; Rights of Women; and Genocide, to name only a few. Often the declarations did not lead to agreed obligations, and often agreed obligations undertaken in treaties were not lived up to. Yet, the very definition of standards for life on the planet by humankind assembled offered new hope— standards to be fulfilled, to be appealed to. *Why did the spirit of hope and mutual responsiveness embodied in these efforts collapse?*

Some Answers

The *samizdat* is filled with speculative answers to these questions.   Some say that the widespread surge for self-determination was subdued by secret collaboration among centers of overwhelming political and military power—particularly in Washington and Moscow—and by centers of economic power, in cities such as New York, London, Paris, Tokyo, Sao Paolo, Lagos and Bombay.   Not only did leaders of big powers and big corporations fear the challenge to their domination of the world, but they also feared that the worldwide surge for self-determination would lead to chaos.   Epitaphs such as anarchic, chaotic or terrorist were applied to self-determination movements.   But others say far more important was the lack of visions that would offer perspective on the global movement for self-determination.   Actually the movement implied a new kind of world order in which all states, nations and ethnic groups would have a place and in which all individuals would have avenues for influencing the policies of world political, economic and communication systems.   Not only those with political and economic power, but also leaders in science, education and the arts had no vision beyond the existing state system.   This system seemed inevitable, and any challenge to it looked messy, unrealistic and disorderly.

The Committee of Correspondence, in particular, makes much of the striking contrast between the lack of a future vision by leaders in the Twentieth Century in the United States and the vision of leaders in 1776.   It is observed that the lack of vision in the late Twentieth Century was not only a failing of those in power but also of those involved in various self-determination movements themselves.   Each seemed to operate in its own little sphere, largely unmindful of the global uprising of which it was a part.

Some blame the rapid rise and fall of the global education movement on PAX LINC in particular, and the compulsive drive of educators for a "state of the art" technology in general.   It is charged that the content of education became less and less important as continual "improvement" of the delivery system became the most important preoccupation.   But there are those who say that the leaders of the global education movement themselves cannot avoid blame. It is said that strong global education leadership could have prevented the spread of PAX LINC had there been steadfast commitment to the spirit of cultural equity at the heart of the movement. But the vision was corrupted as global educators "bought in" to PAX LINC as a strategy for keeping resources flowing into global education. But in the process of becoming a part of PAX LINC, leaders in global education lost their critical insight on the impact of the worldwide spread of PAX LINC culture on global education. Undermined was the great spirit of cultural equity that had produced a vision of a global education movement to which all cultures contributed.

The demise of the global education movement is pointed to by some *samizdat* writers as a key factor in the collapse of efforts in the late Twentieth Century to develop solutions to global issues and problems based on standards for human life on the planet developed cooperatively by the representatives of the peoples of the world. These standards had, of course, been developed primarily in the organizations of the UN system. The rights of individuals and peoples inscribed in the great human rights declarations and treaties of the late Twentieth Century are viewed as the high water mark in humanity's long pursuit of rights for all. Twenty-First Century historians are puzzled why this achievement was recognized by so very few people living in the late Twentieth Century. Were some fearful that rights for others would mean loss of advantages for themselves? Were some too preoccupied with amassing material advantages for themselves? Were some cynical, noting that not all involved in the enterprise really intended to fulfill the standards set forth in human rights documents? Did some have unrealistic expectations, not realizing that promulgation of standards necessarily would proceed their fulfillment by many years?

It is remarkable how many contributors to *samizdat* in the United States mention the significance of an event in the 1980s not widely noticed by people in the United States at the time—the withdrawal of the United States from UNESCO. Up to this time the UN system had been spared the debilitating pattern of withdrawals that plagued the League of Nations. But the United States set a withdrawal trend, followed by numerous withdrawals of other countries from various UN agencies, rendering it a far less significant force than it had been in the late Twentieth Century. But most attention in the present crisis is given to the fact that U.S. withdrawal from UNESCO was specifically related to Third World demand for a New World Information and Communication Order. Historical analysis reveals that U.S. citizens, the media and even the government never really understood the deep significance of the movement for a NWICO. There was a tendency for the press in particular to focus on specific Third World proposals (such as one for licensing journalists) often tossed out in desperation because of the lack of responsiveness by Western countries. But the critical underlying issue was a dispute between "freedom of information" (meaning the right of existing powerful communications organizations to disseminate information with restraint) versus communications equity (a vision of all people and cultures not only receiving worldwide communications but communicating back).

Some in the Committee of Correspondence have written that the inability of most sectors of U.S. society to understand the deep significance of the NWICO dispute was an early warning signal that U.S. society was on a path that would lead to PAX LINC. There was insensitivity to the fact that equity in global communications was a necessary foundation for self-determination and all other human rights. Importantly, withdrawal from UNESCO signified diminishing U.S. interest in working with the rest of the world in developing global communications/educational systems responsive to the needs of all. Instead, U.S. government and corporation leaders, often in cooperation with leaders from Western Europe and Japan, sharply increased U.S./European/Japanese domination of global communication/education. At the end of this line of development, present critics say, is the coming Armageddon between PAX LINC and NIC PAX, and possibly the collapse of civilization as it is known today.

While we have given considerable attention to these dissident writers, and their efforts to point out "where we went wrong," it must be said that most people aware of this literature (and they are not numerous) view it as a rather useless exercise. What use does it make to have these answers now, they say? Never again, at least for a thousand years, will humanity have the conditions that the late Twentieth Century offered for creating a human community based on widespread self-determination, cultural equity and evolving standards for life on the planet shaped by participants from throughout the world. Would that our generation, now in mid-2025, could witness the flowering of human potential equal to that which enriched the life of our predecessors in the 1980s. Would that they had the vision to perceive the possibilities of their age, thus sparing us from . . .

REFERENCES

Gerald Benjamin, *The communications revolution in politics, proceedings of the academy of political science*, Vol. 34, No. 4, New York, 1982.

Kaarle Nordenstreng, *The mass media declaration of UNESCO.* Norwood, N.J.: Ablex Publishing Corp., 1984.

Kaarle Nordenstreng, *National sovereignty and international communication.* Norwood, N.J.: Ablex Publishing Corp., 1979.

Aurelio Peccei, *The human quality.* New York: Pergamon Press, 1977.

John Wicklein, *Electronic nightmare: The new communications and freedom.* New York: The Viking Press, 1981.

13

On the Limits of Visual Communication: A Case Study*

Glenn Hudak
Curriculum Theory
SUNY at Albany

In this paper I will report the findings from a larger study which investigated the use of video equipment as a means of visual communication at the secondary school level.[1] The primary objectives for that study were first to provide practitioners and researchers in the areas of media studies, visual literacy, and educational media technology much needed descriptions of how students learn about, use, and produce a video project. And second, to generate a grounded theory[2] from a concrete situation which would explain and identify conceptual linkages between the specific events which occurred during planning sessions, production sessions, and presentation of video tapes produced by students (*i.e.,* links between planning, production, and text). To this end, this paper will present both description and theory and show how the social and communicative interactions between

---

*Reprinted with permission from the *Journal of Visual/Verbal Languaging,* 7(1), © 1987. The author wishes to acknowledge and thank Jill Casler, Harriet Powers, and Beverly Solseng of the Center for Teaching and Learning for their assistance in the preparation of this manuscript.

[1]Glenn M. Hudak, "Communicating, Learning and Discourse Production in the Classroom: A Case Study of a Mass Media Curriculum." (Ph.D. dissertation, University of Wisconsin-Madison, 1985).

[2]Methods pertaining to the gathering of data and the organization of materials are discussed in Hudak (1985), Chapter 2. Also the discussion of grounded theory is found in Barney Glasser and Anselm Strauss, *The Discovery of Grounded Theory* (New York, Aldine Publishing Company, 1980).

students came to establish boundaries on the form of the video texts produced. Due to the length of this undertaking, I will not focus the analysis on the content of the video texts. Instead, I will describe the content of student video texts to situate the reader and analyze the structure of these student productions.

Data Collection

The data for this study was collected by observing a single high school mass media course. The course met for a full semester, sixteen weeks; five days a week; for 50 minutes each day. Since data was collected on a daily basis for the entire semester, the total time I was in contact with members of this class was approximately 105 hours. In order to investigate the social and communicative dimensions of the class, data was obtained from three sources: first, through written descriptions of classroom activities; second, through formal interviews with students and teacher; and last, by obtaining reproductions of the video projects completed by the students.

With regard to classroom descriptions, my aim was to provide the reader with a complete picture of life in a media course. However, it is important to keep in mind that while I attempted to be 'open-minded' in making my observations, certain events were selected and amplified as more important than others. This process of selection was, of course, determined *a priori* by the conceptual framework of the study. For such a framework acted as a lens or a filter through which events were described and later selected for closer examination. While I will explicate the conceptual framework for this study in the following sections of this paper, it is important to note that at the time of data collection, Basil Bernstein's categories of restricted/elaborated speech codes acted as a conceptual lens.

Setting

The setting for this study was a single high school mass media course. There were 24 students enrolled—13 were male, 11 were female. The instructor was male. Throughout the study he is identified as Mr. Albert, a pseudonym. Likewise, all student names used in the study are pseudonyms. The media course was offered as an elective within the English department. Only high school juniors and seniors (11th and 12th grades) were allowed to register for the course. There were no formal prerequisites for the course. No texts were used in the course; the instructor presented material from his notes, or through the use of films. The curriculum for regular classroom lessons initially focused on the social and cultural foundations of contemporary media practices, and later on the technical aspects of film and video production. During these lessons students were asked to identify technical terms associated with various components found in production, *e.g.*, pan, tilt, fade in/out. After students completed the unit on production terms, the instructor gave students a video assignment to complete. Three and a half class periods were set aside for students to plan and then produce a video tape.

For this project the class was structured in the following manner: a) Mr. Albert, the teacher, divided the class into three production groups. (To limit this article, I will focus on only two of the three student groups.) b) Each group had to produce a video project. c) The groups had to discuss their projects in class and taping had to be completed at the school studio. d) Approximately two and a half class periods were devoted to planning the project, and one class period to taping.

Mr. Albert also made "suggestions" to students regarding their projects. These suggestions pertain to the procedures and to the content of the productions. The suggestions include the following: a) "Remember, this is a group effort." Here Mr. Albert is suggesting that all members of the group ought to contribute to the project. b) The projects are to be completed in "good taste." This suggestion refers to the content of the tape. c) The tapes should be "visually" interesting. Here Mr. Albert is suggesting that students try employing some of the concepts developed during the regular classroom sessions. He does not require that students use classroom information. And d) Mr. Albert suggests that students copy a commercial TV program. He believed that students in the past enjoyed copying a format with which they were familiar and had fewer production problems to solve (*e.g.*, plot development, roles for actors). I call these remarks made by Mr. Albert "suggestions" because, unlike the explicit guidelines, they do not place formal constraints or requirements on students.

Within the context of the media course, Mr. Albert's agenda provided students with some degree of autonomy. The framework for the project was sufficiently vague to allow students ample "space" to develop a script, shoot it, and to enjoy themselves in the process. In essence, the transition from regular classroom sessions to the video production project represents a fundamental shift in the type of knowledge considered legitimate for use in the classroom and a break in routine classroom procedures. The transition from regular classroom sessions to video production indicates a "deregulation" of knowledge and practices found in the media course.

With regard to classroom knowledge, deregulation shifts the source of knowledge from teacher to student. During regular classroom sessions, Mr. Albert was the primary definer of the classroom agenda. Legitimate classroom knowledge was essentially teacher owned knowledge. However, in video production the boundary between student and school knowledge weakens. Students are allowed to draw from their own pool of information about the media. Indeed, the tacit assumption of video production is that students will draw upon and utilize their familiarity with commercial television programs, for Mr. Albert never discussed nor analyzed commercial TV during regular classroom sessions. Rather, he wanted students to explore, and use equipment on their own. This "free" exploration appears to be founded in the assumption that students are familiar enough with commercial TV to have a common foundation upon which to build a group project, without much guidance from teachers. The deregulation of classroom knowledge encourages students to utilize their knowledge of TV.

Along with the deregulation of knowledge, there occurred a deregulation of routine social practices in the classroom. This shift in social practice meant that students no longer had to sit in assigned seats and address their comments to Mr. Albert. Video production allows students to communicate with each other. As I shall describe shortly, the group discussion format allowed students to interact in a less restricted manner. The description of events indicates that, for the most part, Mr. Albert remains in the background; he does not monitor the discussion sessions. In essence, discussions which would have previously been curtailed by Mr. Albert are tolerated. As long as students do not disrupt the class as a whole, they can usually do what they want.

Planning Sessions

Deregulation signals a shift in knowledge orientation (from teacher to student) and social practices (greater student autonomy less teacher control). The question which arises is, "Given increases in student autonomy and responsibility to define their own agenda, what will students do? How will they interact as a group?"

After reviewing my extensive descriptions of the planning sessions, I found that without Mr. Albert's guidance, these sessions can best be described as spontaneous and unorganized. That is, students did not methodically plan their projects. There was no evidence of any student writing a detailed outline, writing a script, or discussing the technical aspects of production (material presented in regular classroom sessions). Instead, group interactions appeared to vacillate between socializing, arguing, sitting quietly, doing homework, and sporadically discussing the video project.

The planning sessions, in turn, were defined to a great extent by the social interaction of each group. From the data I collected, two forces seem to guide group interaction. They are: a) *effort* students were willing to put into the project and b) strong reliance on *familiarity* with commercial television formats. The specific configuration of effort and familiarity found in each discussion group defines what I call the *general characteristic* of that group.

Group A consisted of eight students: three girls (Terry, Sally, and Pam) and five boys (Bob, Steve, Bill, Ted and Ed). The tape made by this group is titled "The Newlywed Game." The length of the tape is eight minutes and 45 seconds. The general characteristics of Group A can be defined as consensus. Consensus was derived from the lack of conflict found in this group. The absence of conflict appears to be partially grounded in the level of effort expended by members and their strong reliance on a familiar format for the video project.

The degree of effort expended by this group can be characterized as "low." My observations indicate that this group does not appear eager to begin their project. For example, Bill's comment, "Well, let's go to sleep," seems to sum up the group attitude. During the two and a half days set aside for planning, Group A students spent the majority of their time either sitting quietly, doing homework, talking with friends, or sleeping. Deregulation allows students the "space" to socialize. These students appeared to take advantage of this situation.

The "low" degree of effort coincides nicely with the format adopted by the group— "The Newlywed Game."

Bob: "There was nothing on our minds. She (Terry) said how about the 'Newlywed Game.' We saw no objection so we went with it. It was something we'd all seen."

Ted: "Well, we didn't have many ideas. The girls started naming off TV programs. Finally the group narrowed it down. And we said OK to the 'Newlywed Game.' We figured it would be like TV."

The group adopts a format that is very familiar and the familiarity allows them to continue to socialize without having to put much effort into the actual planning of the project. The adopted format guides the group. The group picks an emcee, divides into couples, makes cue cards for the emcee and answer cards for the contestants. There is little question on the part of students about their roles, or the procedure they will follow. On the last day set aside for planning the group still appeared fairly confident, even though no script had been written and there had been no discussion of the technical aspects of production. On this day, Bill listens to the radio, Bob sleeps, Pam stares into space, and others talk among themselves. One gets the impression that it is almost out of boredom that the group decides to rehearse. A rehearsal is chosen instead of writing a script. Planning which would require more work is vetoed by the group. The rehearsal is quicker and easier. (Interestingly enough, they rehearse only five minutes!)

In sum, this project is guided by a strong familiarity with the "newlywed" format. The format provides an informal outline for the group to follow and it allows the group to successfully complete the project without exerting a great deal of mental effort. The parameters of the group's agenda are defined by knowledge which is immediately available. The planning of the project does not require, nor rely upon, knowledge derived from the mass media class.

Group B consisted of nine students: three girls (Connie, Kathy, and Cindy), and six boys (Brian, Rob, Fred, Will, Don, and Dan). The project completed by this group was titled, "Hockey-Commercials." The length of the project was two minutes and 53 seconds.

Group B was characterized as consensus/exploring. Consensus was derived from the lack of conflict exhibited by the group. As with Group A, consensus is grounded in the level of effort expended by members of the group, however the degree of effort expended by Group B is somewhat higher than Group A. Exploring accentuates the relative strength of the group effort. Based on the observations, I found that this group immediately begins discussing the project. All members appear to be both eager and interested. While Brian assumes the role of group leader, other members of the group offer suggestions. Their suggestions are not only listened to, but are discussed by others. The members of the group appear willing to participate in the group process.

The description of the initial planning session clearly illustrates this group's energy. As the class breaks into discussion groups, the room is full of noise, yet Mr. Albert does not tell students to be quiet. Group B forms a circle near the blackboard at the front of the classroom. This group is rather animated. They begin discussing the project immediately.

Don: "Are we going to have someone turn on the TV then change channels? Then we can have other skits, just like TV."

Brian: "Well, we can have 35 seconds for each skit. That way we can have everyone do stuff."

Rob: "How about one commercial throughout—the stuff that we keep coming back to, to tie up stuff."

Brian: "Okay . . . a commercial to end it."

Cindy: "Hold on. I'll be secretary. Let me write our ideas down."

The group settles down.   As Cindy writes ideas down, Brian assumes the role of group leader as he rattles off a possible list of things to do.

Brian: "First we turn the TV on . . . then a commercial . . . then a hockey game . . . then a commercial . . . then HBO movie . . . then Family Feud . . . then commercial . . . then turn off the TV set."

Other members of the group sit quietly as Brian outlines the format of the project. All members of the group are listening. Even though Brian is talking, others are not drifting off into their own conversations or doing other school work as in Group A. Group B is willing to let Brian lead; at the same time they appear eager to contribute to the discussion.

Along with effort, strong familiarity with commercial television serves to establish a consensus for Group B. The observations I collected reveal that students are very familiar with television programs. Commercial television provides the foundation from which the group can begin to discuss their project. Strong familiarity also enables students to continue exploring various possibilities. For example, Brian adds several "twists" to some TV commercials. He discusses with Fred and Will variations on battery, beer, and watch commercials.

However, familiarity with commercial television is not sufficient for Group B to go beyond the exploring stages of the project. It appears that by the second and third day of the planning sessions the group has reached a "plateau of understanding." By the last day of the planning session the initial enthusiasm is gone. Members of the group sit quietly. Bill comes over from Group A to borrow Brian's headphones. They talk and joke for a few minutes.

Fred and Will are still discussing the beer commercial.

Will: "I'll do the announcing.   You get drunker as the commercial goes on."

Fred: "Yeah."

Brian: (interjecting) "We need to do some violence in the commercial, like smashing a watch or something."

Fred: "Whose watch are we going to use? Yours?"

Brian: "Okay. How about a battery commercial where I break
        something?"
Will: "Nah, we'll do the beer thing."
      As Will, Fred, and Brian discuss the commercial,
Connie, Cindy, and Kathy talk about their commercial, "Mr.
Faggy Waggy."
Connie: "This is so dumb!"
Cindy: "Yeah, but it's funny. And all we need is toilet paper."
      Rob listens to their conversation. Don sits quietly by
himself, listening to the sub-conversations in the group.
      As the period comes to a close, Brian becomes the center of
the male discussion. The boys talk about variations in the beer
and battery commercial. They laugh and appear to be having fun
imagining different items that can be smashed in the
commercial. There is no mention of camera shots or writing
scripts.
      On the other hand, Cindy is the center of the female
conversation. The girls do not talk about the project. Instead
Connie, Kathy and Cindy talk about social events, such as parties
and events that happened in other classes. As a whole, the
impression I got from this group is one of confidence. They know
they will do something on production day. They do not appear
worried about how they will do it.
Brian: "Something will be done."
      In Group B, students are able to merge social knowledge
with a school assignment, therefore, the group appears more
dynamic, more energetic than Group A. Members of Group B
appear to be having fun. Unlike Group A, they do not appear bored.
However, the energy and enthusiasm of Group B, exhibited by
their exploration, does not aid in planning and organizing the
particulars of their project.

Communicative Interaction

      Thus far, the deregulation of knowledge and actual
classroom practices have been discussed. It had been found that
deregulation afforded students 'space' to define and articulate a
project.
      Next, we must link the social organization of the
discussion groups with the events of production day. As a start, I

will focus on the common ground between discussion and production, that is the students' reliance on material that is familiar.

It is helpful to begin by quoting at length an observation made by Basil Bernstein. In this passage Bernstein links understanding, communicative form, and social practices. He writes:

> "The greater the range of shared interest, the
> more probably speech will take a specific form. The
> range of syntactic alternatives is likely to be reduced
> and the lexis to be drawn from a narrow range. Thus,
> the form of these social relations is acting selectively
> on meanings verbally realized. In these relationships
> the intent of the other person can be taken for granted
> as the speech is played out against a back-drop of
> common assumptions, common history, common
> interests. As a result, there is less of a need to raise
> meanings to the level of explicitness or elaboration . . . .
> The *restricted codes* have their basis in condensed
> symbols, whereas the elaborated codes have their basis
> in articulated symbols."[3]

This is an important passage, for it provides a key with which to understand the events of the planning session and the video production. Bernstein states that in communicative interaction where participants share common assumptions, common history, common interests . . . the intent of the other person can be taken for granted. In this classroom situation, participants do share the common interest of familiarity with commercial television. Due to this shared orientation, the communicative interaction is likely to be condensed. That is, information and the transmission of messages are likely to be compressed. A simple utterance or a gesture may be able to convey enough information to form meaningful statements. And there may be less of a need for participants to have to make meanings

---

[3]Basil Bernstein, "Social Class, Language and Socialization," in *Power and Ideology in Education*, eds., Jerome Karabel and A. H. Halsey (New York: Oxford University Press, 1977), p. 478.

explicit in order to be understood. For users of the restricted code, the bulk of their communicative interaction is grounded in a familiar context shared by the users. This situation is analogous to an iceberg. If the tip of the iceberg is only 10 percent of the total mass, the greater mass lies beneath the surface. Likewise, the actual utterance in the restricted code becomes a compressed symbol; it represents the tip of the iceberg. The bulk of meanings and associations, which give meaning to the utterance, lie 'beneath the surface' of the interactions. Participants need not make explicit statements in order to be understood. Therefore, in this passage, Bernstein links familiarity (common assumptions/interests) with the form of the communicative interaction (*condensed communication*).

It can also be said that since condensed communication conveys meanings efficiently, the selection of lexicon used is likely to be simple. And for our purposes, the range of syntactic structure employed in a communicative interaction is likely to be restricted. For example, if I meet an old friend, all that may be required on my part to communicate meaningfully with him/her is simply "Hi!" "Hi!" expresses my joy in seeing my friend, a joy which is based on years of shared experiences. Since "Hi" communicates my joy and reestablishes old ties, there is no need for me to have to rely on more complex syntactic structures to convey my message. Simultaneously, the immediacy (the context) of my encounter with my friend adds to the communication. As I say "Hi!" I may pat my friend on the back, or have a smile on my face. All of this is compressed (condensed) and transmitted with the utterance. Since my friend is familiar with me and has shared experiences with me, he/she is able to understand the intent of my communication. Therefore, familiarity and context diminish the *necessity* of having to rely upon complex syntactic structures in order to convey messages.

By expanding Bernstein's notion of restricted speech codes, I have been able to derive the concept of condensed communication. The key terms in condensed communication are 'familiarity' (common assumptions/interest) and 'necessity' (the need to make meanings explicit in order to be understood). A project exhibiting a strong degree of condensation (CC+) in a communicative interaction would be characterized by: a) a strong familiarity with the format adopted, b) little necessity to make explicit the directions for coordinating the structure of the text produced. In essence, students will know how to re-create the format adopted, but may not necessarily understand the principles or rationale which constitute that format.

A project exhibiting a weak degree of condensation (CC-) would be characterized by: a) movement away from a familiar format, b) the need to make explicit directions for both actor and cameraperson (*i.e.*, coordination of project), and c) the visual syntactic structure of the text may be more complex. Within the confines of the media class the shift from familiar to unfamiliar knowledge means that students will appropriate the technical aspects of production, therefore, the syntactic structure of the text will be relatively more complex. Of importance here is the realization that as the syntactic structure of the text becomes more complex, there is a shift in the way in which messages are conveyed through the text. In a project exhibiting a strong degree of condensation (CC+), students will attempt to convey information through acting. For projects exhibiting a weak degree of condensation (CC-), students will begin to incorporate camera techniques into their agenda. Here the camera will highlight the action of the skit.

Production Session

In this section I shall present a description and analysis of the production session for each student project. The analysis will attempt to ascertain the degree of condensation for each group project to provide a link between mode of production and mode of communication. To this end, the analysis of the production session is divided into four components: a) quality of acting, b) interaction among actors, c) boundary between actors and camerapersons, d) dominant mode of communication. Taken together, these components (a-d) define the degree of condensation for the production session.

Group A. At 12:40, the members of group A assemble in front of the recording studio. Mr. Albert unlocks the door and with him students enter the room. The studio resembles a classroom. There is no special lighting for production. The space available is approximately the same except that the room is not cluttered with desks and book shelves. Instead, there are five tables, a podium, and the video equipment. The portapack is set up and ready to go. Mr. Albert talks with Steve (cameraperson). Others look over the cue cards made in class. They are very quiet.

Mr. Albert:	"We'll keep the tape running, that way we won't ruin it."

Steve:		"Okay."

Steve begins to explore the equipment. This is the first opportunity he has had to do so. He starts by trying to focus the camera. Mr. Albert stands back and allows Steve to explore. Others in the group are watching their images appear on the monitor. Penny sees herself and giggles. The others look embarrassed and a bit nervous.

Mr. Albert:	(walking over to Steve.) "I'd like it if you fill the screen with the couples. Don't leave too much empty space."

Steve:		(shaking his head nervously) "Okay."

Mr. Albert then stands back and watches as Steve renews his attempts to focus the camera.

Other members of the group take their places. They quietly wait as Steve practices panning the camera from left to right.

Terry:		(to Steve) "Do you want us (the girls) to practice leaving?"

Steve:		"No, you all leave at once . . . remember you're not supposed to hear the answers the guys give."

Terry:		"Yeah, but you know (laughter) we can't do this realistically . . . We'll just walk away. Don't follow us."

The room is very quiet.

Steve:		(yelling) "Okay, let's go."

To capture the "guys' " answers, Steve tells the group that he is going to go from the M.C. to couple #3 (Rob), then to couple #2 (Ted), and finally couple #1 (Bill). Then he will pan back to the announcer. For the girls' answers, he will begin with couple #3 (Sally), and then pan right, gradually working back to the M.C. From these instructions, we find that Steve will employ pans (L-R). The camera will be stationary.

Just as they are ready to begin, Mr. Albert asks:

Mr. Albert: "This is all going to be done continuously?"

Steve: "Yeah."

Mr. Albert: "No commercial breaks?"

Steve: "Ah, no."

Mr. Albert: "Remember to speak up to be heard."

Since the tape has been running, Steve must now stop the tape, rewind, and then record again. Steve has a hard time with this procedure. Mr. Albert shows him how to do it. They begin taping.

The M.C. is standing. He leans over the podium, holding cue cards in his hand. His gestures are very relaxed.

M.C.:   "Welcome to the Newlywed Game. Okay . . ."

He introduces the three couples. Steve makes a quick pan to the couples, as they are introduced. Then returns to the M.C.

M.C.:   "Okay (M.C. giggles), first round of questions . . . Okay. I'll ask questions worth five points. Ladies will you leave?"

We hear shuffling of chairs as they leave. The room is very quiet.

M.C.:   "All right guys, what is your wife's waist size? Uhm, we'll start with you Mr. A."

Bob is seated farthest from the M.C. Steve pans left across the tables.

Bob: "I think it's ah . . . I think it's 30 . . . yeah, I say 30."

M.C.:   "Okay, Mr. C." (Steve pans right)

Ted: "I would say 28, yeah a 28."

M.C.:   "Ok, Mr. B?" (Steve pans right)

Bill: "Uhm, that's a tough one. I'm not really sure. I'll have to take a shot at 31."

M.C.:   "Okay. That completes the first round of questions . . . Now we'll go on to the second round and ask the guys . . . Where did you meet your wife? Mr. B?" (Steve pans left to Bob)

The above procedure is repeated. Steve, with the camera, follows each contestant's response.

Bill: "At a gas station."

Ted: "At a family reunion."

The M.C. then calls the "ladies" back.

M.C.:   "Okay ladies . . . let's see here . . . okay ladies (giggles) . . . okay, where did you meet your husband? Mrs. B?" (Steve pans left across the tables)

Sally: "If he really knows it'll be a family reunion."

She sits staring. Bob holds up the answer card, which reads, "Family Reunion."

Sally: "Oh wow." (said with no emotion)

M.C.:   "Okay, Mrs. C."

Pam: "Visions."

Ted holds up card and "Visions" is written on it. He puts his arm around Pam to give her a hug. Pam looks a little shocked by this move. She giggles. Ted flushes red, obviously a little embarrassed for his having hugged her.

    The M.C. moves on to Terry and Bill. Terry guesses the right answer, "a gas station." Bill gives Terry a big hug, Terry hugs him back. This couple gets very excited.

    Next, the M.C. asks the ladies, "What is your waist size?" The M.C. begins with Terry (sitting closest to him). Terry doesn't guess the right answer. Bill/Terry shake their heads as he holds up the answer card. Then Steve pans to Pam. She guesses the right answer. This time Ted taps her on the shoulder, obviously afraid to hug her again. Finally, the M.C. asks Sally. Sally guesses the wrong answer.

M.C.:   "At the end of the second round we have 10 points for couple number 2 (Ted/Pam); the others have five points each . . . okay, now we'll ask the ladies a question—will the guys leave?" (The guys leave the set. We hear them shuffle out.) ". . . ladies, where were you when you first told your husband you were pregnant?" (He starts with Sally.)

Sally: "It was in bed."

Pam: "Uhm, it was my mother's house for dinner."

Terry: "At the movies."

M.C.   "All right. The second question . . . what is your favorite romantic restaurant?" (He begins with Terry.)

Terry:	"The Hatch Over."
Pam:	"The Edgewater."
Sally:	"No doubt about it, I'll have to say McDonalds."
M.C.:	"Okay, now for the bonus question worth ten points. Ladies, does your husband leave the toilet seat up or down?"
Sally:	"Always up."
Pam:	"Down."
Terry:	"Probably down."
M.C.:	"Okay, that completes the questions. We'll bring the guys back."

The 'guys' return. Bob is asked the first question.

M.C.:	"Where were you when your wife told you she was pregnant?"
Bob:	"Uhm, it was on our way back from our honeymoon. We were on a plane and she mentioned she was pregnant." (He laughs.)

Sally holds up the answer card— "in bed."

Sally:	"It was in bed . . . it was the night before we left!"
Bob:	"No it wasn't."
M.C.:	"Okay, Mr. C?"

Ted guesses the right answer.

Ted:	"At family's house."

He is about to embrace Pam, but doesn't.

Bill guesses "at home." Terry holds up the answer card— "at the movies." Bill and Terry overact their parts, having a prolonged discussion about who was right.

M.C.:	(second question): "What is your favorite restaurant?"

Bill does not guess the right answer. Likewise Ted misses the answer. Bob guesses the correct answer— "McDonalds." Finally the M.C. asks the bonus question.

Bob:	"I leave it down."
Sally:	"You leave it up!"
Bob:	"I leave it down." (They bicker back and forth for a while.)
Ted:	"I leave it down."

	Pam holds up card—"down" is written on it. Ted gives her a quick embrace.
Bill:	"I'd say I leave it up."
Terry:	"You leave it down. Every time I go in there, there's something on the seat. I have to clean up."
Bill:	"Come on, I always wipe."
M.C.:	"Okay ...now at the end of the game, couple number 2 wins with 25 points (Ted/Pam)... Couple number 2 will win a record from Ronco ...(he throws album to Ted) ...and thanks for playing ..."
Ted:	"What we always wanted!"

Steve zooms out to frame whole group with Ted and Pam in the middle of the frame, both hold the Ronco album. He then fades out for a total time of production at eight minutes, 45 seconds.

Interpretation. For Group A the general characteristic "consensus," is derived from a low degree of effort on the part of students, and strong familiarity with the adopted format— "The Newlywed Game." Low effort and strong familiarity reinforce a strong degree of condensation (CC+) within the communicative interaction. As discussed, the production session will be divided into four components: a) quality of the acting, b) interaction between actors, c) boundary between actors and cameraperson, and d) dominant mode of communication. Taken together they constitute the structure of condensed communication.

a) **The quality of acting** is described as spontaneous. The general format adopted provides the basis for the group's agenda. This format selects and defines the acting options available. These options are tacitly known by the actors; they did not need a script. The "spontaneous" quality of the acting is seen in the specific context of their roles. The format informs the actors, for instance, that when they lose they are to act "annoyed." The spontaneous quality is seen as the actor subtly recreates and effectively expresses this "annoyance." Since the actors did not put a great deal of effort into planning, it is reasonable to assume that they are guided by strong familiarity with the adopted format. The outcome is that the acting appears "natural" and "effortless." The display of spontaneity relies on a strong familiarity with the format, and requires little effort on the part of the actors.

Spontaneous acting is the concrete manifestation of the group consensus.

b) **The interaction between actors** displays a strong degree of condensation. The strong degree of condensation allows actors to "sync" their roles without the necessity of making explicit stage directions. The skit's narrative moves at a steady rate; there is little discontinuity. The actors "instinctively" know their cues, for these cues were provided by the format in the form of question/answer interactions. More importantly, the actors seem to be able to "read" their partners fairly well. When a couple loses a point, the two actors sync their "annoyance" rather well. Of importance is the fact that synchronization of parts did not require or rely upon prior explicit direction. A strong familiarity with the format bypasses the necessity of prior direction. The actors did not need to make explicit the specific content of their roles in the planning stages of the project. This aspect is carried over to production day. The actors are able to convey messages without the necessity of being explicit. Hence, the communicative interaction is very efficient and very condensed.

c) **The boundary between actors and cameraperson** is strong. Of importance is the fact that Steve receives no aid from his peers. The separation signifies a strong boundary between actors and cameraperson. It also signifies two distinct domains which operate simultaneously in the production process. On the one hand, the actors are situated within the domain of the familiar, experiential knowledge. On the other hand, Steve is situated within the domain of the unfamiliar, technical aspects of production. The strong boundary is constituted by the strong degree of condensation among the actors. The actors have implicitly eliminated technical knowledge from their discourse and therefore have isolated Steve from the group. The priorities of the actors are to stay within the familiar, and to exert as little effort as possible. (A high degree of condensation satisfies these requirements.) In order for the actors to aid the cameraperson, they would have to consider the technical aspects of production, the unfamiliar. To do this would require more effort. This would be in contradiction to their own inclinations. Hence, two separate domains operate simultaneously. These two domains constitute a sharp distinction in the division of labor. Steve must struggle with his part in the production process and the actors will do their part.

d) **The dominant mode of communication** for conveying the message of the skit is acting. The strong boundary between Steve and the actors isolates Steve from the group. Ironically, the strong boundary has the potential to give Steve a great deal of autonomy. He can shoot the skit any way he pleases. The actors are not concerned with the technical aspects of production. In actuality, Steve's autonomy is diminished for he is unfamiliar with camera operations. It appears that Steve's response is to use the camera as a "simple recording device." The camera simply follows the narrative of the skit. The syntactic structure of the visual images is very simple. Steve pans from one actor directly to another. The visual quality is rather "flat." The camera is not used to "highlight" the acting in any way. The actors convey their emotions of joy, annoyance, etc., on their own. Hence, acting becomes dominant. A strong sense of condensation amplified what the group as a whole was familiar with, while the unfamiliar aspects of technical production were minimized by a narrow usage of the camera.

Group B. As class begins, Mr. Albert is waiting in the studio. He has set up the equipment. Students enter the room slowly; a few come in late. Will has brought some beer cans. He looks around and gets Brian's attention.

Will: "I brought the cans but I don't know what we're doing."

Brian shrugs his shoulders. Kathy and Don also ask Brian about what they will do.

Brian: "We'll do something like we planned."

The group appears a little nervous. Now that the time is here there appears to be a wave of panic.

Don: "I forgot what we talked about."

Fred: "Yeah, me too!"

Mr. Albert asks who is the cameraperson. Brian walks over to him. Mr. Albert begins to show him how to focus the camera and pan.

Fred has brought in a hockey game. He plays a game with Will. The room is noisy and appears rather chaotic. The students occupy the full space, talking animatedly among themselves.

Mr. Albert: "Okay, would you get started?"

The students become quiet, and begin to stand around.

Chris: "Are we supposed to rehearse first?"

Brian: "I guess we should."

The group finally settles down to rehearse the beer commercial. Fred and Will stand by a table. Brian runs the camera. Don is the off-camera announcer. Brian tells the actors where to sit and gives them their lines. They begin.

Announcer: (off screen) "Fred is usually a Miller drinker. Today he taste-tests generic light." (Will and Fred sit facing the camera.)

Will: "Fred, try brand A." (Will speaks into a microphone.)

Fred: "Okay." (Fred drinks from the can labeled A.)

Will: "What do you think?"

Fred: "Not too bad . . . a little flat."

Will: "Well, try B." (Fred drinks from can B. He shakes his head.)

Fred: "Okay . . . it's hard to say now . . ."

Will: "Try another taste."

Fred: "Yeah, I'll try this one." (Fred drinks from can A.)

Fred: "Okay . . ." (cut)

The commercial is to continue throughout the project. The total time for this segment is 35 seconds.

After this take, students stand around wondering what to do.

Mr. Albert interjects: "Are you going to do "Family Feud"?

Brian: "Right! We know what we're doing . . . Can't we rehearse, then film, then erase and tape again?"

Mr. Albert: "Yes, that's okay . . . I suppose. Do you know how to erase what you did?"

Brian: "Oh, sure, yeah."

Brian now takes charge with the assurance of a director. He begins to order the others around. Interestingly enough, the others seem relieved and follow his command.

Brian: "Okay, Chris you turn on the TV."
Connie: "What do I do?" (she giggles).
Brian: "Turn on the TV and I'll tape you."
She turns on the set as Brian tapes it.
Brian: "Okay, Don and Rob, you guys are up."
Brian tells Don what to say. Thus far, Brian is making up the
dialogue for the group. Don and Rob are ready to do as told. Rob is
standing in front of the curtain. He appears to be waiting for
something. His hands are in his pockets. Don walks on to the
stage.
Don: "Say, I'll give you a $100 for that rag on your back."
Rob: "Okay." (Don proceeds to rip the shirt off Rob's
              back).
Rob: "Hey come on . . ." (Cut)
Total time for this segment is eight seconds. Mr. Albert begins to
tell Brian about the composition of shots. He shows Brian how to
tilt down and zoom.
Mr. Albert: "Try to fill the whole frame up."
Brian: "Uh, okay . . . let's do everything over."
Brian erases the tape, and the group begins anew. First Connie
turns on the TV, next Fred and Will do the commercial, then Don
and Rob retake the shirt commercial.
        As Fred, Rob, Will and Brian set up for the hockey game,
Mr. Albert asks Kathy and Dan what they're doing.
Dan: "Uh, I don't know."
Kathy: (looking rather confused) "I guess . . . an HBO
              commercial."
Meanwhile the confusion among group members is beginning to
increase. A debate begins as to whether Connie should again
change channels to show the hockey game. Brian ends the debate
quickly.
Brian: "Let's do the hockey game and see what happens."
Cindy: "Who's playing the game?" (Brian does not answer
              her.)
Connie: (to Cindy) "This whole thing is weird."
Brian: "Okay, look, Rob and I will announce the game.
              Then Rob will be the announcer and we'll show a

close-up of the hockey board. Everyone else yells in
the background."

This begins the hockey game. Rob and Brian are sitting behind a
desk.

Brian: "Good evening, this is Mike Rorzoini and Phil
              Esposito here at Madison Square Garden. We have
              a heck of a game for you folks.   The Rangers
              against the Boston Bruins. This is a title match.
              This will be a real good one. Ah, we had a fight last
              week when there was a three-game sweep by Boston.
              So the Rangers will be out . . . they will be out for
              revenge." (cut)

Brian takes the camera from Mike.   Rob is off-camera
announcer.

Rob: "Dukie slides out there. What a start for the second
              period."

We see a close-up of a mechanical hockey set. We watch plastic
players moving pucks. In the background we hear members of the
group clapping/yelling.

Rob: "And now here's another face-off . . . and it's over
              in the corner."

The commentary does not match the action we see. The puck sits
at center ice, as Fred and Will set up a shot.

Rob: "Duke heads down the ice . . . yes, it's a goal!"

We see the player moving down the ice, making a goal . . . in the
background loud cheers. Then a beer bottle is thrown onto the
game board.

Rob: "Okay, now a fight is breaking out." (cut)

Total time for this segment is 58 seconds.

Mr. Albert: (after the taping of the hockey game) "You only have
              14 on the meter. Your project isn't very long, and
              you're running out of time!"

Connie looks at Mr. Albert; she looks rather frustrated and
perturbed.

Brian: "Well, maybe we can make it longer . . ."

Connie: "After the goal we can show people in the bleachers."

Mr. Albert: "We have only seven minutes left, and I haven't
              seen everything yet. You'd better continue."

With seven minutes left in the period, Brian tells Connie, Kathy, and Rob to do their commercial. Connie tells Rob and Kathy that the commercial is to be on a new sex change product.

Brian: (to Rob) "Yeah, first we'll wrap up your face. Then after about an hour, we unwrap Kathy to show a sex change."

Rob: "Okay."

They begin. Rob is sitting on a chair; he is wearing a cap and a blue jacket. Connie stands next to him.

Connie: "Here we have Mr. Faggy Waggy. And here we have a new product. Facial Wrap . . . sex change facial wrap." (She holds up a roll of toilet paper. With this, Connie begins to laugh uncontrollably. Then:) "Yes . . . ah . . . yes, we have him here . . . and he's always thought he was a woman in a man's body. Well now we'll start wrapping."

She begins to wrap his face with toilet paper. Cut as Kathy sits in Rob's seat and Connie wraps her face. Kathy is not wearing the cap and blue jacket.

Connie: "Okay . . . one hour later we have our face wrapped. And now we'll see what our product has done." (She unwraps Kathy.) "Unreal! Oh no . . . it works . . . it works!"

Kathy and Connie laugh again. Cut. Total time for this segment is 45 seconds.

Brian: "Okay . . . now let's end with the beer commercial. Fred will have cans lying all over the table and will act drunk. Will, you ready? . . ."

Will: "Let me think of what I'm going to say . . ."

Connie: (interrupting) "Say it is the generic one."

Will: "Okay. I'll say that."

They begin immediately. We see the original set-up for the beer commercial. However, Fred is asleep with his head on the desk. He is surrounded by a number of beer cans. Mike tries to wake him up.

Mike: "Fred, Fred . . . which beer did you like?"

Fred: (slowly wakes up) "What . . . what . . ."

Will: "Which is your favorite beer?"
Fred: "This one . . . I think." (He grabs the can closest to his hand. Then goes back to sleep)
Will: (unwrapping the label) "Brand B . . . yes, folks, Generic Light beer is Fred's favorite beer." (cut)
Total time of this segment is 23 seconds.
Brian: "Well, we did rehearse, but we didn't do everything."
Mr. Albert: "Well, you had a week to put stuff together."

Group B wishes to reshoot their project. Since the period was coming to an end, this was not possible. The 1:30 bell rings. The tape made by Group B remains as a series of rehearsals. The group felt it was incomplete.

Interpretation. The degree of condensation exhibited by Group B is weak (CC-). The weak degree of condensation displayed in the communicative interaction was derived from the group's attempt to go beyond the familiar (to incorporate technical knowledge) and the necessity for explicit communication to organize the project. Oddly enough, the group's attempt to incorporate technical knowledge into the agenda appears to stem from their lack of organization.

By the end of the discussion sessions, the group had written a very brief outline for the project. The outline listed only the names of the shows to be taped. The specifics of each skit were not written into the outline nor, for that matter, were they ever really discussed by the group. Instead, the group used this tie to explore variations on different themes. These explorations generated enthusiasm and, more importantly, allowed students to socialize, hence, the general characteristic—consensus/exploring. However, the group could not/would not go beyond this stage of exploration. As mentioned, they had reached a plateau of understanding. The group appeared to be guided by the faith that somehow they will "get the job done," and that explicit planning for the project was not really necessary.

On production day, members of the group came to the studio with some idea of what the project would look like. Many of them brought props; Fred and Will brought beer cans for the beer commercial; Fred also brought a hockey game for part of the project; Rob brought an old shirt; and Connie brought a roll of toilet paper. Members have a very general idea of the project. However, the group is again confronted with the problem of how to organize and articulate the specific content of the project. To explicate this point, I will again divide the production session into the four components constituting condensed communication.

a) **Quality of acting**. After a period of chaos and confusion in the studio, the group begins to tape their skits. The quality of the acting was spontaneous. The actors draw from the experiential knowledge (the familiar). There is no evidence of the actors spending any length of time preparing for or rehearsing their roles. Once in front of the camera, the actors recreate their roles almost instinctively. The very familiarity with commercial television provides the actors with a tacit agenda to follow. In this sense, Group B's project is very similar to all previous projects.

b) **Interaction among actors.** Strong familiarity with commercial television provides the group with an agenda for the specific skits. However, it does not provide members with information regarding the organization of the whole project. From the descriptions we know that the first skit is the beer commercial. After this skit is shot, disorder, confusion, and general chaos reappear in the group. Brian asserts himself as group director and leader. In order to reorganize the group, explicit directions are necessary. It can be seen that Brian gives Don and Rob explicit directions. Also, the communicative interaction between actors becomes more explicit as they organize their skits. Hence, it is out of necessity that the group begins to work together to create a project. In this instance, the group effort demands explicit directions.

This "group effort" was constituted by two forces on production day. On the one hand, the social interactions of the discussion sessions had already established a pattern of members working together. On the other hand, Mr. Albert plays a significant role in defining the production process of this group. From the data, it can be seen that Mr. Albert's presence is more visible. For Group A he remains in the background of events. For

Group B Mr. Albert exerts both a positive and a negative influence on the project.

Initially, Mr. Albert's presence exhibits a negative influence on the project and he continually reminds the group that they are not organized, that time is running out, and that they have not accomplished much. It is reasonable to assume that this pressure from Mr. Albert did create some anxiety for the students. His presence amplified the disorder and chaos already felt by students. As a result, Mr. Albert's pressure actually brings the group closer together. The data show that halfway through the period the majority of students were working together, and that once students begin to organize and work together, Brian is no longer the sole definer of the project. In order to complete the project, Fred and Will discuss their skit. Connie begins to take a more active role in giving directions. Out of necessity members are required to work together and be more explicit in their communicative interactions.

c) **Boundary between actors and cameraperson.** It can be seen that Mr. Albert offers advice on camera operation, which represents his positive influence. Throughout the production he offers Brian "pointers" on how to use the camera. The "pointers" are made after a skit has been taped, but if the group is to incorporate the advice they must re-shoot the skit. Paradoxically, the discovery of different ways of using the camera serves only to increase the anxiety felt in the studio. Each time students retake a skit to incorporate new camera techniques, they use up time without increasing the actual length of their project. I noted by the end of the period the project consisted of a series of rehearsals. And, Mr. Albert complained that the length of their project was only 14 on the VTR counter.

Mr. Albert's presence not only brings the group closer together, but it also serves to push the group beyond the familiar. That is, the actual skits rely heavily upon acting to convey messages. The camera is used as a simple recording device. With Mr. Albert's help, the camera becomes the means to manipulate images seen on the monitor. It is interesting to note that by the time the hockey game is taped, the camera is used to manipulate the location of the action. At first we see Brian and

Rob in the sportscasters box and then there is a cut. In the next scene, the action is the hockey game. Initially, Rob's face is wrapped in Sex Change paper and then there is a cut. In the next scene, one hour later, the tissue is removed and Rob's face is transformed to Kathy's. As the period progresses, a developmental process from disorder to discovery can be seen. The initial disorder dissolves as the group discovers new ways of using the camera. However, the discovery process does not decrease student anxiety. Initially student anxiety is created by the fact the students did not know what to do. By the end of the period, student anxiety is the result of trying to finish before the period ends.

d) **Dominant mode of communication.** The process of disorder to discovery is paralleled by a weakening in the degree of condensation. It can be seen that as the period progresses the communicative interactions become more explicit. Explicitness corresponds with the incorporation of technical knowledge (the unfamiliar) and I find the visual syntax of the skits evolves from simple to complex. Hence, the dominant mode of communicating messages for the skit evolves from acting to camera. The skits at the end of the period rely heavily on camera manipulation to convey messages.

In sum, the short period of discovery exhibited by Group B was not student initiated but teacher initiated. Mr. Albert's presence implicitly pushes the group to go beyond the familiar. By doing so, the communicative interaction becomes more explicit, and the form of the video text becomes more complex.

Conclusion

The aim of this study has been to generate a grounded theory which would explain and identify conceptual linkages between planning, production, and the form of the video text. In many ways this study substantiates the claim made by Raymond Williams.

> As a matter of general theory it is useful to recognize that means of communication are themselves means of production. It is true that means of communication, from the simplest physical forms of language to the most advanced forms of

communications technology, are themselves always
socially and materially produced, and of course
reproduced.[4]

The problem, of course, was how do we show concretely the
relationship between means of production and means of
communication? What sense does it make to state that modes of
communication embody social and material relations?

To accomplish this task, the analysis shows that there is a
strong correspondence between knowledge orientation,
communicative interaction, and the specific *form* of the video text.
Briefly it was noted that the deregulation of school knowledge and
classroom practices allowed specific social interactions to occur
within each group (*i.e.*, the general characteristics). The social
interactions are manifestations of specific knowledge
orientations. For Group A the orientation is within the domain of
the familiar (experiential knowledge). For Group B the
orientation attempts to expand beyond the familiar by
incorporating technical knowledge in the project.

The distinct knowledge orientations correspond to specific
modes of communication among members of each group. The
mode of communication specifies the actual production process by
regulating the interactions among actors, and between
cameraperson and actors. The communicative interaction
ultimately establishes the dominant mode of conveying messages
for each skit. For Group A the dominant mode is acting. For
Group B the dominant mode is the manipulation of the camera.

By establishing the dominant mode for conveying
messages, I find that the knowledge orientation and
communicative interaction of each group plays a decisive role in
determining the *form* of the visual text. Specifically, for Group A
a strong degree of condensation (CC+) restricts the visual syntax
(*i.e.*, the syntax is simple) by relying heavily on acting to convey
messages. For Group B a weak degree of condensation (CC-)
allows for a more complex visual structure by incorporating

---

[4]Raymond Williams, *Problems in Materialism and Culture* (London: Verso
Editions, 1980), p. 50.

technical knowledge into the project's agenda. (Table 1 provides a summary of the analysis presented.)

Table 1
Social and Communicative Structure of Video Production

	Group A	Group B
General Characteristics	Consensus	Consensus/ Exploring
Degree of Condensed Communication	CC+	CC-
Quality of Acting	Spontaneous	Spontaneous
Interaction Among Actors	Little explicit directing	Much explicit directing
Boundary Between Actors & Cameraperson	Strong	Weak
Dominant Mode of Communication	Acting	Acting to Camera

Finally, it is important to realize the paradoxical role familiar knowledge plays in the production of video texts. Consider the claim made by Murdock and Phelps.

> The evidence we have been able to gather indicates that most pupils have an active rather than a passive relationship with the media ... Far from accepting what they are offered wholesale, or just letting material wash over them, most people are constantly making judgments selecting those elements which in some way speak to them, and rejecting those that do not.[5]

Prior to entering the media course, students were not only familiar with the media, but were discriminating consumers. Logic would indicate that this familiar knowledge ought to enhance the learning process by virtue of the fact that this

---

[5]Graham Murdock and Guy Phelps, *Mass Media and the Secondary School* (London: McMillan and Basingstoke, 1974), p. 141.

information was judged important to the student (*i.e.,* "it somehow spoke to them"). Given the "relevance" of this material, it should somehow motivate the student to learn about the media (*i.e.,* to communicate visually).

Ironically, the opposite appears to be the case. The study suggests that student reliance on the familiar inhibits reflective thought and acts as a powerful deterrent to change. The key to understanding this situation lies in the common sensical status of familiar knowledge. For the problem is that,

> You cannot learn through common sense, how things are: you can only learn where they fit into the existing scheme of things . . . Common sense does not require reasoning, argument, logic, thought; it is spontaneously available, thoroughly recognizable, widely shared. It *feels,* indeed, as if it had always been there . . . It is precisely its 'spontaneous' quality, its transparency, its refusal to be made to examine the premises on which it is founded . . . (that leads to) resistance to change or correction.[6]

By relying on the familiar and the immediate, Group A students were able to spontaneously recreate TV formats which required little effort. Students had obviously learned the "existing scheme of things." However, by relying on that which is "natural" and "familiar," students were denied access to the technical aspects of production. As such, there was little need to reflect, logically order, or rationally construct their agenda. As a result, within the production context, modes of expression were restricted. The "familiar" media feel comfortable; they require little effort. Hence, what impetus is there for students to break out of this pattern of socialization? Students in Group A not only completed the projects within the allotted time, but did rather well. Common sense knowledge creates a "safe" harbor for students, a harbor where students gain control over material and reinforce their familiarity with that material. It is for this reason that

---

[6]Stuart Hall, "Culture, the Media and the 'Ideological Effect,'" in *Mass Communication and Society,* eds. James Curran et al., (Beverly Hills: Sage Publications, 1977), p. 325.

Group B projects were so stressful for students. To be sure, Mr. Albert's presence contributed to anxiety and tension. But, apart from this, Group B's projects attest to the immense difficulty required to break out of the parameters of the familiar. And to begin to use video in a creative manner.

14

The Production and Distribution of Knowledge Through Open and Distance Learning*

Stephen Fox
University of Lancaster, Lancaster, UK

Abstract

Open and distance learning (ODL) technology offers a new form of market mechanism for the distribution of knowledge which is increasingly presented as a commodity like any other. Information technology (IT) is also having an impact on the technical and social production of knowledge and higher learning in general. This paper will explore a range of issues arising from this 'mercantilization' of learning by which is meant the tendency for knowledge and learning to be seen as products, skills and competencies produced for sale by what Berger (1987) has called the 'knowledge industry.'

The paper argues that the nature of knowledge is changing under the impact of IT and ODL, as, for example, the Renaissance and subsequent scientific revolution replaced divine revelation with personal human speculation, conjecture and refutation; the current proliferation of new technology is replacing the agency of human speculation with a kind of impersonal, disembodied, free-floating, public dissemination of information.

It is also argued that the purpose of knowledge is changing too. Since the eighteenth century American and French revolutions, education has been used to induce

---

knowledge in learners on a mass scale as a necessary social prerequisite to political democracy. Members of society were inducted into a knowledge of their culture as a 'thinking system' and were free—indeed encouraged—to understand and criticize its basic socio-political and cultural forms, for the sake of freedom, liberty and emancipation. However, 'knowledge' and information are increasingly produced and sold to contract in a market economy ruled by an international class of decision makers in governments, multi-national companies, public institutions, world religions, and media. The purpose of this new form of 'knowledge' is 'performativity'— that is, the capacity to efficiently augment power by producing 'competitive edges' for the decision makers. The role of social, moral or even spiritual critique has been vastly reduced compared to pre-scientific revolution emphasis on theology, medicine and law—then the staple curricula in European universities.

It is further debated that post-modern knowledge and open and distance learning have an ambiguous relationship. On the one hand ODL as an educational movement often espouses a rhetoric of 'learner-centredness', 'open access' and 'freedom to learn' which harks from the social goals of the revolutionary eighteenth century. On the other hand, it espouses 'life skills', 'self-help', 'self-development' and 'continuing vocational education', which echoes the nineteenth century rhetoric of the utilitarianism of Bentham and Samuel Smiles. It is ambiguous whether ODL as an educational movement has thought through the implications of its activities since; it seems to quote even-handedly from these two traditions. Is it for enlightened social critique or rampant industrialization—rapidly becoming post-industrialization? It seems that the large ethical and social issues are being effectively lost in the technological race. Several questions are left hanging.

The paper also argues that Larsen (1986) has reasoned that there is need for a 'revised "educational sociology." ' In the light of the preceding discussion, this paper suggests two directions for such an approach vis-a-vis education and training technologies such as ODL and expert systems: first, a micro level of analysis employing ethnographic (participant observation) methods and interpretive (e.g., ethnomethodological, conversation-analytical and phenomenological) perspectives, and second, a macro level of analysis, utilizing the emerging body of social critique found in the current debate on 'postmodernity' which seeks to explore the cultural effects on the changes being wrought by new information and communicational media.

The paper concludes by observing that IT, in the production of knowledge, and ODL in its distribution/dissemination, are hastening disciplinary specialization within the institutions of higher learning. This leads to a fragmentation of the cultural core of Western civilization—universities no longer provide a unity of learning, and Renaissance man ('homo universale')—as an idealized product of the humanistic educational mission and regime— has been replaced by communities of specialized experts and their students, employed by a class of decision-makers who themselves have risen through specialized ranks without a general education in the sense that it was meant earlier in this century. Those 'specific intellectuals' who are at work within the open and distance learning educational movement are likely to be the architects of the educational institutions of the twenty-first century (such as electronic universities and learning organizations). If they cannot rise to the task of social and educational critique and tackle the big moral and social questions to which their industry gives rise, almost a thousand years of humanism will end in collapse.

Introduction

It has been argued that, in the postindustrial age, that is since the post-war period of European reconstruction, since around the 1950s, the status of knowledge is changing (Bell, 1974; Lyotard, 1984). The rapid growth of computerized information technology is both a product and hastener of this alleged change. By providing new techniques for both the production and distribution of knowledge, it is argued, IT has increased the tendency for us all to see knowledge as a commodity like any other, to be bought, sold and exchanged. We now see it with a price tag attached. More and more knowledge and the opportunity to learn are benefits to be bought by private individuals rather than fundamental rights belonging to every member of a democracy.

Lyotard (1984) reminds us that the beginning of mass education, like mass health programmes, came in the wake of the French Revolution. At this time the social theorists and experimenters, such as Rousseau, Helvetius and La Chalotais saw widespread educational reform as a necessary precondition for democracy. Education became increasingly a State responsibility, and the legitimation for the increase in the production and distribution of knowledge was the emancipation of the people.

This legitimating strategy competed with and/or complemented an older justification for the pursuit of learning, namely that knowledge in itself was good. Speculation, from the Renaissance on, had needed no instrumental purpose—not even the laudable one of the emancipation of the people; rather, it was to be pursued for the sake of truth alone.

Against these legitimating narratives, it is contended by various current writers (Lyotard, Rorty, Foucault), that the advent of what is variously called post-modernism, neo-pragmatism and post-structuralism is producing a revised justification for knowledge. Lyotard has coined the word 'performativity,' meaning that knowledge is to be legitimated by its effects, and not simply its effects but the efficiency of those effects. For the value now placed on learning is no longer primarily its emancipatory influence, nor even truth for its own sake, but its valency in attaining and keeping a competitive edge for whoever purchases it.

Such is the broad thrust of many post-modern arguments and, if they hold, certain implications follow for open and distance learning. For if these arguments are sound then knowledge has become the possession of the powerful. IT becomes the major means for knowledge manufacture and ODL becomes a 'dream instrument' for the control of the ruled. A counter-argument is that ODL is simply a medium for the transmission of learning and does not necessarily promote the 'mercantilization of knowledge.' However, to focus on the technical excellence of the medium without regard to the socio-political context is to collude, however unwittingly, with the performativity principle, allowing the efficiency of the means to blind one to the effects.

Much of the literature on ODL focuses on the technicalities of the technology and ignores the socio-political implications. To help rectify this imbalance, the present paper will appraise three issues: (a) the nature of knowledge, (b) the purpose of knowledge, and (c) the implications for ODL in the light of the post-modernist challenge to humanistic education.

The Nature of Post-Modern Knowledge

What is at issue under the post-modern condition is the meaning of knowledge in Western society. Looking back we can identify periods of transformation in the rules concerning what counts as reliable knowledge. Each of those periods was 'post-modern' in its day, in the sense that they were periods in which what was previously the 'modern' world view came under radical attack. For example, the fourteenth century Italian Renaissance inaugurated the subsequent rise of humanistic education which spread to Northern Europe through intermediaries such as Geert Groot, Thomas à Kempis and Desiderius Erasmus. Humanistic thought undermined the previous status quo of scholasticism which as a species of knowledge was intimately bound up with the political power of the Church of Rome and the Christian world view. Human speculation gradually replaced divine revelation as the fundamental ground of reliable knowledge in the West.

The argument of many current post-modernist thinkers is that we in the West have reached the end of humanism. IT and ODL are pivotal among many changes in our society in that they are radically shifting the ground of reliable knowledge. The databanks and computerized communications systems offer an operative knowledge without a necessary human agent. This is not to say that there will be no more human decision makers but that the impact of telematics is such that our concept of the 'human self' is undergoing a radical change. For just as humanism gradually sapped the divine element in the nature of knowledge, the current post-modernism is sapping the human element. What

is it to be human? The technological hardware is not simply 'out
there'; increasingly the iron is in the soul. Lyotard (1984) writes:

> The old principle that the acquisition of knowledge is
> indissociable from the training of minds, or even of
> individuals, is becoming obsolete and will become
> ever more so . . . Knowledge is and will be produced in
> order to be sold . . . Knowledge ceases to be an end in
> itself . . . Knowledge has become the principle force of
> production over the last few decades.

In this view knowledge is now produced as a commodity, the
principle value of which is its productive capacity—that is, its
ability to hasten the advance of productive technology through such
devices as computer-assisted design, and thereby gain a
competitive edge for the purchaser. Performativity (the ability to
be efficient and therefore competitive) has become the rationale
legitimating knowledge production and distribution, and ODL
represents the market mechanism through which knowledge and
expertise are bought, sold and exchanged.

It is therefore incumbent upon those who are developing the
technology of ODL not to cut themselves off from the educational
debate surrounding their specialist activity. For if the result of
their efforts is to bring an end to humanistic education which has a
thousand-year history, at least some of their time could be spent
reappraising the value of what their activities are in the process of
terminating. Simultaneously, some of their time could be spent
considering what sort of 'post-modern' values they might be
creating. For just as it behooves the genetic scientists from time to
time to evaluate the moral as well as the technical side of their
tinkerings with the human embryo, it behooves the technologists of
ODL to evaluate the moral and educational side of their
tinkerings with the human learner.

During the Second World War, humanist educationalists
such as F. R. Leavis (1943) were already sounding warning bells
against rampant technocratic specialization:

> . . . the social and cultural disintegration that has
> accompanied the development of the inhumanly
> complex machinery is destroying what should have
> controlled the working. It is as if society, in so

complicating and extending the machinery of organization, had incurred a progressive debility of consciousness and of the powers of coordination and control—had lost intelligence, memory and moral purpose.

In short what has been undermined by the spectacular growth of the 'machine'—bureaucratic as well as technological—has been the coherent cultural centre to Western society (see Bell, 1976). The acceleration of technical and professional specialization has fragmented norms and values in the West, as the period of the 1960s epitomizes. In the process the nature of knowledge has begun to change and with it the nature of the university institution, which as the name implies has for centuries been the point in society where a unity among disparate disciplines has been maintained.

This unity of learning has for centuries been vouchsafed by the cultural values of humanism, which combines a respect for speculation and a belief in human unity. As Matthew Arnold (1897) expressed it:

. . . because all men are the members of one great whole, and the sympathy which is in human nature will not allow one member to be indifferent to the rest or to have a perfect welfare independent of the rest, the expansion of our humanity, to suit the idea of perfection which culture forms, must be a general expansion. Perfection, as culture conceives it, is not possible while the individual remains isolated. The individual is required, under pain of being stunted and enfeebled in his own development if he disobeys, to carry others along with him in his march towards perfection, to be continually doing all he can to enlarge and increase the volume of the human stream sweeping thitherward.

Within this humanistic philosophy the institutions of education and learning have a unique responsibility to maintain the central cultural values of Western society and to maintain these as human values 'separable from any particular religious frame or basis' (Leavis, 1943). And it is within this tradition that most educational reform has been carried out including curriculum development. Stenhouse (1975), for example, argues that:

> Education enhances the freedom of man by inducting
> him into the knowledge of his culture as a thinking
> system. The most important characteristic of the
> knowledge mode is that one can think with it. This is
> in the nature of knowledge—as distinct from
> information—that it is a structure to sustain creative
> thought and provide frameworks for judgment.

This stance is equivalent to what Lyotard has called 'the old
principle that the acquisition of knowledge is indissociable from
the training of minds, or even of individuals.' It is this position
that is under threat by the ceaseless trend toward the
commodification and mercantilization of knowledge and
learning that ODL technology promotes.

In brief, the post-modern condition is arguably changing
the meaning of knowledge in our society; IT and ODL through
packaging the 'goods' are reducing knowledge to information.
The difference between knowledge and information is not always
clearly recognized, as Larsen (1986) observes. While noting that
frequently the two words are simply used as synonymns he makes
the point that:

> This is perhaps one of the most serious and widespread
> mistakes in the current use of information technology,
> and it leads to the attitude that giving students
> information is identical to giving them knowledge.

He clarifies the distinction by arguing that knowledge is
essentially personal while information is essentially public.
Knowledge therefore cannot be transmitted, for as soon as it is
formulated in communication it is transformed into information.
Knowledge can be induced in the learner but cannot be
transmitted as such. Knowledge is always a product of the
individual's personal transformation of information. In this
view, Larsen describes the teaching process in three stages:

1. the knowing person's transformation of personal
    knowledge into public information;
2. transmission and distribution of information;
3. the learner's transformation of the obtained public
    information into personal knowledge.

This process of transformation is essentially one of judgment, as Stenhouse put it, and it is the central preoccupation of traditional education—as opposed to training—to induce in the learner the capacity for critical judgment.

This much has already been recognized by those such as Larsen at work within the field of educational studies of information technology. But as it stands this distinction merely acknowledges the role of personal judgment in recognizing and deciding matters of technical 'fact' within the 'truth games' of scientific discourse. There is also the wider point that increasingly—precisely because of the proliferating specialisms of the learner 'into the knowledge of his culture as a thinking system' is disappearing. This is the claim of the post-modernists who recognize the demise of high culture in the fragmentation of specialisms in higher learning. Thus the humanistic notion of 'Renaissance man' (homo universale: the universal man—courtier, politician, explorer, artist, scientist and financier all rolled into one) as a cultural ideal is dissipating. The secular sense of human responsibility for human welfare and, indeed, the husbandry of the universe, which is the Christian spiritual sense of responsibility, is breaking down.

As a result technical 'truth games' are the only ones we feel sure about how to play. Judgment in relation to ethical and moral questions is too difficult in the absence of the moral idealism of Christianity and the evaporation of humanism in the West. (See MacIntyre, 1985, for a recent diagnosis of these issues.) The social role played by the educated class and by scholars themselves increasingly has little to say about value judgments. Pronouncements on such matters are left to the expertise of parliamentary lobby groups such as Greenpeace, CND, the anti-abortion lobby and so on, and to religious sects and cults. Increasingly there is no 'establishment view' on these matters.

It is not my purpose here to lament this state of affairs but to highlight it as one of the social, cultural by-products of information technology and a concern with public information rather than personal knowledge.

The unresolved issue that this leaves is from what centre, if any, of shared cultural values and ground can we begin to evaluate and come to some judgment on whether or not this is a good or bad direction for Western society to be taking. For the very fragmentation that needs to be critically appraised can no longer be so from any central grounds such as the university institution used to be able to provide, because the fragmentation of the proliferating specialized disciplines has eroded the place of the University in the cultural life of society. The current state of the university institution—in which tenure is disappearing and individual disciplines, to survive as intellectual enterprises, have to compete for research and teaching funds in a corporate economy—is indicative of the cultural fragmentation of society brought about by disciplinary technical specialization in the production system of 'information' and the media of ODL technology in the distribution system.

The Purpose of Postmodern Knowledge

The contention of some postmodern thinkers, as we have seen, is that knowledge is less and less good in itself or because it is emancipatory, but is good for its performativity value. This raises the question 'good for whom?' There are no doubt many liberal humanists in the world, occupying posts within the 'knowledge class' (Berger, 1987), many of whom still espouse humanistic values and believe them to be at work within their educational practice. If these people embody humanism in their professional practice how can the 'postmodernists' claim that humanism is at its end, or that the purpose of knowledge has changed? (I use the label 'post-modernists' broadly to condense the argument, recognizing that there are fundamental differences of opinion among so-called post-modernist writers—for example, between Foucault and Derrida as well as between Derrida and Searle.) Norris (1987) provides an interesting discussion of these debates.

The postmodernists seem to have recourse to a modified version of class analysis. Lyotard (1984), for example, writes:

> The ruling class is and will continue to be the class of
> decision makers. Even now it is no longer composed
> of the traditional political class, but of a composite
> layer of corporate leaders, high level administrators,

and the heads of the major professional, political, and religious organizations.

Lyotard seems to be recognizing the divorce of ownership and control argument (Berle and Means, 1933), or the 'managerial revolution' thesis (Burnham, 1942), both of which imply that possession of the means of production no longer resides in the family hands of individual capitalists, but is spread widely through the agency of large institutions such as pension funds, banks and corporations. In short, the argument is that the proportion of owner capitalists is so small in terms of their voice in corporate and national decision making that they no longer comprise 'the ruling class' in Western society. The ruling class that Lyotard identifies nevertheless seeks to act in its own interests, which it claims are identical with the interests of the total social system. It is within this revised version of a form of class analysis that the post-modernists argue that humanism is at its end.

The ruling class pays for research to be done and determines what sorts of research will be done. The higher education system, as a sub-system of the supposed social system, is governed increasingly by the performativity criteria of the corporate and political decision makers, that is: "The desired goal becomes the optimal contribution of higher education to the best performativity of the social system." (Lyotard, 1984).

Thus university research agendas are increasingly directed to producing arguments and proofs which benefit the paymasters. Technical (that is, politically and ethically neutral) questions will raise funds for solutions to be found—speculative and emancipatory concerns will not, unless they also can demonstrate in advance how they might contribute to the performance of the social system. Radical research which might question and criticize the status quo or the principle of the market economy might therefore find difficulty in applying successfully for funds among the high-level administrators, corporate leaders and so on who so obviously have little vested interest in inquiring too deeply in such directions.

Central to the postmodernist argument is that there is an equation between knowledge and power. Funds for knowledge

production and distribution are made available only for those
kinds of knowledge that promise to enhance the performance of the
company or national economy: knowledge, in other words, that
augments the power of the decision makers. 'Scientists,
technicians, and instruments are purchased not to find truth, but to
augment power' (Lyotard, 1984).

Under the postmodern condition, knowledge is
increasingly produced and distributed for utilitarian, functional
reasons. The economic motive has become the legitimation for
learning and education. The overall performance of the social
system may depend on the sub-optimization of parts of the system.
If the index of performance is, say, 'living standards' then
optimal absolute levels may be impossible without sub-optimizing
living standards in parts of the system. As Lyotard (1984) writes:

> . . . the system can count severity among its
> advantages. Within the framework of the power
> criterion, a request . . . gains nothing in legitimacy by
> virtue of being based on the hardship of an unmet need.
> Rights do not flow from hardship, but from the fact that
> the alleviation of hardship improves the system's
> performance.

Humanistic values do not enter into the legitimation of knowledge
production and distribution, since increasingly these are geared
to the performance 'needs' of the system rather than, say,
questioning the politico-ethical basis of the system. The
possibilities for the enlightened criticism of the social system are
becoming fewer since it is not clear that they contribute in any way
to the performance of the system. The decision makers who
control research budgets and directions pay increasingly for
information that will have clear instrumental use and which is
amenable to easy and systematic dissemination. In this way
education becomes an induction into a 'culture as a thinking
system' (in Stenhouse's phrase) in which speculation and
emancipation which enhance the freedom of man are less and less
pivotal concerns. Moreover, the culture into which people are to be
inducted, and which is thereby being created, because of the very
specialization of technical, instrumental disciplines, is becoming

increasingly fragmented. As the ex-president of Johns Hopkins University has protested:

> The failure to rally around a set of values means that universities are turning out potentially highly skilled barbarians: people who are very expert in the laboratory or with the computer or in the surgery or in the law courts, but who have no real understanding of their own society . . . Higher education has done itself a disservice by selling itself in terms of economic return. (Rehder, 1982).

Therefore, even professional training, as well as technical training, is becoming shorn of any central integrating ground which might put the specialist skills within a more general understanding of society including an appreciation of ethics, justice and politics.

Summing up the issues raised in this and the previous section, the post-modernist contention is, first, that the nature of knowledge is changing, becoming more like an informational commodity to be produced and distributed, and second, that the purpose for knowledge is also changing, being increasingly geared to the power requirements of the decision makers: thus, the *raison d'être* of knowledge is its performative value, namely the competitive edge it gives the decision makers in the arenas of economic, industrial, social and political struggle.

Postmodern Knowledge and Open and Distance Learning

ODL, as an educational innovation costing large sums of investment finance, has, like other forms of education, been subject to a wide-ranging debate about legitimation and justification. As Snell (1987) has portrayed, the rhetoric and certain interpretations of practice are, at the very least, ambiguous. On the one hand ODL represents 'freedom to learn,' 'learner centredness' and 'open access,' all of which are species of rhetoric belonging to the emancipatory narrative of legitimation which arose within humanism through the events of the French Revolution, and which Snell has identified with the rhetoric of some kind of 'Marxist Utopia.' On the other hand, ODL represents 'self-help,' 'self development,' 'lifeskills' and the opportunity to equip (or reequip) oneself with the knowledge, skills and competencies with which to flexibly navigate the vagaries of the labour market.   In this sense ODL adopts the legitimating narrative of performativity, by which learning is valued for its pragmatic effects in enhancing the efficiency of the social machine as managed by the decision makers.

ODL is therefore an educational movement with competing versions of its social and educational mission; it is not simply a new medium of distribution, the technological problems of which seem to be the main focus of current research. Indeed, the key issue raised by ODL is that of the nature and purpose of knowledge *vis-à-vis* power in contemporary society. As Lyotard (1984) has said regarding the computerization of society, of which ODL technology is a part:

> It could become the 'dream' instrument for controlling
> and regulating the market system, extended to include
> knowledge itself and governed exclusively by the
> performativity principle.

Thus, as the product and labour markets are constantly transforming themselves, requiring new skills on the part of the participants, ODL represents an efficient means whereby individuals can gain a vocational 'retread.' As the ex-director of the Foundation for Management Education has put it:

> Every company, and every individual working within
> the company, should embrace the concept that education
> does not take place in a discrete period of time
> preceding employment, but is a continuous process
> which lasts through most of the employee's working
> life . . . (Nind, 1981).

Or again, as Lyotard (1984) puts it:

> . . . knowledge will no longer be transmitted en bloc,
> once and for all, to young people before their entry into
> the work force: rather it is and will be served *à la carte*
> to adults who are either already working or expect to be,
> for the purpose of improving their skills and chances of
> promotion, but also to help them acquire information,
> languages, and language games allowing them both to

widen their occupational horizons and to articulate their technical and ethical experience.

In this context, of which ODL is a significant part:

> the question . . . now asked by the professional student, the State, or institutions of higher education is no longer 'Is it true?' but 'What use is it?' . . . 'Is it saleable?' . . . 'Is it efficient?' (Lyotard, 1984).

ODL is one of many technological pressures towards the commodification of knowledge into utilizable bits of the total body of knowledge. On the one hand it offers an emancipatory solution to the problems of access to higher education, thereby breaking the monopoly power of the university institution. On the other hand, the kinds of knowledge most amenable to efficient packaging and the current wants of the 'consumer' are those which are of immediate instrumental use in surviving in a severe market system, rather than the kind of knowledge which provides a structure for enlightened or radical critique. For:

> As much as it is in the interests of the system and therefore of its 'decision makers,' to encourage professional advancement (since it can only improve the performance of the whole), any experimentation in discourse, institutions, and values . . . is regarded as having little or no operational value and is not given the slightest credence in the name of seriousness of the system. (Lyotard, 1984).

It is not in the interest of the system's decision makers to distribute the intellectual wherewithal to criticize the system from within unless this is with an eye on improving its efficiency, nor of questioning and formulating judgments on its moral, judicial and political basis. Consequently, ODL as an educational movement might question its effects with the intention of responsibly distinguishing which legitimating rhetoric is the 'Trojan Horse' for what hidden political agenda and what, anyway, are the merits of the cases. For as the disciplines of knowledge production fragment in proliferating technical specialisms destroying the unity of knowledge within the university, and the means of knowledge distribution are widened by ODL technology—again undermining the coherence of the

university institution in its dissemination function—several
questions are left hanging:

- If the purpose and nature of knowledge and its
  acquisition are changing in the ways suggested by
  the post-modernists, is that a good or bad thing?
  That is, should knowledge be reduced to
  information on sale to the highest bidder?
- Should there be an institutional centre which
  functions to produce a unity among the disparate
  disciplines, as the University has to some extent?
- Should there be a kind of meta-discipline, such as
  philosophy, which functions as a centre ground for a
  discourse on the assumptions underlying the
  knowledge claims of the many disciplines?
- How should questions of values be taught and learnt,
  if at all?
- As ODL in particular offers an alternative market
  mechanism to the traditional university/higher
  educational institution, how should (if at all) the
  'training of minds, or even of individuals' aspect of
  the acquisition of knowledge be maintained in the
  new media, given the tendency of ODL to
  commodify bits of the total body of knowledge into
  discrete packs of information?

The purpose of this paper has not been to propose solutions to
these questions but to raise them as issues for those involved in
researching the technology of ODL.

How Might We Proceed from Here?

It is perhaps becoming hackneyed to point out that open and
distance learning technology may well be as significant in our
own period as the invention of popular printing and
pamphleteering was in the Renaissance and Reformation of
Northern Europe.

Nevertheless this seems to be the case, and this very
information technology which is increasingly of use in both the
production and distribution of 'knowledge' is transforming our
ways of learning. Amid the race to produce the most performative
'teaching and learning machines' possible it is the suggestion of

this paper that those researching open and distance learning should seek to exercise critical judgement in their activities. It is not the intention of this paper to prejudge these issues but as Larsen (1986) has pointed out:

> . . . information technology is just an aspect of the social setting in which education is taking place. Thus what is needed now is not more sophisticated technology or stronger interest towards its characteristics and use, but a revised 'educational sociology.'

I would like to offer two potentially fruitful and interesting lines of educational sociological inquiry to those researching open and distance learning.

First, at the micro level of analysis, there is a tradition of ethnographic (participant observation) research in the sociology of education, for example: Hargreaves (1967; 1972), Lacey (1970), Delamont (1976), Ball (1981), Burgess (1983), Burgoyne and Hodgson (1983), Hammersley (1985), Fox (1987). Much of this has taken place in secondary schools, while in Burgoyne and Hodgson's case it has investigated managers learning from 'live' work experience, and in my own case concerning managers learning in the context of a part-time MBA programme at a major international business school. In addition there have been studies investigating scientists at work in their laboratories—Latour and Woolgar (1979), Gilbert and Mulkay (1980), and Mulkay and Gilbert (1982a; 1982b).

The approaches to data collection and analysis, particularly in terms of the small-group ethnography found in these studies, may well be of use to those involved in, say, the development of expert systems. Self (1987) describes how expert systems are produced iteratively through lengthy discussions with experts, who seek to formulate through this process the personal, tacit knowledge they have acquired over many years, in terms of 'if-then' statements or rules. The set of rules thus produced is called the 'production system' and essentially comprises:

> . . . formal statements of informal knowledge such as:
> *if* the pain is throbbing, *and* its history is paroxysmal repetitive, *and* the prodromal syndrome is

scintillation scotoma, *and* there is no concurrent
neurological sign during paroxysm, *then* the case is
probably migraine. (Self, 1987).

Those involved in investigating the development of expert
systems could, perhaps, benefit from a deeper and more detailed
analysis of how experts—managers or scientists for instance—
are socially constructed through ethnographic studies of their
work and learning experiences. Sociological perspectives which
provide the requisite level of fine-grained analysis within such
studies include ethnomethodology, conversation analysis,
symbolic interactionism and phenomenology.

Self (1987) cites Moralee's (1986) study of the use of expert
systems within a research laboratory, the idea being that
researchers could browse through it using it as a 'knowledge
reservoir' by which they could refine their own expert judgement
and look for new relations between concepts. In such cases it is
likely that the sense made through such browsings will be within,
and part of the ongoing social life of the laboratory. In such cases
also, ethnographic studies could be of use to investigators seeking
to observe the use of expert systems in the everyday lives of expert
communities. Similar studies could, of course, focus on the use of
information technology among aspirant experts as in, say,
Masters of Doctoral programmes or indeed among any
community of learners where the technology of open and distance
learning is part of their everyday context.

In the second instance, at a macro level of analysis, there
is an expanse of sociological theorizing and social criticism
concerned with the issues of cultural modernity and postmodernity—whether or not humanism is at the end of its tether
and how the emergence of new forms of scientific discipline and
their technologies are transforming our ideas about the nature of
the human self, knowledge and information, as well as the
productive and distributive processes. These features of the
variously named post-industrialist, post-modernist era are
explored in the work of many major social and cultural
thinkers—for instance see Derrida (1974), Bell (1976), Foucault
(1977; 1980), Lyotard (1984), Foster (1985), Lyotard and Thebaud

(1985), Berger (1987) and Baudrillard (1988) to selectively name but a few.

It would be impossible here to outline all the issues raised by these writers in connection with how we might understand the relationships between the nature of information technology and society. However, simply to illustrate, Foucault (1977; 1980) explores the emergence, over the past hundred years or so, of the social sciences in the demographic studies of eighteenth and nineteenth century social reformers, as urbanization occurred emphasizing the importance of mass record-keeping by administrators of all kinds in government, education, the military, hospitals, prisons and more. This produced a new and pressing social demand for collecting, storing and retrieving mass statistics, fueling the administrative need for breakthroughs in computer technology able to handle these massive amounts of data.

As another example, Derrida (1974) examines in a novel way the relationship between the spoken word and text, providing a new understanding of meaning, authorial intention (compare the authority of the teacher), writing, dissemination, reading and interpretation. Out of such analyses emerges the possibility of free-circulating information, unowned and uncontrolled by any human agent, Renaissance man or otherwise—a general dissemination without a fundamental source.

Baudrillard (1988) explores the emergence of new cultural forms of mass media such as cinema and television and the impact such technologies are making on how we relate to the printed word, face-to-face interaction, how we experience time, attention spans and the presence or lack of coherent narrative story lines in information we receive, tolerance of ambiguity, and sense of multiple realities.

All these writers express an interest in the fragmentation of the Western cultural tradition under the impact of new media for communication, data storage and education, often in a way far removed from those hardware and software engineers whose main concern is simply to produce 'effective' and 'efficient' programmes and technological innovations. Lyotard (1984) is particularly explicit in linking the narrow pragmatic concerns of systems engineers and managers with social patterns and analyses of far wider social and ethical import.

It would seem that there is a task yet to be achieved: namely an understanding of how the parts of society relate to the whole, not simply in terms of economic efficiency but in terms of cultural meaning. Information technology in the production and distribution of knowledge is hastening the specialization and fragmentation of the disciplines and expert knowledge communities. Those involved in the development of open and distance learning may well be the architects of the next century's institutions and networks of learning. Although the writings of contemporary social theorists may seem far removed from immediate pressing problems such as how to replace the role of the human expert with a machine, nonetheless the attempt to make sense across the disciplinary divide may repay both sides.

Conclusion

This paper points to, but does not attempt to solve, many 'educational sociological' issues raised by the development of open and distance learning and information technology in the production and distribution systems of learning. It demonstrates a cultural fragmentation and an increasing disunity in higher education which is the product of specialization in natural and social scientific communities as well as in the arts, humanities and management studies. The humanistic ideal of a unified body of knowledge which may be grasped by any one universal intellectual or educated person has given way in this century. It is not clear whether there is an educational ideal to replace it; yet educational innovators and systems designers in open and distance learning, as they seek to design futuristic 'electronic universities' and subsequent learning organizations, are perhaps among the few in a position to do so.

REFERENCES

Arnold, M. (1897) *Culture and anarchy.* Smith, Elder, London.
Ball, S.J. (1981) *Beachside comprehensive.* University Press, Cambridge, UK.
Baudrillard, J. (1988) *Jean Baudrillard: Selected writings.* M. Poster (ed.) Polity Press, Cambridge, UK.

Bell, D. (1974) *The coming of postindustrial society.* Peregrine, Harmondsworth.

Bell, D. (1976) *The cultural contradictions of capitalism.* Heinemann, London.

Berger, P.L. (1987) *The capitalist revolution.* Wildwood House, Aldershot, UK.

Berle, A.A. and Means, G.C. (1933) *The modern corporation and private property.* Macmillan, New York.

Burgess, R.G. (1983) *Experiencing comprehensive education: A study of Bishop McGregory School.* Methuen, London.

Burgoyne, J.G. and Hodgson, V.E. (1983) National learning and managerial action: A phenomenological study in the field setting. *Journal of Management Studies, 20,* 3, 387-399.

Burnham, J. (1942) *The managerial revolution.* Wyman and Sons, London.

Delamont, S. (1976) *Interaction in the classroom.* Methuen, London.

Derrida, J. (1974) *Of grammatology.* (Trans. G.C. Spivak) The Johns Hopkins University Press, London.

Foster, H. (1985) *Postmodern culture.* Pluto Press, London.

Foucault, M. (1977) *Discipline and punish: The birth of the prison.* (Trans. A. Sheridan) Penguin, Harmondsworth, UK.

Foucault, M. (1980) *Power/knowledge.* (C. Gordon (ed.); trans. C. Gordon, L. Marshall, J. Mephan, K. Soper). The Harvester Press, Brighton, UK.

Fox, S. (1987) Self knowledge and personal change: The reported experience of managers in part-time management education. Unpublished Ph.D. Thesis, University of Manchester, UK.

Gilbert, G. N. and Mulkay, M. (1982) Warranting scientific belief. *Social Studies of Science, 12,* 363-408.

Hammersley, M. (1985) From ethnography to theory: A programme and paradigm in the sociology of education. *Sociology, 19,* 2, 244-259.

Hargreaves, D.H. (1967) *Social relations in a secondary school.* Routledge and Kegan Paul, London.

Hargreaves, D.H. (1972) *Interpersonal relations and education.* Routledge and Kegan Paul, London.

Lacey, C. (1970) *Hightown grammar.* Manchester University Press, Manchester, UK.

Larsen, S. (1986) Information can be transmitted but knowledge must be induced. *PLET, 23,* 4, 331-336.

Latour, B. and Woolgar, S. (1979) *Laboratory life: The social construction of scientific facts.* Sage, Beverley Hills, California, USA.

Leavis, F.R. (1943) *Education and the university.* Chatto & Windus, London.

Lyotard, J.F. (1984) *The postmodern condition: A report on knowledge.* Manchester University Press, Manchester, UK.

Lyotard, J.F. and Thebaud, J.L. (1985) *Just gaming.* (Trans. Wlad Godzich). Manchester University Press, Manchester, UK.

MacIntyre, A. (1985) *After virtue: A study in moral theory (2nd edn.).* Duckworth, London.

Moralee, S. (1986) Expert systems—some user experience. In O'Shea, T., Self, J. and Thomas, G. (eds.) *Intelligent knowledge based systems: An introduction.* Harper and Row, London.

Mulkay, M. and Gilbert, G.N. (1982a) Accounting for error: How scientists construct their social world when they account for correct and incorrect belief. *Sociology, 16,* 165-183.

Mulkay, M. and Gilbert, G. N. (1982b) Joking apart: Some recommendations concerning the analysis of scientific culture. *Social Studies of Science, 12,* 583-613.

Nind, P. (1981) Preface In Cooper, C. (ed.) *Developing managers for the 1980s.* Macmillan, London.

Norris, C. (1987) *Derrida.* Fontana Press, London.

Rehder, R.R. (1982) SMR forum: American business education— is it too late to change? *Sloan Management Review,* Winter 63-71.

Self, J. (1987) Expert systems and computer tutors. In Hodgson, V.E., Mann, S.J. and Snell, R.S. (eds.) *Beyond distance teaching towards open learning.* SRHE and Open University Press, Milton Keynes, UK.

Snell, R. (1987) Open learning at work: MSC con or Marxist utopia? Paper presented at the EGOS Managing Learning in Organizations AWG Inaugural Conference, 'critical stances in management learning', November, University of Lancaster, UK.

Stenhouse, L. (1975) *An introduction to curriculum research and development.* Heinemann, London.

15

A Grammar of Educational Television

Ann DeVaney
Educational Technology
University of Wisconsin-Madison

Part I: Theory

Over the past 15 years certain discourses about the forms of television have emerged in England and the United States. TV theorists and analysts, Williams (1975), Tuchman (1978), Fiske and Hartley (1978), Heath and Skirrow (1977), Gitlin (1980), Ellis (1982), Hall (1980) among others, have established the tenor for inquiry about that cultural medium which pervades our personal lives and our institutions of schooling. Although these authors articulate their theories along diverse lines, they all work within a social/cultural paradigm. For them television is a cultural form around which unique aesthetic practice, institutional organization and social roles coalesce. Rather than focusing on one neutral medium, they see the practice of television embodying powerful change and inherent contradictions. Although many of these scholars' ideas are disparate, they would agree on key concepts, namely that television produces meaning by interaction with socially constituted groups and that television is a cultural form distinct from film. The former concept situates them outside the psychological domain of knowledge which highlights individual brain processes, and locates them squarely within a social domain which emphasizes group membership and the construction of meaning. In fact, the social domain suggests that certain knowledge occurs only because of one's membership in a group. The latter concept allows them to give television and film separate readings.

The dominant domain within which educational television has been studied is a psychological one and it has produced a vast number of helpful findings about how the medium interacts with individual students and how those students learn from television. Whether the theories which informed this research were behavioral or cognitive, researchers focused on individual brain processes. Work within this domain will continue to illuminate the specific area of learning as psychology. What that research neglects to answer is the question of how meaning is constructed when groups view television. It neglects social knowledge. In a 1985 *ECTJ* issue Stephen Kerr writes:

> There is a blind spot in the way we typically think
> about technology, learning and education. Over the
> past 65 years a considerable body of theory, research
> and practice has grown up around the use of
> technology toward educational ends, but most of that
> work has focused on a dyadic relationship between
> the learner and the medium or the materials
> intended to induce learning. (Kerr, 1985, p. 3)

He initiates a call for the study of educational technology and the social issues which surround it. For a particular study of educational television as a cultural form, guidelines might be drawn from the social domain mentioned above.

Purpose

This essay will present a method for analyzing the manner in which student viewers read educational television and subsequently construct meaning. It will do this by employing semiotic theory and social science methods of observation to build an analytical model. Part I will offer theory for this analysis by reviewing the salient literature on instructional television, differentiating film and television forms, introducing semiotics and identifying those structures of television which might indicate a unique grammar. Part II will offer a method for the semiotic analysis of television by reviewing the salient literature on the structural analysis of film and television, and by presenting a precise method of observation drawn from the social sciences. It will cite two studies in which this model was used to investigate narrative and documentary forms of educational television.

Separate Media

Before the model can be proposed a key question must be answered. Is the practice of reading television sufficiently different from reading film to warrant a separate analysis? (The term "reading" is employed here because a television program may be thought of as a text in which meaning has been intentionally encoded. It is ripe for decoding or interpretation. Text is a term borrowed from literary analysis and suggests the concepts of "author's intent," "reading" and "interpretation.") If one considers television and film as cultural forms, their practices are easy to separate. John Ellis (1982) describes four types of differences in the aesthetic realm, namely, the viewing experience, the combination of forms and sound, the modes of narration and the producers' attitude toward the audience.

Viewing Differences

Film viewing, he points out, is usually a single public event which takes place in a darkened theater. Although films are viewed in groups, the experience is privatized by the darkness and viewers can react without the knowledge of their neighbors. One can add to that description the fact that the viewer's foveal and peripheral visual systems are usually both engaged by the screen. Since distractions are few, the viewing experience is intensified. Television, on the other hand, is usually viewed at home, in a lighted room, often in groups, whose members can see others' reactions to the screen. The viewer's peripheral vision falls outside the screen, therefore, the environment can easily provide distractions. This viewing is certainly a less intense event than film viewing. If the viewing events are different, the manner in which each medium envisions its audience must also be different. Cinema is produced, as Ellis (1982) notes, for expectant and curious viewers who are anxious to discover resolutions to stories. The TV viewer, on the other hand, often glances rather than looks steadily at the TV image, which is the reason TV is sometimes called a distraction. Different forms of communication must be employed to address such different spectators.

Structural Differences

Structural differences between film and television abound. Ellis (1982) writes that film presents a large scale, highly detailed photographic image to the viewer, while television presents a small image of relatively low definition in which sound is important to hold the viewer's attention. (Forms of cinema and television are changing. Large screen, high definition TV screens have been developed, but are not readily available yet. If television is a cultural form, its current practices rather than its future practices must be described. One can also note that Hollywood is producing films for television viewing. Since the forms of those films are noticeably different, one could suppose that Hollywood directors tacitly recognize the fact that film and television have separate grammars.) A consideration of image, frame and editing might be added to Ellis' list of structural differences. The image in film is projected and fixed in emulsion on a strip of acetate, while the video image is neither projected nor fixed. It is an electronic creation of dots which breaks down and is stored magnetically on mylar tape. Although film and TV directors each rely on similar structures, such as frame, shot composition and editing, in the creation of an image, both have differing periods of time, modes of editing and conventions of viewing available to them when producing these structures.

Frame composition is constrained in the two media by technical restrictions as well as viewing conventions. Film depicts not only a greater range of greys than does black-and-white TV, but a greater range of colors than does color TV; therefore, video images appear flatter than film images and display colder colors than film.

Frame composition is influenced by viewing conventions as well. Television directors cannot take full advantage of the long shot, because of the size of the conventional screen. Small subjects in a lingering long shot are not likely to maintain a TV viewer's attention, yet close ups work well on television. Many frames are composed around faces, so the viewer does indeed come face to face with the TV personality.

When editing film, directors have at their fingertips a simultaneous linear presentation of pictures to arrange, rearrange, cut or superimpose as they choose. Although TV editors have the same capabilities, they can only see one frame projected on one monitor. If there are two monitors, two frames can be viewed at once. This is hardly a simultaneous linear presentation, so editors must remember preceding frames and hold the visual superstructure in their mind's eye while making editing decisions. There is a great reliance in television on the mental editing process, whereas, in film literal cutting and sequencing can be accomplished by the interaction between hand and eye.

Differences between commercial film and television can also be located in educational film and video. The aesthetic differences described above do not change in the classroom. Sixteen millimeter film is usually projected in a darkened classroom which affords the viewer a somewhat privatized experience and the projection screen is larger than the TV screen. What does not pertain to the classroom is the difference in envisioning the viewer. Both educational film and video producers most likely address students whom they think form a captive audience.

Elements of Instructional Television

The notion that television is a unique medium with its own production and reception practices is not new. More researchers have investigated instructional television than any other educational medium, except print. This review of the salient literature on instructional and educational television highlights the studies which considered at first the unique characteristics of television, then the structural elements of the medium and finally how the encoding and decoding process occurs with instructional television. This review represents an evolving concern with the structures of television and closes with a consideration of the issue of structuralism in media research.

Unique Characteristics

Instructional media researchers have been concerned with the unique forms of video for some time. Post World War II research (Sykes, 1964; Williams, Paul and Ogilvie, 1957; Pflieger and Kelly, 1961; and Schramm, 1962) pitted instructional television against live lecture with hopes of better understanding the medium. Such gross comparisons netted little knowledge about the unique characteristics of television, yet Chu and Schramm (1967) noted case studies which yielded enough information to suggest that the use of television in the classroom was worthwhile. Although research on the unique features of television was scarce in the early 70s, Anderson (1972) understood the need for a "visual rhetoric" of instructional television. Noting the heavy use of audio in television, he called for a more effective use of the visual track through graphics, set lighting, camera movement and composition, animation, special effects and color. He had identified some of the structural elements of television and hoped to see a study of their pattern of usage or their rhetoric.

It was not until research and program design became more sophisticated that elementary knowledge about the elements of the medium started to accrue. The creation of *Sesame Street,* for example, and the ensuing research (Lesser, 1974) added information about the effects of pacing, linearity, non linearity and sequencing upon viewing.

Another attempt at a grammar of media (Morrow, 1975) was derived from an investigation of the structures found in film, comics, and radio. Morrow charted shots, cuts, actors and sound in film and grouped those features under the headings of representation, symbolism, distance and structure to present his model of media grammar. Like Anderson (1972) he realized that the way to describe a grammar was to start with structural elements.

Baggaley and Duck also experimented with features of television which may be called structural elements. Basically, they were manipulating elements of the medium and this manipulation allowed them to describe some of the structures and their background behind a speaker. In one study (Baggley and Duck, 1974) they described the effects of edited cutaways on the credibility of the speaker and in another (Duck, S. and Baggeley, 1975) they examined the effects of editing interviews. By manipulating these structural elements, they attempted to uncover their unique function in television.

Aptitude treatment interaction studies using television as a treatment (Koran, Snow, and McDonald, 1971 and Salomon, 1979) also raised questions about the unique characteristics of television as well as the information processing skills of the viewer. Attention, subsequently, to instructional elements embedded in television programs, rather than to television programs as a whole allowed media researchers to gain finer control across sets of independent variables. Instead of asking, "What is the effect of an instructional television program on the viewer?" they were able to ask "What is the effect on the viewer of unique characteristics found in the programs?" There occurred within the instructional technology field a minor shift in the old research model which matched task with a medium to a new model which considered the ability of a medium with unique characteristics to perform specific tasks for specific learners. This model opened up in response to the growing interest in learner aptitudes in the area of educational research, in general.

Symbol System

Gavriel Salomon (1970), working with this new model, posited a cognitive-functionalistic theory of learner media interaction. Since this theory was validated in the area of television, it is relevant here. Salomon proposed that learning from media involved processing schematized information that had been coded for a symbol system, such as television, by a viewer who exercised decoding skills. In three separate studies which addressed the interaction between the information processing skills of the viewer and the codes of television, Salomon (1979) found that the symbolic coding elements of television could affect the mastery of specific mental skills. Salomon not only recognized that television had codes, but isolated some and attempted to test their interaction with learning. Among other things, he considered how camera functions, such as zooming in and out, could be used to code information for visual identification and comparison.

Recognizing the structural nature of this process, that is recognizing the contribution of form to meaning, Salomon alerted instructional television (ITV) designers to the necessity of attending to the symbol system of television to aid and abet learners. Salomon provided ITV designers with the option, if they cared to exercise it, of working with rather than against the natural decoding skills of the learner. Salomon's mandate, then, was to use the medium properly by investigating the interaction between the coding and decoding process.

In another important work which addressed the coding and decoding process, Howard Levie (1978) cut across media by categorizing symbol systems. His helpful classification included digital signs, iconic signs and non-sign stimuli. As did Salomon, Levie recognized the interactive aspects of learning from media. He noted that elements of a particular symbolic code are a) type of pictorial cue, b) the mental imagery this cue invokes and c) mental operations required to make the translation from one pictorial cue to the mental representation. And as Salomon did, he called for the consideration of coding and decoding as a whole. Even Levie's (1978) central question of: What pictorial cues serve to evoke what mental operations? suggests an investigation and description of pictorial cues as they exist and as they are employed in media today. His description appears, to this investigator, to be the first step in studying the interactive process of coding and decoding.

The first suggestion for a frame by frame analysis of television appears to be that of Metallinos (1979) who asked for a study of the field forces of the frame, such as asymmetry, main direction and figure/ground relationships. Metallinos (1985) also suggests a grammar of television in an essay which differentiates TV from other media and names some of the unique characteristics of the medium. For him, they are immediacy, spontaneity, intimacy, small size, treatment of space, the ability to replay instantly and to deliver slow motion.

The common strand within this instructional television research of the seventies was a consideration of coding and decoding of information, in other words, the study of a symbol system. Again it was Gavriel Salomon (1981, 1982, 1984) who took the lead in investigating the symbol systems of instructional television. His prior research on television, discussed above, had already addressed the coding and decoding of television messages. He defined a symbol system as follows:

A symbol system consists of two classes of components—the syntactic component (the atomic and compound symbols) and the rules or conventions of combining them, which together constitute the symbol scheme and the semantic component (or the correlation of the symbol scheme with a field of reference) which makes the scheme into a system. (Salomon, 1979, p. 32)

Salomon argues that the concept of symbol is essentially psychological. To substantiate his argument, he (1979) cites studies (Tversky, 1977; Palmer, 1975; Kahneman and Tversky, 1973; Neisser, 1976; Gombrich, 1974; Shepard, 1978; and Kosslyn and Pomerantz, 1977 in Salomon, 1979) which address a feature of symbol systems, namely resemblance or similarity in a psychological mode. Salomon and these researchers work within a psychological domain when considering learning and the interpretation of signs and symbols.

Structuralism

Symbol system research developed concurrently but separately in Europe and the United States. Separate views about the psychological and the social nature of knowledge created two distinct strands of research. Basically, the European approach to symbol systems was structural in nature and followed Ferdinand de Saussure's call for an establishment of a general science, semiotics, for treating "sign systems."

Although Saussure worked between 1906 and 1911, his ideas were not translated into English until 1956. Two world wars hindered the interaction of structural scholars; therefore, American structuralists were primarily influenced by Whorf and Sapir, while European structuralists were influenced by Levi-Strauss and Saussure (Hawkes, 1977). Since most symbol system research employs a structural model, it is wise to look at that term for a moment. Structuralism has been appropriated by theorists in both the psychological and social domain because, loosely conceived, it is "the perception and description of structures." (Hawkes, 1977, p. 17) This means that the cognitivist, Piaget, could be considered a structuralist, as well as those practitioners of the new behaviorism, sociology.

In the social domain, however, structuralism provides a framework for any study concerned with the production of meaning. "Meaning" here is that which one intends to convey by a human act of speech or of another communicative system. Structuralism focuses on those human acts or behaviors that involve cultural construction the way that speech acts involve sentences. (Pettit, 1977) This approach to the concept of meaning is well articulated in two works on film and one video study.

Symbols and Meaning "Film as a Meeting Place of Multiple Codes," (Kjorup, 1977) is a good example of a structuralist essay. Kjorup draws on aesthetic theory from Goodman and on semiotic theory from Ferdinand de Saussure to describe the many languages and unique codes of cinema. He indicates that the unique nature of film depends on the interaction of the elements within this system; therefore, he believes that meaning is created by the interaction of structural elements. An assumption underlying structuralism here is that the film viewer constructs meaning in a social manner.

Worth and Adair (1972), in a now famous study with Navajo Indians, asked questions about which compositional style novices would use when asked to tell a story with film. They found that native narrative styles used to tell existing Navajo myths and stories emerged in film composition. In fact, certain grammatical structures were transferred intact to film composition. It was disclosed, then, that codes of storytelling, narrative codes that were embedded in Navajo tradition, dominated the new medium. Codes from another medium had supplied some of the infrastructure of the new medium, film.

A study similar to the Worth and Adair study was conducted by ethnomethodologists Beryl Bellman and Bennetta Jules-Rosette (1977) in Africa. They asked approximately the same questions (as Worth and Adair had asked) of natives selected from two African communities in Liberia and Zambia. Questions about compositional style of novices were posed. Video cameras were given to the minimally trained participants who then created their own stories on tape. Traditional narrative codes which appear in the oral literature of both of these tribes were transferred to the composition of videotape. As with the Navajo's, their compositional style was narrative. When Bellman and Jules-Rosette conducted this same study with American TV production novices, they found that their dominant compositional style was dramatic, not narrative. The value, however, of both the Navajo and African studies can be found in the methods. Both studies developed methods for reading motion visuals, for describing form cues and their patterns of usage, their codes. In fact, Bellman and Jules-Rosette gave a detailed reading of the motion cues contained in the narrative style of videotaping. Patterns which emerged on the tapes were extensive use of panning for establishing shots, slow panning throughout, an absence of zooms (whereas Americans used the zoom), use of dollying and use of hesitations. What Bellman and Jules-Rosette are describing for the first time are codes of narration in documentary videotape.

Worth and Adair (1969) and Bellman and Jules-Rosette (1977) relied on individual interpretation of their findings. Social scientists have long eschewed the methods of individual interpretation, whether it was application of "new criticism," structuralism or semiotics. Even though the current method of applying semiotic analysis does not provide verification nor generalizability, the theory is too rich to ignore.

Theoretical Model

Following Saussure's (1966) call for an establishment of a general science of testing "sign systems," structural analysts, such as Barthes (1977), Eco (1975) and Metz (1974) elaborated theories of semiotics and applied them variously to analyses of speech, literature, music, road signs, dress codes, cinema and other communicative systems (for description of their work see Part II). Television itself could safely be classified as a "sign system," since it employs linguistic and musical signs in the audio track and primarily iconic signs in the visual track. In his *Structuralism and Semiotics*, Terrance Hawkes (1977) notes that television is a sign system and, as such, an appropriate medium for semiotic analysis.

Semiotics

Semiotics attempts to delineate the unknown parameters of a sign or symbol system, such as television, by close observation of the existing medium. Basic objectives call for a logical description of the codes and signs that give meaning to the system. Units of construction such as frame, shot and sequence in television may be considered signs, and as such they have two types of meaning, syntagmatic and paradigmatic. Syntagmatic meaning refers to the way in which these units are organized. Among other things, it considers the order of shot presentation and the way in which a frame is constructed. This organization is called syntax, just as the organization of a sentence is called syntax. If within this syntax, patterns of use appear, they may be called codes. Codes can be original to the medium in which they are found, but are more frequently derivative and borrowed from other media or other domains. Meaning borrowed from other sources is called paradigmatic meaning. For example, a fade between shots in drama on television usually means a change of location and possibly a passage of time. It has paradigmatic meaning, since it is derived from early cinema. At the same time, that fade has syntactic meaning, since it moves the action from one shot to the next. Derived codes may be described as categories of choice which abstract their meaning from categories rejected as well as categories accepted. If a poet, for example, selects a sonnet for his/her poetic structure, it carries with it traditional codes which suggest themes of love, requited and unrequited, and subjects of beautiful women, nature and death. Such codes carry part of the infrastructure of a communication and supply a paradigm for that communication. Units of television construction, then, such as frame, shot and sequence could be described along syntagmatic as well as paradigmatic lines in a semiotic analysis. An understanding of the sign system of TV depends on an articulation of the elements that already exist and an accounting of their contribution to the whole system.

Grammar

Film grammar has been partially defined, but rules for television grammar have not been identified. If one considers, however, the structures which are differentially incorporated in the production of the video image, it may be hypothesized that the grammar of the two media are different.

   Screen. If the conventional television screen is small, its size restricts the kinds of shots it can portray effectively. In other words the shot range for conventional television is usually between medium and very tight. That is not to say there are no long shots on television, but directors do not linger on them. They usually present them quickly to establish location. If one doubts that television capitalizes on this "medium to tight" range, an examination of current Hollywood films that are made ultimately for home viewing will prove the point. Certain Hollywood films distributed to theaters are produced to realize a larger profit from sales and rentals as video cassettes. These films rely heavily on that "medium to tight" shot range. Another concession to the small size of the TV screen appears in these films. Physical action abounds and the editing pace is swift; therefore, directors realize that quite a bit of motion is necessary to hold the attention of TV viewers who watch small screens. What, then, has the small screen contributed to the grammar of television? If shots can be primarily described within the "medium to tight" range, shot syntax is limited. It precludes the description of that rich "long to medium" shot range in which large scenes and comparisons can be viewed. While the small screen is syntactically limiting, it does give the tight and very tight shot greater power or weight in TV scene composition than they are given in film scene composition. Also, if the small screen needs motion for attention, it limits a number of elements. In the dramatic narrative format, plots which move slowly or in which characters slowly develop are usually avoided. Emphasis on physical motion in dramatic presentations limits the number of subjects TV can portray, or induces directors to include physical action at inappropriate moments. When talking about choice of plot, character development or subjects for portrayal, one is speaking of paradigmatic meaning. These are categories of choice and bring with them meaning from their domains of origin. The small screen, then, is also paradigmatically limiting. At the same time, this screen opens up avenues of exploration for the unique grammar of television. Such an exploration is the current MTV (music television).

Editing. The nature of television editing also influences its grammar. If a television editor does indeed have to keep much of the visual superstructure in mind, he/she is limited in range of sequential effects. Smaller numbers of sequences may then be used to express the same range of messages that film expresses. Sequencing becomes syntactically powerful, therefore, in the shaping of the television message.

Television formats also influence its grammar, since codes are specific to formats. One way of analyzing paradigmatic elements is to examine the codes enforced by the selection of a format from a set of formats. Dramatic narrative form is a popular selection for both commercial and instructional television and could be examined readily. Drama, for example, brings with it a set of codes from theater and cinema, yet unique video codes for drama have not been described. Such a description is currently possible. One can observe that plots in commercial television drama are episodic as in theater, but not as in film. Pacing of plot action is slowest in theater, faster in film and faster yet in television. Climaxes appear to occur more frequently in TV than in either of the other two media.

Semiotics, with its power to describe stated and derived meaning, appears to offer a sound theoretical base for the analysis of the language of television. The application of semiotics to television is not new, but has been employed by Fiske and Hartley (1978) in *Reading Television* and by Heath and Skirrow (1977) as well as other analysts. What has been suggested here is the idea that educational television is ripe for semiotic analysis. The first part of this essay has explored the unique nature of the medium by reviewing salient television literature, differentiating the form of television from that of film, identifying television as a cultural form, situating the proposed analysis within semiotic theory and describing units of television construction which might signify a unique grammar. Part II of this essay will present the model for the grammatical analysis of television. It could be said that the grammar of television is already functioning in the creation of hours of daily commercial and instructional programming. A study of the orderings and functionings of this system is necessary before one can evaluate and design effective video programs for the classroom.

Part II: Method

This section of the essay will propose an analytical model for the grammatical description of television. It will not attempt to present a rationale for the formulation of such an analysis, since arguments for the support of that analysis were mounted in the theory section. The author will offer a background to the current discussion on the semiotics of film by focusing on the use of cinematic codes for appropriation for television when comparisons are evident. The proposed model will be discussed in terms of the selection and validation of structural levels, the formation of program segment and focus questions, the definition and use of sequence, shot and frame, the study procedures and data analyses. Since the analytical model was refined during the conduct of several studies, the author will cite those studies when it is necessary to operationalize abstract concepts. The scope of this essay, however, does not permit a full report of those studies, since the intention here is to propose an analytical model. Since the model relies heavily on the language of semiotics, key concepts will be defined within the body of this text.

Analysis

Arguments for and a delineation of a theory for the analysis of television were presented in the first half of this essay. Briefly stated, the theory section of this paper borrows concepts from semiotics and suggests a grammatical analysis of television. Such an analysis would describe units of television construction such as frame, shot and sequence, along syntagmatic as well as paradigmatic lines. Syntax would provide a description of the patterns of construction found between and among these units for a given television program(s). It would provide the viewer with a method for reading the television image and understanding the actual relationships in the construction of that image. Since syntax exists only within and because of a communication, analysis would be conducted within one program format at a time. Focus questions, instead of hypotheses, would constitute the inquiry and identify the program format and segments to be investigated. Since semiotics is a structural communication theory, and as such, lends itself well to the investigation of social/cultural learning, focus questions would arise from a consideration of knowledge as a product of social interaction.[1]

In conjunction with syntactical analysis which examines the actual relationships among the categories of construction, paradigmatic analysis would be conducted. Paradigmatic analysis would provide a description of the potential relationships between and among the units of television construction. Frame, shot and sequence would be examined as categories of choice. In other words, the domains or paradigms from which they were selected would be traced. Paradigmatic analysis would emerge from informal comparison of structural levels and their sources of origin. This analysis would provide the viewer with a method for decoding the potential or suggested relationships in the construction of television images.

Film and Television Codes

Language of Production

That the structures of film or television communicate in a language based on shared knowledge can be verified by recourse to the vast writings on film and television production. In a popular television production text, (Millerson, 1983) the author speaks in a familiar context. He notes that the use of high key lighting gives a light, fresh, brittle and gay atmosphere to the shot. In his instruction on frame composition, Millerson (1983) repeats the fact that a wide angle shot gives establishing information, but lacks detail for the television audience. That fact is brought home by the small size of the television screen. To convey details, he notes, close up shots are needed. Frame

---

[1]This does not deny the psychological aspects of learning. It simply suggests that there is a tradition of social learning which states that knowledge accrues because of one's membership in a group, not because of one's individual psychological makeup. Semiotic theory is offered here as a base to accommodate social learning issues.

composition is also addressed by Kjorup (1977) when he indicates that composition of the film frame can communicate much information about the people within and their relationships. He notes that a method of drawing attention to a person within a shot is employed when the director points to him or her with a line constructed by background features which may form a vector, or when the director has other people gaze at the person, or when the director allows that person to occupy an area larger than others around him or her. Spatial relations, then, are readily perceived as meaningful and confirm the fact that codes of composition are widely shared.

Shot construction in television and film is not the only structure that communicates its message through an established language, but chains of shots or sequences also partake of that language. Although, as Snow notes (1967), the ability to arrange image events in a fashion to produce implications is almost infinite, known conventions of coherence lead directors to construct a small number of sequence compositions. Television film directors and viewers appear to be in agreement about the meaning of certain "within sequence" structures. A dissolve signifies a short time lapse is occurring. If the dissolve is fast, it indicates concurrent parallel action. If the dissolve is slow, there is an uninterrupted flow of picture which indicates a quiet restful transition and transfer in time and space. (Millerson, 1983; Fiske and Hartley, 1978) Cutting between shots makes instant comparisons about subject and viewpoint. (Millerson, 1983) Slow motion shots indicate that analysis is called for, or signify lyrical beauty. (Fiske and Hartley, 1978) It is not necessary here to continue to cite the existence of the language of film or television, but it is important to note that the syntax of this language is a result of usage, not a determinant of it. The conventions of practicing film and television have supplied a language.

Semiotics

The most thorough and promising description of the language of media has been conducted within a semiotic framework. Although semiotics is diverse so that literature does yield some guidelines for the description of television structures, one might ask about the nature of structural units which have been

insightfully described in the semiotics of any visual
communication system.

Barthes

Roland Barthes (1977) described structural units and their
relation to the culture in which they are found. Not only did his
analysis include visual systems, *i.e.*, photographs, street signs,
film, but music and writing as well. His sweep is broader than
some other semioticians, with emphasis on orders of
signification. Since he deals primarily with these orders of
signification, that is, levels of meaning in the work presented, his
techniques lend themselves to the investigation of the social and
cultural meanings embedded in media. His first level of
signification is the representation of the image. He moves swiftly
through it to second and third order significations where his
contribution is strong. Units of meaning addressed in the second
order are immediately social, *i.e.*, myth or shared cultural
meaning and connotation. His third order addresses the manner
in which this shared cultural meaning is organized into a belief.

Barthes has contributed an awareness of the social
meaning of media and his contribution has not been ignored.
Many current literary and media analyses are indebted to
Barthes, but two outstanding treatments which owe a partial debt to
him are *Reading Television* (Fiske and Hartley, 1978) and
Ideology and the Image (Nichols, 1981). Fiske and Hartley
describe units of British television news, their patterns of usage
and social meaning. They tend to address smaller units than
does Barthes, but their analysis is still social. *Reading
Television* unveils the "myths" or shared cultural meanings
embedded in video images, describes television "reality" and
compares the manner in which television interacts with the
culture itself. A more complex treatment of social meaning and
visual media can be found in *Ideology and Image* (Nichols, 1981)
which draws upon perception theory and psychoanalysis as well as
Barthes' principles of semiotics to complete its task. Working
quickly through communication signs, perception theory, and
essentially the Lacanian perception of self, Nichols (1981)
carefully relates this discussion to advertisements and then leaps
to an analysis of many forms of cinema. His strokes are broad,

but his message is clear. Cultural values are embedded in all media.

   Metz and Codes. If one concentrates only on the semiotics of film, a number of analysts emerge. Successful attempts to "read" film have been made by Christian Metz (1974a, 1974b) and others (Wollen, 1969; Monaco, 1977; Bettetini, 1973; and Carroll, 1980). Metz has developed a sophisticated analytical model for "reading" film, but it is one based on individual interpretation. The challenge in borrowing some of Metz's rich concepts about interpretation would be to introduce the elements of verification and generalization demanded by research in the social sciences. Metz, however, begins his analysis with a helpful code set theory. *This essay will refer to codes as the tacit rules or regulations which develop in the practice of constructing the units of frame, shot and sequence within television or film. Codes are rules of relationships and derive from specific syntax.* They do, however, have paradigmatic meaning embedded in them. For example, McLuhan (1964) notes that early television practice imitated old film practice. Rules or codes for the presentation of plot or dialogue were borrowed intact. Not only were these televison syntax codes, but they borrowed embedded meaning, paradigmatic meaning, from their usage in film. Codes, therefore, cannot be considered solely in a syntactical sense. Codes can be culturally derived, shared, or unique and the presence of a unique code in a medium would indicate a new grammar.

   Metz believes that one must distinguish the source of codes involved in the construction of a sequence, consequently he has developed a code set theory. His theory attempts to trace those codes which are derivative or not unique to cinema, and to describe those unique to the medium of film. He does this to provide a fuller understanding of the contribution of one medium to another and to highlight the new use of an old code. Codes he believes are constructed within domains, such as the domains of general culture, cinema and theater. Within those domains he lists shared and non shared codes. Codes of lighting and narration, for example, would be shared by general culture, cinema and theater. Montage would be non-shared, specific to cinema (see Figure 1). "Domain" for Metz has vast implications and can mean another genre as well as something he calls general culture. His next step is to identify which codes, specific to cinema, are found in all films and which are found in a few. It is easy to see that film relies heavily on theater, as well as the domains of general culture and the novel for its system of codes.

Educational Television and Codes

Since television incorporates so many borrowed codes, a model similar to the Metz code set theory may be applied to television. One of the reasons for identifying the origin of codes is to see how they were originally employed. If they are being used

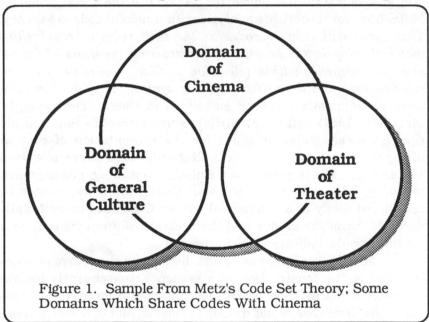

Figure 1. Sample From Metz's Code Set Theory; Some Domains Which Share Codes With Cinema

differently in the new medium, it implies a new grammar. If they are not being used differently, they carry meaning from other domains and indicate a partially borrowed infrastructure.

ITV. The domain of instructional film, for example, was coded early in its history and shares codes with Hollywood film, military training, instructional methods and behaviorism as well as codes from theater, novels, documentaries and many other areas (see Figure 2). The "Yale Chronicles" (Saettler, 1968) were silent photoplays used in 1918 to teach concepts about the American

Revolution in college history classes. They employed dramatic narrative as well as primitive documentary techniques. These photoplays were, of course, imitating the silent films of the day, but it was no accident that history and social studies became favorite topics for instructional films and that dramatic narrative and documentary became favorite styles of presenting these films. Likewise, the "Why We Fight" (Saettler, 1967) series of documentaries, directed in part by Frank Capra, employed dramatic narrative codes used in Hollywood films of the day. A

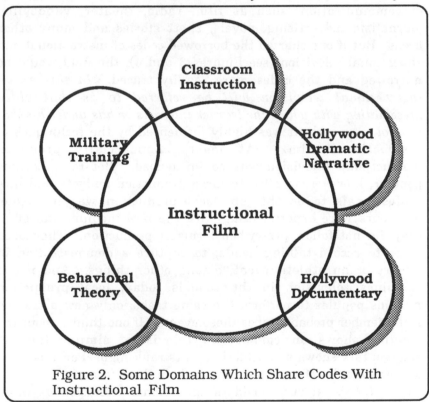

Figure 2. Some Domains Which Share Codes With Instructional Film

new type of instructional documentary film grew out of this experience. The application of dramatic narrative codes, in other words, codes of fiction, became a favorite technique for documentary filmmakers. The technique was and is favored in the composition of instructional and noninstructional documentaries which seek to influence opinion and change or formulate attitudes. Yet, documentaries claim to be factual. Training films, on the other hand, employed not only guidelines from behavioral theory, but from established methods of military training. Today instructional films often employ documentary, dramatic narrative and training techniques. Yet, as these techniques are incorporated in film production, they bring with them their own codes. Borrowed meaning, then, is embedded in the new film production.

Commercial television shares codes with numerous forms of communication, such as film, radio, theater, vaudeville, journalism, advertising, novels, short stories and many other areas. But if one charted the borrowed codes of instructional and educational television (see Figures 3 and 4), the field would be narrowed and the codes more readily traced. *In this essay, instructional television will be referred to as that video presentation with which the learner interacts or has under his/her control.* As such, it was highly influenced by the techniques of instructional film. At least, commercially produced instructional television was so influenced. Before it became popular, however, to allocate large production budgets and hire professionals to do the job, local production was in vogue. Amateurs were experimenting with the new medium and often they did not follow prescribed forms of production. They used video to record talking heads, to capture a demonstration in science or an athletic event, among other things. And if one examines television in the schools today, local production remains popular to perform the same tasks, only now a trained staff member probably tapes these events. If one thinks about the popular shows on commercial television, similar formats emerge; talk shows and athletic events rank high. Perhaps some of the new codes of the television reside in these formats.

ETV. If one considers educational television as those video presentations produced for and broadcast or cablecast on educational television channels, a wider range of codes is included. That range may appear closer to the shared codes of

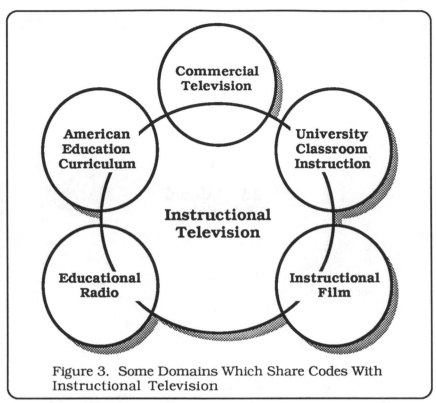

Figure 3. Some Domains Which Share Codes With Instructional Television

commercial television listed above. The introduction of Sesame Street by the Children's Television Workshop expanded the definition of educational television (see Figure 5).

If one were to consider the proximate sources of the codes within one format of instructional or educational television, at a given time, and define these origins with some specificity, then the code set theory would offer a way of decoding meaning within that format. It is conceivable that what Metz calls the Domain of General Culture (Metz, 1974) could include subdivisions addressing those social and economic forces, as well as instructional forces, which shape the construction of an ITV or ETV format. The television analyst who knew the origin of the codes would be able to make informal comparisons between its use in the old and the new medium, or make comparisons between similar codes in separate television formats. Charting of these

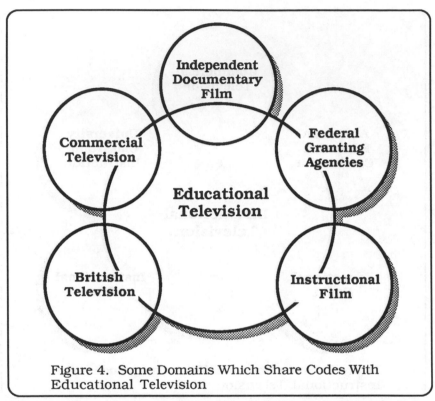

Figure 4. Some Domains Which Share Codes With
Educational Television

codes need not be accomplished by individual "reading" of the
medium, as is now taking place in semiotics, but can be recorded
and verified by use of computer programs. An understanding of
the structure of ETV and ITV might grow in this manner.

Syntax

A television program segment does not only derive its
meaning from codes, but from syntax as well. Levels of
television construction, such as frame, shot and sequence are
meaningful because of their position within the program.
Organizations of these levels of construction may be called
syntax. A focus on those units which relate to one another and
which involve cultural construction the way speech involves
sentences is necessary when considering syntax. Language is
the basic metaphor for semiotic analysis, but the metaphor of
language for film or video analysis is weak at the smallest unit.

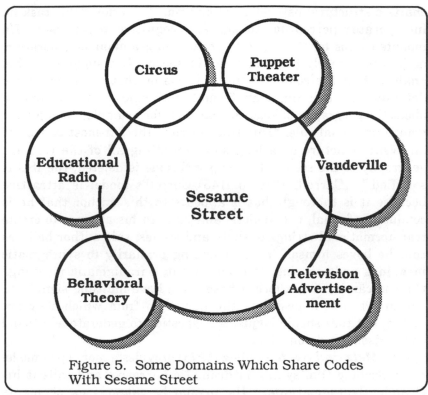

Figure 5. Some Domains Which Share Codes
With Sesame Street

A picture is not like a word; it contains numerous bits of information, while a word usually contains one or two bits of denotative information. A picture is highly denotative, while a word can be moderately denotative, but highly connotative. The strength of the language metaphor exists, however, because the concept of grammar can be understood by the layperson and the researcher alike. The unit of the sentence or the paragraph is generally understood. The communicative links, then, between words, phrases, sentences and paragraphs are understood and used daily in common speech and writing. The metaphor gains strength from a comparison of this linkage.

Film syntax has undergone various analyses (Wollen, 1969; Spottiswoode, 1950; Eisenstein, 1949; Balazs, 1970; and others), but the theorist who has employed the language metaphor most literally is John Carroll (1980). Borrowing theory and method from current transformational grammar, he rigorously charts a structural psychology of cinema. To perform this task he incorporates perceptual theory and cognitive psychology. He mounts claims for the argument that film grammar is generative, as it was formerly believed to be in speech, but suggests by his analysis that the combinations of frame or shot or sequence are definable by existing transformational rules. When writing about the geography of space in the shot, for example, he applies a transformational rule. "This rule rewrites the left-most A node of an event structure as a long shot, revealing all of the relevant geography of the scene. The empty N node is deleted, the ISC is satisfied." (Carroll, 1980, p. 145) Carroll's model is attractive because it is thorough, but it appears to this author that he is conducting formal, not semiotic analysis. In his attempt to create transformational strings of shots and scenes, this author believes that he boxes himself in by attending primarily to syntagmatic meanings and ignoring, to some extent, paradigmatic meaning. Cinema can be an art form whose signs have multiple signifiers. An analyst might postulate the paradigm from which they are drawn, but that should be just a suggestion to generate additional comparisons and contrasts.

Metz and Syntax. Metz (1974) provides a more open model for describing film syntax in dramatic narrative and calls it his Grande Syntagmatique. He primarily categorizes segments according to the relation between and among shots, scenes and sequences. Relations are described in terms of time, chronological or achronological; presentation style; narrative or descriptive; linearity; and episodic or non episodic techniques. He also describes autonomous segments and shots. His categories leave room for much interpretation, and Metz (1974), along with Michele Lacoste, applied them to the reading of two films.

Metz's model supplies rich conceptual information for the analysis of dramatic narrative within educational or commercial television, but it can become cumbersome if used intact. (This author applied it intact for a pilot study in educational television and abandoned it.) The other shortcoming of the model is that it is exclusive to the dramatic narrative format and that format constitutes only a small portion of educational television programs of instructional and TV presentation styles. Metz himself finally abandoned it in favor of a reader theory (Metz, 1975).

A Proposed Model

This section of the essay will describe the method, procedures and data analyses for the model proposed for the grammatical analysis of television. The analysis will seek to answer questions posed about communications in the visual track of specific television programs. Since the method of analysis is based on a structural theory of communication it will address social/cultural issues presented in selected instructional television programs.

The first stage of study procedures begins with several viewings of the program(s) in question. After viewing, a panel of experts generate focus questions and identify program format(s) (see Figure 6). Program segments which are part of the format

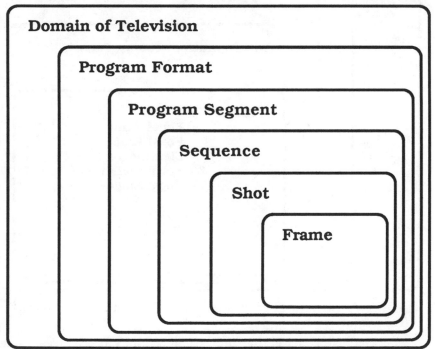

Figure 6. Structures Analyzed in the Grammar of Television

structure and dependent upon the focus questions are then
identified and validated.

During the second stage the panel of experts, trained as
observers, view and record segment structures by employing
Plexyn, a program for recording and analyzing interactions.
During the first pass of the television program, in real time, the
observers note agreed upon program segments and record their
openings and closings. During the second pass, in slow motion
and using the VCR pause button to freeze frame when necessary,
the observers record additional segment structures
(see Figure 7). A reliability check is run on these data and this
completes the second stage of study procedures.

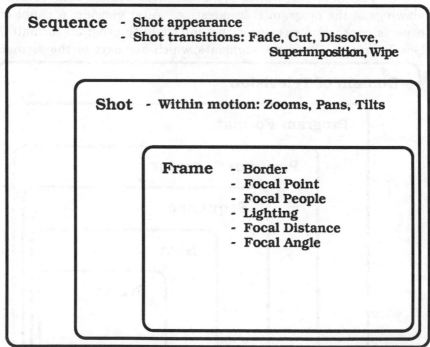

Figure 7. Structural Properties Recorded in the Grammar of
Television

Data analysis is the final stage of study procedures. The
data collected are formally appraised for patterns emerging
within and between program segments and within and between
programs where multiple programs are being studied. Informal

comparisons and contrasts of within patterns, syntax codes, are made with existing syntax codes in similar program formats. The existence of borrowed codes in the program segments is noted and their syntactical origins are traced. Social/cultural origins or paradigmatic meaning(s) of the borrowed codes are also traced. The existence of any new within-program patterns or syntax codes is described. And finally, the social/cultural content or paradigmatic meaning of any new syntax code is examined.

Formats

Semiotic analysts, when employing the method of individual interpretation, work within one format at a time. Indeed, they work to describe one communication at a time, within that format. Syntagmatic analysis, then, takes place initially at the micro rather than macro level. If one postulates that unique patterns exist within television, it would seem appropriate to study these patterns' similarity within the format of television. These formats are variously described in the television literature. One survey of this literature and an appraisal of television programming[2] recommended the following categories for consideration as formats: instructional television, dramatic narrative, situation comedy, documentary, news, advertisements, variety shows, talk shows, soap operas, game shows, musical presentations, sports presentations, dance and MTV. Educational television is a broader category which may incorporate the techniques of any of the formats listed above. In no way is this classification proposed as all-inclusive, nor are the categories always discrete. It is a classification which allows this structural analysis to begin. As production within a format matures, conventional methods of communication or codes develop. Format codes supply the infrastructure in which to examine syntax. The assumption here is that syntax is developed differentially within varying formats. For example, zooms on talk shows have a different meaning than zooms in dramatic narrative. Words can only be linked for the purpose of communication, otherwise one

---

[2]It is not the intent of this analysis to address the possibilities of TV programming, but to consider television in practice, as it is viewed today.

has nonsense phrases. So then can television syntax only be studied and situated within a communication in a given format.

The question, of course, could eventually be posed about the similarity of syntax between or among formats. For example, units of frame construction might be similar across formats. There is a danger, however, in pursuing that question in the early stages of the research.   Since one is analyzing units of communication, it must be remembered that these units take their meaning from format codes. A series of fast cuts from a close-up framed face to close-ups of another framed face has no meaning of its own. It may exist only in relation to the communication within the format in which it is found. For example, it may exist to advance the plot by displaying tension between the central characters whose faces are framed, if these cuts exist within a dramatic narrative.

Program Segment and Focus Question

Within a given television program format there are segments whose construction is oftentimes unique to that format. For example, plot in dramatic narrative usually has a beginning, a middle, and an end, and it is advanced by pitting a protagonist against an antagonist or an antagonistic force. Yet, the viewer can observe the varying unfolding of plot in theater, film or television. One might ask, as this author did in a pilot study, what educational television does to plot construction. The answer would allow television writers, producers and directors more control over their format and classroom teachers more control over the description of meaning in dramatic narrative.   The segments studied within plot included beginning, climax, denouement and ending. In other words, the segments were drawn from the structure of the format.

In an educational television social studies series which describes the culture of three countries, the question was asked "From what point of view is each culture presented to 6th and 7th graders?" (Salcedo, 1984) The first step, then, was to look at the format in which these series were presented. Since it is this author's contention that instructional and educational formats are not discreet structural units, but contain presentation styles drawn from varying formats (see Figures 2 and 3) such as documentary, advertising, dramatic narrative and situation comedy, it is necessary to identify the formats included in the series. Since the presentation format in the social studies series was of a documentary nature, documentary structures were identified. These included noting whether participants or narrators were on screen and for what length of time are they there. Whether events are staged or actual was noted and the nature of the events described. These and other documentary structures provided the program segments within which to do the analysis. By looking at these structures analysts were able to indicate whose knowledge was being communicated in the series. The assumption here is that a television program is a visual text in which meaning has been encoded.

Observers

Since this model incorporates social science research requirements of validity and generalizability, the selection and training of the observers should follow the rules for any observational study. Bias can be reduced and reliability boosted if a) there is precise and similar training for the observers, b) observers are included in the generation and identification of structures, c) there is discussion and agreement among observers about the language and the definitions of the structures to be employed, d) samples are increased and e) reliability checks run on the data. (Becker, 1977) Observers may be selected for their expertise in two areas, television and program format, such as dramatic narrative, news, documentary and education. In pilot studies conducted by this author, the observers had courses and production experience in small format as well as studio television. Those who worked with dramatic narrative had knowledge of literary analysis as well as knowledge of television. They had completed graduate courses in literature and had taught English. Those working with a social studies series for elementary school students had taught elementary social studies, in addition to being knowledgeable about television.

By viewing and discussing the videotaped programs observers reach consensus about the definitions and presentation of structural units before the coding begins. They have practice sessions of entering the codes on the keyboard to gain facility in rapid recording, coding and running reliability checks of their files.

Sequence, Shot and Frame

After identifying program segments to be analyzed, the observers proceed to the next level of analysis. Those structures which are common to all television formats and, consequently, offer themselves for grammatical analysis are sequence, shot and frame.

Selection and Validation. This researcher, after reviewing the literature on television production, compiled an extensive list of structural units. The list was informally presented to educational video directors and camera people. Their task was to prioritize these units, so that a sense of which units were most important in practice would emerge. Their knowledge about usage existed at such an intuitive level that it was hard to elicit a response to that list. When interviewed, however, and asked "What do you shoot?" or "How do you construct your shot, your scene?" they replied in the language of television structure. This suggests that a television grammar probably exists at an intuitive level and remains as yet undescribed. In a circuitous way, they returned to the original list. Mentioned most frequently were frame, shot and scene or sequence. Within a frame the distance, angle, lighting and focal point received most mention. Motion within shots was spoken of in conventional terms of zooming, panning, tilting, and dollying or trucking. And motion between shots was mentioned in conventional terms of cutting, fading, wiping and dissolving. If this research were not conducted with social science methods, the author could have selected conventional units of structure from the research. The validation process used here appears circuitous, since it returns to conventional units. The step was, however, necessary. The list which will constitute the base of a computer program for micro analysis of television has content validity.

Frame, shot and sequence may be described as levels of video construction (see Figures 6 and 7). To discover the existing relationship among these levels, it is necessary to name the smaller units of construction within these. First, however, a definition of the levels should be included.

A *frame* is the image which the cameraperson selects and borders within the boundaries of his/her lens (production 525 lines traced in 1/30 of a second = 1 frame (repeat rate of 30 stills/second), 262.5 alternately traced 1/60 second = field frequency of 60/second reduce flicker). Each line is scanned in 635 microseconds or at rate of 15,750 lines/second). (Millerson, 1966)

A *shot* is identified within camera movement (subjective motion) or within set movement (objective motion) from frame to frame.

Sequences are a self-contained series of shots achieved technically by, within, or between camera switches.

Subcategories can be listed and programmed as follows:

1. *Opening and Closing Frame*
    a. Border (Open, Closed)
    b. Focal Point
    c. Focal People #
    d. Lighting (Back)
    e. Focal Distance (Long, Medium Long, Medium, Medium Close, Close)
    f. Focal Angle (Top, High, Level, Low, Low Level)
2. *Shot*
    a. Opening Frame
    b. Transition
        (1) Between—Fade, Cut, Dissolve, Superimposition, Wipe
        (2) Within—Zoom, Pan, Dolly, Truck, Tilt
    c. Closing Frame
3. *Sequence*
    a. Opening Shot
    b. Closing Shot

Coding

A computer grammar processing program, Pleyn, is employed to code representative sequences and shots, transitions, frames and the within frame components of border, focal point, focal people, lighting, focal distance and focal angle. The program processes these notations through a set of syntactic rules which allows the complex coding properties to be formatted in real time and error corrected. It verifies, completes and reformats the recorded data for subsequent data analysis.

Properties of the structural components of sequence, shot and frame were identified by reference to television production texts, especially Millerson (1976), and to the director/cameraperson survey conducted. Within-sequence properties were limited to fade, cut, dissolve, superimposition and wipe. Objective within-shot motion was categorized as zooms in and out, pans left and right, tilts up and down, and tracking.

The six properties of shots recorded were wide, medium wide, medium, medium tight, tight and very tight. Since television screens are usually small, shots in the practice of television are more fully articulated in the medium to close range. This model emphasizes that range. Properties of frame were recorded as follows; border, open or closed; focal point, upper, middle or lower third of the frame; focal people, one, two, three or group; lighting, back or no back lighting; focal distance; focal angle, high, medium high, level, medium low and low. These structural properties control the Pleyn program as it checks the use of each unit in the observation record. They also manage the recorded data and enhance error correction (Stephenson, 1979). If a property in a category, for example, is mutually exclusive of another property, then as the one property is recorded the other property is automatically terminated. If a frame has a level focal angle, the program will automatically shut off other angles, since they cannot be presented simultaneously.

Data Analyses

Formal. A file printout can be read to ascertain how many and when a structural property appeared to within 1/20th of a second. The first pass of the program segments is noted in real time while the second pass is one in which the videotape is freeze-framed and started again. The program MERGOR allows the second pass to be merged with the first, synchronizing them both to form a third file with a real time base. Additional files on similar properties may be merged if necessary. The additional programs associated with Pleyn supply the frequency and duration of individual properties and can categorize the duration of shots and sequences noting the percent of total program time. It allows the researcher to read the structure of these representative shots and sequences, identify relations and finally syntactical patterns as they emerge.

Informal. Patterns emerging between and among the structural units of sequence, shot and frame constitute the syntax of the program format studied; but syntax will only partially answer the focus questions posed about the television program. Analyses here which must bridge the gap between formal and informal use, as is customary, quantitative techniques to support some of the qualitative conclusions. If a syntactical pattern emerges, it may represent a borrowed code and the social/cultural origins of that code must be traced. If within the study on what television does to plot an over the shoulder reverse angle dialogue code emerges, it can be traced to 1940-50s Hollywood film. Questions about what it meant originally and what part of that meaning it retains in television need to be asked. Why it continues to be used is an important question. If in the study of "Across Cultures," a documentary code, such as—the narrator frequently emerges on camera, the origin of that code should be traced and compared to its use in the program. Tracing social/cultural origins of codes will supply some paradigmatic meaning.

If new syntax emerges within or between television programs (as this theory hypothesizes that it will) the social/cultural context in which it emerges needs to be examined. If within the study of plot in dramatic narrative, suspenseful sequences are short and there are several climactic moments before the climax of a story, new syntax might be claimed. An examination of the current practice of television as a social/cultural institution might shed light on the new syntax. If within the "Across Culture" series, one culture is consistently shot from a high angle, at a distance, and has several non-native narrators on camera, a specific syntax for presenting that culture emerges. Investigation of program objectives, scripts, budget, production techniques and constraints might contextualize that syntax. These examinations supply paradigmatic meaning.

Conclusion

This model has been offered as a replacement for the method of individual interpretation which is conventionally employed in the investigation of social/cultural issues in media studies. It incorporates some theory from media studies, namely semiotics, while borrowing method, observation, from the social sciences. It proposes to study television as it is practiced, looking at syntactical meaning in the construction of programs and paradigmatic meaning in the social/cultural origins and present context of the syntax.

The two studies cited, namely one which asked the question, "What does television do to the plot structure in dramatic narrative?" and another which asked the question, "Are three cultures presented equitably in the social studies series 'Across Cultures?' " are samples of the type of focus question which may be asked when this model is employed. It should be stressed that they are simply samples, but represent a type of question that the model can address. Often researchers in the field of educational technology have abdicated their responsibility to handle social/cultural issues encountered in learning with instructional media. This oversight was in some ways a historical accident since most research in this field was and is based on psychological learning models. Other areas of educational research and media studies do, however, employ social learning models and it is this outside research that has prompted a growing interest in social issues in educational technology. If the issues concern themselves with television, this model could address them. If the research is interested in questions such as "Whose knowledge is presented in a television program?" or "What social messages are embedded in the visual track?" or "How are social messages framed or structured in the visual track?" this model would be appropriate.

REFERENCES

Anderson, C. M. (1972). In search of a visual rhetoric for instructional television. *AVCR, 19,* 43-63.

Baggaley, J. and Duck, S. (1974). Research notes: Experiments in ET: Effects of adding background. *Educational Broadcasting International, 7,* 208-209.

Baggaley, J. and Duck, S. (1975). Research notes: Experiments in ET: Effects of edited cutaways. *Educational Broadcasting International, 8,* 36-37.

Balazs, B. (1970). *Theory of the film.* New York: Dover Press.

Barthes, R. (1977). *Elements of semiology.* Translated by Annette Lavers and Colin Smittz. New York: Hill and Wang.

Becker, A. (1986). A teaching model for the grammar of television. *Journal of Visual and Verbal Languaging 6*(1) 41-47.

Bellman, B. and Jules-Rosette, B. (1977). *A paradigm for looking: Cross cultural research with visual media.* Norwood, NJ: Ablex Publishing Corporation.

Bettitini, G. (1973). *The language and technique of the film.* The Hague: Mouton.

Carroll, J. M. (1980). *Toward a structural psychology of cinema.* The Hague: Mouton.

Chu, G. C. and Schramm, W. (1967). *Learning from television: What the research says.* Stanford: Institute for Communication Research.

de Saussure, F. (1966). *Course in general linguistics 1906-1911.* New York: McGraw-Hill.

Duck, S. and Baggaley, J. (1975). Research notes: Experiments in ETV: Interviews and edited structure. *Educational Broadcasting International, 8,* 93-94.

Eco, U. (1976). *A theory of semiotics.* Bloomington: University of Indiana Press.

Eisenstein, S. (1949). *Film form.* Translated and edited by J. Leyda. New York: Harcourt Brace World.

Ellis, J. (1982). *Visible fictions.* London: Routledge & Kegan Paul.

Fiske, J and Hartley, J. (1978). *Reading television.* London: Methuen.

Gitlin, T. (1980). *The whole world is watching.* Berkeley: University of California Press.

Goodman, N. (1968). *The languages of art.* Indianapolis: Hackett.

Hall, S. (1980). Encoding/decoding. In S. Hall, D. Hobson, A. Lowe, & P. Willis (Eds.), *Culture, media, language.* London: Hutchinson & Company, 128-138.

Hawkes, T. (1977). *Structuralism and semiotics.* Berkeley, CA: University of California Press.

Heath, S. & Skirrow, G. (1977). Television: A world in action. *Screen, 18*(2), 7-59.

Kervin, D. (1985). Structure and meaning: A semiotic analysis of network television news. *Dissertation Abstracts, 47(3),* 70l.

Kjorup, S. (1977). Film as a meeting place of multiple codes. In D. Perkins and B. Leandar (Eds.), *The arts and cognition.* Baltimore: Johns Hopkins University Press, 20-46.

Koran, M. T., Snow, R. E., and McDonald, F. J. (1971). Teacher aptitude and observational learning. *Journal of Educational Psychology, 62,* 219-228.

Lesser, Gerald S. (1974). *Children and television.* New York: Random House.

Levie, H. (1978, Spring). A prospectus for research on visual literacy. *ECTJ, 26,* 1, 25-35.

McLuhan, Marshall. (1964). *Understanding media: The extensions of man.* New York: McGraw-Hill.

Metallinos, N. (1979). Composition of the TV picture: Some hypotheses to test the forces operating within the television screen. *ECTJ, 27,* 205-214.

Metallinos, N. (1985). The idiosyncrasies of television: An overall view. *Journal of Visual and Verbal Languaging,* 5(1), 43-5l.

Metz, Christian. (1974). *Language and cinema.* Translated by Donna Jean Umiker-Sebeok. The Hague: Mouton.

Millerson, G. (1976). *Effective TV production.* New York: Hastings House.

Morrow, James. (1975). Toward a grammar of media. *Media and Methods,* October, 78-80.

Nichols, Bill. (1981). *Ideology and the image.* Bloomington: Indiana University Press.

Pettit, Phillip. (1977). *The concept of structuralism: A critical analysis.* Berkeley, CA: University of California Press.

Pflieger, E. F. and Kelly, F. C. (1961). *The national program in the use of television in the public schools.* New York: The Ford Foundation and the Fund for Advancement of Education.

Saettler, P. (1967). *A history of instructional technology.* New York: McGraw-Hill

Salcedo, A. (1984). A rhetorical and structural analysis of an instructional television series. Unpublished doctoral dissertation, University of Wisconsin, Madison, Wisconsin.

Salomon, G. (1979). *Interaction of media cognition and learning.* San Francisco: Jossey-Bass.

Salomon, G. (1981a). *Communication and education: Social and psychological interactions.* Beverly Hills, CA: Sage.

Salomon, G. (1981b). The use of visual media in the service of enriching mental thought processes. *Instructional Science, 9*(4), 327-39.

Salomon, G. (1982). Television literacy and television vs. literacy. *Journal of Visual and Verbal Languaging, 2(*2), 7-16.

Salomon, G. (1984). Predisposition about learning from print and television. *Journal of Communication, 34*(2) 119-35.

Schramm, Wilbur. (1962). Learning from instructional television. *Review of Educational Research,* 156-167.

Spottiswood, R. (1950). *A grammar of the film.* Berkeley: The University of California Press.

Stephenson, G. & Roberts, T. W. (1977). The SSR system 7: A general encoding system with computerized transcription. *Behavior Research Methods & Instrumentation, 9,* 434-441.

Sykes, R. E. (1964). The effectiveness of closed circuit television observation and of direct observation of children's art classes for implementing elementary teacher's training in art education. *Dissertation Abstracts, 25,* 2387.

Tuchman, G. (1978). *Making news.* New York: The Free Press.

Weiss, B. (1985). A visual analysis of the coverage given the 1984 presidential campaign by CBS television on CBS evening news with Dan Rather. An unpublished doctoral dissertation, University of Wisconsin, Madison, Wisconsin.

Williams, D. C., Paul, J. and Ogilvie, J. C. (1957). Mass media, learning and retention. *Canadian Journal of Psychology, 11,* 157-163.

Williams, R. (1975). *Television: Technology and cultural form.* New York: Schocken Books, 1975.

Wollen, P. (1972). *Signs and meaning in the cinema.* Bloomington: Indiana University Press.

Worth, S. and Adair, J. (1972). *Through Navajo eyes: An exploration in film communication and anthropology.* Bloomington: Indiana University.

Section 4

Computers and the
Critical View

✱✽✱✽✱✱

16

A Critical Analysis of the Use of Computers in Education*

Michael J. Streibel
Educational Technology
University of Wisconsin-Madison

Microcomputers are being introduced into public and private schools at an exponential rate and this trend shows no signs of abating (Becker, 1983). It is therefore crucial that we examine the nature of computer use in education and what implications this has for the future of education (Sloan, 1984). In this article, I will present a critical analysis of the three major approaches to the use of computers in education: the drill-and-practice approach, the tutorial approach, and the simulation and programming approach. I will do this by presenting the characteristics of these approaches and then by examining their assumptions and contexts of use. The focus will not be just on the nature of instructional strategies, but on the nature of these strategies in a computer environment. The computer, as I will try to show, is not just another "delivery system" but an environment that has certain values and biases associated with it. Finally, I will try to uncover a common framework that runs throughout the three approaches and discuss the implications of this framework for education. The analysis will not, however, deal with the social, political, or economic dimensions of education even though such dimensions are ultimately involved (Apple, 1979, 1982).

A number of philosophical questions helped guide me in the course of this analysis. For example, what is the logic behind each of the computer-based approaches to education mentioned above, and how does this logic express itself in a learning situation? These and other questions helped me understand that computerized drill-and-practice approaches to education are a behavioral form of learning technology which may not be the best way to supplement instruction. That is, the logic of computerized drill-and-practice programs may run counter to the dialectics of learning. I also asked myself how the various approaches mentioned above treated the human learner, and what consequences this could have for education. My analysis revealed that a concept of an individual as a generic information-processor was embedded in each of the three approaches. This, in turn, revealed how systems' goals (*e.g.,* efficient production of learner performance) were invariably masked behind the rhetoric of individual "mastery" and individual "needs." It also revealed that the learner's personal intellectual agency was decreased rather than increased in the case of computer-based tutorials even though the rhetoric promised the exact opposite.

Finally, I asked myself how the "intellectual tool" use of computers helped or hindered us to formulate, understand, and solve problems. That is, what kinds of "solutions" were legitimized when we formulated problems in computable form? This was part of the larger question about the potential that computer languages and simulations had for thinking and learning about problems. My answer to this question required a very careful analysis of the "expressive potential" of computer languages.

I have explored the underlying assumptions of the three most common approaches to the use of computers in education in order to understand the potentials and limitations of this technology within education. This should provide a basis for further critical study of the subject.

A Personal Statement of Assumptions and Values

A paper such as this is as much a journey outward toward some external goal as it is a journey inward toward one's personal values and assumptions. Since the latter are so inextricably woven into the fabric of the entire paper, a brief statement of my values is in order.[1]

I teach a variety of courses on the use of the media and computers in education and carry on an empirical and critical line of inquiry into this area. I therefore see myself as a teacher, teacher educator, and scholar in the area of educational technology. In each of these roles, I am motivated by a desire to teach others how to think about media and computers (but not what to think) and how to become empowered, life-long learners.

Empowered learning, in my view, is a form of human liberation in so far as the latter is possible. It goes beyond the ability to encode and decode abstract meanings and focuses on the ability to *create* meanings within an interpretive community. This, in turn, presumes certain epistemological commitments for its realization.

My epistemological commitments are derived from critical theory which states that knowledge is the result of a social construction of reality (Habermas, 1981). That is, what we *know* to be real is the result of historical and social processes of meaning-making, language-making, and symbol-system making (Goody, 1977; Ong, 1982). This social construction of reality applies to our knowledge of physical realty (i.e., scientific and technological knowledge) as well as to our knowledge of social reality (i.e., what we know about ourselves and others) (Kuhn, 1962; Berger & Luckmann, 1966). In both cases, the social construction of reality entails a process of human collaboration and dialogic engagement with interpretive communities (Greene, 1982b). This collaboration and engagement creates a "public space" in the minds of the people involved which then leads to the further evolution of shared meanings and shared symbol systems. In a sense, collaboration and engagement within

---

[1]I would like to thank an anonymous reviewer for suggesting that I add this section and also for making many helpful comments.

interpretive communities define our very humanity because we are participating in the creation of history, our language, and our values (Greene, 1982a).

What is the role of education within this framework? I see formal education as a social process of nurturing cognitive, affective, physical, aesthetic, and moral growth and diversity in children (Kohlberg & Mayer, 1972). The latter are dimensions of "meaning-making" and therefore can only happen within the community. The development of factual knowledge and skills is important, of course, but always in a subordinate role to personal and communal growth and development. A simple way of saying this is to state that "a teacher teaches people and not subjects"— even within the daily routine of classroom schedules, organizational structures, and curricular guidelines (Berlak & Berlak, 1981).

Learning, in my view, is an intentional and constructive act on the part of the learner. Here again, dialogue and critical thinking with the members of one's interpretive community play a central role. Hence, even though a student may be learning a simple fact or skill in a drill-and-practice activity, he or she is still using the linguistic and intellectual tools of the larger community in order to make sense out of the world. Mindfulness and meaningfulness are interconnected as are mind and the social construction of reality. Otherwise, skill-building and knowledge acquisition become mechanical and mindless processes.

Students are active participants in their own knowledge-creation in another sense. Learning is as much a process of accommodation as assimilation (Piaget, 1970; Furth, 1969). Accommodation requires the active creation of new meanings and the active construction of new symbol systems to give expression to these meanings. Assimilation is also an intentional and constructive act even though it entails a process of plugging new information into existing schemas. My reason for believing the latter derives from an ontology which views all events—both physical and social—as unique, historical and irreversible (Whitehead, 1929). A student who is learning facts or skills is more than a receiver of knowledge or a manipulator of predefined puzzles. He or she is an intentional agent. This beings me to the heart of my epistemological commitments.

I believe that our knowledge encompasses more than discrete, objective, rational symbolic representations. I will describe some of these other types below. I also believe that cognition entails more than formal operations which operate on explicit knowledge structures. An individual's cognitive processes are always subordinate to meaning-making which in turn takes place within the context of the social construction of reality. Since cognition deals with meaning-making, it is always open to the future and new ways of representing meaning (Greene, 1982a). Even quasi-formal systems are never complete. I am always reminded of this when I recall how many 19th century physicists believed that Newtonian Mechanics gave them a complete understanding of the world.

There are many types of knowledge besides discrete, objective knowledge. This is not meant to diminish the importance of objective knowledge but rather to indicate that objective knowledge is interconnected with other forms of knowledge. Some other forms of knowledge are:

1. *Tacit Knowledge*—through which explicit knowledge is viewed (Polanyi, 1958, 1966).

2. *"Ambiguous" Knowledge*—which is grasped through a variety of "intelligences" (Gardner, 1983). The word ambiguous is in quotes only because what is explicit in one symbol system (*e.g.*, music) may be ambiguous and inexplicable in another system (*e.g.*, verbal).

3. *Problematic Knowledge*—which is often the starting point for new paradigms of knowledge (Greene, 1982a). Reflection, dialogue, and critical thinking help make certain routine assumptions about the world problematical. This is the case for scientific knowledge, as well as for social knowledge, and it results in "revolutionary science" in science and "social empowerment" in society (Kuhn, 1962; Freire, 1970).

4. *Experiential Knowledge*—which can be combined
    with rigorous reflection, analysis, and inquiry and
    results in robust and ecologically valid
    understanding (Kolb, 1984).

5. *Knowledge of Individual Differences*—which leads
    to the tolerance, understanding, and furtherance of
    individual and cultural diversity and not just to
    finer-grained control of the learner (Bloom, 1976).

Finally, I believe that formal education is more than a
"rationally managed process." Schooling should not be modeled
on an industrial assembly line because schooling deals with
"meaning-making" (and ultimately with "people-making") and
not with widget production (Apple, 1975). I therefore do not view a
teacher as an "instructional manager" who equates certainty with
predictability and power with control over process and product.
Such concepts (predictability and control) are appropriate for the
efficient production of identical products.

In my view, a teacher is a central agent in a dialectical
community of learning and one who forms a triadic relationship
with the learner and the subject matter (Greene, 1978). This
maintains a learning community that extends backward and
forward in time. I do not wish to ignore the daily routine of
teaching. I merely wish to reiterate the craft status of teaching—a
status that is particularly important today because a technological
environment tends to leave most people "powerless" and unable to
articulate their state of being (Greene, 1982a; Ellul, 1980a).
Learning, empowerment, and community, in my view, all go
together.

A teacher is also someone who nurtures various types of
intelligence in students. A teacher is not someone who stands
over and above the learning process or who separates the
conception from the execution of learning (Apple, 1982). In short,
a teacher is not someone who adopts a theoretical stance toward the
learner. Rather, a teacher is a life-long learner who engages and
guides others along a similar path.

One can see from the foregoing discussion that my deepest
commitments center on valuing individual and cultural
uniqueness and diversity while at the same time valuing the

knowledge and skills that contribute to the social construction of reality. Maintaining a balance between uniqueness and uniformity (of person, culture, knowledge, and skills) is a daily struggle for a teacher that will be profoundly affected by the computer (Berlak & Berlak, 1981). It is with these personal beliefs and values that I now turn to a critical analysis of the use of computers in education.

Drill and Practice Computer Programs

Drill-and-practice courseware programs (*i.e.*, computer programs that guide learning with a drill-and-practice instructional strategy) are the dominant use of computers in education today (Suppes, 1966; Coburn, Kelman, Roberts, Snyder, Watt & Weiner, 1982). They are currently run on mainframe, time-sharing, and microcomputers (Murphey & Appel, 1977; Alderman, 1978; Stewart, 1979). I will deal with this topic by first describing the major characteristics of the drill-and-practice approach and then by discussing a number of related issues. The latter issues, however, warrant some preliminary remarks.

The most general issue deals with how drill-and-practice courseware programs are biased toward behavioral forms of learning. I will demonstrate this by showing how such courseware programs combine several broad traditions such as the mastery-learning paradigm, the philosophy of individualized learning, and the concepts of educational work and efficiency. I will then show how such programs represent a very one-dimensional form of education because they restrict the goal structures, reward structures, and meaning structures of educational events to the domain of educational productivity. This, in turn, undermines the possibility of integrating sub-skill performances into other educational experiences.

Finally, I will deal with the issue of how drill-and-practice courseware programs work best in a learning culture that legitimizes behavioral performances over other types of educational goals. Ironically, behaviorally oriented learning cultures must still be created, mediated, and sustained by interpersonal interactions which have the potential for forming alternate cultures (and thereby alternate types of educational goals). Drill-and-practice courseware programs, however, do not permit these alternate goals to develop. My discussion of the importance of dialogue will then lead to an analysis of the "dialogue" component of human-computer tutorial interactions.

Description of Drill-and-Practice Courseware

Drill-and-practice courseware programs make a number of assumptions about instruction (Bunderson, 1981; Salisbury, 1984):

a. Previous instruction in the concept or skill has already taken place,

b. Regular instruction is only being supplemented and not replaced,

c. Instruction is to follow a controlled, step-by-step linear sequence of sub-skills according to an algorithm embedded in the computer program. This algorithm does *not* constitute a model of a student or an expert but constitutes a model of: i) rote skill-building in the case of drill, and ii) patterned skill-building according to the logic of the content and an instructional theory in the case of practice (Skinner, 1968; Gagné, Wager & Rojas, 1981),

d. There exists a right/wrong answer dichotomy in the logic of the content,

e. The basic unit of instructional interaction is a question-answer-branch episode (Dennis, 1979a). Continuous learner responses in the form of correct answers are therefore expected, and

f. The best feedback by the program from an instructional point of view is an immediate check on a student's responses according to the logic of the content:

 i.   Positive feedback when the answer is correct,

 ii. corrective (rather than judgmental) feedback when the answer is incorrect.

The characteristics described above make several things clear: drill-and-practice courseware programs are designed to provide immediate corrective interventions in the learning process when continuously monitored performance measures indicate incorrect responses. The learner is viewed as a "black box" and his or her behaviors are shaped by an external, mechanical process (i.e., by an instructional algorithm that uses feedback mechanisms to guide the learner towards a pre-specified behavioral goal). Drill-and-practice courseware programs therefore constitute a deterministic form of behavioral technology (Skinner, 1968). This may be adequate for beginning skill-building but not for higher levels of learning (Dreyfus & Dreyfus, 1984). Within the beginning skill-building domain, however, drill-and-practice programs do result in significant performance gains (Kulik, Kulik, & Cohen, 1980).

The characteristics described above also make another thing clear: drill-and-practice courseware programs are a one-dimensional form of education. The reasons for this are simple and take us into broader issues:

     a.   They contain a uni-dimensionality of *goal structures* since:

         i.   They only focus on *pre-specified* behavioral performances,

         ii.   They are designed for *convergent uniformity of outcomes* and not a multiplicity of divergent outcomes,

         iii.   They exclude non-behavioral educational goals (*e.g.,* emergent attitudinal and cognitive strategy outcomes),

         iv.   They are conceptualized and designed before any interaction with the actual learners takes place,

     b.   They contain a uni-dimensionality of *reward structures* because:

         i.   They only reward successful performance on one sub-skill with an opportunity to work on the next sub-skill,

         ii.   They define "individualized" feedback in generic terms rather than in terms of personal, semantic, and affective engagement,

     c.   They contain a uni-dimensionality of *meaning structures* because:

i.   They only define "mastery" (i.e., success
         at any point) in terms of objective
         performance (*e.g.,* total number of correct
         responses),
ii.   They do not acknowledge the legitimacy of
         qualitative aspects of performance (*e.g.,*
         expert performance) except in so far as it
         results in better quantitative performance.
In order to understand the consequences of this one-
dimensionality for education, I will delve into the philosophy
behind drill-and-practice courseware programs as well as into the
context of their use. I will do this by examining the mastery
learning paradigm, the philosophy of individualized learning,
and the concepts of educational work and efficiency.

Mastery Learning and Drill-and-Practice Courseware
The mastery learning paradigm assumes that most
students can learn most things to a specific level of competence in
varying amounts of time (Bloom, 1976). It therefore bases
differences in the *amount* of learner performances at any point in
time on differences in the *rates of learning.* Second, the mastery
learning paradigm assumes that instruction can be consciously
designed to guarantee specific outcomes. It therefore places a
heavy emphasis on the *quality of instructional materials.*
Finally, the mastery learning approach uses criterion-referenced
tests with each objective to decide whether a student has met the
criterion of success. Students are then permitted to go on to the
next set of objectives.

You can see from this description that the mastery
learning paradigm closely resembles a rationally managed
input/output model of educational performance (Apple, 1979, 1982).
It therefore makes a number of assumptions about the pedagogical
principles, classroom practices, and instructional arrangements
involved (Barr & Dreeben, 1978; Bolvin, 1982). These
assumptions elaborate the input/output model.

a.   *Pedagogical principles:*
       The mastery learning paradigm assumes
       that students vary in their aptitude, ability to
       understand   instruction,   motivation,   and

perseverance. These factors contribute to the distribution of performances by students at any given point in time. Furthermore, these factors are only considered in so far as they affect educational performance. They are not, for example, considered in terms of their contribution to non-performance educational goals (*e.g.*, growth in consciousness, growth in aesthetic appreciation, moral growth, etc.).

Although all students are believed to be able to achieve mastery *given enough time,* the amount of time it takes to achieve mastery is normally distributed. In comparison, in a norm-referenced learning paradigm, the actual performance scores are also distributed normally at any particular point in time, but there is no claim that low-achievement students will *ever* reach higher levels of performance (Bloom, 1971, 1976).

The pedagogical assumption that all students are able to achieve mastery given enough time allows learning to be treated as a rationally managed process since only time and resources have to be considered in order to guarantee a predictable performance outcome. Considerations such as the dialectics of learning, accommodation to individual uniqueness, and the possibility of emergent goals have been factored out of the process. I will show later that these considerations are essential for learning—even at the level of simple skill-building.

b.   *Classroom and school practices:*

The mastery learning paradigm manipulates the *time* allowed for learning and the *quality of instructional stimuli* as the main factors to help students achieve mastery. It therefore entails the rational planning of classroom time, schedules, organization, and conditions of instruction, as well as the rational design of instructional materials

(Nunan, 1983). Such design and planning activities are only called rational to the extent that they are guided by the pragmatics of instructional and organizational theories. Such design and planning are *not* guided by the pragmatics of classroom teaching (Wolcott, 1977). For example, predictability and manageability of process and product are a prime consideration and not whether some unique classroom event becomes an occasion for further learning. Hence, the conception of instructional events is separated from the execution of such events, and the conceptual phase directs and controls the execution phase (Apple, 1982). In this scheme of things, we would eventually expect teacher performance (and ultimately administrator and even system performance) to be evaluated in terms of student performance since correct student behavior is the ultimate output. However, I will show later that this in fact serves the system's needs more than the learner's needs.

c.   *Instructional arrangements:*

The mastery learning paradigm follows a number of procedures to guarantee that students will perform at pre-specified levels (Bloom, 1976):

    i.   Pre-instructional assessment procedures are used to measure the presence or absence of prerequisite knowledge in the learner,

    ii.   Initial teaching methods are used to inform the learner of the objectives and prerequisite knowledge,

    iii.   Training procedures are used to help the learner acquire the appropriate knowledge and skills,

    iv.   Continual assessment procedures are used to assure the presence of sub-skills,

    v.   Immediate remediation procedures are used if the sub-skills are not present, and

vi.   Certification of mastery is added when some predetermined criterion performance is reached by the learner.

You can see from all of these techniques that the mastery learning paradigm conceptualizes the instructional process in quality control terms. Each step in the paradigm is expressed as a procedure and all instruction is arranged to maximize output. All that is left for humans to do is to get to work!

The mastery learning paradigm described above therefore provides a broad theoretical framework for drill-and-practice courseware. It specifies *what kinds* of things are to be achieved (*i.e.,* measurable performance gains) and *how* these things are to be achieved (*i.e.,* through the manipulation of time and instructional stimuli). Drill-and-practice courseware functions as the training and remediation component within this framework. Although group work is permissible within the mastery paradigm, drill-and-practice courseware is usually individualized. This leads me to the philosophy of individualization.

Individualization and Drill-and-Practice Courseware

Individualization can mean many things: independent study, individual pacing, individual diagnosis, individual educational outcomes, etc. (Bolvin, 1982). It arises out of the larger recognition that individuals differ from each other (Sperry, 1972; Messick, 1976; Cronbach & Snow, 1977). Within computer-based forms of individualized learning, however, it refers to generic outcomes for generic individuals rather than to personal goals for unique individuals. More of this later.

The philosophy of individualization, as it has developed within individualized systems of education, contains a number of specific assumptions (Lukes, 1973; Talmadge, 1975):

a.   A belief that each person has a unique set of characteristics or aptitudes that ultimately influence the *rate* at which competent performance in a particular skill is achieved,

b.   A belief that a well-defined and well-structured sequence of instructional events can be designed for

each individual to facilitate his or her progress
toward preplanned outcomes,

c.   A belief that time and quality of instructional
     materials will influence successful completion of
     an objective,

d.   A belief that assessment procedures of student
     "needs" and characteristics will indicate a
     readiness for the objectives by the learner,

e.   A belief that an evaluation mechanism can be found
     for constantly monitoring the student's progress
     toward a pre-planned outcome (these same
     evaluation mechanisms also provide data for the
     instructional system's performance), and

f.   A shift in the role of the teacher *from* a pedagogical
     one *toward* that of instructional decision-maker
     (i.e., placement of students; selection, use and
     allocation of space, time, and materials; data
     collection and report-writing, etc.)

These assumptions are implemented in a number of ways.
In some systems of individualized learning such as the Keller
Plan, students have a great amount of flexibility in setting
schedules, getting help from student tutors, and following any
number of paths toward a predefined goal (Keller, 1968). Each of
these factors is adjusted for the sake of individual rates of
learning. In the Skinnerian version of the philosophy of
individualization, on the other hand, instruction is broken down
into much smaller units, and instructional events are more
controlled and automated (Skinner, 1968). It is this latter version
that is most often implemented in drill-and-practice courseware.

Drill-and-practice courseware programs overwhelmingly
use rate of progress as their major dimension of
individualization although they sometimes also include level of
difficulty (Suppes, 1966). Other dimensions such as cognitive
style are often called for but rarely implemented because of the
difficulty of specifying these factors in computable form (Scriven,
1975).

Drill-and-practice courseware programs also break the
instructional process into very small steps. They then assess each

response by the learner and specify a finite number of paths for the learner to follow. They are therefore "individualized" in a very narrow sense of the term. That is, they have restricted the meaning of individualization to a finite set of choices within a measurable and computable domain (i.e., individual rates of progress along finite, forced-choice paths that lead to pre-specified, measurable outcomes). Since they control both the *presentation of information* as well as the learner's *interactions with that information,* they control the individual's total attention during the time that they are used.

Finally, drill-and-practice courseware programs relegate the teacher to a managerial function (*e.g.,* resource manager or exception handler) (Boyd, 1983a, 1983b). This is not to suggest that a teacher or school system is forced by the computer to organize the classroom according to the Skinnerian philosophy of individualization, only that drill-and-practice courseware programs are biased towards such an orientation. In many schools, the shift toward teacher-as-manager has already taken place without the computer (Apple, 1975; Berliner, 1982).

In many ways, the philosophy of drill-and-practice courseware is consistent with the movement in the curriculum field toward the "technical control" of learning (Kliebard, 1971; Franklin, 1974, 1982; Carlson, 1982). I will describe this notion under the rubric of the "technological framework" through-out the rest of my discussion. For now, the concept of replicated work will help us begin to understand the concept of "technical control" in courseware.

Courseware as Replicated Work

Victor Bunderson has developed one of the most thorough analyses of the concept of courseware as replicated work (Bunderson, 1981). The following discussion owes much to his analysis and perhaps will add to his ideas. Computer courseware, he argues, has both a product and a process dimension. As a *product,* courseware consists of the "consumables [materials of instruction] that operate on and with a technologically mediated instructional delivery system." As a *process,* courseware constitutes (Bunderson, 1981):

an economically replicable and easily portable package which when used in combination with a technologically mediated instructional delivery system, is capable of performing work related to training and performance improvement.

An instructional delivery system, on the other hand, consists of both *the physical objects and structures* "designed to perform or facilitate the work necessary to achieve educational and training goals," and, a *human culture* of "traditions, values, and habits that inform and constrain the use of the physical artifacts" (Bunderson, 1981). The instructional delivery system is therefore the broadest category within which all other components of the ensemble are situated and from which they derive their meaning.

We can see from the description above that the concept of computer courseware contains a "technological control" orientation. That is, the technical structure of the delivery system shapes the form and function of the human culture and the physical artifacts. The technical structure also orients these components toward some external goal (i.e., educational performance) and then tries to maximize the levels of this goal. A technological delivery system will therefore ultimately influence the nature of the classroom culture—unless, of course, the classroom is already organized as a work culture.

From my earlier discussion, we can begin to see that the student's control over the pace of learning is really a form of pseudo-control because he or she can only choose from a finite number of paths toward a pre-determined goal. Bunderson acknowledges this somewhat by saying that "learner-centered will emphasize learner productivity, not necessarily learner-control" (Bunderson, 1981). This restricts the meaning of "individualized learning" to that of "individualized productivity level."

Bunderson continues his discussion of educational work by criticizing the inability of current teacher-centered "delivery systems" to be more "productive." The teacher-centered culture, he argues, has reached the "limits of [its] improvability." His solution is a technological one: "when education is analyzed into the work that is required, technology is seen as the *only* way to make a fundamental difference" (Bunderson, 1981). Bunderson's argument is very general and even applies to book-based technology (*i.e.*, a teacher with books can accomplish more than a teacher without books). His argument has to be analyzed very carefully, however, for book-based as well as computer-based technologies.

Before turning to my analysis, some general comments are in order. First of all, conceiving of the classroom as an "instructional delivery system" (rather than, say, an instructional setting for the dialectical encounter of mutually respected and unique individuals) narrows the debate about what can happen in such a setting. The classroom, in effect, becomes a place for training and development. I mentioned earlier that the mastery learning paradigm turned the classroom into a workplace for both teachers and students. The concept of the classroom as a workplace is further compounded by highlighting the work potential of classroom technologies. Second, the discussion by Bunderson about classroom instructional delivery systems lays the conceptual groundwork for accepting computer courseware as more efficient versions of the same thing.

Another general theme deals with books. Looking at books as "productivity tools" has a number of problems—some of which also apply to computers:

a. What really counts in books (even for the restricted productivity paradigm of education) is the *intelligence* embodied in the print medium and *not* the presence or quantity of print information. This intelligence goes beyond procedural knowledge and is the key to what is transmitted during learning. Hence, teachers with unintelligent books are not better off than teachers without books. They may, in fact, be worse off because they might be tempted to assume that they can accomplish more than before.

b. The fact that teachers with books can accomplish more than teachers without books does *not* mean that the "work potential" of book-based technology *determines* what a teacher does. True, reading skills might be required simply because books are used, but this does not mean that books need only be used for training. Conceptualizing books in terms of their work potential, however, forces them into a productivity scheme.

c. Analyzing books in terms of their work potential diverts attention away from their dialectical potential (*i.e.*, their ability to confront one with alternate points of view from one's taken-for-granted reality). Books, for example, also have the ability to reveal how other humans have integrated the dialectical tension between, say, justice and love or between wisdom and courage. In these instances, books become guides for experiential learning that point the way to personal and communal integration. All of this is hidden when we look at books in terms of their work potential. We are then only left with an image of a book as a training aid.

d. Finally, books as such leave open the choice of interactions which a person can carry out. Hence, books leave open the way an individual uses and makes sense out of the information. They are therefore not a good analogy with computer courseware programs which control both the presentation of information as well as the user's interactions with that information.

Bunderson's argument permits one to compare teacher-delivered instruction and technology-delivered instruction because both are conceptualized in similar terms. Computer courseware is then seen as a more efficient mechanism. I must admit that when I observe certain classrooms which contain hierarchical authority, rigid schedules, and mindless workbooks, I am inclined to agree with Bunderson. But I must also point out that even in such classrooms, students still have some opportunity for personal integration of experiences and skills. That is, students can still integrate their drill-and-practice activities with exploration, planning, negotiation, and collaboration—even if it is done as a subterfuge. These latter characteristics are essential for education (Kolb, 1984). In individualized drill-and-practice courseware, on the other hand, where a student's total time, attention, and interactions are controlled by the computer, such integrations are no longer possible (Dreyfus & Dreyfus, 1984). Is this loss worth the price—even for low levels of learning where only the acquisition of procedural rules is involved?

When we examine the actual characteristics of Bunderson's concept of educational work, we find that they all embody the *extensional* side of education (i.e., the measurable and procedural). For example, according to Bunderson, a teacher: presents information to students, models processes for students, provides students with trials and feedback, discusses "individual needs" with students, uses affective appeals to motivate learning, trains students in the use of the delivery system, assesses student performance, manages the assessed information, and manages classroom interactions. Where, here, is there a teacher's affective and semantic engagement with students beyond maximizing performance gains? All that Bunderson describes are procedural skills and information processing functions. When conceptualized in this way, such functions *can* be carried out more efficiently and effectively by technology (*e.g.*, video, microcomputer, etc.). Efficiency here means maximizing educational productivity at the lowest financial cost. Effectiveness means reliably reproducing the process and the product (Bunderson, 1981). Efficiency and effectiveness, in effect, are no longer subject to the qualitative criteria of excellence and expertise within a particular subject area but to the quantitative criteria of economics (Eisner, 1979). No wonder teachers cannot compete!

There is a fundamental contradiction in Bunderson's point of view, however. The rhetoric stresses the "needs" of the individual, but the terms of the debate emphasize instructional systems concerns. By shifting the educational interactions away from the intensional logic of interpersonal interactions and toward the extensional logic of procedural skills and information-processing functions, the following criteria are emphasized:

a. *Systems efficiency* (*i.e.,* maximizing the throughput
    of students for the time and resources invested—
    rather than developing individual talents),

b. *Systems reliability* (*i.e.,* quality control and
    replicability of input—rather than the establishment
    of individual, communal, or cultural diversity),
    and,

c. *Systems economy* (*i.e.,* more scholar for the dollar—
    rather than personally-determined pursuit of
    excellence).

Hence, *only those "individual needs" amenable to
systems logic are served.*

There is another contradiction in Bunderson's concept of
educational work. The very work culture which has to exist in a
classroom for a technological instructional system to operate can
only result from intensional human engagement, negotiation,
and interaction. Students and teachers are therefore essential
and continuous agents in the creation of a classroom work culture
(Sarason, 1982). However, the very processes that are required to
produce the work culture then have to be *denied* because they
contradict the technological framework. This is the case because
an instructional delivery system embodies a technological
culture that tries to shape the human culture to its own ends
whereas human cultures shape their own ends (Nunan, 1983).

A good illustration of the contradiction described above
can be seen in the teacher roles which Bunderson believes will
predominate in a technological environment: corrector of
imperfect and outdated information, illustrator and augmenter of
delivered instruction, illustrator and augmenter of the expert
algorithms embodied in the instructional system, creator of a
technologically acceptable setting, and interpreter of
automatically tested and recorded results. Each of these roles
shows how the technological delivery system has become the
central organizing factor in classroom life. The classroom has
thereby been structured as a workplace by someone other than the
teacher (Wolcott, 1977; Nunan, 1983). A simple drill-and-practice
courseware program is therefore not all that innocent an aid to
teaching in a classroom community (Benne, 1975). In fact, such

programs may ultimately conflict with the nature of teaching because teaching is *not* a highly rational decision-making affair.[2]

Summary of Drill-and-Practice Courseware

Drill-and-practice courseware programs embody a deterministic form of behavioral learning technology. They also embody narrow aspects of the mastery-learning paradigm, the philosophy of individualization, and the concepts of educational work and efficiency. That is, they convert the learning process into a form of work that tries to maximize performance-gains, and they restrict the meaning of individualism to rate of progress and level of difficulty (and ultimately to individualized levels of productivity).

Computerized drill-and-practice courseware programs may also *not* be the best way to supplement instruction even though they maximize sub-skill performance. The reason for this is simple: drill-and-practice courseware programs restrict the type of interactions involved to a decontextualized performance domain and diminish integration of sub-skills with higher-level skills.

Finally, drill-and-practice courseware programs are part of a behavioral learning culture that mitigates against non-behavioral goals. Hence, such programs do not lead to critical thinking or personal empowerment. The question therefore arises whether computer-based tutorials have such a potential or whether they simply develop the behaviorally oriented learning philosophy in a more sophisticated way. Many authors have argued that computer-based tutorials do in fact solve some of the limitations of drill-and-practice programs (O'Neil & Paris, 1981).

---

[2]Some scholars have suggested that the prevalence of drill-and-practice in our schools is not incidental. The hidden curriculum of drill-and-practice courseware, they claim, prepares a certain segment of the student population for similar types of computer-controlled jobs in society (Apple, 1979; Olds, 1982). However, such an argument involves socio-political evidence and is beyond the scope of this paper.

Tutorial Computer Programs

Do tutorial courseware programs go beyond drill-and-practice approaches to education? They do in an obvious sense because they are intentionally *designed* to "take total responsibility for instruction" and to contain a "mixed-initiative dialogue" (Dennis, 1979b; Bork, 1980a; O'Shea & Self, 1983). But what exactly do the terms "dialogue" and "initiative" mean here? I will examine the nature of "dialogue" in human-computer interactions as a way of analyzing the nature of tutorial programs. My reason for this is simple: dialogue is seen by many authors to be the basic building block for higher levels of learning (Freire, 1973; Greene, 1978; Shor, 1980). I will also examine the *types* of "quality-control" procedures which are used and the *nature* of the tutorial engagement. I will then show that many of the themes which I uncovered in my analysis of computerized drill-and-practice re-emerge in computerized tutorials in a more sophisticated form. This will stand in sharp contrast to the rhetoric about tutorial courseware programs which claims that such tutorials resemble real conversations and real teaching (Bork & Franklin, 1979; Dennis, 1979b; Bork, 1980b).

Before dealing with these larger issues, however, I would like to describe the various types of human-computer interactions in tutorial courseware programs: on-line tests, remedial dialogues, and interactive proofs (Bork, 1980b).

On-Line tests are initiated by a computer as part of the tutorial interaction. They involve a comparison between a model of the student (which was either pre-programmed into the computer or constructed by the computer on the basis of student performances) and a model of an expert. In simpler tutorials, on-line tests only involve a comparison between student performances and pre-specified, content-determined performance levels (O'Shea & Self, 1983). In either case, however, on-line tests provide continual diagnoses of students' performances.

An immediate consequence of having on-line tests in computerized tutorials is that the learner is subject to constant "quality control." This does not seem unreasonable since, in interpersonal interactions, humans also check out their inferences about each other (Nisbett & Ross, 1980). Why shouldn't a computer do the same? However, in interpersonal dialogues, such monitoring takes place in the context of semantic engagement and conjoint intentions. In human-computer interactions, on the other hand, such monitoring is guided by an external agent's (i.e., author, instructional designer, or programmer) intentions which are fixed *for the duration of the interaction.* These external intentions establish pre-set, non-negotiable, and measurable performance outcomes *for the learner.* Constant monitoring is therefore not intended to understand the learner and his or her messages (as in interpersonal dialogue) but rather intended to guarantee a behavioral outcome. In drill-and-practice courseware, this was rather obvious. In "mixed-initiative" computer "dialogues," this is not always so evident.

The constancy and immediacy of diagnosis and feedback in on-line tests has several other consequences:

a. It emphasizes accretion learning because the computer is constantly assessing evidence of normal progress toward a pre-specified goal. This tends to discourage "messing around" with the subject matter because "messing around behavior" is not evidence that a learner is building up an experiential basis for a quantum leap of understanding (Hawkins, 1974).

b. It tends to focus learning on generic *means* as well as generic *ends* in spite of the fact that tutorials are individualized. The reason for this is simple: by continually measuring and diagnosing educational performances with context-free response analysis, on-line tests pre-empt personally constructed means. The computer, in effect, *controls the means as well as the ends* and constitutes a powerful "other" that structures and dominates the entire interaction (Weizenbaum, 1976; Scheibe & Erwin, 1979; Gardner, 1979; Turkle, 1984).

In interpersonal interactions, on the other hand, learning tends to focus on the ends-in-view and not on the means (Polanyi, 1958; Greene, 1978). Hence, learning incorporates personally constructed means and meanings. This is not to suggest that human teachers cannot dominate an interaction with a learner but only that learners have the opportunity to develop personal ways to reach a particular goal.

c.   It tends to accelerate the learning process because it creates a set of temporal expectations (notice that rate of learning was the major dimension of individuality, and faster rates were considered better because of the efficiency orientation of the system. This in turn, biases the tutorial interaction *against* reflectiveness and critical thinking (Freire, 1973; Shor, 1980). Some courseware authors have suggested that this bias can be countered by using "individualized" wait loops in the courseware programs (Schneidermann, 1980).   However, reflectiveness is *not* a matter of waiting longer.

Remedial dialogues are initiated by the computer when the learner's performance does not match some pre-specified performance criteria (Bork, 1980b). They assume that the student already knows the area and can work with the information which is presented.   Here again, this parallels what happens in interpersonal dialogues but with some very important distinctions:

a.   In interpersonal tutorials, remedial dialogues are initiated by a teacher on the basis of his or her tacit knowledge about the unique characteristics of the learner.   Furthermore, the teacher tries to understand the learner's state of mind by "thinking like the student" in order to unravel the student's conceptual bind or misunderstanding (Hawkins, 1974).   This is a unique, constructive, and intentional act of empathy and engagement by the teacher and *only nominally entails the student's behaviors.*

b. In human-computer tutorials, remedial "dialogues" are initiated on the basis of a set of explicit and computable rules (expert or content-related algorithms) (Sleeman & Brown, 1982; O'Shea & Self, 1983). The tutorial courseware program, in effect, constitutes a generic, rule-driven process that engages an internal, *generic* model of the learner. The actual human agent (i.e., student) in this "dialogue" only provides the data for the computer's generic model of the learner. This is even the case when the computer builds up a model of the student based on a history of student performances. The resulting model of the student is still a formal, rule-oriented, generic model. Remedial "dialogues" therefore do not involve *this* student but rather this *type* of student. I will explain this in greater detail below.

Interactive proofs are a type of computer-based tutorial that permit the learner to make decisions beyond a pre-defined set of choices (Bork, 1980b). Hence, students can ask for information, work through a variety of examples that embody some concept, and even construct their own models of the problem. However, the very nature of the computing environment still constrains the terms of the debate. The best examples of interactive proofs usually come from mathematics and science where the nature of the content parallels the nature of the computing environment (i.e., a computable formula captures both). This in turn permits an author (or instructional designer or programmer) to create an interactive proof out of the formula. Of course, even non-mathematical subject areas can be reformulated to be amenable to interactive proofs. Hence, the socio-political problem of hunger can be recast into economic terms and then reduced to a formula that relates an arbitrarily chosen set of variables. The interactive "proof" then proceeds *as if* it were a mathematical problem. This ultimately treats a problem such as hunger as if it were a computerized numbers game—no matter how complex the mathematics. However, computational complexity will *never* match real-world complexity unless the processes in the world are controlled by comparable mathematical or procedural rules.

Human-Computer "Dialogues" in Tutorial Courseware

We now come to the central assumption of computer-based tutorials. Namely, that human-computer "dialogues" should resemble interpersonal conversations. Bork has modified this claim somewhat by saying that the student is really dialoguing with the author of the computer tutorial rather than with the computer itself, but this is a facile reformulation. Bork also admits that the author of a computer tutorial is trying to manipulate the student by "stimulat[ing] meaningful responses which contribute to learning (Bork, 1980b). Hence, human-computer "dialogues" are a form of behavioral technology where dialogic interactions are controlled by an author who *is not part of the actual interaction.* Responses are only meaningful in light of their contribution to educational performance-gains. The actual confrontations between humans and computing are therefore one-sided affairs because the computers have fixed goal structures, interactive strategies, and deductive capabilities.

What *should* human-computer interactions in a tutorial be called?   To answer this we have to compare them with interpersonal interactions. Interpersonal dialogues contain an essential component of *conjoint control* (in spite of the power differentials that may exist between students and teachers). Such conjointness is missing in human-computer interactions.   In human-computer "dialogues," students only control the:

    a.   *Rate* (*i.e.*, pacing of pre-defined sequences),
    b.   *Route* (*i.e.*, any one of a finite number of predefined, or algorithmically constrained, paths toward a predefined goal), and
    c.   *Timing* (*i.e.*, speed of individual responses).

All other control resides in the courseware program. Students therefore only have a form of pseudo-control because the actual interaction follows a pre-planned, goal-oriented procedural network. Hence, human-computer tutorial interactions are best called *"utilogs"* rather than "dialogues" (Shneidermann, 1980). Of course, utility here is defined by a courseware author who in turn is restricted to certain categories within the technological framework (Ellul, 1980b; Turkle, 1984).

What are the deeper implications of having utilogic interactions in a computer tutorial shaped by the external intentions of an author? I will summarize a number of these implications for education by comparing them with interpersonal interactions:

a. *Humans are treated as data-based, rule-following, symbol-manipulating, information processors:*

This implication emerges from the nature of the computer technology that is used to carry out the actual tutorial interactions. Machine processes can only operate on explicit information according to algorithmic rules (Weizenbaum, 1976). Computers cannot semantically or affectively engage human beings. Humans therefore have to adapt to the *nature* of the computational environment—although within that framework, computer processes can be designed to adapt to the "individual differences" of humans.

Earlier, I mentioned that computers only engage *data* from an individual and not the actual person. These data are organized by the program into a model of the learner (in simpler programs, this is merely a data-base of variables and values). The particular model of an individual which the program contains (or builds up) always remains a formal and abstract *type*. Furthermore, this model is a *means* to an end. This is even the case when many models of students (i.e., many generic types) are programmed into the computer. This has serious implications for education.

Since human beings develop personal intellectual agency through dialogic interactions (Greene, 1983), the learner in computer-based tutorial interactions can *never* develop such agency. The only control a learner ever has is a form of pseudo-control within a technological framework. More significantly, since human beings tend to

model the "other" in dialogic interactions (Scheibe &
Erwin, 1979), computer-based tutorials may actually
teach students to treat other dialogic partners as
anthropomorphized processes and *means* rather than
as ends (Turkle, 1984).

In interpersonal dialogic interactions, on the
other hand, individuals encounter, confront, accept
(to a greater or lesser degree), and engage each other
as unique individuals. True discourse, in this case,
requires the acceptance of the "other" in the discourse
as a unique and intentional being. It also requires a
similar image of self. The individual, in
interpersonal dialogues, is therefore a *unique
ontological entity* (rather than a generic type) and an
end (rather than a means). This sets the stage for
personal agency in learning. Interpersonal
dialogue can, of course, become mechanical if the
humans involved act on the basis of some
stereotypical inferences about each other. However,
the potential for true discourse is *always* present in
interpersonal interactions. This potential can *never*
exist in human-computer interactions
(Weizenbaum, 1976).

Another consequence of viewing humans as
rule-following information-processors (as opposed to
individuals with unique intentionalities) is that
uniform education goals, methods, and outcomes are
legitimized. Uniformity in education is enforced
not only because the instructional systems attempt to
shape a uniform product (*i.e.,* pre-specified learning
outcomes) but also because the very conceptualization
of the individual places "semantic and syntactical
constraints on acceptable language for the
discussion of human beings" (Strike, 1974). This in
turn makes it impossible to express and legitimize
other conceptions of human beings, educational
goals, and methods outside of the technological

framework (Ellul, 1980b). A simple example of an alternative framework can make this clear.

In order to create a community and carry out community action, we must (Newmann & Oliver, 1967):

    i. Unconditionally accept individual uniqueness and diversity.

    ii. Carry out an on-going dialectical synthesis of opposing viewpoints with the actual members of the community, and

    iii. Respect emergent community goals.

The technological framework makes this perspective impossible to conceptualize (let alone operate) because it is based on an opposing set of assumptions. The community framework builds on three things: the uniqueness of each individual and his or her viewpoint, a dialectical rationality that tries to synthesize opposing views, and emergent community goals. The technological framework, on the other hand, builds on: the generic characteristics of individuals, a means-end rationality, and a pre-determined set of performance goals.

  b. *Machine processes will eventually match human processes:*

This second implication derives from the first implication: if humans are ultimately rule-following information processors, then computers will eventually do everything that humans can do. Human-computer utilogs will then in fact become dialogues because both sides of the interaction will have identical ontological status.

This statement has some serious problems for education, however, even if we only restrict ourselves to the cognitive domain. If we as educators accept the responsibility for the growth of young minds, then we are obligated to ask how such minds do in fact grow. Furthermore, if we find that mental development at all levels requires a dialectical

synthesis of personally and socially constructed
meanings, then we can see that the very ontology of
the technological framework (*i.e.*, the world is made
up of specifiable and controllable processes) is
inadequate for the whole domain of intentions and
interpersonal meanings (Greene, 1983). *Machine
processes*, in this case, *will never replace
interpersonal interactions*!

Finally, if we find that human skills and
knowledge are ultimately based on tacit beliefs and
judgments which cannot be analyzed into
components, then computational processes (which by
their nature reduce similarity *judgments* to
computable comparisons of component identities)
will never match human processes (Dreyfus, 1979).

c.   *Education will be viewed as a form of training and
will be subject to explicit, extensional logic:*

Having an expert author design the goals,
rules, and actual messages for a human-computer
interaction means that the logic of prediction and
control (i.e., the technological framework) is applied
to developing pre-planned performance outcomes.
The whole educational enterprise is then reduced to
means-end rationality because the ends are
specified first and then the most efficient means are
employed to guarantee a quality product (Nunan,
1983; Apple, 1982). The resulting mechanization of
interaction is sometimes transparent when
computers carry out the actual interaction because of
the sophistication, speed, and variety of media
involved (Weizenbaum, 1976). But we should never
confuse sophisticated technique with sophisticated
instruction (Amarel, 1983). Technique does not have
a tacit dimension whereas all human knowledge
and learning does (Polanyi, 1966). Technique is
solely subject to extensional logic whereas
knowledge is subject to *both* intensional and
extensional logic.

We can see the implications of this view for education most clearly when we examine the nature of experiential learning within the technological and non-technological frameworks (Kolb, 1984). I will do this by comparing the following notions: the nature of experience, events, and activities; the concept of individual; the methods of knowledge; and the types of thinking involved. My discussion will necessarily be brief.

When restricted to a computational environment, "experiences" take on the form of puzzles *of the same type (i.e.,* computable, quantifiable, procedural). Events are non-historical because they are reversible (*i.e.,* declarative and procedural) and activities are restricted to a non-dialectical "artificial reality" (Kreuger, 1983). Furthermore, an individual is only trivially unique (i.e., the variables of a student model in the computer are generic; only the *values* of the variables are unique). Finally, an individual needs only the ability to decode abstract symbols because the "text" and "context" are pre-determined by an external agent, and because knowledge is expressed in an explicit, abstract form. Critical and dialectical thinking are not needed because they make too many things problematical, ambiguous, and non-controllable.

In a natural environment, on the other hand, "experiences" are made up of indefinite *types.* Events are ambiguous, historical, and irreversible (Whitehead, 1929). Activity involves a confrontation between persons and events, and meanings are personally and interpersonally constructed. Experiences and actions are dialectical and historical. Furthermore, natural experiences entail an accommodation to, and assimilation of, an indefinite variety of uniqueness in persons, ideas, and events (Piaget, 1970). These in turn become the experiential basis for further critical and dialectical thinking. Finally, individuals need interpretive as well as decoding skills because they are forced to construct as well as deconstruct the meanings-in-use of others (Greene, 1978). Interpersonal dialogue plays a central role here because knowledge is dialectical, historical, and subject to transformation.

This brief discussion of experiential learning points out the tremendous restrictions that the technological framework places on the variety of educational experiences. Computer-based tutorials therefore seem to rule out everything that is of value to the individual in the natural and social worlds.

Summary of Tutorial Courseware Programs

I began my discussion about tutorial courseware programs with the question of whether human-computer "dialogues" go beyond drill-and-practice approaches. The answer is both yes and no: such tutorials do go beyond because they are a more sophisticated form of interaction, but they also stay well within the bounds of behavioral and technological framework. That is: behavioral outcomes are still pre-specified by expert agents outside of the actual interaction, "quality control" procedures are still used to guarantee that the learner will reach the intended outcomes, and learners are still only given a form of pseudo-control (*i.e.*, rate, route, and timing). Furthermore, although the actual interaction is less rigid than a drill-and-practice courseware, the interaction is still constrained by a computable algorithm, is still focused on maximizing education performance gains, and still treats the learner as a means toward someone else's end. Computer-based tutorials are biased against experiential learning (outside of the technological framework), quantum leaps in learning, and reflective thinking. Their value in education is therefore very limited.

The question now arises about the case where computers are used as "intellectual tools." Does *this* use of computers go beyond the limitations discussed so far? On first reflection, personal intellectual agency seems to be a natural concomitant of the "tool" use of computers, but this conclusion requires a more careful analysis.

Computers as Intellectual Tools

What is the intellectual dimension, if any, of computers (Luehrmann, 1980)? To answer this question, I will build on my earlier discussion and then examine the nature of the computer as an intellectual, problem-solving tool. I will *not* deal with the computer as a personal productivity tool (*e.g.*, word processor) but rather with the computer as an "object to think with" (Papert, 1980). This brings me into the realm of computer languages and simulations.

So far, I have described how drill-and-practice and tutorial courseware programs introduce a means-end rationality into the learning process. Knowledge acquisition and skill building (the terms themselves are revealing) become subject to efficiency and performance criteria, and learning becomes a systematically designed and rationally managed process. Furthermore, knowledge and skills become commodified because they are conceptualized in utilitarian terms and because the design and the conception of instruction are separated from the execution of instruction. This commodification, in turn, permits a fine-grained control of the learner's, the teacher's, and even the system's performance. The computer formalizes this whole process and makes it capital intensive.

Does the situation described above apply to the case where the learner programs his or her own solutions to problems (Critchfield, 1979)? Surely here, we will not see the means-end rationality of an external agent conceptualizing, designing, and managing the learning process. After all, the *learner* is now in control of the whole process!

The general question therefore becomes whether the student who controls the computer can go beyond the technological framework of the computer (the values associated with the computer and the symbol systems that can be manipulated by the computer). My answer will proceed as follows: tools tend to insist that they be used in certain ways and intellectual tools tend to define the user's mental landscape (Bruner, 1975; Greene, 1978). Computational intellectual tools (i.e., computer programming and simulations) therefore bias our ways of knowing and dealing with the world toward extensional knowledge (i.e., the quantitative, declarative, and procedural kinds of knowledge) and hide other kinds of knowledge. Intensional knowledge, of course, will not go away. It will only be delegitimized by computers.

The Computer as an Intellectual Problem-Solving Tool

Before answering the general question, I would like to discuss how a computer might bias our ways of knowing. A computer is basically a box that manipulates symbols (and information) according to a plan. When someone else writes the plan (i.e., the program), then we are forced to follow their set of procedures. When we write the plan, then we are forced to use the computer's language. In both cases, we are confronted with a question about the nature of the plans and the types of symbols which the computer can manipulate. We therefore need to explore how programming a particular problem in a computer language helps us learn and think about a problem (Taylor, 1980).

Computers, as I mentioned, are boxes that manipulate symbols according to a plan. The symbols are actually only energy states in an electronic machine which are transformed according to formal, algorithmic rules. Hence, a *computer does not add* "1+1" to get "2." Rather, the computer initiates an electronic process where two energy states, which we identify as representing the numeric unit "1," are transformed according to an internal structural process (hardwired or software, it matters not) into another energy state which we identify as representing the numeric unit "2." I am belaboring this point because of its generality. If a computer manipulates two high-level representational constructs such as "All men are mortal" plus "Socrates is a man" and ends up with "Therefore Socrates is a mortal," then *nothing has been added by the computer beyond my first example*. The computer only manipulates semantically empty energy states (which we call input or data or symbols) according to syntactical rules—no matter how high-level those rules. It is *we* who actively construct and ascribe meaning to these semantically empty mechanisms. A computer language is therefore *not* a language in the traditional sense of the term (i.e., expressive, intentional, and connotative as well as denotative and based on qualitative knowing, etc.) but rather a set of syntactical notations to control computer operations (Wirth, 1976; Iverson, 1980). Hence, *a computer's expressive potential only extends over the syntactical dimension of its formal operations.* Of course, for those who equate cognition with computation, the expressive potential of computer languages extends into the semantic domain because "all relevant semantic distinctions [are] mirrored by syntactic distinctions" (Pylyshyn, 1980, 1984). Semantics, in the latter case, become a set of rule-governed, cognitive operations that act on symbolic representations.

What are the epistemological implications of using computer languages to represent events in our world? It is clear that if humans are going to use computers as intellectual tools, then they must work within the epistemological limitations of these tools (Mowshowitz, 1976). Since computers can only manipulate explicit data and symbols according to formal, syntactical rules, computers tend to legitimize those types of knowledge that fit into their framework and delegitimize other types of knowledge (Strike, 1974). The latter types of knowledge can only be processed when they are reformulated into computable terms. I described such a transformation earlier with the hunger example. Hence, computers tend to *legitimize* the following characteristics of knowledge (Broughton, 1984; Olson, 1985): rule-governed order, objective systematicity, explicit clarity, non-ambiguity, non-redundancy, internal consistency, non-contradiction (i.e., logic of the excluded middle), and quantitative aspects. They also tend to legitimize deduction and induction as the only acceptable epistemological methods.

By way of contrast, computers tend to *delegitimize* the following characteristics of knowledge (Streibel, 1983): emergent goals, self-constructed order, organic systematicity, connotation and tacitness, ambiguity, redundancy, dialectical rationality, simultaneity of multiple logics, and qualitative aspects. And finally, they tend to delegitimize the following epistemological methods: abduction, interpretation, intuition, introspection, and dialectical synthesis of multiple and contradictory realities. The more computers are used as intellectual tools, therefore, the more this process of legitimization and delegitimization takes hold. The more we rely on the formal characteristics of knowledge, the less we rely on the tacit and interpretative dimensions of knowledge. It is almost as if the technological framework is not only incompatible with other ways of knowing, but inevitably excludes them from our mental landscapes as well (Ellul, 1980b). Of course, the formal and the tacit dimensions of knowledge can never be separated from each other (Polanyi, 1966). The tacit dimension can only become hidden.

The foregoing discussion brings us back to an earlier conclusion: computers force us to act *as if* we were rule-governed information processors. They also force us to construe thinking as " 'cognitive problem-solving' where the 'solutions' are arrived at by formal calculation, computation, and rational analysis" (Broughton, 1984). Even if we are active and constructive and intuitive in our approach to the world, we must still analyze and reduce problems into explicit and procedural terms. Hence, we must restrict our thinking to cognitive operations. The concept of the computer as an intellectual tool is therefore *not* a neutral formulation because it forces us to objectify ourselves as agents of prediction, calculation, and control (Weizenbaum, 1976). Personal intellectual agency has thereby been limited to the technological framework. This has serious consequences for education.

Computer Programming and Computer Simulations

We can easily see how programming is a paradigm of *thinking* in the context of the tool use of computers. If the only legitimate knowledge entails objective facts, explicit representations of facts as data, and formal operations on these representations, then programming is the ideal way to process such knowledge. The same can be said of programming as a paradigm for *learning*. If the only way to think about things is through analysis and procedural debugging, then programming is also the ideal way to *learn* how to deal with the world. After all, we are not just learning to act *as if* we were computers, we are developing operational and representational cognitive structures to deal with *any* aspect of the world. Gone are aesthetic, metaphoric, artistic, affective, interpretive, and moral structures for dealing with the world!

We can therefore understand how many of the chief advocates of the tool use of computers see computer literacy as the ability to "do computing" (Luehrmann, 1981) and see computer programming as the best way to shape a child's cognitive development (Papert, 1980). However, in this scheme of things, we can also see that our rational life is thereby reduced to a set of operational, problem-solving skills—to say nothing about our emotional life.

Is there anything positive to be gained from programming aside from the actual technical skills? In several studies, very little positive transfer was found from programming to other domains of cognitive problem-solving (Coburn et al., 1982; Pea & Kurland, 1983). However, this conclusion is only tentative because the field is still too new (Linn, 1985). We must therefore fall back on an analysis of the nature of programming in order to see what is possible with this approach.

Computing, as Arthur Luehrmann, one of the chief advocates of programming, argues (Luehrmann, 1981):

> belongs as a regular school subject for the same reason as reading, writing, and mathematics. Each gives the student a basic intellectual tool with wide areas of application. Each gives the student a distinctive means of thinking about and representing a problem, of writing his or her thoughts down, of studying and criticizing the thoughts of others, whether they are embodied in a paragraph of English, a set of mathematical equations, or a computer program. Students need practice and instruction in all these basic modes of expressing and communicating ideas.

This certainly is an admirable statement because it integrates computing (*i.e.*, algorithmic, procedural thinking) into the other "basics" of education (*i.e.*, reading, writing, and arithmetic) (Kroener, 1981; Ershov, 1981). Luehrmann's argument also casts programming as an aid to understanding.

Given the arguments described above, how could anyone possibly object to programming as a subject matter in our schools?

The answer is very simple and applies to the other "distinctive means of thinking and representing a problem": whenever technique is emphasized over grappling with content, then the innermost principles of that content are lost (Ershov, 1972). Although this is also true for reading and writing, this is especially true for computer programming because the computer is an instrument of technique *par excellence*. The computer can *only* manipulate content-free symbols according to formal procedures. Hence, although computer programming may force one to structure *information* in precise and systematic ways and carry out *logical operations* on abstract representations of that information, it tells us *nothing* about *what* information should be treated in this way. It also tells us nothing about the *nature* of the real world. A simple computer-simulation example should make this clear. The same argument applies to programming the simulation.

    Oregon Trail is a popular computer simulation that records the problems which the pioneers had in crossing the American frontier (Grady, 1983). It provides a simplified environment for elementary-aged school children where they can make "decisions" and watch the consequences of their "actions." Hence, forgetting to "buy" enough bullets inevitably leads to program termination. A student can "win" if he or she keeps a careful record of the "purchases" and analyzes the relationships between events, supplies, and mileage. What we have here, however, is quantitative, artificial reality with no hint of the lived reality (Grady, 1983). The simulation, in fact, represents the abstract world of algorithmic logic rather than the lived-experience of historical logic. Hence, whether one is simply using the finished simulation to learn about history or whether one is programming the simulation, historical logic is incapable of being represented. It would be more justifiable to say that winning here (i.e., solving the problem) is more the result of looking for patterns among the numbers than developing a sense of history (Grady, 1983). The simulation is simply a well-disguised numbers game.

    One might object to the foregoing discussion on a number of grounds:

a. The algorithmic logic of simulations does in fact parallel a similar logic in *some* content areas (such as mathematics) so that computer simulations have a place in education.

b. All learning proceeds from the known to the unknown (and from the simple to the complex) so that simulations are a stepping stone to life.

c. Persons can learn to become autonomous inquirers within the limitations of a safe and simple artificial reality—a skill that they can later use in real life.

Each of these objections has an intuitive appeal and therefore warrants our attention. Each of these statements, however, can also be interpreted in several ways, so each deserves a careful analysis.

The first objection is easy to handle. It is certainly the case that many real-world activities contain the same logical and procedural structure that is found in the realm of computation. Hence, learning to subtract can be modeled in a computer program because procedural rules are all there is to the *process* of subtraction (Dreyfus & Dreyfus, 1984). But what does this tell one about the *reasons* for these procedures?

Brown & Burton have developed an "intelligent" computer tutor that recognizes over ninety ways to make a mistake during subtraction (Brown & Burton, 1979). Each of these procedural bugs models one way in which a person can go wrong in the process of subtraction. This is certainly a very sophisticated approach and may be very useful in some cases. However, it only elaborates the procedures surrounding subtraction. A logical positivist would say: fine, this will help establish the automaticity of the subtraction skill more efficiently. But an educator would say: wait a minute—subtraction is not an isolated, de-contextualized skill that leads to nothing but itself. At a minimum, it should lead to competence in *using* subtraction with real-world problems. At a maximum, it should lead to mathematical understanding. In both cases, it should be connected to experiences that ultimately generate personal expertise. And expertise *cannot* be reduced to procedures because it involves judgment as well as calculations. As Dreyfus and Dreyfus (1984) conclude:

> at the higher stages of skill acquisition, even if there
> are rules underlying expertise, the rules that the expert
> has access to are not the rules that generate his
> expertise . . . [Hence], trying to find rules or
> procedures in a domain often stands in the way of
> learning *even at the earliest stages* [my emphasis].

Developing procedure-following skills, therefore, does *not*
facilitate broader learning.   I have used subtraction as an
example in this discussion because it involves a procedural skill.
My argument applies even more for non-procedural kinds of
expertise and understanding (*e.g.*, historical expertise and
understanding).

The second objection is more difficult to handle: all
learning proceeds from the known to the unknown and from the
simple to the complex. But we have to be very careful how we
define simple so that we do not prejudge the *nature* of the complex.
This problem is a perennial concern in the philosophy of science:
should we base our scientific concepts on our intuitions and lived
experiences, or should we base them on counter-intuitive
conceptual constructions that happen to fit empirical facts (Kuhn,
1962)? This problem emerges in education in a number of forms.
For example, in science education, should we teach young
children to be Artistotelians before Newtonians—let alone before
Einsteinians (DiSessa, 1982)?

In the context of this discussion, the simplicity question
becomes: is a simple, context-free, quantitative, and procedural
simulation *ever* an adequate preparation for a complex,
contextual, qualitative, and non-procedural lived-experience
(Megarry, 1983)? If we wanted to prepare children to understand
and deal with the real world, shouldn't we develop simple
learning situations *of the same kind* as those they will later
encounter in a more complex form? Isn't problem-solving, in
fact, domain-specific no matter how high-level the activity
(Newell & Simon, 1982; Lester, 1980; Pea & Kurland, 1983)? The
"ivory tower" aspect of schooling might be just the right protection
against the harsh realities of life, but this does *not* mean that
schools should become "artificial realities." Using the computer
to develop problem-solving skills, however, sets up just such a

dichotomy between *"simple* artificial reality" and *"complex* natural reality." Notice that the *artificial-natural* dimension of the above dichotomy is usually hidden in the debate on the matter (Noble, 1984). Learning to program the computer may therefore not be the best way to prepare children for real life.

The final objection is the most difficult to answer: can persons develop analytical and inquiry skills within the limitations of a computational environment that can then be used in real life? After all, analytical and inquiry skills are very general and more like "frames of mind" than simple procedures (Streibel, 1985). The question can be reformulated, however, to reveal what has been hidden: are the analytical and inquiry skills which are developed within a non-contextual, non-dialectical, and judgment-free computational environment useful within the lived environment that requires tolerance for ambiguity, interpersonal construction of new meanings, dialectical thinking, the acceptability of incomplete solutions, and judgment-based actions? When the question is reformulated in this way, a positive answer becomes doubtful. The reason for this is twofold: the computer embodies a technological framework that crowds out other forms of conceptualizing and understanding problems, and thinking is only ever thinking about something (*i.e.,* problem-solving is domain-specific).   Hence, mature analysis and inquiry can therefore only be the result of a history of dealing with similar *kinds* of things. Flight simulators work so well for this reason—both the simulation and the real-world event are controlled by the same kinds of procedures. Furthermore, the flight simulator is *both* simpler as well as true to the nature of the real world situation.

A final answer to the third objection remains to be seen. It does seem, however, that the computer restricts our rational life to utilitarian, problem-solving skills. Saying that such skills are under our control does not help very much because these skills have delegitimized other ways of knowing. Saying that such skills display "intelligence" does not help either because intelligence itself has been redefined in a restricted manner. As Broughton laments (Broughton, 1984):

one can measure the educational impact of computers,
and particularly of learning to program them, in
terms of what is lost in the process. To the curriculum
is lost the arts and the humanities. To pedagogy is lost
the hermeneutic art and language that allows us to ask
about the meaning of things and of life, to interpret
them in their many and various cultural horizons. To
both is lost the self and the autonomous capacity to
examine critically what we interpret.

Hence, although problem-solving with a computer appears more
desirable and high-level than computerized drill-and-practice,
programming still limits us to the technological framework.
Using a computer as an intellectual tool is therefore a more subtle
form of behavioral learning technology because the computer and
its "languages" (*i.e.,* information, symbol systems, and
activities) shape the very categories with which we apprehend and
think about the world, and because it is also done with the active
consent and participation of the learner. It represents, as one
author has called it, the "industrialization of intellectual work"
(Ershov, 1972). This is particularly disturbing because
programming (as well as drill-and-practice and tutorial
courseware) is being introduced to children in their most plastic
and formative years (Bitter, 1982/83; Cuffaro, 1984).

Summary of the Tool Use of Computers

I began this section with the question of whether the
"intellectual tool use" of computers went beyond the limitations of
tutorial interactions. The answer again is both yes and no.
Computers do help us develop a limited personal intellectual
agency by forcing us to structure information in precise,
systematic ways and specific logical operations on that
information (Linn, 1985). However, this agency only develops
within the computational domain. Hence, we are left with an
under-developed intellectual agency within the qualitative,
dialectical, and experiential domain of natural and social
events. Learning to program is therefore only a good way to learn
and think about procedural problems, although even here there are
some limitations.

The root of the difficulty seems to reside in the nature of computer languages: the expressive potential of computer language only extends over the syntactical dimension of computer operations. This contrasts sharply with the expressive potential of natural languages which extend over the aesthetic, metaphoric, artistic, affective, and moral domains (Ong, 1982). Why can't these various languages co-exist? The answer boils down to this: computer languages are part of a technological framework, which, when applied to a number of problems, delegitimizes other frameworks. We are then left with a very restricted mental landscape.

General Summary

I have examined the three major approaches to the use of computers in education and found serious limitations with each approach. The drill-and-practice approach was shown to embody a deterministic, behavioral technology that turned learning into a systematically designed and quality-controlled form of work. Although drill-and-practice courseware programs were only intended to supplement instruction, they in fact introduced a technological framework into the classroom culture that mitigated against non-behavioral educational goals. Computerized tutorial programs were shown to extend the behavioral and technological approach to learning even further. That is, in tutorial courseware programs, interactions were still shaped by an external agent's intentions in order to maximize the learner's performance gains and still constrained by computable algorithms. Furthermore, the human learner was still treated as a means toward someone else's ends and only given a form of pseudo-control in the interaction. Most seriously, computerized tutorial interactions pre-empted personal intellectual agency and ultimately inner-directed learning. Finally, the use of computer programming and simulations in education was shown to limit the learner's mental landscape to objective, quantitative, and procedural "intellectual tools." This left the learner with an under-developed intellectual agency within the qualitative, dialectical, and experiential domains of natural and social events.

Each of the approaches described above may have some short-term gain associated with them, but taken together, they represent a shift toward technologizing education. Drill-and-practice courseware programs alter the nature of sub-skill acquisition, tutorial courseware programs restrict the full range of personal intellectual agency, and computer programming and simulations delegitimize non-technological ways of learning and thinking about problems. Taken together, is this worth the price?

REFERENCES

Alderman, D. L. (1978). *Evaluation of the TICCIT computer-assisted instructional system in the community college.* Princeton, N.J.: Educational Testing Service.

Amarel, M. (1983). The classroom: An instructional setting for teachers, students, and the computer. In A. C. Wilkinson (Ed.), *Classroom computers and cognitive science.* New York: Academic Press.

Apple, M. W. (1975). The adequacy of systems management procedures in education. In R. H. Smith (Ed.), *Regaining educational leadership.* New York: John Wiley & Sons.

Apple, M. W. (1979). *Ideology and curriculum.* London: Routledge & Kegan Paul.

Apple, M. W. (1982). *Education and power.* London: Routledge & Kegan Paul.

Barr, R., & Dreeben, R. (1978). Instruction in classrooms. In L. Shulman (Ed.), *Review of research in education* (Vol. 5). Ithaca, IL: F. E. Peacock.

Becker, H. J. (1983). *School uses of microcomputer: Reports from a national survey.* Nos. 1-5. Baltimore, MD: Center for Social Organization of Schools, the Johns Hopkins University.

Benne, K. D. (1975). Technology and community: Conflicting bases of educational authority. In W. Feinberg & H. Rosemont, Jr. (Eds.), *Work, technology, and education: Dissenting essays in the intellectual foundations of*

American education. Urbana, IL: University of Illinois Press.

Berger, P. L., & Luckmann, T. (1966). *The social construction of reality: A treatise in the sociology of knowledge.* New York: Doubleday.

Berlak, A., & Berlak, H. (1981). *The dilemmas of schooling.* New York: Methuen.

Berliner, D. (1982). Viewing the teacher as manager. *Education Digest, 47,* 20-23.

Bitter, G. S. (1982/93). The road to computer literacy. *Electronic Learning.* Sep., 60-63; Oct., 34-68; Nov.-Dec., 41-91; Jan., 40-48; Feb., 54-60.

Bloom, B. S. (1971). Mastery learning. In J. H. Block (Ed.)., *Mastery learning: Theory and practice.* New York: Holt, Rinehart, and Winston.

Bloom, B. S. (1976). *Human characteristics and school Learning.* New York: McGraw-Hill.

Bolvin, J. O. (1982). Classroom organization. In H. M. Mitzel (Ed.), *Encyclopedia of educational research. 5th edition,* Vol. 1. New York: Macmillan, pp. 265-274.

Bork, A. (1980a). Interactive learning. In R. Taylor (Ed.), *The computer in the school: Tutor, tool, and tutee.* New York: Teachers College Press.

Bork, A. (1980b). Preparing student-computer dialogs: Advice to teachers. In R. Taylor (Ed.), *The computer in the school: Tutor, tool, and tutee.* New York: Teachers College Press, pp. 15-52.

Bork, A., & Franklin, S. D. (1979). The role of personal computer systems in education. *AEDS Journal,* Fall.

Boyd, G. M. (1983a). Education and miseducation by computer. In J. Megarry, E. R. F. Walker, S. Nisbet, & E. Hoyle (Eds.), *World yearbook of education, 1982/83: Computers and education,* pp. 50-54.

Boyd, G. M. (1983b). Four ways of providing computer-assisted learning and their probable impacts. *Computers and Education, 6,* 305-310.

Broughton, J. M. (1984). Computer literacy as political socialization. Paper presented at the annual meeting of

the *American Educational Research Association*. New
Orleans, April 23-27.

Brown, J. S., & Burton, R. R. (1979). Diagnostic model for
procedural bugs in basic mathematical skills. *Cognitive
Science, 2*, 155-192.

Bruner, J. S. (1975). Language as an instrument of thought. In
A. Davis (Ed.), *Problems of language and learning*.
London: Heinemann. pp. 61-80.

Bunderson, V. (1981). Courseware. In H. F. O'Neil (Ed.),
*Computer-assisted instruction: A state of the art
assessment*. New York: Academic Press.

Carlson, D. (1982). 'Updating' individualism and the work ethic:
Corporate logic in the classroom. *Curriculum Inquiry,
12*(2), 125-160.

Coburn, P., Kelman, P., Roberts, W., Snyder, T., Watt, D., &
Weiner, C. (1982). *Practical guide to computers in
education*. Reading, MA: Addison-Wesley.

Critchfield, M. (1979). Beyond CAI: Computers as personal
intellectual tools. *Educational Technology, 19*(10), 18-25.

Cronbach, L. J., & Snow, R. E. (1977). *Aptitudes and
instructional methods*. New York: Irvington.

Cuffaro, H. K. (1984). Microcomputers in education: Why is
earlier better? *Teachers College Record, 85*(4), 559-568.

Dennis, J. R. (1979a). The question-episode: Building block of
teaching with a computer. *The Illinois series on
educational applications of computers*, Vol. 4e. Urbana,
IL: College of Education, the University of Illinois.

Dennis, J. R. (1979b). Tutorial instruction on a computer.
Illinois series on educational applications of computers,
Vol. 6e. Urbana, IL: College of Education, The University
of Illinois.

DiSessa, A. (1982). Unlearning Aristotelian physics: A study of
knowledge-based learning. *Cognitive Science, 6*(1), 37-
75.

Dreyfus, H. H. (1979). *What computers can't do* (2nd Ed.). New
York: Harper & Row.

Dreyfus, H. H., and Dreyfus, S. E. (1984). Putting computers in their proper place: Intuition in the classroom. *Teachers College Record, 85*(4), 578-601.

Eisner, E. W. (1979). *The educational imagination.* New York: Macmillan.

Ellul, J. (1980a). The power of technique in the ethics of non-power. In K. Woodward (Ed.), *The myth of information: Technology and post-industrial culture.* Madison, WI: Coda Press.

Ellul, J. (1980b). *The technological system.* New York: Continuum.

Ershov, A. P. (1972). Aesthetics and the human factor in programming. *Datamation, 18*(7), 62-67.

Ershov, A. P. (1981). Programming: the second literacy. In R. Lewis & E. D. Tagg (Eds.), *Computers in education: Proceedings of the 3rd IFIP world conference.* Lausanne, Switzerland, July.

Franklin, B. (1974). *The curriculum field and the problem of social control, 1918-1938. A study in critical theory.* Unpublished Ph.D. Dissertation. Madison, WI: University of Wisconsin.

Freire, P. (1970). *Pedagogy of the oppressed.* New York: The Seabury Press.

Freire, P. (1973). *Education for critical consciousness.* New York: Seabury Press.

Furth, H. (1969). *Piaget and knowledge: Theoretical foundations.* Englewood Cliffs, NJ: Prentice-Hall.

Gagné, R. M., Wager, W., & Rojas, A. (1981). Planning and authoring computer-assisted instruction lessons. *Educational Technology, 21,* 17-26.

Gardner, H. (1979). Toys with a mind of their own. *Psychology Today,* Nov., 101.

Gardner, H. (1983). *Frames of mind: The theory of multiple intelligences.* New York: Basic Books.

Goody, J. (1977). *The domestication of the savage mind.* London: Cambridge University Press.

Grady, D. (1983). What every teacher should know about computer simulations. *Learning, 11*(8), 34-46.

Gray, L. (1983). Teacher's unions and the impact of computer-based technologies. In J. Megarry, E. R. F. Walker, S. Nisbet, & E. Hoyle (Eds.), *World yearbook of education, 1982/83: Computers and education*. pp. 29-41.

Greene, M. (1978). *Landscapes of learning*. New York: Teachers College Press.

Greene, M. (1982a). Literacy for what? *Phi Delta Kappan, 63*(5), 326-329.

Greene, M. (1982b). The University and the public. Lecture given at the Pennsylvania State University, University Park, PA. October 14-15.

Greene, M. (1983). The literacy that liberates. Tape No. 612-20312. *Association for Supervision and Curriculum Development*. Alexandria, VA.

Habermas, J. (1981). *The theory of communicative action. Vol. 1. Reason and the rationalization of society*. Boston: Beacon Press.

Hawkins, D. (1974). *The informed vision: Essays on learning and human nature*. New York: Agathon Press.

Iverson, K. (1980). Notation as a tool for thought. *Communications of the ACM, 23*, 444-465.

Jackson, P. W. (1968). *Life in classrooms*. New York: Holt, Rinehart, and Winston.

Keller, F. S. (1968). Goodbye teacher. *Journal of Applied Behavior Analysis, 1*(1), 79-89.

Kliebard, H. M. (1971). Bureaucracy and curriculum theory. In V. F. Haubrich (Ed.), *Freedom, Bureaucracy, & Schooling. Yearbook of the Association for Supervision and Curriculum Development*. New York: National Education Association. pp. 74-93.

Kohlberg, L., & Mayer, R. (1972). Development as the aim of education. *Harvard Educational Review, 42*(4), 449-496.

Kolb, D. A. (1984). *Experiential learning: Experience as the source of learning and development*. Englewood Cliffs, NJ: Prentice-Hall.

Kroener, J. D. (Ed.), (1981). *The new liberal arts: An exchange of views*. New York: Alfred P. Sloan Foundation.

Krueger, M. W. (1983). *Artificial reality.* Reading, MA: Addison-Wesley.

Kuhn, T. S. (1962). *The structure of scientific revolutions.* Chicago: University of Chicago Press.

Kulik, J. A., Kulik, C. L. C., & Cohen, P. A. (1980). Effectiveness of computer-based college teaching: A meta-analysis of findings. *Review of Educational Research, 50,* 525-544.

Lester, F. K. (1980). Research on mathematical problem solving. In R. J. Shumway (Ed.), *Research in Mathematics Education.* Reston, VA: National Council of Teachers of Mathematics.

Linn, M. C. (1985). The cognitive consequences of programming instruction in classrooms. *Educational Researcher, 14*(5), 14-29.

Luehrmann, A. (1980). Should the computer teach the student or vice versa? In R. Taylor (Ed.), *The computer in the school: Tutor, tool, tutee.* New York: Teachers College Press, pp. 129-140.

Luehrmann, A. (1981). Computer literacy: What should it be? *Mathematics Teacher, 74*(9), 682-686.

Lukes, S. (1973). *Individualism.* Oxford: Basil Blackwell.

Megarry, J. (1983). Thinking, learning, and educating: The role of the computer. In J. Megarry, E. R. F. Walker, S. Nisbet, & E. Hoyle (Eds.), *World yearbook of education, 1982/83: Computers and education.* New York: Kogan Page, pp. 15-28.

Messick, S. (Ed.). (1976). *Individuality in learning.* San Francisco: Jossey-Bass.

Mowshowitz, A. (1976). *The conquest of will: Information processing in human affairs.* Reading, MA: Addison-Wesley.

Murphey, R. T., & Appel, L. R. (1977). *Evaluation of the PLATO IV computer-based educational system in the community college.* Princeton, NJ: Educational Testing Service.

Newell, A., & Simon, H. (1972). *Human problem solving.* Englewood Cliffs, NJ: Prentice-Hall.

Newmann, F., & Oliver, D. (1967). Education and community. *Harvard Educational Review, 37*(1), 61-106.

Nisbett, R., & Ross, L. (1980). *Human inference: Strategies and shortcomings of social judgment.* Englewood Cliffs, NJ: Prentice-Hall.

Noble, D. (1984). Computer literacy and ideology. *Teachers College Record, 85*(4), 602-614.

Nunan, T. (1983). *Countering educational design.* New York: Nichols Publishing.

Olds, H. F., Jr. (1982). The microcomputer—an environment that teaches: Exploring the hidden curriculum. In *Proceedings. The computer: Extension of the human mind.* Third Annual Summer Conference. College of Education. University of Oregon. Eugene, Oregon, pp. 73-85.

Olson, D. R. (1985). Computers as tools of the intellect. *Educational Researcher, 14*(5), 5-8.

O'Neil, H. F., Jr., & Paris, J. (1981). Introduction and overview of computer-based instruction. In H. F. O'Neil, Jr. (Ed.), *Computer-based instruction: A state of the art assessment.* New York: Academic Press.

Ong, W. (1982). *Orality and literacy. The technologizing of the word.* New York: Methuen.

O'Shea, T., & Self, T. (1983). *Learning and teaching with computers.* Englewood Cliffs, NJ: Prentice-Hall.

Papert, S. (1980). *Mindstorms: Children, computers, and powerful ideas.* New York: Basic Books.

Pea, R. D., & Kurland, D. M. (1983). On the cognitive effects of learning computer programming. *Bank Street technical report #18.* New York: Bank Street College.

Piaget, J. (1970). *Genetic epistemology.* New York: W. W. Norton.

Polanyi, M. (1958). *The tacit dimension.* Garden City: Doubleday.

Pylyshyn, Z. W. (1980). Computation and cognition: Issues in the foundations of cognitive science. *The Behavioral and Brain Sciences, 3*, 111-169.

Pylyshyn, Z. W. (1984). *Computation and cognition.* Cambridge, MA: MIT Press.

Salisbury, D. F. (1984). Cognitive psychology and its implications for designing drill-and-practice programs for computers. Presented at the annual conference of the *American Educational Research Association*, New Orleans, April.

Sarason, S. B. (1982). *The culture of the school and the problem of change*. 2nd Edition. Boston: Allyn & Bacon.

Scheibe, K. E., & Erwin, M. (1979). The computer as altar. *Journal of Social Psychology, 108*, 103-109.

Scriven, M. (1975). Problems and prospects for individualization. In H. Talmadge (Ed.), *Systems of individualized instruction*. Berkeley, CA: McCutchan, pp. 199-210.

Schneidermann, B. (1980). *Software psychology: Human factors in computer and information systems*. Cambridge, MA: Winthrop.

Shor, I. (1980). *Critical teaching and everyday life*. Boston: South End Press.

Skinner, B. F. (1968). *The technology of teaching*. Englewood Cliffs, NJ: Prentice-Hall.

Sleeman, D., & Brown, J. S. (1982). *Intelligent tutoring systems*. New York: Academic Press.

Sloan, D. (1984). On raising critical questions about the computer in education. *Teachers College Record, 85*(4), 539-547.

Sperry, L. (Ed.). (1972). *Learning performance and individual differences*. Glenview, IL: Scott Foresman.

Stewart, J. T. (1979). Drill-and-practice on a computer. *Illinois series on educational applications of computers*. Vol. 7e. Urbana, IL: College of Education, The University of Illinois.

Streibel, M. J. (1983). The educational utility of LOGO. *School Science and Mathematics, 83*(6), 474-484.

Streibel, M. J. (1985). Beyond computer literacy: Analytical skills, inquiry skills, and personal empowerment. *Technical Horizons in Education, 12*(10), 69-73.

Strike, K. A. (1974). On the expressive potential of behaviorist language. *American Educational Research Journal, 11*(2), 103-120.

Suppes, P. (1966). The uses of computers in education. *Scientific American, 215*(3), 206-220.

Talmadge, H. (1975). *Systems of individualized instruction.* Berkeley, CA: McCutchan Publishing.

Taylor, R. (Ed.). (1980). *The computer in the school: Tutor, tool, tutee.* New York: Teachers College Press.

Turkle, S. (1984). *The second self: Computers and the human spirit.* New York: Simon & Schuster.

Weizenbaum, J. (1976). *Computer power and human reason.* San Francisco: W. H. Freeman.

Whitehead, A. N. (1929). *The aims of education and other essays.* New York: Free Press.

Wirth, N. (1976). *Algorithms & data structures = programs.* Englewood Cliffs, NJ: Prentice-Hall.

Wolcott, H. F. (1977). *Teachers versus technocrats.* Eugene, OR: University of Oregon.

17

The Use of Computers in Education: A Response to Streibel*

Robert Heinich
Instructional Systems Technology
Indiana University

This article is a reply to Michael Streibel's "Critical Analysis of the Use of Computers in Education" [*ECTJ 34*(3), Fall 1986]. I congratulate Streibel for forcing us to consider issues we prefer to sweep under the intellectual rug. Too often we act as "mindless technicians," as James D. Finn once put it, with little thought given to our philosophical assumptions about learning, the organization of instruction, and instructional vehicles (including teachers). The level of discourse in the article is at a consistently high level.

However, I am afraid that Streibel has fallen into the trap described by Charles Kettering as using logic to go wrong systematically. It is a trap that I have been caught in myself on more than one occasion. There is an irresistible urge to push an argument too far, with a consequent loss of touch with experience. For example, Streibel's analysis of the logic of computer-based instruction (p. 285) is driven by his own assumptions, a common enough beginning and one we all engage in. But what evidence (as opposed to the testimony, speculation, assertions, or logical inferences of others) is offered that these assumptions are correct and the conclusions confirmed?

My reply to Streibel touches on these points: (1) his assumption of total reliance on one instructional mode; (2) his underestimation of student capabilities to make instrumental use of knowledge; (3) his overestimation of the ability of teachers to engage students in high-level behaviors; and (4) the knotty problem of the relationship between how we learn and what we believe.

Students are seldom taught by only one method. For example, three years ago my wife and I were studying Chinese in preparation for an extended stay in China. During our beginning Chinese class, we engaged in drill and practice in pronouncing and learning Chinese words; practice in writing Chinese characters on prepared worksheets; practice in stroke order of Chinese characters using a PLATO program; practice in listening to Chinese dialogues in the language lab; listening to explanations of Chinese grammar in class; participating in conversations in Chinese in small, supervised groups; feebly participating in conversations with Chinese people at lunches and dinners. All of the practice led to our ability to speak, write, and read Chinese and obviously contributed to our handling of the language. The more secure we were in the fundamentals, the more we could venture on our own, a goal with which I assume Streibel would agree.

No course that I know of is taught entirely by one instructional mode (although lecturing does come close to that). The question is one of mix, not of exclusivity. Streibel needs to answer these questions: At what point does drill and practice have the stultifying effect ascribed to it? Does the intrusion of drill and practice nullify other instructional efforts?

Most surprising to me is Streibel's underestimation of the student's ability to transcend instructional limitations. Streibel stresses the "active participation of learners in their own knowledge-creation" (p. 286), but apparently this active participation ceases as soon as the learner sits down at a terminal. He gives the learner no credit for being able to go beyond instructional methods, although many researchers are now realizing that the student's ability to do just that confounds many treatment studies. In discussing the "Oregon Trail" simulation, he assumes the student cannot build on the simulation experience, but is forever trapped in the program.

If I follow Streibel's argument, somehow the computer program prevents the student from engaging in discussions with other students or with the teacher, from seeking more information, or from simply evaluating the ultimate effects of the variables in the program. Oddly enough, neither teachers nor books, according to Streibel, have this stifling effect. ("Oregon Trail" and a number of other simulations are often played in groups whose members are very active indeed.) I would agree that the extent to which the student can expand and go beyond instruction depends on his or her ability, but it also depends on the richness of experiences. Which brings me back to the "Oregon Trail." What would be "the lived-experience of historical logic?" A book? A teacher? Time travel?

Not surprisingly, Streibel's idealized (romanticized?) view of teachers (p. 288) is at considerable variance with reality. According to the various reports on what's wrong with the schools, "poorly prepared teachers" heads the list. Furthermore, the evidence is incontrovertible that teacher education programs are tapping the bottom fourth of the undergraduate barrel. By and large, many teachers in the schools and in training are incapable of performing in the manner spelled out by Streibel. If I were asked to identify Streibel's philosophical position on this basis alone, I would have to say he is an Idealist.

Curriculum faculty tend to spin out instructional strategies far beyond the capabilities of the people in their classrooms to implement. I firmly believe that the widest gap in education is between the dreams of curriculum faculty and the reality of the classroom. But they want us to buy the dream, not the reality. Something is always preventing teachers from unleashing their creativity: to the NEA, it's the bureaucracy, to Streibel, it's technology. The reality is that creativity is a rare commodity among teachers, and we need to identify the really creative teachers and, wherever possible, extend the range of their talents by incorporating their skills in mediated forms, thereby benefiting more students. A word to researchers in instructional psychology: the more we learn about learning and the more sophisticated our instructional strategies become as a result, the less likely it is that teachers will be able to implement those strategies. Carefully designed, technologically based experiences will be our only assurance that the integrity of those strategies, including any that give students great control, will be retained.

Now to the question that I am still grappling with, and one which I would like to see Streibel and others address: What is the relationship between how we learn and what we believe? How direct is the translation of philosophical positions into teaching practice and, further, what is the effect of that practice on the learner? Some easy assumptions are sometimes made. Vander-Meer, in an article in *Audiovisual Communication Review* [8(5)], came to the conclusion that instructing with films is based on the ontological position of realism. But he assumed, like Streibel, that the student is trapped in the film and that the film is the end point of the student's experience in that content. Yet the student can go in many directions with information, regardless of source, and more information will allow the student to modify what was learned in the film. I will readily agree that instructional methods differ in how effectively they facilitate students' "active participation in their own knowledge-creation." But is this a philosophical proposition, or is it a conviction that certain instructional methods are superior to others, regardless of the philosophical orientation of the one who devises them?

Does a pragmatist teach pragmatically? John Dewey didn't. Does a student, to become a pragmatist, have to be taught pragmatically? I wasn't. When I enrolled in Colorado State College of Education in 1946, the College was a bastion of progressive education. I became a convert to progressive education, and, more important, a disciple of John Dewey. (I have since given up progressive education, but I'm still with John Dewey.) How did this come about? By being lectured to, not by the "project method" or any of the other trappings of progressive education. The arguments presented made intuitive good sense to me and I assimilated and accommodated like crazy. On the other hand, Mortimer Adler, a confirmed Idealist, created an adult education program on a pragmatically based instructional method, which he hoped would lead the participants to Idealism.

Does a philosophical position dictate instructional methods? Various philosophical positions are represented among professors in a university philosophy department, but does this mean that their instructional methods differ? Do instructional methods reveal a philosophical position? If I walk into a philosophy teacher's classroom, could I observe his or her instructional methods and be able to say, "Now there's an existentialist"? Do instructional methods, not content, shape one's view of reality (ontology), how one goes about knowing (epistemology), and what one values (axiology)? I don't have answers to these questions. I am seeking dialogue.

Streibel's article is certainly stimulating. The important issues he raises should evoke discussion in the field. I regret that he doesn't apply the same logic to the reality of teacher-led instruction. Twenty years ago I stated the principle "technology makes instruction visible," meaning that technologically based instruction, by definition, can be examined and tested and its effectiveness and effects judged. Teaching is invisible. We don't know what goes on, specifically, in classrooms. Relationships between instructional efforts and learning are exceedingly difficult to determine (and much harder to modify). Consequently, it is easy to romanticize about classroom instruction, especially when one has a vested interest in those who do the instructing and in the methods they are supposed to use. But there is also strength in being visible. Technologically based instruction can be revised until it does work. How much more difficult it is to change people!

To me, the best chance of accomplishing what Streibel would like to see accomplished is through technology and not through the teachers we now have and those on the horizon. Their built-in "programs" are more severely limited.

18

Recontextualizing Computers in Education: A Response to Streibel*

Suzanne K. Damarin
Instructional Design & Technology
The Ohio State University

Streibel's article, "A Critical Analysis of the Use of Computers in Education " [*ECTJ 34*(3) FALL 1986] is a welcome addition to the discussion of educational computing. His careful explication, both of his own educational philosophy and of the effects of three approaches to educational computing in relation to that philosophy, provides a bridge between broad-scale criticisms of educational computing (*e.g.,* Dreyfus & Dreyfus, 1984; Taylor & Johnsen, 1986; Weizenbaum, 1976) and the pragmatic reality of courseware available to schools. The purpose of this article is not so much to argue with Streibel's philosophy, nor to quarrel with the implications he draws, but to continue the discussion which he has begun.

In a sense, Streibel's paper is guilty of some of the epistemological limitations which he attributes to the use of computer languages (p. 317). His arguments isolate types of software in order to seek regularities and deduce consequences; thus, these arguments tend to legitimize non-ambiguity, internal consistency, and non-contradiction, as well as deduction and induction. While arguing that computer programming decontextualizes the knowledge that student programming activities are intended to convey, Streibel has decontextualized educational computing in (at least) two important respects. He fails to consider the effects of computers on society at large, and he

---

analyzes the effects of computer-based lessons without reference to the many other social and political variables which shape the larger educational context we call schools.

The Context of Computing

At the outset of his article, Streibel asserts: "The computer, as I will try to show, is not just another 'delivery system,' but an environment that has certain values and biases associated with it" (p. 283).

If this statement is true—Streibel argues well that it is—then it is true not only in the realm of education, but even more so in those aspects of society which use not only more computers, but more powerful computers, than education. The computer is a well-established "tool" of business and industry, social service agencies, the scientific community, and government. The computer has changed each of these environments by bringing its values and biases not only to the activities within each of these domains of society, but also to the ways in which individuals understand them, interact with them, and reform them. To the extent that educational systems prepare students for their multiple roles in society, they must prepare students for roles in computer-saturated environments.

Many issues are related both to these roles and to Streibel's arguments. Three of these issues are (1) the declining importance of decontextualized skills, (2) the use of mathematical models in simulations, and (3) the information explosion and associated issues related to access to information.

Drill-and-practice programs are used to promote the student's acquisition of decontextualized skills, rote skill-building in the case of drill and patterned skill-building in the case of practice (p. 289). The usefulness of these programs in education is related to the value placed upon the skills themselves and upon the one-dimensional Mastery Learning paradigm which Streibel details. In the computer-saturated workplace of today, the decontextualized skills of arithmetic and of precise spelling are relegated to computers. As more sophisticated software (symbol manipulators and text analyzers) becomes widely available, the skills of algebraic manipulation and calculus, as well as many technical writing skills, can also be performed by computer. Some educators (*e.g.*, Commission on

Standards, 1987; Steen, 1987) project that these developments will eventually eliminate decontextualized skills from formal education. In any case, the very existence and availability of software capable of performing tasks which formerly required human skill development changes learners' relationships to those skills, and thus to the drill-and-practice software designed to teach them.

With the increase in power and availability of computers, the use of simulations based upon quantitative models has grown in virtually all parts of society. Businesses, government, and other agencies (including education) rely heavily on such models for both predictive and descriptive purposes. The use of quantitative information to represent situations and relationships is not a new development; many formulae of the physical sciences and quantitative constructs (*e.g.*, IQ) of the social sciences predate electronic computers. However, the computer allows the building of more complex models and the manipulation of these models in more complex ways. In a society which values numbers, a computer-generated printout has persuasive power, even when it results from poorly constructed models or suspect data.

The power relationship between the individual and the computer is dependent, at least in part, upon the individual's understanding of the modeling process and upon her or his beliefs concerning the relationship of computer models to reality. Increasingly, individuals must judge whether a computer model is reality, replicates reality, represents reality, provides a (clear or distorted) view of reality, or has no relation to reality. Insofar as education is the road to individual empowerment, it must provide students with opportunities for assessing this relationship. We will return to this issue in the following paragraphs.

The issue of simulations and mathematical modeling is made more serious by the computer-generated information explosion; the sheer quantity of computerized information is becoming incomprehensible. The relationship of computers to information was once viewed as analogous to that of file cabinets; information was hierarchically ordered, then stored and accessed in a linear manner within that hierarchy. Today computer-based information is stored in data bases using increasingly complex multidimensional structures. The computer allows the building of models which involve complex interrelationships among more variables than the human mind can comprehend simultaneously. Moreover, information has a life of its own, in the sense that it can be used by the computer to generate new information which is then added to the data base. In the very real sense of amount of information available, computers can "know " more than their human users even if they cannot reflect or act upon that "knowledge." The thrust of artificial intelligence can be viewed as allowing computers to act "intelligently," based upon sophisticated knowledge structures. This goal is not unlike a major traditional goal of schooling, to enable students to act intelligently based upon their knowledge.

Taken together, these phenomena create significant issues for formal education. In the past, society relied on individuals for all the knowledge and skills needed to maintain itself; student acquisition of knowledge and skills was, therefore, a major goal of formal education. Today, however, computers surpass humans, not only in the practice of skills such as arithmetic, but also in the amount of "knowledge " acquired in the form of digitized information. The question of how knowledge and skills should and will be shared among people and computers is, therefore, an issue for society in general and education in particular.

A related issue has to do with modeling. As Streibel reminds us, classroom education provides learners with examples of many ways of viewing the world (artistic, metaphoric, historic, moral, and so on). Although computers support only a procedure-driven model or view, this type of model is used increasingly throughout society. The problem for educators is how to preserve a balance among diverse approaches to understanding; this problem is made more compelling by the availability of computer models which purport to teach about other models.

Computers in Education

If computers are to have a place in schools (and it seems apparent that they will), the question is how they should be used for instructional purposes. A common answer from administrators and from the popular and professional presses is: "The computer should be used for what it does best, thus freeing the teacher to do what he or she does best." This very easy and obvious answer begs the very difficult questions of what, exactly, it is that computers and teachers do, and, beyond that, what each does best. Implicit in each of these questions is the notion that what is done will be positive and good. Streibel's article forces us to consider the possibility of powerful but negative, and perhaps even bad, educational consequences of the use of computer-based drill and practice, tutorials, simulations, and programming activities. The remainder of this chapter raises issues regarding his conclusions.

Drill and Practice

Streibel recognizes that drill-and-practice courseware assumes that previous instruction has taken place (p. 289), and he asserts that these programs are "part of a behavioral learning culture that mitigates against non-behavioral goals " (p. 303). Referring to arguments that the technological delivery system becomes the central organizing principle of the classroom, he states "a simple drill and practice courseware program is (therefore) not all that innocent an aid to teaching " (p. 302). In a paper not cited by Streibel, Trumbull (1986) asserts that drill-and-practice programs teach children that knowledge is "objective, determinate, and finite " (p. 21) as well as boring.

Streibel cites evidence (p. 289) that drill-and-practice programs represent the dominant use of computers in education and laments what he sees as the necessary sequelae of this use. He does not ask when drill and practice is the dominant use; the reader assumes that Streibel thinks it is because teachers value it most. A more optimistic view is that, perhaps, teachers are turning away from their roles in the "behavioral learning culture," asserting through their actions that what they do best is not to teach boring, finite, decontextualized facts which are decreasingly important outside the context of Mastery Learning. Perhaps teachers are giving to computers those tasks which best reflect the computer's essential activity: rapid execution of decontextualized—and essential meaningless—operations.

There is some irony in the observation that the computer makes possible the efficient use of behavioral methods for teaching decontextualized skills at precisely the time that these

same skills are being outmoded by the computer itself.   The
primary question for schools seems not to be whether to use drill-
and-practice courseware to teach these skills, but rather to teach
them at all.   If one believes, with Streibel, that a major goal of
education is to teach others "how to become empowered lifelong
learners " (p. 285), the answer is clear and compelling.   The use of
scarce classroom time to train students to perform obsolete skills
is not only wasteful of time and resources; it sends the student
negative messages concerning both the nature of learning and
her or his own potential.

If decontextualized skill mastery is moved from the core of
education, drill-and-practice programs bear a different
relationship to school learning and Streibel's arguments become
much less compelling.   Drill-and-practice courseware may serve
a useful purpose for those who, already understanding the
relationship of a specific skill to a broader area of knowledge,
choose to decontextualize it and to master it through the methods of
behaviorism.

Computational Models

A sophisticated computer-based tutorial and a
computerized simulation each has at its core a set (or sets) of
"explicit and computable rules " (p. 307), a mathematical model
which defines the content intended for the student.   Streibel
observes (correctly) that such a model, applied to a tutorial on
hunger, reduces the sociopolitical problem to economic terms and
arbitrarily selected variables; hunger then becomes a
computerized numbers game.   Similarly, the "Oregon Trail "
simulation "represents the abstract world of algorithmic logic
rather than the lived experience of historical logic " (p. 320).   Both
the tutorial and the simulation are defined by computer models; in
the tutorial the student's learning activity is directed by the model,
while in the simulation students must act as if they were
computers operating on the model.   As Streibel says, "Gone are the
aesthetic, metaphoric, artistic, affective, interpretive, and moral
structures for dealing with the world " (p. 318).

These points are hard to dispute; the problem is that they
are points to be made, not only about education, but about the use of
computational models as representations of "reality " in virtually
all facets of life.   As the use of computational modeling increases

throughout society, it would seem to become more important that students learn not only to differentiate the procedure-driven algorithmic logic of computers from other ways of knowing, but also to distinguish computational models of sociopolitical problems such as hunger from the reality of hunger throughout the world.

Streibel (citing Dreyfus, 1979) argues that "if we find that human skills and knowledge are ultimately based on tacit beliefs and judgments which cannot be analyzed into components, then computational processes...will never match human processes " (p. 312). On the other hand, information scientists argue that when it comes to handling large bodies of interrelated "information," humans cannot match computers. The "information explosion " is a computer-based phenomenon, but one which affects human lives in both mundane and fundamental ways.

If a purpose of formal education is (as Streibel says) to "prepare others for lifelong learning," it appears that the learning of what we hope is a long life ahead must in some way accommodate the reality of computers. Perhaps the best means of preparation for this life is to help learners distinguish clearly between human reality and computerized representations of reality. The very faults which Streibel cites in his discussion of "Oregon Trail " clearly exemplify this distinction, and could be made to do so for students. Streibel's discussion of programming instruction (p. 325) further clarifies the issue and provides an important message for students as well as instructional designers: computing languages and programming activities require that information be structured in procedural ways and are, therefore, appropriate only when dealing with procedural problems. Given all of the issues outlined above, it would seem that a major goal of education for the future is that all learners will understand, for themselves, how to think about what it is that the computer does best and what it is that human beings do best.

Recognizing a dichotomy between human intelligence and "machine intelligence," it is radical, but perhaps instructive, to consider the possibility that all instruction on decontextualized skills and procedure-driven quantitative modeling activities be assigned to computers, and that teachers be encouraged—indeed required—to devote their energies and attention to the development of other nonprocedural abilities and attitudes, including both cognitive and affective comparison of procedural and other approaches to understanding situations. In such a scenario, rather than removing computer simulations and programming from the curriculum, these programs should be recontextualized in two ways: (1) they should stand alone in the sense of being completely self-contained units, requiring no assistance, preparation, preteaching, or follow-up activities by the teacher, and (2) they should be "fair game " as examples in the study of the "technological framework." The teacher is thereby freed from the need to isolate variables, set parameters, gather and analyze data (as well as from the need to rationalize designer/programmer decisions in these matters). He or she can then use the shared "experience " of a computer simulation or programming activity as a vehicle through which to examine with learners the limitations of "reality " as simulated and as printed out.

The virtues of this "solution" lie in the clear and consistent identification of computer capabilities and models with computers and of a broad range of human concerns and thought processes with teachers. Many of Streibel's concerns would, or at least could, be answered; the questions of hunger and of the westward migration, for example, could be revisited by teachers from a variety of perspectives, none of them quantitative in nature. Segregation of computer modeling from other perspectives would help to avoid student confusion of computer models with "the whole picture " and with "reality."

There are, however, two major problems with this solution: (1) the solution ignores the fact that mathematical modeling, and the computer itself, are artifacts of human intelligence, and (2) within the political structures of society and schools, the solution pits the computer against the humans, in the struggle for resources and prestige. These issues, together with the issues raised by Streibel, are not essentially new problems; although specific to educational computing, they are new manifestations of the "two cultures " debate begun 30 years ago.

In the Snow-Leavis controversy of the 1950s concerning the "two cultures " of science and humanities, Snow (1959) argued that there was a growing communication gap between scientists and others, especially intellectuals in the literary tradition, and that this gap would portend the doom of Western civilization. Leavis countered by arguing that there is but one culture with literature at its core and science and technology at its periphery; the job of literature is not to oppose science but to humanize it. This controversy, unresolved and apparently dormant for the past two decades, appears to be re-emerging in intellectual and public discussion. In a recent review of the debate, Ozick (1987) finds that neither position is totally correct, but argues that some methods of science, as well as the tendency of scientists toward specialization, have intruded into the study of literature.

Viewed in the context of this controversy, Streibel's article suggests that, through simulations, science is intruding even further into the humanities. Moreover, because computer models have implicit values and biases, by definition they are incapable of humanization. What Streibel seems to fear is a converse of Leavis' position: that, in schools at least, there is increasingly but one culture with technology at its core and the humanities at its periphery. If this is the case, then Streibel's arguments become more crucial because, indeed, computers can no longer be thought of as mere "delivery systems" of instruction.

REFERENCES

Commission on Standards for School Mathematics of the National Council of Teachers of Mathematics (1987). *Curriculum and evaluation standards for school mathematics: Working draft*. Reston, VA: NCTM

Dreyfus, H. H. (1979). *What computers can't do* (2nd ed.). New York: Harper and Row.

Dreyfus, H. H., & Dreyfus, S. E. (1984). Putting computers in their proper place: Intuition in the classroom. *Teachers College Record, 85*(4), 578-601.

Ozick, C. (1987). Science and letters: God's work—and ours. *New York Times Book Review*. September 27, 1987, 3, 51.

Snow, C. P. (1959). *The two cultures and the scientific revolution*. London and New York: Cambridge University Press.

Steen, L. A. (1987). Who still does math with paper and pencil? *The Chronicle of Higher Education, 34*(7), A48.

Streibel, M. J. (1986). A critical analysis of the use of computers in education. *Educational Communications and Technology Journal, 34*(3), 137-161.

Taylor, W. D., & Johnsen, J. B. (1986). Resisting technological momentum. In J. A. Culbertson & L. L. Cunningham (eds.), *Microcomputers and education. Eighty-fifth yearbook of the National Society for the Study of Education.* Chicago: University of Chicago Press.

Trumbull, D. J. (1986, March). Games children: A cautionary tale. *Educational Leadership,* 18-21.

Weizenbaum, J. (1976). *Computer power and human reason.* San Francisco: W. H. Freeman.

19

A Response to Robert Heinich and Suzanne Damarin*

Michael J. Streibel
Educational Technology
University of Wisconsin-Madison

In this article, I respond to the articles by Robert Heinich and Suzanne K. Damarin that appeared in the *Educational Communications and Technology Journal, 36*(3), 1988.

Response to Robert Heinich

Heinich believes that he detects four presumably crippling assumptions in my original article. My arguments, he claims, assume:

1. A "total reliance on one instructional mode [computers]."
2. An "underestimation of student capabilities to make instrumental use of knowledge [available in a computational environment]."
3. An "overestimation of the ability of teachers to engage students in high-level behaviors."
4. A problematic "relationship between how we learn and what we believe."

I will discuss each of these points in turn.

Total Reliance on One Instructional Mode

Heinich begins by recalling how he learned Chinese through various forms of practice. "No course," he writes, "is taught entirely by one instructional mode." I certainly agree with

---

this, but find two points worth adding. First, practice of component facts and skills should always take place within the context of the learner's intention of achieving some higher level goal (speaking Chinese in Heinich's case). Second, the methods of practice to achieve short-term goals should never undermine long-term goals.

The first point is always brought home to me when I observe my son's music teacher telling him that every drill-and-practice finger exercise should always be an expression of his love of music and not merely a mindless quest for technical excellence. Otherwise the two become disconnected and the qualitative dimension of music gets lost. This analogy holds for all drill and practice in any subject. Is this an unrealistic expectation? Some would argue that it is, because school should be a preparation for adult work, which itself is often fragmented and alienating. I would argue that it is not unrealistic, because the purpose of schooling is not just a conservative function (preparing students for the existing social order), but also a progressive function (preparing students to restructure social relations in order to promote the general welfare and social justice). Furthermore, all actions in school (including drill and practice) should serve both of these functions; otherwise one function will dominate the other.

In my original article, I tried to show how computerized drill-and-practice programs reinforced an authoritarian, behavioral performance culture in the classroom and how this mitigated against the possibility of a general progressive function of schooling. That is, the computer tended to favor the conservative side of education (despite its modern appearance) by focusing on predefined skills and by reinforcing order, control, predictability, rational systematicity, and manageability. The issue in my article was therefore not about one instructional mode (nor about a total reliance on one instructional mode). The issue was about a point of view which categorized the world of learning into a hierarchy of prerequisite skills.

The second point, about means and multiple ends, is also brought home to me when I observe schools that publicly claim they are preparing K-12 students to become autonomous, inner-directed, lifelong learners and critical inquirers but then use authoritarian training methods to establish fragmented knowledge and skills in their students. Yes, such schools are using efficient instructional strategies to achieve short-term performance objectives. But just as certainly, they are undermining their publicly stated, long-term educational goals. Students in such a system never have the experience of democracy, inner-directed learning, or critical inquiry. I therefore conclude that we, as teachers (and instructional designers), should only use (or design) drill-and-practice activities after carefully examining how such activities contribute to long-term as well as short-term (and high-level as well as low-level) educational goals. I am clearly taking a stand here which is at variance with Gagné's belief that we as educators can focus on developing the automaticity of component skills alone. We can't! If the means that we choose to establish the automaticity of component skills subvert long-term (or high-level) goals, then we should not use them.

Heinich then asks the question, "At what point does drill and practice have the stultifying effect ascribed to it?" I did not ask this question in my original article because I was more interested in the effects of instrumental reason on understanding. My proposition was that instrumental reason (as embodied in the computer via calculation, induction, deduction, etc.) was so inherent in computational approaches to education (*i.e.*, drill and practice, tutorials, simulations, etc.) that it became the very way through which a learner would eventually apprehend the world. I argued further that computational ways of apprehending the world tended to legitimize the proceduralization of experience and delegitimize other ways of apprehending the world. Drill-and-practice programs were therefore "stultifying" in an epistemological sense of the word.

Let me put my position in another way. My goal as a teacher, researcher, and instructional designer is always to find ways of developing understanding in the mind and action of the learner. Understanding is taken here in the broadest sense of the word and includes the notion of praxis. This has led me to subsume the goal of performance improvement under the goal of understanding. The larger (and largely qualitative) goal of understanding places its own set of unique constraints on a teacher (and instructional designer) that go beyond (and sometimes seemingly contradict) the constraints of the goal of efficient performance improvement. I first realized this on reading David Hawkin's book, The Informed Vision, in which he makes a strong case for a "messing around" phase in instruction. I don't recall ever seeing "messing around" as one of Gagné's instructional events.

Understanding Students' Ability to Transcend Instructional Limitations

Heinich claims that I underestimate students' ability to transcend the instructional limitations of computers. I certainly hope not! Heinich also fears that I believe a student's "active participation [in their own knowledge creation] ceases as soon as the learner sits down at a terminal." Both of these claims are red herrings and divert attention away from the real issue. The issue is not whether students can construct knowledge when they sit down at a terminal (they can and do—see Turkle's book, The Second Self) or whether they get "forever trapped in the program." The real issue is: What counts as legitimate knowledge within the computer environment?

Let me summarize my argument as follows. Assume, with Polanyi, that tacit knowledge is the foundation of explicit knowledge and the means through which instrumental knowledge is understood and applied. Let us assume further, along with Piaget, that body knowledge gained through multisensory play and exploration is the foundation for later formal operations. Computers then put a tremendous restriction on the creation, development, use, and understanding of knowledge because:

1.   Computers bypass the learner's direct experience of their own bodies (except in the most minimal and distancing ways—e.g., facts about the body, etc.).
2.   Computers narrow the whole range of sensory experience (which in its natural state has multiple, overlapping modalities and

ambiguities that call for the learner's active resolution).

3. Computers impose a premature formal manipulation of abstract symbols (*i.e.,* "symbol pushing") onto the learner. (Piaget believed that formal operations came at the end of a long developmental process.)

4. Computers constrain the learner to use instrumental reason as the *modus operandi* (*e.g.,* cognitive problem solving is favored over problem posing).

Does this mean that students can never go beyond these limitations of computers? Of course not! But if we realize that many people (Heinich included) are calling for technology-based experiences to overcome the limitations of teacher-generated educational experiences, then we realize that the whole culture of schooling is becoming technologized to the point where the epistemological constraints of technology are shaping the dominant forms of legitimate knowledge. I tried to show this in my original article by describing how the computer was contributing to the technologizing of education. Clearly, the computer is not the only factor involved, but it is becoming a cultural paradigm for the very way that we are conceptualizing education. I therefore find it somewhat capricious of Heinich to place so much burden on the learner and his or her ability to "transcend instructional limitations." How, exactly, is a student supposed to construct ways of knowing that "go beyond the instructional methods" when the whole structure of education in a future classroom is so thoroughly technologized?

Overestimation of Teachers' Ability to Engage Students in High-Level Behavior

Heinich also believes that I overestimate the ability of teachers to engage students in high-level behaviors. "The evidence is incontrovertible," he writes, "that teacher education programs are tapping the bottom fourth of the barrel." What are we to make of this? Heinich's solution is straightforward: Find ways to use technology to overcome the natural limitations of teachers!

My first response to all of this was to find Heinich's attitude toward teachers simply appalling. Why does he have such profound disdain for teachers? His approach seems to be one of "blaming the victim" (*i.e.*, looking for personality defects in teachers to account for the problems of education) and then reconceptualizing teachers' work into technological terms and proposing technological solutions to solve the problem. In my original article, however, I tried to show that a technological approach to education (with or without computers) was itself a major structural part of the problem. The computer only systematized and reified the technologizing of education.

On a deeper level, however, Heinich's arguments require a more reasoned response. Heinich begins with an innocent and uncontroversial claim. We should "identify the really creative teachers and, whenever possible, extend the range of their talents by incorporating their skills in mediated forms." All well and good! However, something is missing. Good teachers achieved their expert status over many years of experience and labor. They did not become experts by following other people's "expert rules" but by carefully (and often painfully) constructing their own expertise within a community of learning. Why not foster this social process of teachers helping each other to become more professional practitioners? Seeing the creative strategies of other teachers is useful here but does not guarantee success.

Heinich then continues on a more disturbing note. "The more we learn about learning, and the more sophisticated our instructional strategies become," he writes, "the less likely it is that teachers will be able to implement those strategies." In other words, the more we as researchers and instructional designers know about learning, the less we will need the expertise of teachers (the actual experts after all). So much for the personally constructed expertise of each teacher! So much for the craft status of teaching! Teaching will then be a process where theories of learning determine instructional behaviors. Furthermore, teaching will be a rationally managed process where "carefully designed technologically based experiences will be our only assurance that the integrity of those strategies...will be retained." Wait a minute! Why have we suddenly shifted attention from the purposes of education to the methods employed? Why have questions about the integrity of the triadic relationship between teacher, learner, and subject, as Maxine Greene calls it, suddenly been replaced by questions about the integrity of the strategies used?

I sense a subtle but very deep shift in what Heinich and others are claiming. Namely, the certainty and control of educational outcomes reside in the instructional strategies that are used and not in the people (teachers and students) who labor to bring about these educational outcomes. If we accept this shift, then we are buying into the belief that the theoretical knowledge as constructed by behavioral and cognitive scientists (and dispensed via instructional delivery systems and instructional designers) is more fundamental, more useful, and more legitimate than the practical expertise embodied in teachers. I do not accept the legitimacy of this belief. I also do not want to make this an either-or situation. I merely (what a deceptive word!) believe that the practical knowledge as constructed, developed, and used within the community of teachers is as legitimate (if not more legitimate for the purposes of education) as the theoretical knowledge of behavioral and cognitive science (which, after all, was constructed by a community of scientists to serve their human interest). This "mere belief" will take much more thought and scholarship, however, because, if it is warranted, it will have a profound effect on our conduct as teacher educators and educational technologists.

The parameters of this "mere belief" are becoming clear: Theories of behavioral or cognitive science that "psychologize" learning (*i.e.*, conceptualize learning as an individual psychological process in theoretical terms) are an inadequate basis for curriculum. Furthermore, when such behavioral and cognitive theories of learning are used to design instruction, they tend to legitimize the conservative function of education and the forms of knowledge that go along with the conservative function of education. I therefore find it more than ironic that Heinich believes that the "widest gap in education is between the dreams of curriculum faculty [such as myself] and the reality of the classroom."

The Relationship Between How We Learn and What We Believe

Heinich gets right to the heart of the matter by bringing up this issue, although I would probably phrase the question as follows: What do our behaviors as teachers and instructional designers reveal about our beliefs about learning? The question should be asked in this way because our behaviors are much better indicators of our beliefs, attitudes, and values than our publicly stated philosophies. The question should also be asked in this way about computers because computers are behaving systems. A computer's "instructional behaviors" therefore reveal something about the values, attitudes, and beliefs of the community of instructional designers and about the human interests that this community serves. I will not recount all of the arguments from my original article, but present those that address specific points which Heinich makes.

Heinich begins this section by making a very popular claim. "Technology," he writes, "makes instruction visible." How can one object to this? I certainly agree with this statement, but I would add one important point. Computers first force us to reconceptualize instruction in terms of instrumental reason. Hence, computers only make one aspect of instruction visible. Furthermore, the craft aspect of teaching is only "invisible" within the framework of technologized instruction. It is not invisible within the lived experience of teachers. I therefore conclude that the more technologically minded we become about teaching (and learning and instruction), the more invisible teaching (and learning and instruction) will become. This view is not directed by romanticism, idealism, or pessimism, but by a realization that a social-critical framework can do more justice to the phenomena of teaching and learning than a behavioral or a cognitive one. Clearly, much more work needs to be done to articulate a social-critical framework for teaching, learning, and instruction.

Finally, Heinich claims that "technologically based instruction can be revised until it does work." This makes me very uneasy for a number of reasons. On the surface, it sounds innocent and pragmatic enough. However, on a deeper level, it tries to solve human problems (of which education is one) with technological solutions. Hence, rather than restructuring the social processes that led to our current forms of education and empowering the people who are charged with the responsibility for education, Heinich advocates bypassing these very people and using technological solutions. Whose interests are being served by his proposals? Heinich's ideas are all the more ironic because if we succeed in technologizing education as thoroughly as he suggests, it will still require the unacknowledged, unrewarded, and "invisible" yet creative labor of teachers to make computers have the appearance of teaching.

Response to Suzanne Damarin

Suzanne Damarin's article raises a number of other important issues in educational computing. First, she expands the debate by focusing on the "effects of computers on society at large" and how these will affect the use of computers in education. Second, she expands the debate by showing how it is not enough to "analyze the effects of computer-based lessons without reference to many other social and political variables which shape the larger educational contexts we call schools." I will address each of these issues in order to continue the debate. But first, I will deal with a methodological concern.

Damarin begins by pointing out that I "may be guilty of some of the epistemological limitations which [I] attribute to the use of computer languages." Namely, my arguments first "isolate types of software in order to seek regularities and deduce consequences" and then "tend to legitimize non-ambiguity, internal consistency, and non-contradiction as well as deduction and induction." Is there something to this charge? I believe not, for two reasons. First, although I did select various types of software for analysis in my original article (*e.g.*, drill and practice, tutorial), I did so in the belief that they were the most prevalent (in terms of actual usage) and the most exhaustively representative types of educational software. I then tried to show how all of these types of software had a common set of assumptions about the learner, the teacher, and the teaching/learning process. I called this set of assumptions the technological framework because each type of software emphasized behavioral performance improvement and system efficiency at the expense of other types of educational goals. My analysis was therefore not restricted to a selective subset of educational software.

I did not, of course, deal with software such as word processors, data bases, and spreadsheets, although I believe that many of my conclusions also apply in these cases. I also did not deal with more recent developments such as intelligent tutoring systems, even though I believe that my conclusions also apply. Intelligent tutoring systems, in fact, bring the technological framework in education to new heights by explicitly creating computational models of the student, the expert, the content domain, the tutor, and the communication interface.

As to the second point, my own methodology of trying to be unambiguous, internally consistent, and non-contradictory should not be confused with the non-ambiguity, internal consistency, and non-contradiction of computational approaches to solving problems. For example, the non-ambiguity that I demand of myself during a philosophical critique is different from the non-ambiguity that I would demand of myself were I to reconceptualize a problem in computational terms. The former tends to problematize experience and uncover taken-for-granted assumptions. The latter tends to hide category judgments in order to get on with the job. If the distinction that I have drawn were not the case, then a clear, consistent, and thorough phenomenologist would also be "guilty of some of the epistemological limitations which [could be] attributed to the use of computer languages." I tried to show in my original article, in fact, how a clear, consistent, and thorough computationist (what an awful word!) would be incapable of dealing with the phenomenological dimension of our personal and social lives. This brings me to the issue of computers and society.

The Effects of Computers on Society

Damarin begins this section by claiming that "educational systems...must prepare students for roles in computer-saturated environments." I agree with this, but disagree with the means that are proposed. That is, I question the assumption by Damarin and many others in my field of educational technology that a computer-saturated society requires the use of computer-saturated learning environments. In an ironic and somewhat dialectical way, I want students to become empowered and liberated citizens in a computer-saturated society—not by buying into it from birth, but by being able to stand above it and shape it to their own ends. My original article can be seen as an attempt to spell out the consequences for learning if we saturate learning environments with computers. Learners will become more efficient performers within a classroom where a technological mentality has become the "central organizing framework," but they will have done so at the expense of understanding and real-life intellectual agency. Hence, just because a technological mentality operates in the workplace does not mean that it should operate in our schools.

I am therefore somewhat taken aback by Damarin's proposal to use computerized drill-and-practice programs to "promote the student's acquisition of decontextualized skills." Decontextualization of skills is one of the major consequences of technologizing a process. Automating and reifying this step in computer courseware only makes the whole approach more entrenched. Let me reiterate my position: All decontextualized skill acquisition in schooling is wrong because it leads to a lack of integrated and inner-directed learning. If I were to conduct a critique of computer use in industry, I would make a similar case for the inadvisability of decontextualized skill application. But that is another story which has been told far better by others such as Edwards (Contested Terrain) and Noble (Forces of Production).

Damarin continues by claiming that computer-based "simulations based on quantitative models have grown in virtually all parts of [our] society" and that many "agencies (including education) rely heavily on such models for both predictive and descriptive purposes." This leads her to conclude that "increasingly, individuals must judge whether a computer model is reality, replicates reality, represents reality, provides a (clear or distorted) view of reality, or has no relation to reality." I have several things to add to her observations.

First, notice how artifacts made possible by the computer (*i.e.*, complex simulations) have become an important issue for education rather than the use to which they are put or the human interests which they serve.   Yes, one aspect of personal empowerment requires the ability to discriminate various dimensions of computer models and simulations.   However, and much more certainly, personal empowerment requires the integration of many other ways of understanding the world besides computer simulations.   These other ways of dealing with the world (*e.g.*, affective, moral, aesthetic, scientific, and political structures) do not just have to be judged as to whether they are, represent, picture, or have no relation to reality.   They have to be constructed interpersonally within a community through a historical process of personal and political struggle, negotiation, and conflict resolution.   Such constructions of knowledge and understanding get lost in a sanitized and rationally reconstructed computer simulation whether one learns about things within someone else's simulation or one programs one's own computer solution to problems.   Hence, I would not recommend focusing on how to judge computer models in a discussion of educational computing (no matter how much such models are used in society) because it restricts the debate about educational goals to quantitative, procedural, and performance outcomes.

I realize that Damarin does not intend to restrict education as I have suggested, but others, such as Heinich, clearly have this in mind when they call for technology-based education. I always keep one question in mind when I hear such proposals: Whose interests (i.e., which social groups) are served by reframing educational goals into technical terms?   I mentioned earlier in response to Heinich's article that the technological approach to education may very well be carrying out the conservative function of schooling at the expense of the progressive function.   This brings me to Damarin's second major theme.

The Social and Political Context of Educational Computing

Damarin continues her discussion with a very important proposal: We cannot afford to "decontextualize educational computing" because "social and political variables...shape the larger context we call schools."   She then draws an obvious conclusion—since computers are permeating all aspects of society, "schooling must [therefore] accommodate to the reality of computers." I would like to address each of these points by focusing on what they imply for me.

I began my original article with a simple question: How are computers used in education? This question quickly evolved into further questions: How can computers be used and how should computers be used in education? My article therefore reflects a personal history that began with an analysis of specific applications of educational computing and reached outward toward the goals and purposes of education. Along the way, however, several things slowly dawned on me: technology is not neutral; teaching is not a form of rationally managed work; computer languages are not models for linguistic or cognitive development; and a learner's empowerment and intellectual agency are not a matter of skills alone. Each of these statements, first formulated in a negative way because I was reacting to my own taken-for-granted assumptions, then became the nucleus for a positive position: Computer technology (and not only its design and application) embodied the values of efficiency and performance improvement; teaching was first and foremost a complex craft, no matter how technological the environment; natural language dialogue and communicative competence were at the heart of education and development; and empowerment and intellectual agency were primarily a matter of critical thinking and critical praxis within an interpretive community. All of these positions clearly need to be developed further before they are accepted, because they challenge the dominant assumptions of educational computing. All of these positions, however, have already been spelled out in greater detail by other scholars within the fields of curriculum history, curriculum theory, and critical social and cultural studies. I cited many of these scholars in my original article, even though I did not begin with a summary of their findings. Were I to rewrite my original article, I would do as Damarin suggests and begin with an analysis of the social and political context of educational computing. Specifically, I would look at the structural relationships of power and domination in both the workplace and in schooling and then examine how the computer plays an increasing role in these structural relationships.

In dealing with the specifics of educational computing, I would (if I were rewriting my original article) examine the political agenda within technological solutions to education. The concept of political analysis implied here does not deal with the interaction of state politics or ideology and education (although these are legitimate issues in their own right). It deals with the social choices and social consequences of the structure and practices of schooling. Schooling is not politically neutral in this sense of the term, just as technology is not neutral. The structures and practices of schooling serve someone's interests just as do the structures and practices of the workplace. These structures and practices are not inevitable or predetermined except insofar as they are unexamined.

The question then becomes: How should we accommodate to the fact of computers in our social life and how should we use computers in education? Damarin makes a number of tentative suggestions. We should acknowledge the limitations of computers and "consider the possibility that all instruction on decontextualized skills and procedure-driven quantitative modeling activities be assigned to computers." Computers would then be "recontextualized" by "stand[ing] alone in the sense of being completely self-contained units, requiring no assistance, preparation, preteaching, or follow-up activities by the teacher." Computers could also be "recontextualized" by being "fair game" as examples in the study of the technological framework.

I am sure that Damarin will anticipate my response to each of these proposals. The purpose of schooling is not just a conservative function of elaborating, inculcating, critiquing, and transmitting existing forms of knowledge (of which "decontextualized skills and procedure-driven quantitative modeling activities" are a part), but a progressive function of constructing new ways of formulating, understanding, and using knowledge. Furthermore, the conservative function of education should not undermine or divert attention away from the progressive function. These "shoulds" constitute a "political" agenda for teachers. Hence, I would not propose that we "recontextualize" computers by using them to instruct "decontextualized skills" or by using them as "fair game...in the study of the technological framework." Rather, I would propose that we get right to the heart of knowledge construction in schooling and encourage teachers and students to develop multiple modalities of thinking about a problem (of which quantitative modeling is one). For example, I would much rather see children in elementary school experience beginning levels of scientific thinking through problem posing and data definition activities than through the puzzle-solving and data-manipulation activities of computer simulations. The former approach (as described by David Hawkins) legitimizes a much broader view of knowledge and a much broader view of the learner as an intentional agent. The former view also treats the learner as a participant in his or her own education.

Damarin ends her response to my article with a rather shrewd but unwarranted comment. My arguments, she suggests, revive the "two cultures" debate of the 1960s—only this time with technology as the agent of science's intrusion into the humanities. Would that life were so simple! My concern, if it can be called such, is actually for both the sciences and the humanities. My concern is that a managerial and technological point of view (as fostered, systematized, and reified by the computer) becomes so entrenched at the center of education that both the sciences and the humanities are relegated to the periphery of education.

20

Critical Evaluation of Educational Software from a Social Perspective: Uncovering Some Hidden Assumptions*

J. Peter Rothe
Research Manager
Insurance Corporation of British Columbia

Introduction

Recently, the Educational Research Institute of British Columbia completed a study on communications technology and education. A major thrust of the project was the critical examination of educational software according to hidden assumptions. When the literature was reviewed, it became apparent that articles featuring a sociological analysis of educational software were limited. This article is a response to that limitation.

Critical Evaluation: An Analytic Framework

Most evaluation research on technology and education focuses on learning outcomes, such as measurable improvement in students' attention, perception, retention, attitude, and cognition. This evaluation focus is based on the definition of educational technology as the use of materials, energy sources, tools, and systems for the achievement of educational goals. Hardware such as microcomputers, interactive television, and videotape systems, and software such as computer programs, videotapes, and videodiscs, are examples of such a view of

---

* Reprinted with permission from *Educational Technology*, September 1983, copyright © Educational Technology Publications, 1983.

educational technology. For this article, software is viewed as the programs of instruction housed in and directed by the hardware.

Whenever educational software is evaluated, it is usually done according to the criteria of effectiveness, efficiency, documentation, appeal, and compatibility to the hardware (Axtell and Walker, 1982). Questions on social implications of the software have not yet received high priority in educational literature. Hence, there is a need to respond to this shortcoming by developing a critical evaluation design which explicates hidden assumptions underlying educational software.

Software is shaped within a social context. Therefore, there is little neutrality in the selection of knowledge, content, learning outcomes, language, ethics, or cultural perspectives. These features comprise assumptions underlying software which serve as the guide for student thinking and acting with the software. Since programmers' assumptions, value stances, and perspectives become incorporated in the software in an implicit sense, educators should critically evaluate educational software so that they can better recognize the consequences that hidden assumptions may have on student activities.

Critical evaluation accounts for educational software in terms of hidden perspectives which undergird programs. Evaluators undertake a comprehensive assessment in the form of evaluative inquiry directed toward the foundation of the software. Although many critical frameworks can be applied, for the purpose of this article a modified set of criteria based on sociology will be described.

Six analytic categories are developed. Although the categories may be viewed as interdependent and overlapping, for the purpose of analysis and description, they are considered distinct:

1. *Language Usage.* This includes dominant metaphors included in software which reaffirm hidden assumptions. For example, computer-based programs are advertised as operating under the interactive instructional presentation system. In everyday life, interaction reflects a common-sense view of two or more people acting with each other and

mutually influencing each other in a socially meaningful way. However, within educational software, interaction means students responding in structured formats to a rigidly-defined progression of statements programmed within microcomputer software.

2. *Knowledge.* This includes transmitted knowledge content which assumes a political, social, economic, or geographic perspective. Excluded are knowledge sources which contradict a point of view promoted in the software. For example, the IBM (PC) software package titled "The Speed Reader" is a practical program that systematically enhances reading skill. The knowledge is presented according to the assumption that increased reading speed makes individuals more efficient processors of information. It is based on the foundation of efficient time management. Knowledge pertaining to the psycholinguistic structure of understanding words is omitted, as is reading for leisure, literary appreciation, and memory. Hence, ten-year-old students (recommended in the advertisement) are removed from word understanding and appreciation.

3. *Ideology.* Included are forms of reasoning which assume a certain world view within the subject matter. An ideology may be evident from the learning models that are promoted in the software. For example, a software package titled "Snooper Troops: The Disappearing Dolphin," for students aged ten to adult, is based entirely on the analytic thinking model comprised of a careful, well-defined, rigidly-structured process of reasoning. This model is linked to problem-solving which arises from science. Omitted entirely is the opportunity for intuitive thinking embracing understandings, conclusions, and solutions. If the software relies on science as the only method for

solving socially-defined problems, the ideology of
scientism would arise. Examples of other ideologies
which may be found underlying some educational
software are consumerism, systems-management,
technologism, and militarism.

4. *Profit*. This includes the economic perspective
underlying software. Marketing strategies are
included in software descriptions which promote the
quality of education as being efficient, cost-effective,
and accountable—objectives which are economics-
based. Development of software corresponds to
profitability, which equates to mass sales of
marketable programs. Much of the educational
software focuses primarily on skills such as basic
reading, spelling, and arithmetic, because these can
be more easily programmed and targeted to the
greatest audience for a quick return on investment.
Programs for special students whose needs cannot be
produced on justifiable economic terms may be
omitted.

5. *Culture*. Included are culture-specific assumptions on lifestyle, community, language, family,
history, etc. Also included are implicit perspectives
on culture-relevant concepts such as adaptation,
accommodation, segregation, acculturation, and
homogenization. For example, the abundance of
IBM microcomputer software packages presents an
American point of view on matters such as
individual competition (*e.g.*, in contrast, some
Canadian cultural groups proceed on consensus
rather than individual competition for success),
community organization with a systems approach
(*e.g.*, but numerous northern Canadian
communities are organized around a patriarchal
system), lifestyle (*e.g.*, Canadian views on leisure
activities, friendship, and standards of living often
differ from the American view of the same), and
cultural individuality (*e.g.*, Canadians believe in a

mosaic structure compared to the American melting pot philosophy). Yet, because there is a shortage of Canadian-developed software for use by American hardware, many foreign cultural concepts are imported to Canada and may be received by Canadian students as "fact."

6. *Ethics.* This includes value assumptions which underlie the knowledge content and learning activities of a software package. For example, values reflecting competition are often found in educational software packages such as "Word Challenge" and "Arithmetic Game Set 1 and 2." Although competition is the basis for instruction, students who respond to the program may live in a community where cooperation and consensus are the dominant values.

Discussion of the Categories

Language Usage

Although all language may be considered metaphorical, the specific intentional use of a metaphor can screen the world or filter the perception by suppressing some facts and emphasizing others (Turbayne, 1962). Describing events, features, or products through a metaphor may imply something is the case when it is not, or give a thing a name which belongs to something else (Aristotle).

Software incorporates metaphors which implicitly provide students with a framework of judging their surroundings. A relevant example is the metaphor "computer literacy," included in a software package titled "BASIC: An Introduction to Computer Programming." Traditionally, people convey meaning by communicating through a language rooted in culture. Literacy means the ability to use this language proficiently in a process of interaction between people. Literate individuals have the learning to describe their cognitive orientations toward the world in appropriate discourse patterns.

The metaphor "computer literacy" means the ability to understand and use computers. Within the software package titled Basic: An Introduction to Computer Programming, literacy refers to a general knowledge of the capabilities, limitations, and implications of computer use and familiarity with the capacity of computers to perform specific information-processing functions applied to a variety of circumstances. The computer language BASIC includes a vocabulary which is artificially designed and specific to technology, whereas everyday language is context-specific. Meanings of words continuously change according to sentence structure, topic, location of interaction, purpose of interaction, intonation, etc.

By translating a common-sense concept like literacy into a metaphor for technology, students may tend to interpret everyday language which is comprised of human meaning, creativity, romance, and description according to technically precise, logically-ordered structures. According to Davison (1959), students' discourse systems are closely linked to their concepts of identity. Any change in the discourse system is likely to have a demonstrable change in their personalities or even their view of culture and communication.

The possibility of changing students' ways of thinking through the implicit meaning of metaphors can also be illustrated with videotape software. For example, a British Columbia distance education media company features a video program titled "Stress Management." Throughout the program, the metaphor stress management is divided into "stress" and "management." Stress is presented as if it were a given social event or fact of life. Management is discussed as the use of expedient techniques to order and direct events. Their combination as stress management implies that stress is a tangible object or event that can be ordered and directed, much as one would order and manage a bank account. Repeated use of this metaphor may lead to its acceptance and establishment in a student's way of thinking, and it may discourage asking vital questions such as: What are the causes of stress? Who is responsible for stress? And can causes of stress be eliminated at their source (Rothe, in press)?

Knowledge

The tasks of developing educational software cannot be accomplished with a blank mind, without prior beliefs, with an interest-free stance, or with empty anticipations (Werner, 1978). Everyone brings a viewpoint to the selection, translation, and transmission of knowledge. In educational software, the knowledge is translated for use by the new technology. To illustrate, most of the computer course work places knowledge within a design of rote learning and memorization. Examples of such software can be found in social studies ("How to Read in the Content Areas: Social Studies"), science ("Circulation System"), English ("Capitalization, and English Basics: Synonyms and Antonyms"), and mathematics ("SRA Computer Drill and Instruction: Mathematic Level C").

According to Dede (1981), knowledge content in future educational software will be increasingly molded into the intellectual skills of analysis, synthesis, and evaluation. Dede writes:

> Being able to select the best option from the menu of choices, analyze the data's implications, synthesize it with other knowledge, and evaluate the outcome will be crucial to successful intellectual endeavor (1981, p. 208).

When knowledge is translated according to an educational technology design, there appears to be limited teacher and student involvement in the selection and interpretation of knowledge. This tends to place knowledge into a commodity framework whereby teachers buy suitable software without input into software content. For example, the "Chemistry I Series" microcomputer software packages consist of six instructional units designed to help develop basic chemistry skills and assist with mathematical calculations required in laboratory experiments. Although the experiment simulated in the courseware can be made more relevant if a teacher exchanges certain elements, the software is developed so that a teacher cannot add or delete elements or radicals, or adapt a simulation of a similar type of reaction (British Columbia Ministry of Education,

1982). The courseware is a complete package which the teacher must use according to design.

Furthermore, hidden assumptions are not only found within the software but also within the process of accessing and storing the knowledge (Innis, 1951). A simple example may suffice. With more microcomputers in homes and their interface with centralized master computers, educational software addressing citizens' literacy will emerge as a powerful tool for handling societal crises. According to Dede (1981), courseware which addresses, for example, possible gasoline shortages, will be developed, stored, and transmitted when a gasoline availability crisis occurs. Timing of knowledge transmission, therefore, may be based upon defined perspectives of what knowledge should be made public for maximum emphasis.

Ideology

Interrelated with knowledge perspective is the concept of ideology. In short, ideology means the viewpoints underlying the software which serve as the basis for the process of teaching and learning incorporated in software. Many software packages are developed according to problem-solving, which is the standard in terms of the philosophy of science. However, problem-solving is often the presentation style in the human sciences. For example, effective management, communication skills, leadership, motivation, and time control are considered by IBM as problem areas which require rational problem-solving (IBM, Canada, 1982). If individuals do not meet a level of performance deemed acceptable by an organization, they are perceived to have a problem which can be solved through participation in computer course work. One might consider forms of reasoning which define human problems and processes for solution entirely in technical terms reflecting the ideology of technologism.

Further, educational outcomes of software usage are usually technically defined in terms of increased time efficiency and accountability, acquisition of skills, and more effective cognitive learning. Broadly-based learning outcomes evident in traditional classrooms may be completely omitted. In times of financial restraint, technically-designed learning outcomes become inviting to administrators. Therefore, the possibility exists that education may become based more on a technically-designed educational reality, than, for example, a liberal arts framework.

If features of technology are repeatedly promoted, a mind set may develop among senior administrators, suggesting that in order to attain educational goals synonymous with scrupulous budgeting, they must purchase up-to-date technology. Conversely, if the technology is not purchased, the realization of desirable educational goals may be perceived as being limited. This chain of events reflects consumerism, whereby educators are encouraged to buy a commodity which addresses a defined need, rather than administrators initiating alternative strategies which may also serve the need.

Profit

Market forces underlying most North American ventures may dictate that the educational software produced be designed for the largest and richest body of consumers. The materials developed may well be directed toward the educational needs of the majority of students. Minority groups for whom it would be unprofitable to develop software may well be placed in inferior positions. This may entrench a two-tier system of education, with a profound loss of human potential. Or, minority students may be forced to comply with the structure of a software program. For example, the elementary grade microcomputer software package titled "Domino Grouping," which is designed as a multiplication drill-and-practice program in mathematics, proceeds at a rate appropriate for average or better students. Since even the slowest speed is too fast for remedial students (British Columbia Ministry of Education, 1982), they are left with a choice—either participating with limited benefits, or not participating, and falling further behind in mathematics.

Presently, there is a danger that educational programs may be evaluated according to software marketing. For example, in 1980, the Ministry of Education for British Columbia developed a discussion paper on the evaluation of educational software for school use. Under the heading of marketing, the authors indicated that the value of software to the classroom is dependent on company promotions, allotment of trial periods for software, adequate documentation, and packaging (British Columbia Ministry of Education, 1982). It appears that software may be purchased and implemented on the basis of good marketing rather than complete educational appropriateness. As discussed in the section titled Ideology, a consumer mentality is developed and maintained through marketing devices.

An economic perspective is also evident when the compatibility of software to particular hardware is analyzed. For example, software developed by IBM cannot be operationalized by Apple or TRS-80 computers. Consequently, the availability of software may reflect the monopolization of certain corporations. That is, teachers who desire software, such as "Solar System Astronomy" or "Optics," must have an Apple II computer. If the school has an IBM PC or a TRS-80, this courseware would not be usable. Consequently, the corporation which has the financial resources and expertise to develop or contract the development of maximum software will assure sale of its hardware. Hence, persuasive marketing strategies implicit in economics may be used to sell maximum software for defined hardware. Unfortunately, the zealous salespeople may be unaware that the courseware they wish to sell is excellent for certain microcomputers, but not suitable in some educational environments.

Culture

Educational software is a completed product which passes from producers to consumers. Perspectives of cultural or social life may become incorporated in the courseware as proper interpretive schemes for certain issues. For example, videotape software concerning social studies is often based on a compensatory perspective of culture. Native Indians have been displayed as:

> Culturally deprived, culturally impoverished, educationally retarded, economically impoverished, culturally disadvantaged, chronically poor, educationally deprived, culturally alienated, *ad infinitum* . . . (Callihoe, 1972, p. 36)

Callihoe's statement illustrates why educational software should be critically reviewed for sensitive social issues. Rather than assume that a prescribed definition of poverty be applied, questions which need to be addressed are: What is poverty? Whose values, traditions, and structures should be used as a gauge for measuring poverty?

It appears that as the centralization and standardization of software production grows, instructional units will not address sensitive social issues. Growing uniformity of, for example, computer courseware may reduce the pool of cultural diversity and ethnic pluralism in a country. The extent to which software is developed upon a lowest common denominator of cultural differentiation may be determined by economic factors such as profit and market. Perspectives reflecting the majority culture are likely to be included in educational software. For example, courseware may become based on mainstream society's assumptions concerning such relevant features as responsibility, education, religion, career, family future, etc. Continuous emphasis on mainstream society's perspectives could influence distant rural students to adopt an imposed perspective on life and to reject traditional values and perhaps even their heritage.

On an international level, most microcomputer software is conceptualized and developed in the United States. When Canadians purchase software for their American hardware, in all likelihood they have to import it. This may result in an American point of view prevailing within the software. For example, the microcomputer package titled "George Earl's Readings in Literature" is designed to help students memorize a variety of readings. The British Columbia Ministry of Education evaluated this package and outlined, among other weaknesses, that the program had a great emphasis on American historical and political content. Similarly, the software package "Computorials: Evaluation Unit," intended for high school English, was evaluated as containing too much American jargon and bias.

Already in 1977, UNESCO recognized the inherent danger regarding cultural identity and software. Consequently, it developed Article VII of the "Declaration of Guiding Principles for the Use of Satellite Broadcasting for the Free Flow of Information, the Spread of Education, and Greater Cultural Exchange." The article states:

Cultural programs, while promoting the enrichment of
all cultures, should respect the distinctive character,
the value and the dignity of each, and the right of all
countries and peoples to preserve their cultures as part
of the common heritage of mankind. (Mowlana, 1977,
p. 124)

Ethics

The perspective on knowledge underlying software
packages includes a value stance. If students are required to use a
software program, they may become so structured by the format of
the program that they cannot apply their own value positions. For
example, a senior secondary Physics microcomputer software
package titled "Three Mile Island" deals with the controversial
issue of nuclear energy. This topic may be analyzed according to
values underlying environmental, cultural, industrial, and
political points of view. Yet, this program is designed for students
to monitor the parts of the reactor, receive information on their
condition, and make decisions regarding changes necessary to
supply a stated demand for electricity at a given cost (British
Columbia Ministry of Education, 1982). As such, students are not
provided the opportunity to reason through Three Mile Island or
nuclear energy from their value positions. This may create some
tension within the students. Although some students may be
committed to values on nuclear energies based on an
environmental perspective, to successfully complete the program,
the students may have to give priority to values underlying the
industrial perspective. The acceptance of values underlying a
program may be considered an important step toward adaptation.
Certain values assumed in a software package may become
acknowledged as legitimate societal values.

One of the predominant values which is considered
legitimate is competition. Although students may learn through
self-exploration or consensus, many microcomputer software
programs are based on competition. For example, the IBM
microcomputer software package titled "Arithmetic Set 1" is based
on a competitive game format whereby students compete against
the computer, or two students compete against each other. This

design may create conflict for individuals who believe in values of cooperation.

The possibility of homogenized values is another prominent issue which requires some clarification. Homogenization means forcing values considered out of the mainstream into a middle-of-the-road position. For example, in the QUBE interactive television trials, whenever a controversial issue such as homosexuality was presented to the students, they could answer questions through predefined multiple-choice responses, most of which were not sensitive to people's deeply felt values (Wicklein, 1979). Consequently, the thrust of the computerized interactive program reflected mediated values included in the five defined responses. Similarly, many present-day microcomputer software programs reflect standard instructional designs with predefined variations. Any choice by students to move out of the variations and select a process based on a different value stance is limited.

Procedure for Applying the Critical Framework

The research process which should be activated with the critical framework is content analysis. This involves a systematic analysis of software programs according to the sociological categories previously described. Each category should entail a number of questions which can be applied to the software so that a description of hidden assumptions can be surfaced. The following questions may serve as examples:

1. Language Usage
   (a) What common-sense metaphors are found in the software to describe a technical process?
   (b) Why are these metaphors used?
2. Knowledge
   (a) What knowledge is selected and neglected?
   (b) How is the selected knowledge intended to be used by students?
3. Ideology
   (a) What basic perspective on the knowledge underlies the software's knowledge content and student activities?

        (b) What alternative perspectives can be considered?

        (c) Is the program's basic perspective ethically justifiable?

4.   Profit

        (a) To what extent is a software package marketed according to ideas of efficiency, cost-effectiveness, etc.?

        (b) Is the software linked to the purchase of more software for the accomplishment of objectives?

5.   Culture

        (a) What cultural tastes or attitudes are reflected in the software?

        (b) How do these tastes and/or attitudes relate to the program user?

6.   Ethics

        (a) What teaching structures are found in the software that are based on a basic value stance?

        (b) What are the basic values underlying activities and content?

        (c) How do these values interface with the values held by a community of users?

These questions can be modified and/or expanded according to the type of software evaluated, and the purpose of the evaluation. As the questions stand, they direct the analyst to the foundation upon which software was developed.

Data Gathering Implications

The evaluator can use the critical framework approach to systematically analyze software programs and extract their implicit assumptions. If a trend emerges which merits attention, the data should be made public so that an optimum number of educators can begin to take seriously the process of analysis. On an individual basis, teachers should be encouraged to reflect upon their principles of operation, and administrators should be provided with a new set of lenses through which to view technology, education, and the administrative role.

Conclusion

Evaluators have a moral responsibility to judge a program as thoroughly as possible. With the rapid communications and information surge, evaluators need to engage in critical analysis so that administrators become aware of the wider consequences of their selection of hardware and software. By providing educators a description of hidden assumptions which influence electronic programming, they can make better informed judgments regarding the educational quality of software. Ultimately, this will equip educators to become active agents rather than passive bystanders of educational change.

REFERENCES

Apple, M. *Ideology and curriculum.* London: Routledge and Kegan Paul, 1979.

Aristotle. *Poetics.* Englewood Cliffs, NJ: Prentice-Hall, 1968.

Axell, R. H., and Walker, R. Educational software for the PC. *P.C. Magazine,* December 1982.

Barrett, W. *The illusion of technique.* Garden City, NY: Anchor books, 1978.

Berger, P., and Luckmann, T. *Social construction of reality.* Garden City, NY: Doubleday Co., 1966.

British Columbia Ministry of Education. *Evaluations: Microware.* Vancouver, BC: Provincial Educational Media Center, 1982.

Callihoe, N. A. Rationale for compensatory education in public schools of the Province of Alberta. Unpublished paper for the Alberta Department of Education, Edmonton, Alberta, 1982.

Davison, W. P. On the effects of communication. *Public Opinion Quarterly,* 1959, 23.

Dede, C. Educational, social and ethical implications of technological innovation. *Programmed Learning and Educational Technology,* November 1981.

Ellul, J. *The technological society.* New York: Vintage Books, 1964.

Fagothey, A. *Right and reason.* St. Louis: C. V. Mosby Co., 1976.

Freire, P. *Pedagogy of the oppressed.* New York: Seabury Press, 1974.

Ghatala, M. H. Role of technology in correspondence education. *The Proceedings* of the Ninth World Conference of the International Council on Correspondence Education, 1972.

Gleason, G. Microcomputers in education. The state of the art. *Educational Technology*, March 1981, 7-18.

Gurevitch, H., and Roberts, C. *Issues in the study of mass communication and society.* London: Open University Press, 1978.

Hall, S. The hinterland of science: Ideology and the sociology of knowledge, working papers in cultural studies no. 10, Great Britain, 1977.

Heidegger, M. *The question concerning technology.* New York: Harper Colophon, 1977.

Hetzler, S. A. *Technological growth and social change: Achieving modernization.* London: Routledge and Kegan Paul, 1969.

IBM, Canada. Education course catalogue volume 1-10. Don Mills, Ontario: IBM, 1982.

Innis, H. *The bias of communication.* Toronto: University of Toronto Press, 1951.

Laroque, E. *Defeathering the Indian.* Agincourt, Ontario: Book Society of Canada, 1975.

Leshan, L., and Morgenau, H. *Einstein's space and Van Gogh's sky: Physical reality and beyond.* New York: Macmillan Publishing Company, 1982.

Mannheim, M. *Ideology and utopia.* New York: Harcourt, Brace, and World, 1936.

Moore, B. The society in which we lead. Paper presented at the Fall Forum of the Council for Leadership in Education. Vancouver, B.C., April 1, 1981.

Mowlana, H. Political and social implications of communications satellite applications in developed and developing countries. In J. Pelton and M. Snow (Eds.), *Economic and policy problems in satellite communications.* New York: Praeger Publishers, Inc., 1977.

Rothe, J. P. A critical look at communications technology and distance education. *Journal of Distance Education* (in press).

Ruggles, R., Anderson, J., Blackmore, D. E., Lafleur, C., Rothe, J. P., and Taerum, T. *Learning at a distance and the new technology.* Vancouver, BC: Educational Research Institute of British Columbia, 1982.

Turbayne, C. M. *The myth of metaphor.* London: Yale, 1962.

Werner, W. *Evaluation: Sense making of school programs.* Edmonton: Department of Secondary Education, University of Alberta, 1978.

Wicklein, J. Wired city, USA. *Atlantic Monthly*, February 1979, 243(2).

Young, M. (Ed.) *Knowledge and control.* London: Collier-Macmillan, 1971.

Young, M., Peraton, H., Jenkins, J., and Dodds, T. *Distance education for the third world.* London: Routledge and Kegan Paul, 1980.

21

The Technological World-View and the Responsible Use of Computers in the Classroom*

John W. Murphy
Sociology
University of Miami

and John T. Pardeck
Social Work
Southeast Missouri State University

In this paper it is argued that technology does not merely represent a set of devices that teachers may choose to use, but more importantly advances a world-view that shapes social existence. The image of social life that technology conveys is not currently receiving serious consideration from those who are rushing headlong to incorporate computers into the classroom. As a result, the possible deleterious consequences of a technological education are not being exposed. This paper attempts to correct this deficiency by addressing the philosophy of technology and its impact on education.

Presently technology is proliferating throughout the United States at an unprecedented rate. In particular, the computer has made its way into the home, farm, and factory, not to mention the classroom. Great claims are made by those who favor this increase in computerization, as the particular form of technology is thought to be capable of solving many of our social problems. However, the introduction of this technology into the classroom may have adverse effects which can be anticipated and possibly averted, yet will most likely be overlooked until problems

---

* Reprinted with permission from *Journal of Education, 167*(2), copyright © Journal of Education, 1985.

surface.   This is the case for the following reason: the philosophical world-view of technology is rarely given serious attention and therefore its social impact is obscured. And without an examination of the world-view which accompanies technology, the images of the classroom, learning, and students which are advanced by technological rationality may go undetected.

Therefore, the aim of this paper is to detail the philosophical principles of modern technology so that its *raison d'être* is revealed. Specifically, we argue that technology portrays social existence quite negatively, and may actually stifle the critical and creative style of learning that most educators extol. Moreover, this is not simply a matter of careless pedagogical procedures, but, more importantly, stems from philosophical principles that underlie modern technology. Mere technological changes designed to humanize the use of computers by educators may exacerbate, instead of ameliorate, an unpleasant situation in the classroom.

The Technological World-View

The central difficulty with technology is that it denies the "life-world" from which it originates. As Merleau-Ponty (1964a) states, the life-world (Lebenswelt) is the domain filled by "living history and the spoken word," and therefore is the source of all social meaning. Specifically, the life-world is the living presence to which all persons adhere prior to Cartesian distinctions—that is, the world inscribed by human praxis (Merleau-Ponty, 1964b). This living world, as Schutz and Luckmann (1973) state, embodies the "meaning-strata which transforms natural things into cultural objects, human bodies into fellow-men, and the movements of fellow-men into acts, gestures, and communication" (p. 5).

Of key importance is that the world is not objective in the Cartesian sense, but exists for someone. All knowledge, stated simply, is mediated by the constitutive activity of human experience, and thus represents neither crudely realistic events nor a Kantian "in-itself." The world's meaning is a social product, as human action is at the heart of all phenomena.

As should be immediately noted, when the world is envisioned to be a life-world the significance of human action cannot be diminished, as in theories which maintain that phenomena have a self-same, or objective, identity, immune to the influence of human intentions. When conceived objectively, a phenomenon's identity is not incumbent upon human action, and subsequently individuals are unable to treat it creatively. Yet it is precisely this creative tendency that technology aims to suppress.

What are the central tenets of the technological world-view? Modern writers have described them as follows (Lenk, 1973). First, technology materializes existence, as the world is conceived to be matter, pure extension, and thus an objective thing. Second, mathematics is the language of technology, which means that a rational calculus is employed to conceptualize the world. Third, the logic of matter is assumed to govern individual behavior and social order. And fourth, both individuals and society are portrayed as part of an objective order which is thoroughly asocial.

As a consequence of these traits, Ihde (1979) declares that technology offers a style of social imagery which he calls "instrumental realism." Technology, he suggests, establishes its own form of reason for assessing the world. This technological rationality, as it is sometimes called, is typically thought to represent the paragon of reason, because it is ostensibly divorced from the passion indigenous to human action. Because this modality of reason is assumed to represent objective standards it claims to furnish the most reliable method available for making judgments. Technology, in this sense, defines the world in such a way that a precise and persistent relationship is established among its parts. As Mumford (1963) remarks, this allows phenomena to be controlled in a manner which is impossible when the so-called human element is not checked. With the human side of life rendered ancillary to technical reason, technology becomes an impregnable force. It is in this respect that Ellul (1964) refers to persons as enslaved to modern technology, as its logic becomes synonymous with reason.

When technological thinking comes to dominate the social scene, certain problems begin to appear. Particularly significant is that human cognition, action, and learning begin to assume a technological hue. Human existence becomes technologized, thereby creating the illusion that technology is autonomous or essentially unrelated to the contingencies which are presumed to be indigenous to human action. Because technology instills reason where it is presumed to be missing, humans by definition are enslaved by this rationality.

Accordingly, Heidegger (1967, pp. 14-15) says that technology "sets upon nature" and "makes 'unreasonable demand(s)' on both nature and man." Technology can do this, he contends, because it is not treated as a modality of human existence. Technology established itself as what Marcuse (1964) calls a "veil" that separates human action from the world; or, as Habermas (1978) states, it advances principles that demand universal recognition, and therefore has a status identical to "ideology." Stated simply, technology "de-animates" social life, as it displaces human action by inserting its own form of rationality at the center of existence (Ihde, 1982). This does not mean, as some critics suggest, that individuals are dehumanized by technology merely because they must work with machines, but more importantly because the logic of technology is assumed to be objective, ahistorical, and, thus, undaunted by existential contingencies (Caldwell, 1981).

What this means is that a functional image of social existence is promoted, as exemplified by the work of Talcott Parsons. According to his technological or cybernetic rendition of the social world, the only knowledge that can unite society exists objectively. Consequently, individuals must imagine themselves to be subordinate to the source of order and adjust to its demands, since they are only able to supply the energy required to enliven the social system and cannot give it direction (Parsons, 1966).

When the world is conceived in this way, the "history of transcendental consciousness [is] no more than the residue of the history of technology" (Habermas, 1971). Since human action merely supports an imperious technological system, behavior is considered worthwhile only when this function is adequately performed. Stated otherwise, the goal of human action is the maintenance of the social system and not liberation or self-determination. Marcuse (1964) argues that this results in persons living in a "one-dimensional" world, where only the dominant values and norms are treated as legitimate and all opposition to them is eviscerated. Therefore, the only behavior that is evaluated positively is that which acquiesces to authority and unquestioningly adopts traditional ways of acting.

In short, the obfuscation of the life-world culminates in an externalized locus of social order and the belief that persons are living in a society that exists *sui generis*. Usually this is referred to as social ontological realism, as the system is the only thing that is considered to be real and everything else is assumed to be derived from it. This image of existence requires that the social system be understood to supply individuals with their identity, and therefore they are forever indebted to this source for their meaning (Stark, 1963).

Both Marxists and functionalists, in contending that education serves to sustain the status quo, generally suggest that this process is overtly coercive and manipulative. The world-view advanced by technology, however, may unobtrusively promote an identical policy. Thus, both radicals and conservatives may want to take note of how technology accomplishes this ignoble feat.

Technology and Learning

Atomization. Technology tends to atomize or fragment the learning process, thus resulting in what Sartre (1977) calls "serialization." Because persons must adjust themselves to a mechanical learning device, closely monitor its instructions, follow its commands, and supply appropriate responses at the right time, a state of isomorphism is reached whereby a student's intentions are subsumed by the directives that are issued. This means that the process is ahistorical, since an inanimate object establishes the framework (Lebensraum) for all learning.

Accordingly, as Straus (1963) writes, no "play space" is present between an instrument's instructions and a student's response, but instead all choices are made ex post facto, or after they are legitimized by a machine and cognitively imprinted. This results in a style of technological "forced feeding." And when learning is understood in this manner, the dynamism that is possible in a classroom can never be realized. For example, knowledge cannot be challenged, expanded, and its symbolic nature revealed, as when information is bandied about in a classroom. Particularly, students may miss the importance of interpretation in acquiring knowledge and the role this activity plays in shaping society. For as Sartre (1977) points out, when learning is serialized then brute matter, as opposed to praxis, mediates human relations, leaving persons alone to face what seems to be an intractable reality.

Monological discourse. Technological learning relies on discourse that is thoroughly monological. Communication is monological when it:

> attributes the intersubjectivity of meaning, that is the
> mutual sharing of identical meanings to the fact that
> sender and receiver—each an entity for itself—are
> previously equipped with the same program.
> (Habermas, 1970, p. 131)

Because information proceeds from a single sender to a receiver without the meaning of these transmissions being questioned, everyone is assumed to operate according to universal (ahistorical) principles of logic, rationality, and speech. To use Perelman's (1979) well-known phrase, technological education treats students as if they are members of a "universal audience" and use an identical cognitive style.

Technological pedagogy epitomizes monological discourse. For instance, information is presented by an agent which is not susceptible to critique or interrogation, and thus knowledge can only be recorded and not actively analyzed. Additionally, all transmissions are structured according to the requirements of Aristotelian logic, as all answers to questions are presented as binary alternatives. Although this method of communication eliminates ambiguity from the process of identifying a correct answer, the need for persons to learn how to classify and generalize—in other words to think—is systematically reduced. *A priori* categories are merely mastered, and data placed into them, without students understanding how or why a particular classificatory scheme is used. Consequently, students are unable to cope with situations where the standard cognitive categories do not apply. They have not learned how to improvise, or interpret information in an effective manner, as this requires an active mind.

Instrumental learning. Technology promotes what Horkheimer (1974) calls "instrumental learning." The general aims of computerized learning are to process information rapidly, identify relationships, and reduce a person's response time. Although information passes before one's eyes quickly, as in video games and speed reading, little else is accomplished. All that is fostered is a type of "means-end" rationality, whereby students learn to follow premises to their logical conclusions as expeditiously as possible. Accordingly, it is assumed that a single system of logic underpins all rational thinking, and that educated persons must know its laws. Quickness of response is considered to be a valid index for measuring learning, as efficiency and accuracy are thought to be at the heart of intelligent behavior. Gifted persons, moreover, are believed to be able to master the principles of reason faster than those who are less talented.

Clearly, this style of cognition is advantageous in a modern bureaucratic society like our own (Weber, 1947). A bureaucratic society is characterized by increasing rationality, as rules become more formal and legalistic and social and political distinctions become more detailed. If persons are to function adequately, cognitive complexity must be fostered, yet there are drawbacks to this type of thinking. Most important, learning in this system is discursive and not critical, primarily because the discovery of detail is given the highest priority. This results in mental acuity and not inventiveness, since the mind is not trained to transcend the data that are presented. And without this ability, critical insight, imagination, and creativity are impossible.

Inhibiting of inquiry. When knowledge is conveyed technologically it is presented as a set of fully developed "either/or" options that are understood through repetition. Learning is assumed to have occurred when students are able to apply this logic to concrete situations through problem-solving exercises. As a result, learning is made relevant because knowledge is put into practice. Nevertheless, this type of knowledge application may in fact inhibit rigorous inquiry.

This is the case for the following reasons. First, practice is solely a matter of reiteration and not reflection. Thus, knowledge is adopted and implemented without being thoroughly scrutinized. Second, personal or pragmatic motives do not determine the utility of knowledge. Instead, information is valued because of its clarity, reproducibility, and immediate social utility, as opposed to its thought-provoking character. And third, because the logic that is indigenous to technology is not subject to question, social existence is portrayed abstractly throughout the learning process. This results in reductionism, since any particular rendition of "reality" is given credence only if it conforms to the strictures imposed by technological rationality (Horkheimer, 1982). Therefore, life is dominated and rationalized by a specific logic, while social existence is explained but not necessarily understood. As a consequence of this approach to learning, students are taught not to investigate a situation, but to apply ready-made axioms that may seriously distort the actual intentions of persons. Clearly, this is a poor substitute for investigative integrity.

The marginalization of morality. And finally, technological pedagogy offers an image of social order that is amoral (Apel, 1979), because technology portrays social life as if it were objective and consisted of a fixed set of behavioral and cognitive options. The purpose of education, accordingly, is to acquaint students with these norms so that they become socially competent. Although it is certainly not the aim of educators to curtail divergent thinking through their use of technology, independent thought is not fostered when information is divorced from human action. If persons are not conceived to be self-directed and able to recognize themselves in their actions, the idea of social morality cannot be sustained (Dewey, 1916). Apel (1979) explains how morality is eliminated as a consequence of technology reducing the significance of interpretation.

Because technology "rationalizes" learning, thereby eliminating interpretation from education, social fragmentation is promoted. This happens because knowledge is not viewed to be a collective product but rather is assumed to be individually generated. Because technology does not allow knowledge acquisition to be a "purposive-rational activity," a matter of decision and interpretation, one person alone, involved in a "subject-object" relationship to facts, is believed to be able to discover truth (Apel, 1979). However, when learning is understood to be a thoroughly interpretive activity, and not merely based on perceptual or logical precision, the issue of intersubjective validity is raised. That is, interpretation presupposes the existence of a variety of interpretations, a community of interpreters, the need to recognize all interpretations, since none by definition is absolute. A procedure for merging these interpretations into a common body of knowledge is required. In short, interpretive learning recognizes both self and other as central to obtaining knowledge, as opposed to treating education as an asocial process which stresses the collection of facts.

The Responsible Use of Technology

As might be expected, the plans that are usually proposed to humanize the use of educational technology are preponderately structural (Bjorn-Anderson & Rasmussen, 1980). Attention has been directed to redesigning classrooms in order to integrate technology smoothly into the everyday affairs of both students and faculty members. For example, it has been suggested that curriculum and environmental fragmentation can be corrected by transforming traditional classrooms into seminar rooms or laboratories which facilitate interaction among students and teachers (Kurland, 1968). Some planners argue that opportunities should be provided regularly for students to share their ideas, while they each pursue their own particular program of learning (Brabner, 1970). Most recently this issue of humanizing technology has been raised in terms of establishing an appropriate interface between computers and humans, mostly a logistical undertaking aimed at enabling students to "talk" effectively with computers (Goldes, 1983).

For the most part, these strategies treat technology as a tool that can be humanized if its rules of operation are mastered. What has to be done, accordingly, is to create a setting in which this information can be disseminated to all users. Once a proper environment is furnished, educators assume that a commodious relationship will flourish between technology and those who use it. What this scenario overlooks, however, is that technology is not a tool which can be assimilated readily into the classroom by altering the environment. Technology is not passive, but instead promulgates a world-view which shapes a society's identity. In fact, persons may begin to define themselves and their culture technologically, and when this occurs the usual structural approaches to humanizing technology are ineffective.

Inevitably, an autonomous technology which reduces the importance of human action in learning will severely disrupt and limit the learning process. This is not to say that educators must abandon the use of technology, but it does mean that a responsible rendition must be developed. A human ground for technology must be specified which prevents technological rationality from appearing to be autonomous and the nemesis of praxis. Technology, in other words, must be reintegrated into the human condition and not simply assimilated into the environment of a classroom.

Most important when establishing this new ground for technology is to recognize that the world is neither subjective nor objective, but subtends this Cartesian differentiation. Technological rationality employs the Cartesian distinction and thus projects an image of an objective world that is allowed to control individual behavior. Yet if technology is ever to be responsible to its creators it cannot be perceived as immune to existential claims. Therefore, technology must also be understood to emanate from what Merleau-Ponty (1968) calls the "Chiasm," the intertwining of objectivity and subjectivity that is central to human action. Education must no longer be oriented in terms of those ancient maxims which claim to provide access to ideal or timeless truth. People must not be "led out" of the world as a result of their education, but only out of darkness. In other words, education should return persons to the world, as opposed to starting them on a journey which culminates in their denying their existence.

This world, however, is not the mundane world which students must try to mollify. Rather, this is the world of direct experience, and existential claim, which is the only type of world that individuals can call their own. The world that educators must resurrect, stated simply, is the "lived-world," the pre-objective world that is sustained by human praxis. Education must be understood to be an interpretive process which emphasizes the mystery of inquiry instead of the acquisition of fixed principles. Most important is that technology is implicated in the opacity of the lived-world, and accordingly cannot claim to have a seignorial status above the melange of truths that compete for dominance in everyday life.

When understood as autonomous, technology can only provide an interpretation of knowledge, specifically the rendition which is consistent with its world-view. But when technology is understood to emerge from the lived-world, its image is distinctly altered. It can no longer be viewed as an autonomous entity that can justifiably shape human actions. Human action, instead, sustains technology, and consequently, technological rationality represents merely another modality of praxis, not the ultimate measure of knowledge. Subtending the technological world-view is the human ability to challenge any picture of reality presented; therefore, technology cannot legitimately claim to dictate knowledge.

If we make this theoretical shift, technology assumes what Marcuse (1978) refers to as an "aesthetic" identity. Technology does not supply its own parameters for identifying information; rather, it rests on a base of human action and owes its significance or meaning to this expressive human dimension. With this aesthetic backdrop, technology's attempt to deanimate social existence is sharply curtailed. Only then can technology be used critically, as a facilitator of human imagination, rather than assuming control of learning.

Socratic Questions in the High-Tech Age

Merely adding more technology to an already abstract teaching strategy will not make education more socially responsible. In order to foster the humanization of technology, questions that pertain to the human ground of technology must be addressed. The issues that have always concerned educators are not technological, but those of lived existence, such as the meaning of life, the nature of social relationships, commitment, the need for community, and the value of ethical behavior (Weizenbaum, 1976).

In fact, philosophers have characteristically argued that discussions about these aspects of life have saved humans from barbarism. Although technological rationality may be important in shaping the modern view of pedagogy, these Socratic issues remain at the heart of education. Education, therefore, can never be concerned solely with the acquisition of techniques, because technology is sustained by principles which are much more fundamental than technological rationality. Accordingly, educators must never abdicate their responsibility to raise more than technical questions in the classroom, even though the technological ethic may devalue this type of study.

This shift toward understanding technology to be a social form of reasoning has significant implications for educational policy. First, humanizing technology should not be limited to making logistical adjustments to its presence in the classroom. Second, technology should not be discussed merely in terms of mastering techniques, but more importantly in its relationship to human destiny. Third, the implementation of technology must be understood as replete with social, ethical, and political consequences, in addition to technical difficulties. And fourth, technology should not be allowed to overshadow the Socratic questions which pertain to self-knowledge, as often occurs when persons are enamored of the application of technological rationality.

Anyone who has worked with students recently will recognize that these recommendations post a significant challenge to educators. Students seem to find the ethical, political, and social implications of technology bothersome, as they want to move ahead undaunted with its application. Many programs have been inaugurated which attempt to combine technological training with the arts, so as to provide students with an enlightened perspective on technology. Yet for the most part they have been unsuccessful, primarily because technology is thought to be scientific and conveying truth, while the arts offer opinion. Before the humanization of technology can be taken seriously its world-view must be exposed, as this philosophy is cajoling persons into indifference about their humanity. In this way, technology will be placed in the service of humanity and humanized. It must be remembered that without this philosophical shift technology can never be brought under human control. And as should be noted, merely adding more technology to an already abstract teaching strategy will not make technological education socially responsible. Educators must understand that if the world-view of technology is not examined seriously, technological rationality may promote apathy on the part of students by encouraging them to take a nonreflective attitude toward society. And because this conception of education is unconscionable to most teachers, we must take care not to foster inadvertently this style of learning through our use of technology in the classroom.

REFERENCES

Apel, K. O. (1979). The common presuppositions of hermeneutics and ethics: Types of rationality beyond science and technology. In J. Sallis (Ed.), *Studies in phenomenology and the human sciences* (pp. 35-55). Atlantic Highlands, NJ: Humanities Press.

Ballard, E. G. (1981). Man or technology: Which is to rule? In S. Skousgaard (Ed.), *Phenomenology and the understanding of human destiny* (pp. 3-19). Washington, DC: University Press of America.

Bjorn-Anderson, N., & Rasmussen, L. B. (1980). Sociological implications of computer systems. In H. T. Smith and T. R. Green (Eds.), *Human interaction with computers* (pp. 57-123). London: Academic Press.

Brabner, G. (1970). *The decline of pedagocentricity. Educational Technology,* 10(11), 11-18.

Caldwell, R. (1981). Computers and curriculum promises and problems. In Institute for Educational Leadership (Ed.), *Technology and education* (pp. 257-270). Washington, DC: Institute for Educational Leadership.

Dewey, J. (1916). *Democracy and education.* New York: Macmillan.

Ellus, J. (1964). *The technological society.* New York: Random House.

Goldes, H. J. (1983). Designing the human-computer interface. *Educational Technology*, 23(10), 9-15.

Habermas, J. (1970). Toward a theory of communicative competence. In H. P. Dreitzel (Ed.), *Recent sociology No. 2* (pp. 114-148). New York: Macmillan.

Habermas, J. (1971). *Knowledge and human interests.* Boston: Beacon Press.

Habermas, J. (1978). *Problems of legitimacy in late capitalism.* In P. Connerton (Ed.), Critical sociology (pp. 363-387). New York: Penguin Books.

Heidegger, M. (1967). *Vortrage und aufsatze* [Lectures and Essays]. Teil Pfulligen: Verlag Gunther Neske.

Horkheimer, M. (1974). *Critique of instrumental reason.* New York: Seabury Press.

Horkheimer, M. (1982). *Critical theory.* New York: Continuum Publishing.

Ihde, D. (1979). *Technics and praxis.* Dordrecht: D. Reidel.

Ihde, D. (1982). The historical-ontological priority of technology over science. Paper presented at the International Conference on Philosophy and Science in Phenomenological Perspective, Buffalo, NY.

Kurland, N. D. (1968). The impact of technology on education. *Educational Technology*, 8(20), 12-15.

Lenk, H. (1973). *Technokratie als ideologie* [Technology as Ideology]. Stuttgart: Verlag W. Kohlhammer.

Marcuse, H. (1964). *One-dimensional man.* Boston: Beacon Press.

Marcuse, H. (1968). *The aesthetic dimension.* Boston: Beacon Press.

Merleau-Ponty, M. (1964a). *Signs.* Evanston: Northwestern University Press.

Merleau-Ponty, M. (1964b). *Sense and non-sense.* Evanston: Northwestern University Press.

Merleau-Ponty, M. (1968). *The visible and the invisible.* Evanston: Northwestern University Press.

Mumford, L. (1963). *Technics and civilization.* New York: Harcourt, Brace and World.

Parsons, T. (1966). *Societies: Evolutionary and comparative.* Englewood Cliffs, NJ: Prentice-Hall.

Perelman, C. (1979). *The new rhetoric and the humanities.* Dordrecht: D. Reidel.

Sartre, J. P. (1977). *Life/situations.* New York: Pantheon Books.

Schutz, A., & Luckmann, T. (1973). *The structures of the life-world.* Evanston: Northwestern University Press.

Stark, W. (1963). *The fundamental forms of social thought.* New York: Fordham University Press.

Straus, E. (1963). *The primary world of the senses.* New York: The Free Press.

Weber, M. (1947). *Social and economic organization.* New York: Macmillan.

Weizenbaum, J. (1976). *Computer power and human reason.* New York: W. H. Freeman.

Section 5

Foundations

✳❋✳❋✳

22

A Process for Looking At and Understanding*

Edmund B. Feldman
Art Education
The University of Georgia

Just seeing films and paintings and buildings is not enough. People want to talk about what they have seen. They want to compare their likes and dislikes. Talking about a work of art with friends frequently leads to the discovery of something that was missed. Often, we want to know if we are getting the same message as others. Or we want to persuade someone to agree with our opinion about a work of art. But whatever the reason for talking about art, everyone does it in order to share experiences.

Art criticism can be defined as talk—spoken or written—about art. It is not necessarily negative or destructive talk. It can include praise, comparison, description, and explanation as well as disapproval. Naturally, some people are better critics than others. They can see more in art than others can see, and so their reports about it are more interesting. In fact, a good critic's report about a work of art can add a great deal to your enjoyment of it. He can help you to see things you would not have seen alone. But eventually, you must learn to be a good critic yourself so that you do not become too dependent on "official" opinions. One mark of an educated person is the ability to recognize and evaluate excellence independently. This ability, however, does not come from memorizing lists of so-called masterpieces. It comes from developing sound procedures for analyzing and interpreting art and then applying those procedures as well as you can. This chapter, therefore, will be devoted to explaining some techniques or procedures that you can use to develop your ability as a critic.

---

*Reprinted with permission from *Becoming Human Through Art,* Chapter 12, copyright © Prentice Hall, 1970.

Attending To What We See: Description

There are two ways to draw attention to a work of art you are going to criticize: the first is to identify the work; the second is to describe it. I prefer to emphasize description because that immediately involves us in using our eyes and minds to understand what we are looking at. There are four stages of criticism—description, analysis, interpretation and evaluation—and when they have been completed, the viewer will have a critical identification of the work. This identification is very valuable from an educational standpoint. But there is also the standard, scholarly identification which the critic should know: the title of the work, the artist who made it, the date when it was created, the place where it was made, and, if possible, the medium or materials it was made of. Not all of this information may be known with certainty. In that case, the critic proceeds on the basis of the facts he does have. Usually, art historians or archaeologists have identified a work of art as accurately as they can and the critic can rely on their best judgment. A disagreement among historians about the date of a work, or about who created it, should not seriously affect a critic's interpretation, however. The critic should proceed with the help of the facts that scholars are able to bring out. That is, knowing the country an artist lived in or the period in which he worked can give the critic some clues about the original purpose or use of the art object. Nevertheless, as critics we are mainly interested in the present meaning and purpose of a work of art. We want to know how it affects our lives and our world outlook right now. The historical function of a work of art is useful to us, as critics, only when it points to significant features of life as it is now understood and as we feel it must now be lived.

The most common mistake made in art criticism is jumping to conclusions—deciding too quickly about the value or meaning of what is seen. We have to give ourselves time to see as much as can be seen in a work and then we can decide what it means and is worth. You get this time by describing what you see, that is, by listing what the art object seems to be made of. Making a list, or an inventory, does two things: it slows you down, and it forces you to notice things you might have overlooked. This process of listing is description.

The words you use in description are like pointers; they are not intended to be the exact equivalents of what you see. Instead they draw attention, or point to, something worth seeing. They force you to pause in your race to a conclusion and they help you to notice or attend to inconspicuous details of the art object. A description also gives the critic a chance to get the agreement of a group of people about what they are looking at. One of the reasons why the public may disagree with a critic's judgment is that they have not been looking at the same work of art; they are really noticing different features of the same art object. By describing what he sees, the critic gets his audience or public to examine the same work that he plans to judge. Later on, when he tries to form an interpretation, he can be reasonably sure that he is talking about something his audience has really observed.

In some descriptions, you can get agreement about the names of what you see. That is, you can say that a picture shows a man, a tree, a lake, grass, children, animals, sky, and so on. But sometimes, it may not be clear whether you are looking at men, for example, or women. The forms may be too indistinct to enable you to make that decision. In such a case, you should say you see some people. Your objective is to describe only what you are reasonably sure of. Perhaps other details will enable you to decide, later on, whether you see men or women, children or adults. Right now, during the stage of description, you are more interested in a complete and neutral inventory than in certainty and precision. We would prefer to be vague about some detail rather than take the chance of making an error that might throw off the final interpretation.

Traditional works of art show many recognizable persons and objects—making the job of description easier. (But even recognizable persons and objects may present problems if they are part of a complex system of symbols, as in medieval art. In that case, it is necessary to be a student of iconology in order to know the original meaning and function of the work.) Contemporary abstract and nonobjective works rarely show us things that have common or proper names, so we have to describe the shapes, colors, spaces, and volumes we see. Remember that the purposes of a description are to point out what can be seen (regardless of names) and to slow down the viewer's tendency to form conclusions too quickly. Therefore, the critic has to adjust his language to the level of what he sees: the more abstract the forms, the more general the words he uses to describe them. Fortunately, we have words that call attention to the specific properties of very general things—words like vertical, round, oval, smooth, dark, bright, square, horizontal, and so on. As these adjectives are combined and attached to general nouns like shape, space, and volume, we add precision to our description of a work or art without judging or interpreting it too early.

Another phase of description is technical. That is, the critic tries to describe the way the art object seems to have been made. He discusses the way the paint was brushed on, the kind of tools or manipulation used to create a sculptural surface, the way a building's wall was erected and supported. Naturally, the critic's own experience as an artist or as a person who has studied artistic methods will be very useful in technical description. Technique is important for criticism because it is just as expressive as the shapes and forms we see.

Describing a work of art can be done publicly, just by telling a group of people what you see; or it can be done privately, by telling yourself what is there. But the important feature of a good description is its neutrality. That is, your list or inventory contains only the things other people would agree are there. A description does not have any conclusions about the excellence or the meaning of what you see. It is an impartial inventory.

In order to be impartial or neutral, you have to watch your language, avoiding loaded words or expressions that reveal feelings and preferences. Assume that you are going to be challenged whenever you use adjectives that might suggest your point of view—words like strong, beautiful, harmonious, weak, ugly, disorderly, funny-looking, and so on. Instead use words like straight, curved, small, large, rough, smooth, light, dark. You can use the names of colors in description, too, because colors are neutral until judged in relation to surrounding shapes, sizes, textures, and other colors. Of course, the word "red" may not be an exact description of the particular color you see; it is just a way of saying that a certain area is more like red than some other color. A viewer is affected by the way something seems to be made as well as by what it is; he imaginatively repeats the operations the artist carried out, especially if the artist employs a style that does not cover up or conceal his technique. Your ability as a critic will obviously be increased if you study artistic processes and procedures. You can get more enjoyment out of a film, for example, if you can detect the director's control of acting style, lighting, composition, cutting, camera angles, focus, fadeouts, montage, and so on. It is a mistake to believe that art and technique are separate. One way you can discover ideas in a work of art is by studying the technique that created the art object in the first place.

Observing the Behavior of What We See: Analysis

In the first stage of art criticism we named the things we saw. We tried to make a complete list of the objects and forms everyone would agree are visible in a work of art. Now we must go one step further and try to describe the relationships among the things we see. This whole process is formal analysis.

In this stage we want to find out what the forms do to each other—how they affect and influence each other. Imagine two circles side by side, and two identical circles, one above the other. Although the forms are the same in each case, their relationships are different. One is a horizontal and the other is a vertical relationship. Obviously, these relationships have a different effect on the viewer. The way forms are located, then, is one of the things we try to notice in the formal analysis.

Size relationships are very important. We do not see shapes and objects in isolation, we see them in pairs, groups, or clusters. We notice the largest or the smallest shapes; or we notice whether the sizes are about the same. In any event, comparative size is significant because it gives us clues about importance (large shapes usually seem more important, they seem to have higher "rank" than small shapes). In addition, size is a clue to location in space if you are looking at a picture in which spatial depth is represented.

Shape relationships reveal a great deal, too. What happens when curved shapes are next to each other, or when they are next to square or pointed shapes? How do jagged shapes affect smooth ones? Shape also calls attention to the quality of an edge. There are hard and soft, even and uneven edges. You can study their combination in the same work of art and get valuable evidence for deciding what the total work of art means.

Color and textural relationships should also be described. You have to notice whether the colors of related shapes are similar to, or different from, each other; whether they vary slightly or contrast strongly. You will want to mention their value relationship—whether a color area is lighter or darker than a nearby area. Perhaps the colors are different while the values are the same. That observation may be useful later on when you try to interpret the entire work of art.

Textural and surface relationships are things we notice in everyday life. For example, when you go out on a rainy day, you can usually tell from looking at surfaces whether you are about to step in a puddle, walk on a wet but firm sidewalk, or possibly slip on a thin coat of mud. You can often tell whether a metal surface is dirty or clean, wet or dry, perfectly new or old and bruised, or even whether it is hot or cold. We make the same kind of observation when analyzing the surface qualities of a work of art. Once again, this type of observation helps us discover the emotional qualities as well as the ideas conveyed by the art object.

Somewhat more difficult than describing shape, size, color, and textural relations is analyzing space and volume relationships. In painting, we look for clues to the location of forms—not only on the picture plane, but also in depth, in the implied space that the artist creates by using perspective, size, color, or light-and-shadow relationships. We want to find out whether this implied space is indefinite, seemingly open and endless, or whether it has limits and is enclosed. It is important to know whether the painter's forms seem to rest on the surface, crowd around each other in shallow space, or move far back into the picture's depth. We also want to learn to see the shapes of the empty spaces—the so-called negative shapes—as well as the positive forms or volumes that constitute the art object.

For the artist or designer, negative space must be organized and controlled just as much as positive shapes and volumes. The way a sculptor, painter, or architect treats negative space may offer useful clues to the total meaning of his work, because an artist's space conception is often the controlling factor in his creative expression. He may not be aware of the way he thinks about space. Nevertheless, his space conception—one way or another—will be represented in his work. Consequently, a critic should look for signs of openness or density, clarity or obscurity, darkness or light, and flatness or depth in the over-all treatment of space.

When the description and formal analysis are completed, the critic has probably been able to describe most of the visible features of the art object. These two critical operations accomplish the following purposes:

1. They encourage as complete an examination of the object as it is possible for the viewer to make.
2. They slow down the viewer's tendency to jump to conclusions.
3. They help build skill in observation—a skill that is vital for understanding the visual arts as well as for general personal development.
4. They accumulate the visual facts that will form the basis for a critical interpretation.
5. For public criticism, they help establish a consensus about which features of the art object constitute the subject of interpretation and judgment.

Giving Meaning to Works of Art: Interpretation

This stage of art criticism is the most difficult, the most creative, and the most rewarding. It is the stage when you have to decide what all your earlier observations mean. Of course, your intelligence and sensitivity are needed; but especially important is courage. You must not be afraid to risk being wrong, that is, making an interpretation that does not fit the facts immediately. You can change or adjust your interpretation until it does fit the visual facts, so there is no harm in being wrong or wide of the mark at your first try. It would be bad art criticism only if you changed or ignored a great many facts to make them fit your interpretation. Just what is an interpretation and how do you go about making one?

A critical interpretation is a statement about a work of art that enables the visual observations we have made to fit together and make sense. In other words, what single, large idea or concept seems to sum up or unify all the separate traits of the work? Please notice that an interpretation does not describe the object (we have already done that); and it does not try to translate visual qualities into verbal combinations. We use words now to describe ideas—ideas that, in turn, explain the sensations and feelings we have in the presence of the art object. An interpretation might also be regarded as an explanation of a work of art.

Sometimes an interpretation is a statement of the problem that the work seems to be trying to solve. We pretend that the art object—like a person—has aims and purposes, that it "wants" or "tries" to reach certain objectives. The evidence we have been gathering in our description and analysis seems to point toward those objectives, and as critics we try to state what the objectives appear to be.

In describing the objective or goal of the work, we are often guided by our own artistic experience. We can recognize the technical signs that an artist is trying to solve a certain problem because it is a problem we might have struggled with ourselves. A knowledge of art history and artistic styles is also useful because it helps the critic to recognize problems that artists have persistently tried to solve—problems of meaning or form or social function.

In stating what the goal or aim of the work of art is, we are not necessarily saying what the artist's purpose was. We do not really know the artist's purpose. It is possible that he does not know his purpose either. The artist may believe he knows what he was trying to do, and he may also think he succeeded in reaching his objective. (It is very difficult for any artist to be objective or impartial about his own work.) But as critics, we state only what the visual evidence seems to point to, or mean, regardless of the artist's intentions. Sometimes an artist's statement about his work is useful in suggesting good places to look for visual information. However, it is an important rule of art criticism that your interpretation and judgment be based on what you have seen and felt in the work—not on what someone says about it. After all, you are judging images, not words.

From what has been said, it follows that no one is an absolute authority about the meaning or value of any work of art—

not the artist and not any critic. When the artist talks about his work, or the work of another artist, he becomes a critic and is subject to the same errors as other critics. Some critics, however, are better than other critics because their interpretations are more persuasive and illuminating than others. Therefore, their conclusions about a work of art—especially if they are shared by other good critics—tend to be understood as standard or authoritative judgments. Naturally, we do not want to ignore the ideas and opinions of respected and well-qualified persons. But we must remember that as times change, ways of feeling and thinking change too. Critical interpretations, therefore, will not be the same for all times and places.

Although critical interpretations vary, we should not make the mistake of thinking that any interpretation of a work of art is as good as any other. The best interpretation would be one that (a) makes sense out of the largest body of visual evidence drawn from a work of art and (b) makes the most meaningful connections between the work of art and the lives of the people who are looking at it. Now this second trait of good interpretation is the one which calls for a very creative critic. Of course, he must know enough about the language of art to observe and describe the art object sensitively and completely. But also, he must know enough about people—those who are viewing the work—to understand what interests or concerns them and how a particular work of art meets those interests and concerns. If I tell you things about art that you really do not want to know, I may be speaking truthfully, but not relevantly so far as you are concerned. Therefore the good critic must be able to persuade people of the relevance or significance for them of the observations and meanings he has found in a work of art.

Now how do we build an interpretation? As suggested earlier, it is difficult to be right at the first try. In fact, being wrong—missing the target—is very helpful in arriving finally at a convincing explanation. Testing an idea, even if it doesn't fit all the visual evidence, helps you decide which adjustments to make in your explanation, which visual features are controlling and which are subordinate, which guess or intuition is promising and which looks like a dead end. This process is what I call forming an hypothesis. It is very similar to what scientists do when they have accumulated a body of observations that needs to be explained—except that in art we rely more on our feelings than in science. A scientist can run experiments to test out his hypothesis about a phenomenon. In these experiments he is very careful to separate his feelings from his observations. But an art critic is not pursuing the same kind of truth as a scientist. Instead, he is looking for a statement or explanation that satisfies his feelings about a work of art as well as his observations of it. That is, the critic is not looking for the cause of his feelings, he is looking for an idea that will connect his feelings to each other, and also, connect them with the observations he has been making about the object.

Since feelings are so important in art criticism, we try to pay special attention to any impression that seems to suggest itself while we are interpreting a work. Usually, such impressions come to us in the form of "looks like" and "feels like" reactions. They may be funny, illogical or absurd, but do not reject them. Try to use your far-out impressions. The way to employ these strange, even weird, ideas is to ask yourself what they have in common with the relationships you were able to describe in your formal analysis. Perhaps your "looks like" or "feels like" reaction can be modified so that it fits some or all of the formal relationships in the work of art. Your "looks like" reaction is often a very shrewd response to the work except that it does not sound like what an art critic should say. But if you work on that response—sharpen it, say it in a more general way—you can retain its fundamental insight and sensitivity without sounding silly or stupid.

This method of forming an interpretation is nothing more than a way of trusting yourself—your observation, your hunches, your intelligence. During the stages of description and analysis your mind and imagination were working more than you realized. But you kept them "quiet" and under control in order to concentrate on a full description of the art object. Now, during interpretation, you can draw on those impressions. They are much more useful now because there has been time for them to interact with your whole personality. Your intuitions are richer because you have given yourself a chance to combine them with a greater variety of thoughts and observations.

Clearly, we have been building to the stage of interpretation. This is the stage where you give expression to your natural desire to respond to an experience as completely as possible. Perhaps you thought that a truly complete and intense human response is possible only when another person is involved, as in love, for example. But if you have carefully governed your examination and search into a work of art; if you have tried to see it and feel it and know it; if you have learned to focus your imagination and search into a work of art; then you have discovered what it is like to have an aesthetic experience. You have been able to let a thing—an art object—enter your life and become part of you. Your mental and emotional powers have transformed that thing—that work of art—so that it is yours in a very unique and special sense.

Deciding About the Value of an Art Object: Judgment

From the discussion of interpretation you can see that a viewer or critic puts a lot of himself into the examination of a work of art. That is, if he is serious about it and wants to get something out of the experience. But our time and energy are not endless. We cannot have really close relationships with everyone we know, for example. Life is too short—or so it seems. And for the same reason, we cannot become deeply involved in every work of art we happen to see. Some will mean more to us; some will seem less valuable; some we would like to own, or at least, see again; some appear to be worth talking about; and some are best forgotten.

For many of us, deciding whether a work of art is worth serious attention is one of the most important problems of art criticism. Some people collect art, however, and for them the decision is complicated by the fact that they will risk their money and much of their time on their judgment. That is, they may buy a work because it satisfies them in some way and they expect it to continue to be satisfying. Whenever a collector, dealer, or critic says that a work is good, he is saying, in effect, that it has the power to satisfy or please many viewers for a long time. Naturally, a museum or a private collector would like to own works of this quality.

Most of us do not have enough money to buy really famous works of art, although many of us can afford to own works by artists who are good but not well known. Nevertheless, we seem to be interested in knowing which works are considered outstanding or excellent. Sometimes, we are curious mainly about the cost of a masterpiece—a curiosity that reflects an interest in money more than art. Or we are interested in "great artists"—an interest in the lives of certain men rather than their creations. But usually we want to know if a work is important so that we can decide whether to examine and study it seriously. If we have gained any experience in art criticism, we can make this decision by ourselves. If not, we tend to rely on the word of authorities. But authorities do not always agree, especially about new works that have not been discussed in print. The student of art should take steps toward becoming his own authority, his own guide to artistic excellence.

To become a "judge" of excellence, it is helpful to know how good "judges" or critics decide whether a work is poor or excellent. In other words, you must know the reasons good critics give for their opinions about art. If a critic gives no reasons—directly or indirectly—then he is not a good critic. If he asks you to rely on his judgment because he is famous, important, well traveled, well educated, well acquainted with artists, and so on, then he is not giving good reasons. The reasons for judging a work excellent or poor have to be based on a philosophy of art, not on a man's personal authority. Fortunately, we have a choice of several philosophies of art for justifying critical judgments. You may prefer one or the other, but at least you have some freedom in choosing the philosophy that suits you best: You need not depend on someone's unsupported opinion. And, if you are resourceful, you can develop your own philosophy of art as a basis for judging the merit of any work that interests you.

23

Discursive and Presentational Forms*

Susanne K. Langer

The logical theory on which this whole study of symbols is based is essentially that which was set forth by Wittgenstein, some twenty years ago in his *Tractatus Logico-Philosophicus*:

One name stands for one thing, and another for another thing, and they are connected together. And so the whole, like a living picture, presents the atomic fact. (4.0311)

At the first glance the proposition—say as it stands printed on paper—does not seem to be a picture of the reality of which it treats. But neither does the musical score appear at first sight to be a picture of a musical piece; nor does our phonetic spelling (letters) seem to be a picture of our spoken language. ... (4.015)

In the fact that there is a general rule by which the musician is able to read the symphony out of the score, and that there is a rule by which one could reconstruct the symphony from the line on a phonograph record and from this again—by means of the first rule—construct the score, herein lies the internal similarity between the things which at first sight seem to be entirely different. And the rule is the law of projection which projects the symphony into

*Reprinted by permission of the publishers from *Philosophy in a New Key*, by Susanne K. Langer, Cambridge, MA: Harvard University Press. Copyright © 1942 by the President and Fellows of Harvard College. Copyright renewed by Susanne K. Langer in 1970.

the language of the musical score. It is the rule of translation of this language into the language of the gramophone record. (4.0141)

"Projection" is a good word, albeit a figurative one, for the process by which we draw purely logical analogies. Geometric projection is the best instance of a perfectly faithful representation which, without knowledge of some logical rule, appears to be a misrepresentation. A child looking at a map of the world in Mercator projection cannot help believing that Greenland is larger than Australia; he simply finds it larger. The projection employed is not the usual principle of copying which we use in all visual comparisons or translations, and his training in the usual rule makes him unable to "see" by the new one. It takes sophistication to "see" the relative sizes of Greenland and Australia on a Mercator map. Yet a mind educated to appreciate the projected image brings the eye's habit with it. After a while, we genuinely "see" the thing as we apprehend it.

Language, our most faithful and indispensable picture of human experience, of the world and its events, of thought and life and all the march of time, contains a law of projection of which philosophers are sometimes unaware, so that their reading of the presented "facts" is obvious and yet wrong, as a child's visual experience is obvious yet deceptive when his judgment is ensnared by the trick of the flattened map. The transformation which facts undergo when they are rendered as propositions is that the relations in them are turned into something like objects. Thus, "A killed B" tells of a way in which A and B were unfortunately combined; but our only means of expressing this way is to name it, and presto!—a new entity, "killing" seems to have added itself to the complex of A and B. The event which is "pictured" in the proposition undoubtedly involved a succession of acts by A and B, but not the succession which the proposition seems to exhibit—first A, then "killing," then B. Surely A and B were simultaneous with each other and with the killing. But words have a linear, discrete, successive order; they are strung one after another like beads on a rosary; beyond the very limited meanings of inflections, which can indeed be incorporated in the words themselves, we cannot talk in simultaneous bunches of names.

We must name one thing and then another, and symbols that are not names must be stuck between or before or after, by convention. But these symbols, holding proud places in the chain of names, are apt to be mistaken for names, to the detriment of many a metaphysical theory. Lord Russell regrets that we cannot construct a language which would express all relations by analogous relations; then we would not be tempted to misconstrue language, as a person who knows the meaning of the Mercator map, but has not used one freely enough to "see" in its terms, misconstrues the relative sizes of its areas.

"Take, say, that lightning precedes thunder," he says. "To express this by a language closely reproducing the structure of the fact, we should have to say simply: 'lightning, thunder,' where the fact that the first word precedes the second means that what the first word means precedes what the second word means. But even if we adopted this method for temporal order, we should still need words for all other relations, because we could not without intolerable ambiguity symbolize them by the order of our words."[1]

It is a mistake, I think, to symbolize things by entities too much like themselves; to let words in temporal order represent things in temporal order. If relations such as temporal order are symbolized at all, let the symbols not be those same relations themselves. A structure cannot include as *part of a symbol* something that should properly be *part of the meaning*. But it is unfortunate that names and syntactical indicators look so much alike in language; that we cannot represent objects by words, and relations by pitch, loudness, or other characteristics of speech.[2]

---

[1]*Philosophy*, p. 264.

[2]In the same chapter from which I have just quoted, Lord Russell attributes the power of language to represent *events* to the fact that, like events, it is a temporal series. I cannot agree with him in this matter. It is by virtue of *names for relations* that we can depict dynamic relations. We do not mention past events earlier in a sentence than present ones, but subject temporal order to the same "projection" as, for instance, attribution or classification; temporal order is usually rendered by the syntactical (nontemporal) device of *tense*.

As it is, however, all language has a form which requires us to string out our ideas even though their objects rest one within the other; as pieces of clothing that are actually worn over the other have to be strung side by side on the clothesline. This property of verbal symbolism is known as *discursiveness;* by reason of it, only thoughts which can be arranged in this peculiar order can be spoken at all; any idea which does not lend itself to this "projection" is ineffable, incommunicable by means of words. That is why the laws of reasoning, our clearest formulation of exact expression, are sometimes known as the "laws of discursive thought."

There is no need of going further into the details of verbal symbolism and its poorer substitutes, hieroglyphs, the deaf-and-dumb language, Morse Code, or the highly developed drum-telegraphy of certain jungle tribes. The subject has been exhaustively treated by several able men, as the many quotations in this chapter indicate; I can only assent to their findings. The relation between word-structures and their meanings is, I believe, one of logical analogy, whereby, in Wittgenstein's phrase, "we make ourselves pictures of facts." This philosophy of language lends itself, indeed, to great technical development, such as Wittgenstein envisaged:

> In the language of everyday life it very often happens that the same word signifies in different ways—and therefore belongs to two different symbols—or that two words, which signify in different ways, are apparently applied in the same way in the proposition. (3.323)

> In order to avoid these errors, we must employ a symbolism which excludes them, by not applying the same sign in different symbols and by not applying signs in the same way which signify in different ways. A symbolism, that is to say, which obeys the rules of *logical* grammar—of logical syntax.

(The logical symbolism of Frege and Russell
is such a language, which, however, does still not
exclude all errors.) (3.325)[3]

Carnap's admirable book, *The Logical Syntax of Language,* carries out the philosophical program suggested by Wittgenstein. Here an actual, detailed technique is developed for determining the *capacity for expression* of any given linguistic system, a technique which predicts the limit of all combinations to be made in that system, shows the equivalence of certain forms and the differences among others which might be mistaken for equivalents, and exhibits the conventions to which any thought or experience must submit in order to become conveyable by the symbolism in question. The distinctions between scientific language and everyday speech, which most of us can feel rather than define, are clearly illumined by Carnap's analysis; and it is surprising to find how little of our ordinary communication measures up to the standard of "meaning" which a serious philosophy of language, and hence a logic of discursive thought, set before us.

In this truly remarkable work the somewhat diffuse apprehension of our intellectual age, that *symbolism* is the key to epistemology and "natural knowledge," finds precise and practical corroboration. The Kantian challenge: "What can I know?" is shown to be dependent on the prior question: "What can I ask?" And the answer, in Professor Carnap's formulation, is clear and direct. I can ask whatever language will express; I can know whatever experiment will answer. A proposition which could not, under any (perhaps ideal, impracticable) conditions, be verified or refuted, is a pseudo-proposition, it has no literal meaning. It does not belong to the framework of knowledge that we call logical conception; it is not true or false, but *unthinkable,* for it falls outside the order of symbolism.

Since an inordinate amount of our talk, and therefore (we hope) of our cerebration too, defies the canons of literal meaning,

---

[3]*Tractatus.*

our philosophers of language—Russell, Wittgenstein, Carnap, and others of similar persuasion—are faced with the new question: what is the true function of those verbal combinations and other pseudo-symbolic structures that have no real significance, but are freely used as though they meant something?

According to our logicians, those structures are to be treated as "expressions" in a different sense, namely as "expressions" of emotions, feelings, desires. They are not symbols for thought, but symptoms of the inner life, like tears and laughter, crooning, or profanity.

"Many linguistic utterances," says Carnap, "are analogous to laughing in that they have only an expressive function, no representative function. Examples of this are cries like 'Oh, Oh,' or, on a higher level, lyrical verses. The aim of a lyrical poem in which occur the words 'sunshine' and 'clouds,' is not to inform us of certain meteorological facts, but to express certain feelings of the poet and to excite similar feelings in us. . . . Metaphysical propositions—like lyrical verses—have only an expressive function, but no representative function. Metaphysical propositions are neither true nor false, because they assert nothing. . . . But they are, like laughing, lyrics and music, expressive. They express not so much temporary feelings as permanent emotional and volitional dispositions."[4]

Lord Russell holds a very similar view of other people's metaphysics: "I do not deny," he says:

> the importance or value, within its own sphere, of the
> kind of philosophy which is inspired by ethical
> notions. The ethical work of Spinoza, for instance,
> appears to be of the very highest significance, but
> what is valuable in such a work is not any
> metaphysical theory as to the nature of the world to
> which it may give rise, not indeed anything that can
> be proved or disproved by argument. What is
> valuable is the indication of some new way of feeling

---

[4]*Philosophy and Logical Syntax*, p. 28.

toward life and the world, some way of feeling by which our own existence can acquire more of the characteristics which we must deeply desire.[5]

And Wittgenstein:

Most propositions and questions, that have been written about philosophical matters, are not false, but senseless. We cannot, therefore, answer questions of this kind at all, but only state their senselessness. Most questions and propositions of the philosophers result from the fact that we do not understand the logic of our language. (4.003)

A proposition represents the existence and non-existence of atomic facts. (4.1)

The totality of true propositions is the total of natural science (or the totality of the natural sciences). (4.11)

Everything that can be thought at all can be thought clearly. Everything that can be said can be said clearly. (4.116)[6]

In their criticism of metaphysical propositions, namely such that propositions are usually pseudo-answers to pseudo-questions, these logicians have my full assent; problems of "First Cause" and "Unity" and "Substance," and all the other time-honored topics, are insoluble, because they arise from the fact that we attribute to the world what really belongs to the "logical projection" in which we conceive it, and by misplacing our questions we jeopardize our answers. This source of bafflement has been uncovered by the philosophers of our day, through their interest in the functions and nature of symbolism. The discovery marks a great intellectual advance. But it does not condemn philosophical inquiry as such; it merely requires *every philosophical problem to be recast*, to be conceived in a different

---

[5]"Scientific Method in Philosophy," in *Mysticism and Logic* (1918), p. 109.

[6]Op. cit.

form.   Many issues that seemed to concern the *sources* of
knowledge, for instance, now appear to turn partly or wholly on
the *forms* of knowledge, or even the forms of expression, of
symbolism. The center of philosophical interest has shifted once
more, as it has shifted several times in the past.   That does not
mean, however, that rational people should now renounce
metaphysics.   The recognition of the intimate relation between
symbolism and experience, on which our whole criticism of
traditional problems is based, is itself a metaphysical insight.
For metaphysics is, like every philosophical pursuit, a study of
meanings. From it spring the special sciences, which can develop
their techniques and verify their propositions one by one, *as soon
as their initial concepts are clear enough to allow systematic
handling, i.e.,* as soon as the philosophical work behind them is at
least tentatively accomplished.[7]   Metaphysics is not itself a
science with fixed presuppositions, but progresses from problem to
problem rather than from premise to consequence. To suppose that
we have outgrown it is to suppose that all "the sciences" are finally
established, that human language is complete, or at least soon to be
completed, and additional facts are all we lack of the greatest
knowledge ever possible to man; and though this knowledge may
be small, it is all that we shall ever have.

   This is, essentially, the attitude of those logicians who
have investigated the limits of language.   Nothing that is not
"language" in the sense of their technical definition can possess
the character of symbolic expressiveness (though it may be
"expressive" in the symptomatic way).   Consequently nothing that
cannot be "projected" in discursive form is accessible to the
human mind at all, and any attempt to understand anything but
demonstrable fact is bootless ambition. The knowable is a clearly
defined field, governed by the requirement of discursive
projectability.   Outside this domain is the inexpressible realm of
feeling, of formless desires and satisfactions, immediate
experience, forever incognito and incommunicado.   A

---

[7] I have presented a fuller discussion of philosophy as the "mother of
sciences" in *The Practice of Philosophy* (1930), ch. ii.

philosopher who looks in that direction is, or should be, a mystic; from the ineffable sphere nothing but nonsense can be conveyed, since language, our only possible semantic, will not clothe experiences that elude the discursive form.

But intelligence is a slippery customer; if one door is closed to it, it finds, or even breaks, another entrance to the world. If one symbolism is inadequate, it seizes another; there is no eternal decree over its means and methods. So I will go with the logisticians and linguists as far as they like, but do not promise to go no further. For there is an unexplored possibility of genuine semantic beyond the limits of discursive language.

This logical "beyond," which Wittgenstein calls the "unspeakable," both Russell and Carnap regard as the sphere of subjective experience, emotion, feeling, and wish, from which only *symptoms* come to us in the form of metaphysical and artistic fancies. The study of such products they relegate to psychology, not semantics. And here is the point of my radical divergence from them. Where Carnap speaks of "cries like 'Oh, Oh,' or, on a higher level, lyrical verses," I can see only a complete failure to apprehend a fundamental distinction. Why should we cry our feelings at such high levels that anyone would think we were *talking*?[8] Clearly, poetry means more than a cry; it has reason for being articulate; and metaphysics is more than the croon with which we might cuddle up to the world in a comfortable attitude. We are dealing with symbolisms here, and what they express is often highly intellectual. Only, the form and function of such symbolisms are not those investigated by logicians, under the heading of "language." The field of semantics is wider than that of language, as certain philosophers—Schopenhauer, Cassirer, Delacroix, Dewey, Whitehead, and some others—have discovered; but it is blocked for us by the two fundamental tenets of current epistemology, which we have just discussed.

---

[8]Cf. Urban, *Language and Reality,* p. 164.

These two basic assumptions go hand in hand: (1) That *language*[9] *is the only means of articulating thought,* and (2) that *everything which is not speakable thought, is feeling.* They are linked together because all genuine thinking *is* symbolic, and the limits of the expressive medium are, therefore, really the limits of our conceptual powers. Beyond these we can have only blind feeling, which records nothing and conveys nothing, but has to be discharged in action of self-expression, in deeds or cries or other impulsive demonstrations.

But if we consider how difficult it is to construct a meaningful language that shall meet neo-positivistic standards, it is quite incredible that people should ever *say* anything at all, or understand each other's propositions. At best, human thought is but a tiny, grammar-bound island, in the midst of a sea of feeling expressed by "Oh-oh" and sheer babble. The island has a periphery, perhaps, of mud—factual and hypothetical concepts broken down by the emotional tides into the "material mode," a mixture of meaning and nonsense. Most of us live the better part of our lives on this mudflat; but in artistic moods we take to the deep, where we flounder about with symptomatic cries that sound like propositions about life and death, good and evil, substance, beauty, and other nonexistent topics.

So long as we regard only scientific and "material" (semi-scientific) thought as really cognitive of the world, this peculiar picture of mental life must stand. And *so long as we admit only discursive symbolism as a bearer of ideas, "thought" in this restricted sense must be regarded as our only intellectual activity.* It begins and ends with language; without the elements, at least, of scientific grammar, conception must be impossible.

A theory which implies such peculiar consequences is itself a suspicious character. But the error which it harbors is not in its reasoning. It is in the very premise from which the doctrine proceeds, namely that all articulate symbolism is discursive. As Lord Russell, with his usual precision and directness, has stated

---

[9]Including, of course, its refinements in mathematical and scientific symbolisms, and its approximations by gesture, hieroglyphics, or graphs.

the case, "it is clear that anything that can be said in an inflected language can be said in an uninflected language; therefore, anything that can be said in language can be said by means of a temporal series of uninflected words. This places a limitation upon what can be expressed in words. It may well be that there are facts which do not lend themselves to this very simple schema; if so, they cannot be expressed in language. Our confidence in language is due to the fact that it . . . shares the structure of the physical world, and therefore can express that structure. But if there be a world which is not physical, or not in space-time, it may have a structure which we can never hope to express or to know. . . . Perhaps that is why we know so much physics and so little of anything else."[10]

Now, I do not believe that "there is a world which is not physical, or not in space-time," but I do believe that in this physical, space-time world of our experience there are things which do not fit the grammatical scheme of expression. But they are not necessarily blind, inconceivable, mystical affairs; they are simply matters which require to be conceived through some symbolistic schema other than discursive language. And to demonstrate the possibility of such non-discursive patterns one needs only to review the logical requirements for any symbolic structure whatever. Language is by no means our only articulate product.

Our merest sense-experience is a process of *formulation*. The world that actually meets our sense is not a world of "things," about which we are invited to discover facts as soon as we have codified the necessary logical language to do so; the world of pure sensation is so complex, so fluid and full, that sheer sensitivity to stimuli would only encounter what William James has called (in characteristic phrase) "a blooming, buzzing confusion." Out of this bedlam our sense-organs must select certain predominant forms if they are to make report of *things* and not of mere dissolving sensa. The eye and the ear must have their logic—

---

[10]*Philosophy,* p. 265.

their "categories of understanding," if you like the Kantian
idiom, or their "primary imagination," in Coleridge's version of
the same concept.[11] An object is not a datum, but a form construed
by the sensitive and intelligent organ, a form which is at once an
experienced individual thing and a symbol for the concept of it, for
this sort of thing.

A tendency to organize the sensory field into groups and
patterns of sense-data, to perceive forms rather than a flux of
light-impressions, seems to be inherent in our receptor apparatus
just as much as in the higher nervous centers with which we do
arithmetic and logic. But this unconscious appreciation of forms
is the primitive root of all abstraction, which in turn is the keynote
of rationality; so it appears that the conditions for rationality lie
deep in our pure animal experience—in our power of perceiving,
in the elementary functions of our eyes and ears and fingers.
Mental life begins with our mere physiological constitution. A
little reflection shows us that, since no experience occurs more
than once, so-called "repeated" experiences are really *analogous*
occurrences, all fitting a form that was abstracted on the first
occasion. *Familiarity* is nothing but the quality of fitting very
neatly into the form of a previous experience. I believe our
ingrained habit of hypostatizing impressions, of seeing *things*
and not sense-data, rests on the fact that we promptly and
unconsciously abstract a form from each sensory experience, and
use this form to *conceive* the experience as a whole, as a "thing."

No matter what heights the human mind may attain, it can
work only with the organs it has and the functions peculiar to
them. Eyes that did not see forms could never furnish it with
images; ears that did not hear articulated sounds could never open
it to *words*. Sense-data, in brief, would be useless to a mind whose
activity is "through and through a symbolic process," were they not
par excellence receptacles of meaning. But meaning, as previous
considerations have shown, accrues essentially to forms. Unless

---

[11]An excellent discussion of Coleridge's philosophy may be found in D. G.
James, *Skepticism and Poetry* (1937), a book well worth reading in
connection with this chapter.

the *Gestalt*-psychologists are right in their belief that *Gestaltung* is of the very nature of perception, I do not know how the hiatus between perception and conception, sense-organ and mind-organ, chaotic stimulus and logical response, is ever to be closed and welded. A mind that works primarily with meanings must have organs that supply it primarily with forms.

The nervous system is the organ of the mind; its center is the brain, its extremities the sense-organs; and any characteristic function it may possess must govern the work of all its parts. In other words, the activity of our senses is "mental" not only when it reaches the brain, but in its very inception, whenever the alien world outside impinges on the furthest and smallest receptor. All sensitivity bears the stamp for mentality. "Seeing," for instance, is not a passive process, by which meaningless impressions are stored up for the use of an organizing mind, which construes forms out of these amorphous data to suit its own purposes. "Seeing" is itself a process of formulation; our understanding of the visible world begins in the eye.[12]

This psychological insight, which we owe to the school of Wertheimer, Kohler, and Koffka, has far-reaching philosophical consequences, if we take it seriously; for it carries rationality into processes that are usually deemed pre-rational, and points to the

---

[12]For a general account of the *Gestalt*-theory, see Wolfgang Kohler, *Gestalt Psychology* (1929), from which the following relevant passage is taken:

"It is precisely the original organization and segregation of circumscribed wholes which make it possible for the sensory world to appear so utterly imbued with meaning to the adult because, in its gradual entry into the sensory field, meaning follows the lines drawn by natural organization. It usually enters into segregated wholes. . . .
"Where 'form' *exists* originally, it acquires a meaning very easily. But here a whole with its form is given first and then a meaning 'creeps into it.' That meaning automatically produces a form where beforehand there is none, has not been shown experimentally in a single case, as far as I know" (p. 208).

See also Max Wertheimer, *Drei Abhandlungen zur Gestalttheorie* (1925), and Kurt Koffka, *Principles of Gestalt Psychology* (1935).

existence of forms, *i.e.*, of *possible symbolic material*, at a level
where symbolic activity has certainly never been looked for by
any epistemologist. The eye and the ear make their own
abstractions, and consequently dictate their own peculiar forms of
conception. But these forms are derived from exactly the same
world that furnished the totally different forms known to physics.
There is, in fact, no such thing as *the* form of the "real" world;
physics is one pattern which may be found in it, and "appearance,"
or the pattern of *things* with their qualities and characters, is
another. One construction may indeed preclude the other; but to
maintain that the consistency and universality of the one brands
the other as *false* is a mistake. The fact that physical analysis
does not rest in a final establishment of irreducible "qualities"
does not refute the belief that there are red, blue, and green things,
wet or oily or dry substances, fragrant flowers, and shiny
surfaces in the real world. These concepts of the "material mode"
are not approximations to "physical" notions at all. Physical
concepts owe their origin and development to the application of
mathematics to the world of "things," and mathematics never—
even in the beginning—dealt with qualities of objects. It
measured their proportions, but never treated its concepts—
triangularity, circularity, etc.—as qualities of which so *and so*
much could become an ingredient of certain objects. Even though
an elliptical race-track may approximate a circle, it is not to be
improved by the addition of more circularity. On the other hand,
wine which is not sweet enough requires more sweetening, paint
which is not bright enough is given an ingredient of more white or
more color. The world of physics is essentially the real world
construed by mathematical abstractions, and the world of sense is
the real world construed by the abstractions which the sense-
organs immediately furnish. To suppose that the "material
mode" is a primitive and groping attempt at physical conception is
a fatal error in epistemology, because it cuts off all interest in the
developments of which sensuous conception is capable, and the
intellectual uses to which it might be put.

These intellectual uses lie in a field which usually
harbors a slough of despond for the philosopher, who ventures into
it because he is too honest to ignore it, though really he knows no

path around its pitfalls. It is the field of "intuition," "deeper meaning," "artistic truth," "insight," and so forth. A dangerous-looking sector, indeed, for the advance of a rational spirit! To date, I think, every serious epistemology that has regarded mental life as greater than discursive reason, and has made concessions to "insight" or "intuition," has just so far capitulated to *unreason*, to mysticism and irrationalism. Every excursion beyond propositional thought has dispensed with thought altogether, and postulated some inmost soul of pure feeling in direct contact with a Reality unsymbolized, unfocused, and incommunicable (with the notable exception of the theory set forth by L.A. Reid in the last chapter of his *Knowledge and Truth*, which admits the facts of non-propositional conception in a way that invites rather than precludes logical analysis).

The abstractions made by the ear and the eye—the forms of direct perception—are our most primitive instruments of intelligence. They are genuine symbolic materials, media of understanding, by whose office we apprehend a world of *things*, and of events that are the histories of things. To furnish such conceptions is their prime mission. Our sense-organs make their habitual, unconscious abstractions, in the interest of this "*reifying*" function that underlies ordinary recognition of objects, knowledge of signals, words, tunes, places, and the possibility of classifying such things in the outer world according to their kind. We recognize the elements of this sensuous analysis in all sorts of combination; we can use them imaginatively, to conceive prospective changes in familiar scenes.

Visual forms—lines, colors, proportions, etc.—are just as capable of *articulation, i.e.,* of complex combination, as words. But the laws that govern this sort of articulation are altogether different from the laws of syntax that govern language. The most radical difference is that *visual forms are not discursive*. They do not present their constituents successively, but simultaneously, so the relations determining a visual structure are grasped in one act of vision. Their complexity, consequently, is not limited, as the complexity of discourse is limited, by what the mind can retain from the beginning of an apperceptive act to the end of it. Of course such a restriction on discourse sets bounds to the complexity of

speakable ideas. An idea that contains too many minute yet
closely related parts, too many relations within relations, cannot
be "projected" into discursive form; it is too subtle for speech. A
language-bound theory of mind, therefore, rules it out of the
domain of understanding and the sphere of knowledge.

But the symbolism furnished by our purely sensory
appreciation of forms is a *non-discursive symbolism*, peculiarly
well suited to the expression of ideas that defy linguistic
"projection." Its primary function, that of conceptualizing the flux
of sensations, and giving us concrete *things* in place of
kaleidoscopic colors or noises, is itself an office that no language-
born thought can replace. The understanding of space which we
owe to sight and touch could never be developed, in all its detail
and definiteness, by a discursive knowledge of geometry. Nature
speaks to us, first of all, through our senses; the forms and
qualities we distinguish, remember, imagine, or recognize are
symbols of entities which exceed and outlive our momentary
experience. Moreover, the same symbols—qualities, lines,
rhythms—may occur in innumerable presentations; they are
abstractable and combinatory. It is quite natural, therefore, that
philosophers who have recognized the symbolical character of so-
called "sense-data," especially in their highly developed uses, in
science and art, often speak of a "language" of the senses, a
"language" of musical tones, of colors, and so forth.

Yet this manner of speaking is very deceptive. Language
is a special mode of expression, and not every sort of semantic can
be brought under this rubric; by generalizing from linguistic
symbolism to symbolism as such, we are easily led to misconceive
all other types, and overlook their most interesting features.
Perhaps it were well to consider, here, the salient characteristics
of true language, or discourse.

In the first place, *every language has a vocabulary and a
syntax*. Its elements are words with fixed meanings. Out of these
one can construct, according to the rules of the syntax, composite
symbols with resultant new meanings.

Secondly, in a language, some words are equivalent to
whole combinations of other words, so that most meanings can be
expressed in several different ways. This makes it possible *to*

define the meanings of the ultimate single words, i.e., to construct a dictionary.

Thirdly, there may be alternative words for the same meaning. When two people systematically use different words for almost everything, they are said to speak different languages. But the two languages are roughly equivalent; with a little artifice, an occasional substitution of a phrase for a single word, etc., the propositions enunciated by one person, in his system, may be *translated* into the conventional system of the other.

Now consider the most familiar sort of non-discursive symbol, a picture. Like language, it is composed of elements that represent various respective constituents in the object; but these elements are not units with independent meanings. The areas of light and shade that constitute a portrait, a photograph for instance, have no significance by themselves. In isolation we would consider them simply blotches. Yet they are faithful representatives of visual elements composing the visual object. However, they do not represent, item for item, those elements which have *names*; there is not one blotch for the nose, one for the mouth, etc.; their shapes, in quite indescribable combinations, convey a total picture in which nameable features may be pointed out. The gradations of light and shade cannot be enumerated. They cannot be correlated, one by one, with parts of characteristics by means of which we might *describe* the person who posed for the portrait. The "elements" that the camera represents are not the "elements" that language represents. They are a thousand times more numerous. For this reason the correspondence between a word-picture and a visible object can never be as close as that between the object and its photograph. Given all at once to the intelligent eye, an incredible wealth and detail of information is conveyed by the portrait, where we do not have to stop to construe verbal meanings. That is why we use a photograph rather than a description on a passport or in the Rogues' Gallery.

Clearly, a symbolism with so many elements, such myriad relationships, cannot be broken up into basic units. It is impossible to find the smallest independent symbol, and recognize its identity when the same unit is met in other contexts. Photography, therefore, *has no vocabulary*. The same is obviously true of painting, drawing, etc. There is, of course, a technique of picturing objects, but the law governing this technique cannot properly be called a "syntax," since there are no items that might be called, metaphorically, the "words" of portraiture.

Since we have no words, there can be no dictionary of meanings for lines, shadings, or other elements of pictorial technique. We may well pick out some line, say a certain curve, in a picture, which serves to represent one nameable item; but in another place the same curve would have an entirely different meaning. It has no fixed meaning apart from its context. Also, there is no complex of other elements that is equivalent to it at all times, as "2+2" is equivalent to "4." Non-discursive symbols cannot be defined in terms of others, as discursive symbols can.

If there can be no defining dictionary, of course we have no translating dictionary, either. There are different media of graphic representation, but their respective elements cannot be brought into one-to-one correlation with each other, as in languages: *"chien"* = *"dog,"* *"moi"* = *"me,"* etc. There is no standard key for translating sculpture into painting, or drawing into ink-wash, because their equivalence rests on their common *total reference*, not on bit-for-bit equivalences of parts such as underlie a literal translation.

Furthermore, verbal symbolism, unlike the non-discursive kinds, has primarily a *general* reference. Only convention can assign a proper name—and then there is no way of preventing some other convention from assigning the same proper name to a different individual. We may name a child as oddly as we will, yet we cannot guarantee that no one else will ever bear that designation. A description may fit a scene ever so closely, but it takes some known proper name to refer it without possible doubt to one and only one place. Where the names of persons and places are withheld, we can never *prove* that a discourse refers—not merely applies—to a certain historic occasion. In the non-discursive mode that speaks directly to sense, however, there is no intrinsic generality. It is first and foremost a direct *presentation* of an individual object. A picture has to be schematized if it is to be capable of various meanings. In itself it represents just one object—real or imaginary, but still a unique object. The definition of a triangle fits triangles in general, but a drawing always presents a triangle of some specific kind and size. We have to abstract from the conveyed meaning in order to conceive triangularity in general. Without the help of words this generalization, if possible at all, is certainly incommunicable.

It appears, then, that although the different media of non-verbal representation are often referred to as distinct "languages," this is really a loose terminology. Language in the strict sense is essentially discursive; it has permanent units of meaning which are combinable into larger units; it has fixed equivalences that make definition and translation possible; its connotations are general, so that it requires non-verbal acts, like pointing, looking, or emphatic voice-inflections, to assign specific denotations to its terms. In all these salient characters it differs from wordless symbolism, which is non-discursive and untranslatable, does not allow of definitions within its own system, and cannot directly convey generalities. The meanings given through language are successively understood, and gathered into a whole by the process called discourse; the meanings of all other symbolical elements that compose a larger, articulate symbol are understood only through the meaning of the whole, through their relations within the total structure. Their very functioning as symbols depends on the fact that they are involved in a simultaneous, integral presentation. This kind of semantic may be called "presentational symbolism," to characterize its essential distinction from discursive symbolism, or "language" proper.[13]

The recognition of presentational symbolism as a normal and prevalent vehicle of meaning widens our conception of rationality far beyond the traditional boundaries, yet never

---

[13]It is relevant here to note that "picture language," which uses *separate pictures in place of words,* is a discursive symbolism, though each "word" is a presentational symbol; and that all codes, *e.g.*, the conventional gestures of deaf-mutes or the drum communications of African tribes, are discursive systems.

breaks faith with logic in the strictest sense. Wherever a symbol operates, there is a meaning; and conversely, different classes of experience—say, reason, intuition, appreciation—correspond to different types of symbolic mediation. No symbol is exempt from the office of logical formulation, of *conceptualizing* what it conveys; however simple its import, or however great, this import is a *meaning*, and therefore an element for understanding Such reflection invites one to tackle anew, and with entirely different expectations, the whole problem of the limits of reason, the much-disputed life of feeling, and the great controversial topics of fact and truth, knowledge and wisdom, science and art. It brings within the compass of reason much that has been traditionally relegated to "emotion," or to that crepuscular depth of the mind where "intuitions" are supposed to be born, without any midwifery of symbols, without due process of thought, to fill the gaps in the edifice of discursive, or "rational," judgment.

The symbolic materials given to our senses, the *Gestalten* or fundamental perceptual forms which invite us to construe the pandemonium of sheer impression into a world of things and occasions, belong to the "presentational" order. They furnish the elementary abstractions in terms of which ordinary sense-experience is understood.[14] This kind of understanding is directly reflected in the pattern of *physical reaction*, impulse and instinct. May not the order of perceptual forms, then, be a possible principle for symbolization, and hence the conception, expression,

---

[14]Kant thought that the *principles* of such formulation were supplied by a faculty of the mind, which he called *Verstand;* but his somewhat dogmatic delimitation of the field of knowledge open to *Verstand*, and the fact that he regarded the mind-engendered forms as *constitutive* of experience rather than *interpretative* (as principles must be), prevented logicians from taking serious note of such forms as possible machinery of reason. They abode by the forms of *Vernunft*, which are, roughly speaking, the forms of discourse. Kant himself exalted *Vernunft* as the special gift and glory of man. When an epistemology of medium and meaning began to crowd out the older epistemology of percept and concept, his *Verstandesformen*, in their role of *conceptual ingredients* of phenomena, were lumped with his metaphysical doctrines, and eclipsed by "metalogical" interests.

and apprehension, of impulsive, instinctive, and sentient life? May not a non-discursive symbolism of light and color, or of tone, be formulative of that life? And is it not possible that the sort of "intuitive" knowledge which Bergson extols above all rational knowledge because it is supposedly not mediated by any formulating (and hence deforming) symbol[15] is itself perfectly rational, but not to be conceived through language—a product of that presentational symbolism which the mind reads in a flash, and preserves in a disposition or an attitude?

This hypothesis, though unfamiliar and therefore somewhat difficult, seems to me well worth exploring. For, quite apart from all questions of the authenticity of intuitive, inherited, or inspired knowledge, about which I do not wish to cavil, the very idea of a *non-rational source* of any knowledge vitiates the concept of mind as an organ of understanding. "The power of reason is simply the power of the whole mind at its fullest stretch and compass," said Professor Creighton, in an essay that sought to stem the great wave of irrationalism and emotionalism following the World War.[16] This assumption appears to me to be a basic one in any study of mentality. Rationality is the essence of mind, and symbolic transformation its elementary process. It is a fundamental error, therefore, to recognize it only in the phenomenon of systematic, explicit reasoning. That is a mature and precarious product.

Rationality, however, is embodied in every mental act, not only when the mind is "at its fullest stretch and compass." It permeates the peripheral activities of the human nervous system, just as truly as the cortical functions.

---

[15]See Henri Bergson, *La pensee et le mouvement* (1934), esp. essays ii ("De la position des problemes") and iv ("L'intuition philosophique"): also his *Essai sur les donnees immediates de la conscience* (1889), and *Introduction to Metaphysics* (1912).

[16]J. E. Creighton, "Reason and Feeling," *Philosophical Review*, XXX (1921), 5: 465-481. See p. 469.

"The facts of perception and memory maintain themselves only in so far as they are mediated, and thus given significance beyond their mere isolated existence. . . . What falls in any way within experience partakes of the rational form of the mind. As mental content, any part of experience is something more than a particular impression having only the attributes of existence. As already baptized into the life of the mind, it partakes of its logical nature and moves on the plane of universality. . . .

"No matter how strongly the unity and integrity of the mind is asserted, this unity is nothing more than verbal if the mind is not in principle the expression of reason. For it can be shown that all attempts to render comprehensible the unity of the mental life in terms of an alogical principle fail to attain their goal."[17]

The title of Professor Creighton's trenchant little article is "Reason and Feeling." Its central thesis is that if there is something in our mental life besides "reason," by which he means, of course, discursive thinking, then it cannot be an alogical factor, but must be in essence cognitive, too; and since the only alternative to this reason is feeling (the author does not question that axiom of epistemology), feeling itself must somehow participate in knowledge and understanding.

All this may be granted. The position is well taken. But the most crucial *problem* is barely broached: this problem is epitomized in the word "somehow." *Just how* can feelings be conceived as possible ingredients of rationality? We are not told, but we are given a generous hint, which in the light of a broader theory of symbolism points to explanation.

"In the development of mind," he says, "feeling does not remain a static element, constant in form and content at all

---

[17]*Ibid.*, pp. 470-472.

levels, but . . . is transformed and disciplined through its interplay with other aspects of experience . . . . Indeed, the character of the feeling in any experience may be taken as an index of the mind's grasp of its object; at the lower levels of experience, where the mind is only partially or superficially involved, feeling appears as something isolated and opaque, as the passive accompaniment of mere bodily sensations. . . In the higher experiences, the feelings assume an entirely different character, just as do the sensations and the other contents of mind."[18]

The significant observation voiced in this passage is that *feelings have definite forms, which become progressively articulated.* Their development is effected through their "interplay with the other aspects of experience;" but the nature of that interplay is not specified. Yet it is here, I think, that cogency for the whole thesis must be sought. *What* character of feeling is "an index of the mind's grasp of its object," and by what tokens is it so? If feeling has articulate forms, what are they like? For what these are *like* determines by what symbolism we might understand them. Everybody knows that language is a very poor medium for expressing our emotional nature. It merely names certain vaguely and crudely conceived states, but fails miserably in any attempt to convey the evermoving patterns, the ambivalences and intricacies of inner experience, the interplay of feelings with thoughts and impressions, memories and echoes of memories, transient fantasy, or its mere runic traces, all turned into nameless, emotional stuff. If we say that we understand someone else's feeling in a certain matter, we mean that we understand why he should be sad or happy, excited or indifferent, in a general way; that we can see due cause for his attitude. We do not mean that we have insight into the actual flow and balance of his feelings, into that "character" which "may be taken as an index of the mind's grasp of its object." Language is quite inadequate to articulate such a conception. Probably we

---

[18]*Ibid., pp. 478-479.*

would not impart our actual, inmost feelings even if they could be spoken. We rarely speak in detail of entirely personal things.

There is, however, a kind of symbolism peculiarly adapted to the explication of "unspeakable" things, though it lacks the cardinal virtue of language, which is denotation. The most highly developed type of such purely connotational semantic is music. We are not talking nonsense when we say that a certain musical progression is significant, or that a given phrase lacks meaning, or a player's rendering fails to convey the import of a passage. Yet such statements make sense only to people with a natural understanding of the medium, whom we describe, therefore, as "musical." Musicality is often regarded as an essentially unintellectual, even a biologically sportive trait. Perhaps that is why musicians, who know that it is the prime source of their mental life and the medium of their clearest insight into humanity, so often feel called upon to despise the more obvious forms of understanding, that claim practical virtues under the names of reason which is known as rationalism or intellectualism; and *vice versa*, common-sense and scientific acumen need not defend themselves against any "emotionalism" that is supposed to be inherent in a respect for music. Speech and music have essentially different functions, despite their oft-remarked union in song. Their original relationship lies much deeper than any such union (of which more will be said in a subsequent chapter), and can be seen only when their respective natures are understood.

The problem of meaning deepens at every turn. The longer we delve into its difficulties, the more complex it appears. But in a central philosophical concept, this is a sign of health. Each question answered leads to another which previously could not be even entertained: the logic of symbolism, the possible types of representation, the fields proper to them, the actual functions of symbols according to their nature, their relationships to each other, and finally our main theme, their integration in human mentality.

Of course it is not possible to study every known phenomenon in the realm of symbolism. But neither is this necessary even in an intimate study. The logical structures underlying all semantic functions, which I have discussed in this chapter, suggest a general principle of division. Signs are logically distinct from symbols; discursive and presentational patterns show a formal difference. There are further natural divisions due to various ways of *using* symbols, no less important than the logical distinctions. Altogether, we may group meaning-situations around certain outstanding types, and make these several types the subjects of individual studies. Language, ritual, myth, and music, representing four respective modes, may serve as central topics for the study of actual symbolisms; and I trust that further problems of significance in art, in science or mathematics, in behavior or in fantasy and dream, may receive some light by analogy, and by that most powerful human gift, the adaptation of ideas.

24

The Precession of Simulacra*

Jean Baudrillard
Sociology
University of Paris
Translated by Paul Foss and Paul Patton

> *The simulacrum is never that which conceals the truth—it is the truth which conceals that there is none.*
> *The simulacrum is true.*   *Ecclesiastes*

If we were able to take as the finest allegory of simulation the Borges tale where the cartographers of the Empire draw up a map so detailed that it ends up exactly covering the territory (but where the decline of the Empire sees this map become frayed and finally ruined, a few shreds still discernible in the deserts—the metaphysical beauty of this ruined abstraction, bearing witness to an imperial pride and rotting like a carcass, returning to the substance of the soil, rather as an aging double ends up being confused with the real thing)—then this fable has come full circle for us, and now has nothing but the discrete charm of second-order simulacra.[1]

Abstraction today is no longer that of the map, the double, the mirror, or the concept. Simulation is no longer that of a territory, a referential being or a substance. It is the generation by models of a real without origin or reality: a hyperreal. The territory no longer precedes the map, nor survives it. Henceforth,

---

[1]Cf., Jean Baudrillard. L'echange symbolique et la mort ("L'ordre des simulacres"), (Paris: Gallimard, 1975).

it is the map that precedes the territory—PRECESSION OF SIMULACRA—it is the map that engenders the territory and if we were to revive the fable today, it would be the territory whose shreds are slowly rotting across the map. It is the real, and not the map, whose vestiges subsist here and there, in the deserts which are no longer those of the Empire, but our own: *The desert of the real itself.*

In fact, even inverted, the fable is useless. Perhaps only the allegory of the Empire remains. For it is with the same imperialism that present-day simulators try to make the real, all the real, coincide with their simulation models. But it is no longer a question of either maps or territory. Something has disappeared: the sovereign difference between them that was the abstraction's charm. For it is the difference which forms the poetry of the map and the charm of the territory, the magic of the concept and the charm of the real. This representational imaginary, which both culminates in and is engulfed by the cartographer's mad project of an ideal coextensivity between the map and the territory, disappears with simulation—whose operation is nuclear and genetic, and no longer specular and discursive. With it goes all of metaphysics. No more mirror of being and appearances, of the real and its concept. No more imaginary coextensivity: rather, genetic miniaturization is the dimension of simulation. The real is produced from miniaturized units, from matrices, memory banks, and command models—and with these it can be reproduced an infinite number of times. It no longer has to be rational, since it is no longer measured against some ideal or negative instance. It is nothing more than operational. In fact, since it is no longer enveloped by an imaginary, it is no longer real at all. It is a hyperreal, the product of an irradiating synthesis of combinatory models in a hyperspace without atmosphere.

In this passage to a space whose curvature is no longer that of the real, nor of truth, the age of simulation thus begins with a liquidation of all referentials—worse: by their artificial resurrection in systems of signs, a more ductile material than meaning, in that it lends itself to all systems of equivalence, all binary oppositions, and all combinatory algebra. It is no longer a question of imitation, nor of reduplication, nor even of parody. It is rather a question of substituting signs of the real for the real itself, that is an operation to deter every real process by its operational double, a metastable, programmatic, perfect descriptive machine which provides all the signs of the real and short-circuits all its vicissitudes. Never again will the real have to be produced—this is the vital function of the model in a system of death, or rather of anticipated resurrection which no longer leaves any chance even in the event of death. A hyperreal henceforth sheltered from the imaginary, and from any distinction between the real and the imaginary, leaving room only for the orbital recurrence of models and the simulated generation of difference.

The Divine Irreference of Images

To dissimulate is to feign not to have what one has. To simulate is to feign to have what one hasn't. One implies a presence, the other an absence. But the matter is more complicated, since to simulate is not simply to feign: "Someone who feigns an illness can simply go to bed and make believe he is ill. Someone who simulates an illness produces in himself some of the symptoms." (Littre) Thus, feigning or dissimulating leaves the reality principle intact: the difference is always clear, it is only masked; whereas simulation threatens the difference between "true" and "false," between "real" and "imaginary." Since the simulator produces "true" symptoms, is he ill or not? He cannot be treated objectively either as ill, or as not-ill. Psychology and medicine stop at this point, before a thereafter undiscoverable truth of the illness. For if any symptom can be "produced," and can no longer be accepted as a fact of nature, then every illness may be considered as simulatable and simulated, and medicine loses its meaning since it only knows how to treat "true" illnesses by their objective causes. Psychosomatics evolves in a dubious way on the edge of the illness principle. As for psychoanalysis, it transfers the symptom from the organic to the unconscious order: once again, the latter is held to be true, more true than the former—but why should simulation stop at the portals of the unconscious? Why couldn't the "work" of the unconscious be "produced" in the same way as any other symptom in classical medicine? Dreams already are.

The alienist, of course, claims that "for each form of the mental alienation there is a particular order in the succession of symptoms, of which the simulator is unaware and in the absence of which the alienist is unlikely to be deceived." This (which dates from 1865) in order to save at all cost the truth principle, and to escape the specter raised by simulation—namely that truth, reference and objective causes have ceased to exist. What can medicine do with something which floats on either side of illness, on either side of health, or with the reduplication of illness in a discourse that is no longer true or false? What can psychoanalysis do with the reduplication of the discourse of the unconscious in a discourse of simulation that can never be unmasked, since it isn't false either?[2]

What can the army do with simulators? Traditionally, following a direct principle of identification, it unmasks and punishes them. Today, it can reform an excellent simulator as though he were equivalent to a "real" homosexual, heart-case, or lunatic. Even military psychology retreats from the Cartesian clarities and hesitates to draw the distinction between true and false, between the "produced" symptom and the authentic symptom. "If he acts crazy so well, then he must be mad." Nor is it mistaken: in the sense that all lunatics are simulators, and this lack of distinction is the worst form of subversion. Against it classical reason armed itself with all its categories. But it is this today which again outflanks them, submerging the truth principle.

Outside of medicine and the army, favored terrains of simulation, the affair goes back to religion and the simulacrum of divinity: "I forbad any simulacrum in the temples because the divinity that breathes life into nature cannot be represented." Indeed it can. But what becomes of the divinity when it reveals itself in icons, when it is multiplied in simulacra? Does it remain the supreme authority, simply incarnated in images as a visible

---

[2]And which is not susceptible to resolution in transference. It is the entanglement of these two discourses which makes psychoanalysis interminable.

theology? Or is it volatilized into simulacra which alone deploy their pomp and power of fascination—the visible machinery of icons being substituted for the pure and intelligible Idea of God? This is precisely what was feared by the iconoclasts, whose millennial quarrel is still with us today.[3] Their rage to destroy images arose precisely because they sensed this omnipotence of simulacra, this facility they have of effacing God from the consciousness of man, and the overwhelming, destructive truth which they suggest: that ultimately there has never been any God, that only the simulacrum exists, indeed that God himself has only ever been his own simulacrum. Had they been able to believe that images only occulted or masked the Platonic idea of God, there would have been no reason to destroy them. One can live with the idea of a distorted truth. But their metaphysical despair came from the idea that the images concealed nothing at all and that in fact they were not images, such as the original model would have made them, but actually perfect simulacra forever radiant with their own fascination. But this death of the divine referential has to be exorcised at all cost.

It can be seen that the iconoclasts, who are often accused of despising and denying images, were in fact the ones who accorded them their actual worth, unlike the iconolaters, who saw in them only reflections and were content to venerate God at one remove. But the converse can also be said, namely that the iconolaters were the most modern and adventurous minds, since underneath the idea of the apparition of God in the mirror of images, they already enacted his death and his disappearance in the epiphany of his representations (which they perhaps knew no longer represented anything, and that they were purely a game, but that this was precisely the greatest game—knowing also that it is dangerous to unmask images, since they dissimulate the fact that there is nothing behind them).

This was the approach of the Jesuits, who based their politics on the virtual disappearance of God and on the worldly

---

[3]Cf., Maria Perniola. "Icones, Visions, Simulacres," *Traverses*, no. 10 (February 1978): 39-49. Translated by Michel Makarius.

and spectacular manipulation of consciences—the evanescence of God in the epiphany of power—the end of transcendence, which no longer serves as alibi for a strategy completely free of influences and signs. Behind the baroque of images hides the grey eminence of politics.

Thus perhaps at stake has always been the murderous capacity of images, murderers of the real, murderers of their own model as the Byzantine icons could murder the divine identity. To this murderous capacity is opposed the dialectical capacity of representations as a visible and intelligible mediation of the Real. All of western faith and good faith was engaged in this wager on representation: that a sign could refer to the depth of meaning, that a sign could exchange for meaning, and that something could guarantee this exchange—God, of course. But what if God himself can be simulated, that is to say, reduced to the signs which attest his existence? Then the whole system becomes weightless, it is no longer anything but a gigantic simulacrum— not unreal, but a simulacrum, never again exchanging for what is real, but exchanging in itself, in an uninterrupted circuit without reference or circumference.

So it is with simulation, insofar as it is opposed to representation. The latter starts from the principle that the sign and the real are equivalent (even if this equivalence is utopian, it is a fundamental axiom). Conversely, simulation starts from the *utopia* of this principle of equivalence, *from the radical negation of the sign as value*, from the sign as reversion and death sentence of every reference. Whereas representation tries to absorb simulation by interpreting it as false representation, simulation envelops the whole edifice of representation as itself a simulacrum.

These would be the successive phases of the image:
—it is the reflection of a basic reality
—it masks and perverts a basic reality
—it masks the absence of a basic reality
—it bears no relation to any reality whatever:
it is its own pure simulacrum.

In the first case, the image is a good appearance—the representation is of the order of sacrament. In the second, it is an evil appearance—of the order of malefice. In the third, it plays at being an appearance—it is of the order of sorcery. In the fourth, it is no longer in the order of appearance at all, but of simulation.

The transition from signs which dissimulate something to signs which dissimulate that there is nothing marks the decisive turning point. The first implies a theology of truth and secrecy (to which the notion of ideology still belongs). The second inaugurates an age of simulacra and simulation, in which there is no longer any God to recognize his own, nor any last judgment to separate true from false, the real from its artificial resurrection, since everything is already dead and risen in advance.

When the real is no longer what it used to be, nostalgia assumes its full meaning. There is a proliferation of myths of origin and signs of reality; of secondhand truth, objectivity, and authenticity. There is an escalation of the true, of the lived experience; a resurrection of the figurative where the object and substance have disappeared. And there is a panic-stricken production of the real and the referential, above and parallel to the panic of material production: this is how simulation appears in the phase that concerns us—a strategy of the real, neo-real, and hyperreal, whose universal double is a strategy of deterrence.

Rameses, or Rose-Colored Resurrection

Ethnology almost met a paradoxical death that day in 1971 when the Phillipine government decided to return to their primitive state the few dozen Tasaday discovered deep in the jungle, where they had lived for eight centuries undisturbed by the rest of mankind, out of reach of colonists, tourists, and ethnologists. This was at the initiative of the anthropologists themselves, who saw the natives decompose immediately on contact, like a mummy in the open air.

For ethnology to live, its object must die. But the latter revenges itself by dying for having been "discovered," and defies by its death the science that wants to take hold of it.

Doesn't every science live on this paradoxical slope to which it is doomed by the evanescence of its object in the very process of its apprehension, and by the pitiless reversal this dead object exerts on it? Like Orpheus, it always turns around so soon, and its object, like Eurydice, falls back into Hades.

It was against this hades of paradox that the ethnologists wanted to protect themselves by cordoning off the Tasaday with virgin forest. Nobody now will touch it: the vein is closed down, like a mine. Science loses a precious capital, but the object will be safe—lost to science, but intact in its "virginity." It isn't a question of sacrifice (science never sacrifices itself; it is always murderous), but of the simulated sacrifice of its object in order to save its reality principle. The Tasaday, frozen in their natural element, provide a perfect alibi, an eternal guarantee. At this point begins a persistent anti-ethnology to which Jaulin, Castaneda, and Clastres variously belong. In any case, the logical evolution of a science is to distance itself ever further from its object until it dispenses with it entirely: its autonomy ever more fantastical in reaching its pure form.

The Indian thereby driven back into the ghetto, into the glass coffin of virgin forest, becomes the simulation model for all conceivable Indians *before ethnology*: The latter thus allows itself the luxury of being incarnate beyond itself, in the "brute" reality of these Indians it has entirely reinvented—savages who are indebted to ethnology for still being Savages: what a turn of events, what a triumph for this science which seemed dedicated to their destruction!

Of course, these particular savages are posthumous: frozen, cryogenized, sterilized, protected to death, they have become referential simulacra, and the science itself a pure simulation. Same thing at Creusot where, in the form of an "open" museum exhibition, they have "museumized" on the spot, as historical witnesses to their period, entire working-class *quartiers*, living metallurgical zones, a complete culture including men, women, and children and their gestures, languages, and habits—living beings fossilized as in a snapshot. The museum, instead of being circumscribed in a geometric location, is now everywhere, like a dimension of life itself. Thus, technology now freed from its object, will no longer be circumscribed as an objective science but is applied to all living things and becomes invisible, like an omnipresent fourth dimension, that of the simulacrum. *We are all Tasaday*. Or Indians who have once more become "what they used to be," or at least that which ethnology has made them—simulacra Indians who proclaim at last the universal truth of ethnology.

We all become living specimens under the spectral light of ethnology, or of anti-ethnology which is only the pure form of triumphal ethnology, under the sign of dead differences, and of the resurrection of differences. It is thus extremely naive to look for ethnology among the savages or in some Third World—it is here, everywhere, in the metropolis, among the whites, in a world completely catalogued and analyzed and then artificially revived as though real, in a world of simulation: of the hallucination of truth, of blackmail by the real, of the murder and historical (hysterical) retrospection of every symbolic form—a murder whose first victims were, noblesse oblige, the savages, but which for a long time now has been extended to all Western societies.

But at the same moment ethnology gives up its final and only lesson, the secret which kills it (and which the savages understood much better): the vengeance of the dead.

The confinement of the scientific object is the same as that of the insane and the dead. And just as the whole of society is hopelessly contaminated by that mirror of madness it has held out for itself, so science can only die contaminated by the death of the object which is its inverse mirror. It is science which ostensibly masters the object, but it is the latter which deeply invests the former, following an unconscious reversion, giving only dead and circular replies to a dead and circular interrogation.

Nothing changes when society breaks the mirror of madness (abolishes asylums, gives speech back to the mad, etc.) nor when science seems to break the mirror of its objectivity (effacing itself before its object, as Castaneda does, etc.) and to bow down before "differences." Confinement is succeeded by an apparatus which assumes a countless and endlessly diffractable, multipliable form. As fast as ethnology in its classical institution collapses, it survives in an anti-ethnology whose task is to reinject fictional difference and savagery everywhere, in order to conceal the fact that it is this world, our own, which in its way has become savage again, that is to say devastated by difference and death.

It is in this way, under the pretext of saving the original, that the caves of Lascaux have been forbidden to visitors and an exact replica constructed 500 meters away, so that everyone can see them (you glance through a peephole at the real grotto and then visit the reconstituted whole). It is possible that the very memory of the original caves will fade in the mind of future generations, but from now on there is no longer any difference: the duplication is sufficient to render both artificial.

In the same way the whole of science and technology were recently mobilized to save the mummy of Rameses II, after it had been left to deteriorate in the basement of a museum. The West was panic-stricken at the thought of not being able to save what the symbolic order had been able to preserve for forty centuries, but away from the light and gaze of onlookers. Rameses means nothing to us: only the mummy is of inestimable worth since it is what guarantees that accumulation means something. Our entire linear and accumulative culture would collapse if we could not stockpile the past in plain view. To this end the pharaohs must be brought out of their tombs, and the mummies out of their silence. To this end they must be exhumed and given military honors. They are prey to both science and the worms. Only absolute secrecy ensured their potency throughout the millennia—their mastery over putrefaction, which signified a mastery over the total cycle of exchange with death. *We* know better than to use our science for the *reparation* of the mummy, that is, to restore a visible order, whereas embalming was a mythical labor aimed at immortalizing a *hidden* dimension.

We need a visible past, a visible continuum, a visible myth of origin to reassure us as to our ends, since ultimately we have never believed in them. Whence that historic scene of the mummy's reception at Orly airport. All because Rameses was a great despot and military figure? Certainly. But above all because the order which our culture dreams of, behind that defunct power it seeks to annex, could have had nothing to do with it, and it dreams thus because it has exterminated this order by exhuming it *as if it were our own past.*

We are fascinated by Rameses just as Renaissance Christians were by the American Indian: those (human?) beings who had never known the word of Christ. Thus, at the beginning of colonization, there was a moment of stupor and amazement before the very possibility of escaping the universal law of the Gospel. There were two possible responses: either to admit that this law was not universal, or to exterminate the Indians so as to remove the evidence. In general, it was enough to convert them, or even simply to discover them, to ensure their slow extermination.

Thus it would have been enough to exhume Rameses to ensure his extermination by museumification. For mummies do not decay because of worms: they die from being transplanted from a prolonged symbolic order, which is master over death and putrescence, on to an order of history, science, and museums—our own, which is no longer master over anything, since it only knows how to condemn its predecessors to death and putrescence and their subsequent resuscitation by science. An irreparable violence towards all secrets, the violence of a civilization without secrets. The hatred by an entire civilization for its own foundations.

And just as with ethnology playing at surrendering its object the better to establish itself in its pure form, so museumification is only one more turn in the spiral of artificiality. Witness the cloister of St. Michel de Cuxa, which is going to be repatriated at great expense from the Cloisters in New York to be reinstalled on "its original site." And everyone is supposed to applaud this restitution (as with the "experimental campaign to win back the sidewalks" on the Champs-Élysées!). However, if the exportation of the cornices was in effect an arbitrary act, and if the Cloisters of New York is really an artificial mosaic of all cultures (according to a logic of the capitalist centralization of value), then reimportation to the original location is even more artificial: it is a total simulacrum that links up with "reality" by a complete circumvolution.

The cloister should have stayed in New York in its simulated environment, which at least would have fooled no one. Repatriation is only a supplementary subterfuge in order to make out as though nothing had happened and to indulge in a retrospective hallucination.

In the same way Americans flatter themselves that they brought the number of Indians back to what it was before their conquest. Everything is obliterated only to begin again. They even flatter themselves that they went one better, by surpassing the original figure. This is presented as proof of the superiority of civilization: it produces more Indians than they were capable of themselves. By a sinister mockery, this overproduction is yet again a way of destroying them: for Indian culture, like all tribal culture, rests on the limitation of the group and prohibiting any of its "unrestricted" growth, as can be seen in the case of Ishi. Demographic "promotion," therefore, is just one more step towards symbolic extermination.

We too live in a universe everywhere strangely similar to the original—here things are duplicated by their own scenario. But this double does not mean, as in folklore, the imminence of death—they are already purged of death, and are even better than in life; more smiling, more authentic, in light of their model, like the faces in funeral parlors.

Hyperreal and Imaginary

Disneyland is a perfect model of all the entangled orders of simulation. To begin with it is a play of illusions and phantasms: Pirates, the Frontier, Future World, etc. This imaginary world is supposed to be what makes the operation successful. But what draws the crowds is undoubtedly much more the social microcosm, the miniaturized and religious reveling in real America, in its delights and drawbacks. You park outside, queue up inside, and are totally abandoned at the exit. In this imaginary world the only phantasmagoria is in the inherent warmth and affection of the crowd, and in that sufficiently excessive number of gadgets used there specifically to maintain the multitudinous affect. The contrast with the absolute solitude of the parking lot—a veritable concentration camp—is total.   Or rather: inside, a whole range of gadgets magnetize the crowd into direct flows—outside, solitude is directed onto a single gadget: the automobile.   By an extraordinary coincidence (one that undoubtedly belongs to the peculiar enchantment of this universe), this deep-frozen infantile world happens to have been conceived and realized by a man who is himself now cryogenized: Walt Disney, who awaits his resurrection at minus 180 degrees centigrade.

The objective profile of America, then, may be traced throughout Disneyland, even down to the morphology of individuals and the crowd. All its values are exalted here, in miniature and comic strip form. Embalmed and pacified. Whence the possibility of an ideological analysis of Disneyland (Louis Marin does it well in *Utopies, jeux d'espaces*): digest of the American way of life, panegyric to American values, idealized transposition of a contradictory reality. To be sure. But this conceals something else, and that "ideological" blanket exactly serves to cover over a *third-order simulation*: Disneyland is there to conceal the fact that it is the "real" country, all of "real" America, which *is* Disneyland (just as prisons are there to conceal the fact that it is the social in its entirety, in its banal omnipresence, which is carceral). Disneyland is presented as imaginary in order to make us believe that the rest is real, when in fact all of Los Angeles and the America surrounding it are no longer real, but of the order of the hyperreal and of simulation. It is no longer a question of a false representation of reality (ideology), but of concealing the fact that the real is no longer real, and thus of saving the reality principle.

The Disneyland imaginary is neither true nor false; it is a deterrence machine set up in order to rejuvenate in reverse the fiction of the real. Whence the debility, the infantile degeneration of this imaginary. It is meant to be an infantile world, in order to make us believe that the adults are elsewhere, in the "real" world, and to conceal the fact that real childishness is everywhere, particularly amongst those adults who go there to act the child in order to foster illusions to their real childishness.

Moreover, Disneyland is not the only one. Enchanted Village, Magic Mountain, Marine World: Los Angeles is encircled by these "imaginary stations" which feed reality, reality-energy, to a town whose mystery is precisely that it is nothing more than a network of endless, unreal circulation—a town of fabulous proportions, but without space or dimensions. As much as electrical and nuclear power stations, as much as film studios, this town, which is nothing more than an immense script and a perpetual motion picture, needs this old imaginary made up of childhood signals and faked phantasms for its sympathetic nervous system.

Political Incantation

Watergate. Same scenario as Disneyland (an imaginary effect concealing that reality no more exists outside than inside the bounds of the artificial perimeter): though here it is a scandal effect concealing that there is no difference between the facts and their denunciation (identical methods are employed by the CIA and the *Washington Post* journalists). Same operation, though this time tending towards scandal as a means to regenerate a moral and political principle, towards the imaginary as a means to regenerate a reality principle in distress.

The denunciation of scandal always pays homage to the law. And Watergate above all succeeded in imposing the idea that Watergate *was* a scandal—in this sense it was an extraordinary operation of intoxication. The reinjection of a large dose of political morality on a global scale. It could be said along with Bourdieu that: "The specific character of every relation of force is to dissimulate itself as such, and to acquire all its force only because it is so dissimulated," understood as follows: capital, which is immoral and unscrupulous, can only function behind a moral superstructure, and whoever regenerates this public morality (by indignation, denunciation, etc.) spontaneously furthers the order of capital, as did the *Washington Post* journalists.

But this is still only the formula of ideology, and when Bourdieu enunciates it, he takes "relation of force" to mean the *truth* of the capitalist domination, and he *denounces* this relation of force as itself a *scandal*—he therefore occupies the same deterministic and moralistic position as the *Washington Post* journalists. He does the same job of purging and reviving moral order, an order of truth wherein the genuine symbolic violence of the social order is engendered, well beyond all relations of force, which are only its indifferent and shifting configuration in the moral and political consciousness of men.

All that capital asks of us is to receive it as rational or to combat it in the name of rationality, to receive it as moral or to combat it in the name of morality. For they are *identical,* meaning *they can be read another way:* before, the task was to dissimulate scandal; today, the task is to conceal the fact that there is none.

 Watergate is not a scandal: this is what must be said at all cost, for this is what everyone is concerned to conceal, this dissimulation masking a strengthening of morality, a moral panic as we approach the primal (mise-en-) scene of capital: its instantaneous cruelty, its incomprehensible ferocity, its fundamental immorality—this is what is scandalous, unaccountable for in that system of moral and economic equivalence which remains the axiom of leftist thought, from Enlightenment theory to communism. Capital doesn't give a damn about the idea of the contract which is imputed to it—it is a monstrous unprincipled undertaking, nothing more. Rather, it is "enlightened" thought which seeks to control capital by imposing rules on it. And all that recrimination which replaced revolutionary thought today comes down to reproaching capital for not following the rules of the game. "Power is unjust, its justice is a class justice, capital exploits us, etc."—as if capital were linked by a contract to the society it rules. It is the left which holds out the mirror of equivalence, hoping that capital will fall for this phantasmagoria of the social contract and fulfill its obligation towards the whole of society (at the same time, no need for revolution: it is enough that capital accept the rational formula of exchange).

 Capital in fact has never been linked by contract to the society it dominates. It is a sorcery of the social relation, it is a *challenge to society* and should be responded to as such. It is not a scandal to be denounced according to moral and economic rationality, but a challenge to take up according to symbolic law.

Moebius-Spiraling Negativity

 Hence Watergate was only a trap set by the system to catch its adversaries—a simulation of scandal to regenerative ends. This is embodied by the character called "Deep Throat," who was said to be a Republican grey eminence manipulating the leftist journalists in order to get rid of Nixon—and why not? All hypotheses are possible, although this one is superfluous: the work of the right is done very well, and spontaneously, by the left on its

own. Besides, it would be naive to see an embittered good
conscience at work here. For the right itself also spontaneously
does the work of the left. All the hypotheses of manipulation are
reversible in an endless whirligig. For manipulation is a
floating causality where positivity and negativity engender and
overlap with one another, where there is no longer any active or
passive. It is by putting an arbitrary stop to this revolving
causality that a principle of political reality can be saved. It is by
the simulation of a conventional, restricted perspective field,
where the premises and consequences of any act or event are
calculable, that a political credibility can be maintained
(including, of course, "objective" analysis, struggle, etc.). But if
the entire cycle of any act or event is envisaged in a system where
linear continuity and dialectical polarity no longer exist, in a
field unhinged by simulation, then all determination evaporates,
every act terminates at the end of the cycle having benefited
everyone and been scattered in all directions.

    Is any given bombing in Italy the work of leftist
extremists, or of extreme right-wing provocation, or staged by
centrists to bring every terrorist extreme into disrepute and to
shore up its own failing power, or again, is it a police-inspired
scenario in order to appeal to public security? All this is equally
true, and the search for proof, indeed the objectivity of the fact does
not check this vertigo of interpretation. We are in a logic of
simulation which has nothing to do with a logic of facts and an
order of reasons. Simulation is characterized by a precession of
the model, of all models around the merest fact—the models come
first, and their orbital (like a bomb) circulation constitutes the
genuine magnetic field of events. Facts no longer have any
trajectory of their own, they arise at the intersection of the models;
a single fact may even be engendered by all the models at once.
This anticipation, this precession, this short circuit, this confusion
of the fact with its model (no more divergence of meaning, no
more dialectical polarity, no more negative electricity or
implosion of poles) is what each time allows for all the possible
interpretations, even the most contradictory—all are true, in the
sense that their truth is exchangeable, in the image of the models
from which they proceed, in a generalized cycle.

The communists attack the Socialist party as though they wanted to shatter the union of the left. They sanction the idea that their reticence stems from a more radical political exigency. In fact, it is because they don't want power. But they do not want it at this conjecture because it is unfavorable for the left in general, or because it is unfavorable for them within the union of the left—or do they not want it by definition? When Berlinguer declares: "We mustn't be frightened of seeing the communists seize power in Italy," this means simultaneously:

—that there is nothing to fear, since the communists, if they come to power, will change nothing in its fundamental capitalist mechanism,

—that there isn't any risk of their ever coming to power (for the reason that they don't want to)—and even if they did take it up, they will only ever wield it by proxy,

—that in fact power, genuine power, no longer exists, and hence there is no risk of anybody seizing it or taking it over,

—but more: I, Berlinguer, am not frightened of seeing the communists seize power in Italy—which might appear evident, but not that much, since

—this can also mean the contrary (no need of psychoanalysis here): I am frightened of seeing the communists seize power (and with good reason, even for a communist).

All the above is simultaneously true. This is the secret of a discourse that is no longer only ambiguous, as political discourses can be, but that conveys the impossibility of a determinate position of power, the impossibility of a determinate position of discourse. And this logic belongs to neither party. It traverses all discourses without their wanting it.

Who will unravel this imbroglio? The Gordian knot can at least be cut. As for the Moebius strip, if it is split in two, it results in an additional spiral without there being any possibility of resolving its surfaces (here the reversible continuity of hypotheses). Hades of simulations, which is no longer one of torture, but of the subtle, maleficent, elusive twisting of

meaning[4]—where even those condemned at Burgos are still a gift
from Franco to Western democracy, which finds in them the
occasion to regenerate its own flagging humanism, and whose
indignant protestation in return consolidates Franco's regime by
uniting the Spanish masses against foreign intervention. Where
is the truth in all that, when such collusions admirably knit
together without their authors even knowing it?

The conjunction of the system and its extreme alternative
like two ends of a curved mirror, the "vicious" curvature of a
political space henceforth magnetized, circularized,
reversibilized from right to left, a torsion that is like the evil
demon of commutation, the whole system, the infinity of capital
folded back over its own surface: transfinite? And isn't it the
same with desire and libidinal space? The conjunction of desire
and value, of desire and capital. The conjunction of desire and
the law—the ultimate joy and metamorphosis of the law (which is
why it is so well received at the moment): only capital takes
pleasure, Lyotard said, before coming to think that *we* take
pleasure in capital. Overwhelming versatility of desire in
Deleuze, an enigmatic reversal which brings this desire that is
"revolutionary by itself, and as if involuntarily, in wanting what
it wants," to want its own repression and to invest paranoid and
fascist systems? A malign torsion which reduces this revolution
of desire to the same fundamental ambiguity as the other,
historical revolution.

All the referentials intermingle their discourses in a
circular, Moebian compulsion. Not so long ago sex and work were
savagely opposed terms: today both are dissolved into the same
type of demand. Formerly the discourse on history took its force
from opposing itself to the one on nature, the discourse on desire to
the one on power—today they exchange their signifiers and their
scenarios.

---

[4]This does not necessarily result in a despair of meaning, but just as much in
an improvisation of meaning, of nonsense, or of several simultaneous senses
which cancel each other out.

It would take too long to run through the whole range of operational negativity, of all those scenarios of deterrence which, like Watergate, try to regenerate a moribund principle by simulated scandal, phantasm, murder—a sort of hormonal treatment by negativity and crisis. It is always a question of proving the real by the imaginary, proving truth by scandal, proving the law by transgression, proving work by the strike, proving the system by crisis, and capital by revolution, as for that matter proving ethnology by the dispossession of its object (the Tasaday)—without counting:

—proving theater by anti-theater
—proving art by anti-art
—proving pedagogy by anti-pedagogy
—proving psychiatry by anti-psychiatry, etc., etc.

Everything is metamorphosed into its inverse in order to be perpetuated in its purged form. Every form of power, every situation speaks of itself by denial, in order to attempt to escape, by simulation of death, its real agony. Power can stage its own murder to rediscover a glimmer of existence and legitimacy. Thus, with the American presidents: the Kennedys are murdered because they still have a political dimension. Others—Johnson, Nixon, Ford—only had a right to puppet attempts, to simulate murders. But they nevertheless needed that aura of an artificial menace to conceal that they were nothing other than mannequins of power. In olden days the king (also the god) had to die—that was his strength. Today he does his miserable utmost to pretend to die, so as to preserve the *blessing of* power. But even this is gone.

To seek new blood in its own death, to renew the cycle by the mirror of crisis, negativity and anti-power: this is the only alibi of every power, of every institution attempting to break the vicious circle of its irresponsibility and its fundamental nonexistence, of its *deja-vu* and its *deja-mort*.

Strategy of the Real

Of the same order as the impossibility of rediscovering an absolute level of the real is the impossibility of staging an illusion. Illusion is no longer possible, because the real is no longer possible. It is the whole political problem of the parody, of hypersimulation or offensive simulation, which is posed here.

For example: it would be interesting to see whether the repressive apparatus would not react more violently to a simulated holdup than a real one. For the latter only upsets the order of things, the right of property, whereas the other interferes with the very principle of reality. Transgression and violence are less serious, for they only contest the distribution of the real. Simulation is infinitely more dangerous, however, since it always suggests, over and above its object, that law and order themselves might be nothing more than a simulation.

But the difficulty is in proportion to the peril. How to feign a violation and put it to the test? Go and simulate a theft in a large department store: how do you convince the security guards that it is a simulated theft? There is no "objective" difference: the same gestures and the same signs exist as for a real theft: in fact the signs incline neither to one side nor the other. As far as the established order is concerned, they are always of the order of the real.

Go and organize a fake holdup. Be sure to check that your weapons are harmless, and take the most trustworthy hostage, so that no life is in danger (otherwise you risk committing an offense). Demand ransom, and arrange it so that the operation creates the greatest commotion possible—in brief, stay close to the "trust," so as to test the reaction of the apparatus to a perfect simulation. But you won't succeed: the web of artificial signs will be inextricably mixed up with real elements (a police officer will really shoot on sight; a bank customer will faint and die of a heart attack; they will really turn the phony ransom over to you)—in brief, you will unwittingly find yourself immediately in the real, one of whose functions is precisely to devour every attempt at simulation, to reduce everything to some reality—that's exactly how the established order is, well before institutions and justice come into play.

In this impossibility of isolating the process of simulation must be seen the whole thrust of an order than can only see and understand in terms of some reality, because it can function nowhere else. The simulation of an offense, if it is patent, will either be punished more lightly (because it has no "consequences") or be punished as an offense to the public office (for example, if one triggered off a police operation "for nothing")—but *never as simulation*, since it is precisely as such that no equivalence with the real is possible, and hence no repression either. The challenge of simulation is irreceivable by power. How can you punish the simulation of virtue? Yet as such it is as serious as the simulation of crime. Parody makes obedience and transgression equivalent and that is the most serious crime, since *it cancels out the difference upon which the law is based.* The established order can do nothing against it, for the law is a second-order simulacrum whereas simulation is third-order, beyond true and false, beyond equivalences, beyond the rational distinctions upon which function all power and the entire social order. Hence, *failing the real,* it is here that we must aim at order.

This is why order always opts for the real. In a state of uncertainty, it always prefers this assumption (thus in the army they would rather take the simulator as a true madman). But this becomes more and more difficult, for it is practically impossible to isolate the process of simulation, through the force of inertia of the real which surrounds us, the inverse is also true (and this very reversibility forms part of the apparatus of simulation and of power's impotency): namely, *it is now impossible to isolate the process of the real,* or to prove the real.

Thus all holdups, hijacks, and the like are now as it were simulation holdups, in the sense that they are inscribed in advance in the decoding and orchestration rituals of the media, anticipated in their mode of presentation and possible consequences. In brief, where they function as a set of signs dedicated exclusively to their recurrence as signs, and no longer to their "real" goal at all. But this does not make them inoffensive. On the contrary, it is as hyperreal events, no longer having any particular contents or aims, but indefinitely refracted by each other (for that matter like so-called historical events: strikes, demonstrations, crises, etc.[5]), that they are precisely

---

[5]The energy crisis, the ecological setting, by and large, are themselves a disaster film, in the same style (and of the same value) as those which currently do so well for Hollywood. It is pointless to interpret these films laboriously by their relationship with an "objective" social crisis, or even

unverifiable by an order which can only exert itself on the real
and the rational, on ends and means: a referential order which
can only dominate referentials, a determinate power which can
only dominate a determined world, but which can do nothing about
that indefinite recurrence of simulation, about that weightless
nebula no longer obeying the law of gravitation of the real—power
itself eventually breaking apart in this space and becoming a
simulation of power (disconnected from its aims and objectives,
and dedicated to power effects and mass simulation).

The only weapon of power, its only strategy against this
defection, is to reinject realness and referentiality everywhere, in
order to convince us of the reality of the social, of the gravity of the
economy, and the finalities of production. For that purpose it
prefers the discourse of crisis, but also—why not?—the discourse of
desire. "Take your desires for reality!" can be understood as the
ultimate slogan of power, for in a nonreferential world even the
confusion of the reality principle with the desire principle is less
dangerous than contagious hyperreality. One remains among
principles, and there power is always right.

Hyperreality and simulation are deterrents of every
principle and of every objective; they turn against power this
deterrence which is so well utilized for a long time itself. For,
finally, it was capital which was the first to feed throughout its
history on the destruction of every referential, of every human
goal, which shattered every ideal distinction between true and
false, good and evil, in order to establish a radical law of
equivalence and exchange, the iron law of its power. It was the
first to practice deterrence, abstraction, disconnection,
deterritorialization, etc.; and if it was capital which fostered
reality, the reality principle, it was also the first to liquidate it in
the extermination of every use value, of every equivalence, of
production and wealth, in the very sensation we have of the

---

with an "objective" phantasm of disaster. It is in the other direction that we
must say it is the social itself which, in contemporary discourse, is organized
according to a script for a disaster film. (Cf., Michel Makarius, "La strategie
de la catastrophe," *Traverses*, no. 10 (February 1978): 115-124.

unreality of the stakes and the omnipotence of manipulation. Now, it is this very logic which is today hardened even more against it. And when it wants to fight this catastrophic spiral by secreting one last glimmer of reality, on which to found one last glimmer of power, it only multiplies the signs and accelerates the play of simulation.

As long as it was historically threatened by the real, power risked deterrence and simulation, disintegrating every contradiction by means of the production of equivalent signs. When it is threatened today by simulation (the threat of vanishing in the play of signs), power risks the real, risks crisis, it gambles on remanufacturing artificial, social, economic, political stakes. This is a question of life or death for it. But it is too late.

Whence the characteristic hysteria of our time: the hysteria of production and reproduction of the real.   The other production, that of goods and commodities, that of *la belle epoque* of political economy, no longer makes any sense of its own, and has not for some time.   What society seeks through production, and overproduction, is the restoration of the real which escapes. That is why contemporary "material" production is itself hyperreal. It retains all the features, the whole discourse of traditional production, but it is nothing more than its scaled-down refraction (thus the hyperrealists fasten in a striking resemblance a real from which has fled all meaning and charm, all the profundity and energy of representation).   Thus the hyperrealism of simulation expressed everywhere by the real's striking resemblance to itself.

Power, too, for some time now produces nothing but signs of its resemblance.   And at the same time, another figure of power comes into play: that of a collective demand for signs of power—a holy union which forms around the disappearance of power. Everybody belongs to it more or less in fear of the collapse of the political.   And in the end the game of power comes down to nothing more than the critical obsession with power—an obsession with its death, an obsession with its survival, the greater the more it disappears.   When it has totally disappeared, logically we will be under the total spell of power-haunting memory already foreshadowed everywhere, manifesting at one and the same time the compulsion to get rid of it (nobody wants it any more; everybody unloads it on others) and the apprehensive pining over its loss. Melancholy for societies without power: this has already given rise to fascism, that overdose of a powerful referential in a society which cannot terminate in mourning.

But we are still in the same boat: none of our societies knows how to manage its mourning for the real, for power, for the social itself, which is implicated in this same breakdown. And it is by an artificial revitalization of all this that we try to escape it. Undoubtedly this will even up in socialism. By an unforeseen twist of events and an irony which no longer belongs to history, it is through the death of the social that socialism will emerge—as it is through the death of God that religions emerge. A twisted coming, a perverse event, an unintelligible reversion to the logic of reason. As is the fact that power is no longer present except to conceal that there is none. A simulation which can go on indefinitely, since—unlike "true" power which is, or was, a structure, a strategy, a relation of force, a stake—this is nothing but the object of a social demand, and hence subject to the law of supply and demand, rather than to violence and death. Completely expunged from the political dimension, it is dependent, like any other commodity, on production and mass consumption. It's spark has disappeared—only the fiction of a political universe is saved.

Likewise with work. The spark of production, the violence of its stake no longer exists. Everybody still produces, and more and more, but work has subtly become something else: a need (as Marx ideally envisaged it, but not at all in the same sense), the object of a social "demand," like leisure, to which it is equivalent in the general run of life's options. A demand exactly proportional to the loss of stake in the work process.[6] The same

---

[6]To this flagging investment in work corresponds a parallel declining investment in consumption. Goodbye to use value or prestige of the automobile, goodbye to the amorous discourse which made a clear-cut distinction between the object of enjoyment and the object of work. Another discourse takes over, which is a discourse of work on the object of consumption aiming at an active, compelling, puritan reinvestment (use less

change in fortune as for power: the scenario of work is there to conceal the fact that the work-real, the production-real, has disappeared. And for that matter so has the strike-real too, which is no longer a stoppage of work, but its alternative pole in the ritual scansion of the social calendar. It is as if everyone has "occupied" their workplace or workpost, after declaring the strike, and resumed production, as is the custom in a "self-managed" job, in exactly the same terms as before, by declaring themselves (and virtually being) in a state of permanent strike.

This isn't a science-fiction dream: everywhere it is a question of a doubling of the work process. And of a double or locum for the strike process—strikes which are incorporated like obsolescence in objects, like crisis in production. Then there are no longer either strikes or work, but both simultaneously, that is to say something else entirely: a *wizardry of work*, a *trompe l'oeil*, a scenodrama (not to say melodrama) of production, collective dramaturgy upon the empty stage of the social.

It is no longer a question of the ideology of work—of the traditional ethic that obscures the "real" labor process and the "objective" process of exploitation—but of the scenario of work. Likewise, it is no longer a question of the ideology of power, but of the scenario of power. Ideology only corresponds to a betrayal of reality by signs; simulation corresponds to a short circuit of reality and to its reduplication by signs. It is always the aim of ideological analysis to restore the objective process; it is always a false problem to want to restore the truth beneath the simulacrum.

This is ultimately why power is so in accord with ideological discourses and discourses on ideology, for these are all discourses of truth—always good, even and especially if they are revolutionary, to counter the mortal blows of simulation.

---

gas, look to your security, speed is obsolete, etc.), to which automobile specifications pretend to be adapted: rediscovering a stake by transposition of the poles. Thus work becomes the object of a need, the car becomes the object of work—no better proof of the inability to distinguish the stakes. It is by the very swing of voting "rights" to electoral "duties" that the disinvestment of the political sphere is signaled.

The End of the Panopticon

It is again to this ideology of the lived experience, of exhumation, of the real in its fundamental banality, in its radical authenticity, that the American TV-*vérité* experiment on the Loud family in 1971 refers: seven months of uninterrupted shooting, 300 hours of direct nonstop broadcasting, without script or scenario, the odyssey of a family, its dramas, its joys, ups and downs—in brief, a "raw" historical document, and the "best thing ever on television, comparable, at the level of our daily existence, to the film of the lunar landing." Things are complicated by the fact that this family came apart during the shooting: a crisis flared up, the Louds went their separate ways, etc. Whence that insoluble controversy: was TV responsible? What would have happened if TV hadn't been there?

More interesting is the phantasm of filming the Louds *as if TV wasn't there*. The producer's trump card was to say: "They lived as if we weren't there." An absurd, paradoxical formula—neither true, nor false: but utopian. The "as if *we* weren't there" is equivalent to "as if *you* weren't there." It is this utopia, this paradox that fascinated 20-million viewers, much more than the "perverse" pleasure of prying. In this "truth" experiment, it is neither a question of secrecy nor of perversion, but of a kind of thrill of the real, or of an aesthetics of the hyperreal, a thrill of vertiginous and phony exactitude, a thrill of alienation and of magnification, of distortion in scale of excessive transparency all at the same time. The joy in an excess of meaning, when the bar of the sign slips below the regular waterline of meaning: the nonsignifier is elevated by the camera angle. Here the real can be seen never to have existed (but "as if you were there"), without the distance which produces perspective space and our depth vision (but, "more true than nature"). Joy in the microscopic simulation which transforms the real into the hyperreal. (This is also a little like what happens in porno, where fascination is more metaphysical than sexual.)

This family was in any case already somewhat hyperreal by its very selection: a typical, California-housed, three-garage, five-children, well-to-do, professional, upper-middle-class, ideal American family, with an ornamental housewife. In a way, it is this statistical perfection which dooms it to death. This ideal heroine of the American way of life is chosen, as in sacrificial rites, to be glorified and to die under the fiery glare of the studio lights, a modern fatum. For the heavenly fire no longer strikes depraved cities, it is rather the lens which cuts through ordinary reality like a laser, putting it to death. "The Louds: simply a family who agreed to deliver themselves into the hands of television, and to die from it," said the producer. So it is really a question of a sacrificial process, of a sacrificial spectacle offered to 20 million Americans. The liturgical drama of a mass society.

TV-vérité. Admirable ambivalent term: does it refer to the truth of this family, or to the truth of TV? In fact, it is TV which is the Loud's truth, it is it which is true, it is it which renders true. A truth which is no longer the reflexive truth of the mirror, nor the perspective truth of the panoptic system and of the gaze, but the manipulative truth of the test which probes and interrogates, of the laser which touches and then pierces, of computer cards which retain your punched-out sequences, of the genetic code which regulates your combinations, of cells which inform your sensory universe. It is to this kind of truth that the Loud family is subjected by the TV medium, and in this sense it really amounts to a death sentence (but is it still a question of truth?).

The end of the panoptic system. The eye of TV is no longer the source of an absolute gaze, and the ideal of control is no longer that of transparency. The latter still presupposes an objective space (that of the Renaissance) and the omnipotence of a despotic gaze. This is still, if not a system of confinement at least a system of scrutiny. No longer subtle, but always in a position of exteriority, playing on the opposition between seeing and being seen, even if the focal point of the panopticon may be blind.

It is entirely different when with the Louds. "You no longer watch TV, TV watches you (live)," or again: "You no longer listen to *Pas de Panique, Pas de Panique* listens to you"— switching over from the panoptic apparatus of surveillance (of *Discipline and Punish*) to a system of deterrence, where the distinction between active and passive is abolished. No longer is there any imperative to submit to the model, or to the gaze. "YOU are the model!" "YOU are the majority!" Such is the slope of a hyperrealist sociality, where the real is confused with the model, as in the statistic operation, or with the medium, as in the Louds' operation. Such is the later stage of development of the social relation, our own, which is no longer one of persuasion (the classical age of propaganda, ideology, publicity, etc.) but one of dissuasion or deterrence: "YOU are news, you are the social, the event is you, you are involved, you can use your voice, etc." A turnabout of affairs by which it becomes impossible to locate an instance of the model, of power, of the gaze, of the medium itself, since *you* are always already on the other side. No more subject, focal point, center, or periphery: but pure flexion or circular inflection.   No more violence or surveillance: only "information," secret virulence, chain reaction, slow implosion, and simulacra of spaces where the real-effect again comes into play.

We are witnessing the end of perspective and panoptic space (which remains a moral hypothesis bound up with every classical analysis of the "objective" essence of power), and hence the very abolition of the spectacular. Television, in the case of the Louds for example, is no longer a spectacular medium. We are no longer in the society of spectacle which the situationists talked about, nor in the specific types of alienation and repression which this implied. The medium itself is no longer identifiable as such, and the merging of the medium and the message (McLuhan[7]) is

---

[7]The medium/message confusion, of course, is a correlative of the confusion between sender and receiver, thus sealing the disappearance of all the dual, polar structures which formed the discursive organization of language, referring to the celebrated grid of functions in Jakobson, the organization of all determinate articulation of meaning. "Circular" discourse must be taken literally: that is, it no longer goes from one point to the other but describes a circle that indistinctly incorporates the positions of transmitter and receiver, henceforth unlocatable as such. Thus there is no longer any instance of power, any transmitting authority--power is something that circulates and whose source can no longer be located, a cycle in which the positions of dominator and the dominated interchange in an endless reversion which is also the end of power in its classical definition. The circularization of power, knowledge and discourse brings every localization of instances and poles to an end. Even in psychoanalytic interpretation, the "power" of the interpreter

the first great formula of this new age.   There is no longer any

---

does not come from any external authority, but from the interpreted themselves. This changes everything, for we can always ask the traditional holders of power where they get their power from. Who made you Duke? The King. And who made the King? God. God alone does not reply. But to the question: Who made the psychoanalyst? the analyst quite easily replies: You. Thus is expressed, by an inverse simulation, the passage from the "analyzed" to the "analysand," from active to passive, which only goes to describe the swirling, mobile effect of the poles, its effect of circularity in which power is lost, is dissolved, is resolved into complete manipulation (this is no longer of the order of the directive authority and the gaze, but of the order of personal contact and communication.) See, also, the State/ family circularity secured by the floating and metastatic regulation of images of the social and the private. (Jacque Donzelot. The Policing of Families, trans. Robert Hurley [New York: Pantheon Books, 1979]).

From now on, it is impossible to ask the famous question:

"From what position do you speak?"—

"How do you know?"—

"From where do you get the power?" without immediately getting the reply: "But it is of (from) you that I speak"—meaning, it is you who speaks, it is you who knows, power is you. A gigantic circumvolution of the spoken word, which amounts to irredeemable blackmail and irremovable deterrence of the subject supposed to speak, but left without a word to say, responseless, since to questions asked can come the inevitable reply: but you are the replay, or: your question is already an answer, etc.—the whole sophistical stranglehold of his own questioning, the precession of the reply about the question (the whole violence of interpretation is there, and the violence of the conscious or unconscious self-management of "speech").

This simulacrum of inversion or involution of poles, this clever subterfuge which is the secret of the whole discourse of manipulation and hence, today, in every domain, the secret of all those new powers sweeping clean the stage of power, forging the assumption of all speech from which comes the fantastic silent majority characteristic of our times—all this undoubtedly began in the political sphere with the democratic simulacrum, that is to say with the substitution of the instance of the people for the instance of God as source of power, and the substitution of power as representation for power as emanation. An anti-Copernican revolution: no longer any transcendent instance nor any sun nor any luminous source of power and knowledge—everything comes from and returns to the people. It is through this magnificent recycling that the universal simulacrum of manipulation, from the scenario of mass suffrage to present-day and illusory opinion polls, begins to be installed.

medium in the literal sense: it is now intangible, diffuse, and diffracted in the real, and it can no longer even be said that the latter is distorted by it.

Such immixture, such a viral, endemic, chronic, alarming presence of the medium, without our being able to isolate its effects—spectralized, like those publicity holograms sculptured in empty space with laser beams, the event filtered by the medium—the dissolution of TV into life, the dissolution of life into TV—an indiscernible chemical solution: we are all Louds, doomed not to invasion, to pressure, to violence, and to blackmail by the media and the models, but to their induction, to their infiltration, to their illegible violence.

But we must be careful of the negative twist discourse gives this: it is a question neither of an illness nor of a viral complaint. Rather, we must think of the media as if they were, in outer orbit, a sort of genetic code which controls the mutation of the real into the hyperreal, just as the other, micromolecular code controls the passage of the signal from a representative sphere of meaning to the genetic sphere of the programmed signal.

The whole traditional mode of causality is brought into question: the perspective, deterministic mode, the "active," critical mode, the analytical mode—the distinction between cause and effect, between active and passive, between subject and object, between ends and means. It is in this mode that it can be said: TV watches us, TV alienates us, TV manipulates us, TV informs us. Throughout all this, one is dependent on the analytical conception whose vanishing point is the horizon between reality and meaning.

On the contrary, we must imagine TV on the DNA model, as an effect in which the opposing poles of determination vanish according to a nuclear contraction or retraction of the old polar schema which has always maintained a minimal distance between a cause and an effect, between the subject and an object: precisely, the meaning gap, the discrepancy, the difference, the smallest possible margin of error, irreducible under penalty of reabsorption in an aleatory and indeterminable process which discourse can no longer even account for, since it is itself a determinable order.

It is this gap which vanishes in the genetic coding process, where indeterminacy is less a product of molecular randomness than a product of the abolition, pure and simple, of the relation. In the process of molecular control which "goes" from the DNA nucleus to the "substance" it "informs," there is no more traversing of an effect, of an energy, of a determination, of any message. "Order, signal, impulse, message": all these attempt to render the matter intelligible to us, but by analogy, retranscribing in terms of inscription vector, decoding, a dimension of which we know nothing—it is no longer even a "dimension," or perhaps it is the fourth (that which is defined, however, in Einsteinian relativity, by the absorption of the distinct poles of space and time). In fact, this whole process only makes sense to us in the negative form. But nothing separates one pole from the other, the initial from the terminal: there is just a sort of contraction into each other, a fantastic telescoping, a collapsing of the two traditional poles into one another: an IMPLOSION—an absorption of the radiating model of causality, of the differential mode of determination with its positive and negative electricity—an implosion of meaning. *This is where simulation begins.*

Everywhere, in whatever political, biological, psychological, media domain, where the distinction between poles can no longer be maintained, or enters into simulation, and hence into absolute manipulation—not passivity, but the *non-distinction of active and passive*. DNA realizes this aleatory reduction at the level of the living substance. Television itself, in the example of the Louds, also attains this *indefinite limit* where the family *vis-à-vis* TV are no more or less active or passive than is a living substance *vis-à-vis* its molecular code. In both there is only a nebula indecipherable into its simple element, indecipherable as to its truth.

Orbital and Nuclear

The nuclear is the apotheosis of simulation. Yet the balance of terror is nothing more than the spectacular slope of a system of deterrence that has crept from the inside into all the cracks of daily life. The nuclear cliffhanger only sees the trivialized system of deterrence at the heart of the media, of the inconsequential violence that reigns throughout the world, of the aleatory contrivance of every choice which is made for us. The slightest details of our behavior are ruled by neutralized, indifferent, equivalent signs, by zero-sum signs like those which regulate "game strategy" (but the genuine equation is elsewhere, and the unknown is precisely that variable of simulation which makes the atomic arsenal itself a hyperreal form, a simulacrum which dominates us all and reduces all "ground-level" events to mere ephemeral scenarios, transforming the only life left to us into survival, into a wager without takers—not even into a death policy: but into a policy devaluated in advance).

It isn't that the direct menace of atomic destruction paralyzes our lives. It is rather that deterrence leukemizes us. And this deterrence comes from the very situation which excludes the real atomic clash—excludes it beforehand like the eventuality of the real in a system of signs. Everybody pretends to believe in the reality of this menace (one understands it from the military point of view, the whole seriousness of their exercise, and the discourse of their "strategy," is at stake): but there are precisely no strategic stakes at this level, and the whole originality of the situation lies in the improbability of destruction.

Deterrence excludes war—the antiquated violence of expanding systems. Deterrence is the neutral, implosive violence of the metastable or involving systems. There is no subject of deterrence any more, nor adversary, nor strategy—it is a planetary structure of the annihilation of stakes. Atomic war, like that of Troy, will not take place. The risk of nuclear atomization only serves as a pretext, through the sophistication of arms—but this sophistication exceeds any possible objective to such an extent that it is itself a symptom of nonexistence—to the installation of a universal system of security, linkup , and control whose deterrent effect does not aim for atomic clash at all (the latter has never been a real possibility, except no doubt right at the beginning of the cold war, when the nuclear posture was confused with conventional war) but really the much larger probability of any real event, of anything which could disturb the general system and upset the balance. The balance of terror is the terror of balance.

Deterrence is not a strategy. It circulates and is exchanged between the nuclear protagonists exactly like international capital in that orbital zone of monetary speculation, whose flow is sufficient to control all global finance. Thus kill money (not referring to real killing, any more than floating capital refers to real production) circulating in nuclear orbit is sufficient to control all violence and potential conflict on the globe.

What stirs in the shadow of this posture, under the pretext of a maximal "objective" menace and thanks to that nuclear Sword of Damocles, is the perfection of the best system of control which has never existed. And the progressive satellization of the whole planet by that hypermodel of security.

The same goes for *peaceful* nuclear installations. Pacification doesn't distinguish between the civil and the military; wherever irreversible apparatuses of control are elaborated, wherever the notion of security becomes absolute, wherever the norm of security replaces the former arsenal of laws and violence (including war), the system of deterrence grows, and around it grows a historical, social, and political desert. A huge involution makes every conflict, every opposition, every act of defiance contract in proportion to this blackmail which interrupts, neutralizes, and freezes them. No mutiny, no history can unfurl any more according to its own logic since it risks annihilation. No strategy is even possible anymore, and escalation is only a puerile game left to the military. The political stake is dead. Only simulacra of conflict and carefully circumscribed stakes remain.

The "space race" played exactly the same role as the nuclear race. This is why it was so easily able to take over from it in the 1960s (Kennedy/ Khrushchev), or to develop concurrently in a mode of "peaceful coexistence." For what is the ultimate function of the space race, of lunar conquest, of satellite launchings, if not the institution of a model of universal gravitation, of satellization, whose perfect embryo is the lunar module: a programmed microcosm, where *nothing can be left to chance?* Trajectory, energy, computation, physiology, psychology, the environment— nothing can be left to contingency, this is the total universe of the norm—the Law no longer exists, it is the operational immanence of every detail which is law. A universe purged of every threat to the senses, in a state of asepsis and weightlessness—it is this very perfection which is fascinating. For the exaltation of the masses was not in response to the lunar landing or the voyage of man in space (this is rather the fulfillment of an earlier dream)—no, we are dumbfounded by the perfection of their planning and technical manipulation, by the immanent wonder of programmed development. Fascinated by the maximization of norms and by the mastery of probability. Unbalanced by the model, as we are by death, but without fear or impulse. For if the law, with its aura of transgression, if order, with its aura of violence, still taps a perverse imaginary, then the norm fixes, hypnotizes, dumbfounds, causing every imaginary to involve. We no longer fantasize about every minutia of a program. Its observance alone unbalances. The vertigo of a flawless world.

The same model of planned infallibility, of maximal security and deterrence, now governs the spread of the social. This is the true nuclear fallout: the meticulous operation of technology serves as a model for the meticulous operation of the social. Here, too, *nothing will be left to chance;* moreover, this is the essence of socialization, which has been going on for some centuries but which has now entered into its accelerated phase, towards a limit people imagined would be explosive (revolution), but which currently results in an inverse, irreversible, implosive process: a generalized deterrence of every chance, of every accident, of every transversality, of every finality, of every contradiction, rupture, or complexity in a sociality illuminated by the norm and doomed to the transparency of detail radiated by data-collecting mechanisms. In fact, the spatial and nuclear models do not even have their own ends: neither has lunar exploration, nor military and strategic superiority. Their truth lies in their being models of simulation, vector models of a system of planetary control (where even the superpowers of this scenario are not free—the whole world is satellized).[8]

Reject the evidence: with satellization, the one who is satellized is not who you might think. By the orbital inscription of a space object, the planet earth becomes a satellite, the terrestrial principle of reality becomes eccentric, hyperreal, and insignificant. By the orbital establishment of a system of control like peaceful coexistence, all terrestrial microsystems are satellized and lose their autonomy. All energy, all events are absorbed by this eccentric gravitation, everything condenses and implodes on the micro-model of control alone (the orbital satellite), as conversely, in the other, biological dimension everything converges and implodes on the molecular micro-model of the genetic code. Between the two, caught between the nuclear and the genetic, in the simultaneous assumption of the two fundamental codes of deterrence, every principle of meaning is absorbed, every deployment of the real is impossible.

The simultaneity of two events in July 1975 illustrates this in a striking way: the linkup in space of the two American and Soviet supersatellites, apotheosis of peaceful existence—and the suppression by the Chinese of character writing and conversion to the Roman alphabet. This latter signifies the "orbital" establishment of an abstract and model system of signs, into whose orbit will be reabsorbed all those once remarkable and singular forms of style and writing. The satellization of their tongue: this is the way the Chinese enter the system of peaceful coexistence, which is inscribed in their sky at the very same time by the docking of the two satellites. The orbital flight of the Big Two, the neutralization and homogenization of everybody else on earth.

Yet despite this deterrence by the orbital authority—the nuclear code or molecular—events continue at ground level, mishaps are increasingly more numerous, despite the global process of contiguity and simultaneity of data. But, subtly, these

---

[8]Paradox: all bombs are clean–their only pollution is the system of control and security they radiate *when they are not detonated.*

events no longer make any sense; they are nothing more than a duplex effect of simulation at the summit. The best example must be the Vietnam war, since it was at the crossroads of a maximal historical or "revolutionary" stake and the installation of this deterrent authority. What sense did that war make, if not that its unfolding sealed the end of history in the culminating and decisive event of our age?

Why did such a difficult, long, and arduous war vanish overnight as if by magic?

Why didn't the American defeat (the greatest reversal in its history) have any internal repercussions? If it had truly signified a setback in the planetary strategy of the USA, it should have necessarily disturbed the internal balance of the American political system. But no such thing happened.

Hence something else took place. Ultimately this war was only a crucial episode in a peaceful coexistence. It marked the advent of China to peaceful coexistence. The long sought-after securing and concretizing of China's non-intervention, China's apprenticeship in a global *modus vivendi,* the passing from a strategy of world revolution to one of a sharing of forces and empires, the transition from a radical alternative to political alternation in a now almost settled system (normalization of Peking-Washington relations): all this was the stake of the Vietnam war, and in that sense, the USA pulled out of Vietnam, but they won the war.

And the war "spontaneously" came to an end when the objective had been attained. This is why it was de-escalated, demobilized so easily.

The effects of this same remolding are legible in the field. The war lasted as long as there remained unliquidated elements irreducible to a healthy politics and a discipline of power, even a communist one. When finally the war passed from the resistance to the hands of regular Northern troops, it could stop: it had attained its objective. Thus the stake was a political relay. When the Vietnamese proved they were no longer bearers of an unpredictable subversion, it could be handed over to them. That this was communist order wasn't fundamentally serious: it had proved itself, it could be trusted. They are even more effective than capitalists in liquidating "primitive" precapitalist and antiquated structures.

Same scenario as in the Algerian war.

The other aspect of this war and of all wars since: behind the armed violence, the murderous antagonism between adversaries—which seems a matter of life and death, and which is played as such (otherwise you could never send out people to get smashed up in this kind of trouble), behind this simulacrum of a struggle to death and of ruthless global stakes, the two adversaries are fundamentally as one against that other, unnamed, never-mentioned thing, whose objective outcome in war, with equal complicity between the two adversaries, is total liquidation. It is tribal, communal, precapitalist structures, every form of exchange, language, and symbolic organization which must be abolished. Their murder is the object of war—and in its immense spectacular contrivance of death, war is only the medium of this process of terrorist rationalization by the social—the murder through which sociality can be founded, no matter what allegiance, communist or capitalist. The total complicity or division of labor between two adversaries (who can even make huge sacrifices to reach that) for the very purpose of remolding and domesticating social relations.

"The North Vietnamese were advised to countenance a scenario of the liquidation of the American presence through which, of course, honor must be preserved."

The scenario: the extremely heavy bombardment of Hanoi. The intolerable nature of this bombing should not conceal the fact that it was only a simulacrum to allow the Vietnamese to seem to countenance a compromise and Nixon to make the Americans swallow the retreat of their forces. The game was already won, nothing was objectively at stake but the credibility of the final montage.

Moralists about war, champions of war's exalted values should not be greatly upset: a war is not any the less heinous for being a mere simulacrum—the flesh suffers just the same, and the dead ex-combatants count as much there as in other wars. That objective is always amply accomplished, like that of the partitioning of territories and of disciplinary sociality. What no longer exists is the adversity of adversaries, the reality of antagonistic causes, the ideological seriousness of war—also the reality of defeat or victory, war being a process whose triumph lies quite beyond these appearances.

In any case, the pacification (or deterrence) dominating us today is beyond war and peace, the simultaneous equivalence of peace and war. "War is peace," said Orwell. Here, also, the two differential poles implode into each other, or recycle one another—a simultaneity of contradictions that is both the parody and the end of all dialectic. Thus it is possible to miss the truth of a war: namely, that it was well over before reaching a conclusion, that at its very core, war was brought to an end, and that perhaps it never ever began. Many other such events (the oil crisis, etc.) never began, never existed, except that artificial mishaps—abstracts, ersatzes of troubles, catastrophes, and crises intended to maintain a historical and psychological investment under hypnosis. All media and the official news service only exist to maintain the illusion of actuality—of the reality of the stakes, of the objectivity of the facts. All events are to be read in reverse, where one perceives (as with the Communists "in power" in Italy, the posthumous, "nostalgic" rediscovery of gulags and Soviet dissidents like the almost contemporary rediscovery, by a moribund ethnology, of the lost "difference" of savages) that all these things arrive too late, with an overdue history, a lagging spiral, that they have exhausted their meaning long in advance and only survive on an artificial effervescence of signs, that all these events follow on illogically from one another, with a total equanimity towards the greatest inconsistencies, with a profound indifference to their consequences (but this is because there are none anymore: they burn out in their spectacular promotion)—thus the whole newsreel of "the present" gives the sinister impression of kitsch, retro, and porno all at the same time—doubtless everyone knows this, and nobody really accepts it. The reality of simulation is unendurable—more cruel than Artaud's Theater of Cruelty, which was still an attempt at the dramaturgy of life, the last flickering of an ideal of the body, blood, and violence in a system already sweeping towards a reabsorption of all the stakes without a trace of blood. For us the trick has been played.

All dramaturgy, and even all real writing of cruelty has disappeared. Simulation is master, and nostalgia, the phantasmal parodic rehabilitation of all lost referentials, alone remains. Everything still unfolds before us, in the cold light of deterrence (including Artaud, who is entitled like all the rest to his revival, to a second existence as the referential of cruelty).

This is why nuclear proliferation increases neither the chance of atomic clash nor of accident—save in the interval where "young" powers could be tempted to use them for nondeterrent of "real" purposes (as the Americans did on Hiroshima—but precisely they alone were entitled to this "use value" of the bomb, while all those who have since acquired it are deterred from using it by the very fact of its possession). Entry into the atomic club, so amusingly named, very rapidly removes (like syndicalization for the working world) any inclination towards violent intervention. Responsibility, control, censorship, self-deterrence always increase faster than the forces or weapons at our disposal: this is the secret of the social order. Thus the very possibility of paralyzing a whole country with the flick of a switch makes it impossible that electrical engineers will ever utilize this weapon: the entire myth of the revolutionary and total strike collapses at the very moment when the means to do so are available—but alas, exactly because the means to do so are available. This is deterrence in a nutshell.

Therefore it is altogether likely that one day we shall see the nuclear powers exporting atomic reactors, weapons, and bombs to every latitude. After control by threat will succeed the much more effective strategy of pacification by the bomb and by its possession. "Small" powers, hoping to buy their independent strike force, will only buy the virus of deterrence, of their own deterrence. The same goes of the atomic reactors we have already sent them: so many neutron bombs knocking out all historical virulence, all risk of explosion. In this sense, the nuclear system institutes a universally accelerated process of implosion, it conceals everything around it, it absorbs all living energy.

The nuclear system is both the culminating point of available energy and the maximization of systems controlling all energy. Lockdown and control grow as fast as (and undoubtedly

even faster than) liberating potentialities. This was already the
aporia of modern revolutions. It is still the absolute paradox of the
nuclear system. Energies freeze by their own fire power, they
deter themselves. One can't really see what project, what power,
what strategy, what subject could possibly be behind this enclosure,
this vast saturation of a system by its own hereafter neutralized,
unusable, unintelligible, nonexplosive forces—except the
possibility of an explosion towards the center, or an implosion
where all these energies are abolished in a catastrophic process (in
the literal sense, that is to say in the sense of a reversion of the
whole cycle towards a minimal point, of a reversion of energies
towards a minimal threshold).

25

Metaphorical Roots of Curriculum Design*

Herbert M. Kliebard
Curriculum and Instruction/Education Policy Studies
The University of Wisconsin: Madison

In simplicity or in sophistication man tends to think in metaphors, intuitively drawn from his social and personal experience— J. H. Plumb

The Metaphor of Production

The curriculum is the means of production, and the student is the raw material which will be transformed into a finished and useful product under the control of a highly skilled technician. The outcome of the production process is carefully plotted in advance according to rigorous design specifications, and when certain means of production prove to be wasteful, they are discarded in favor of more efficient ones. Great care is taken so that raw materials of a particular quality or composition are channeled into the proper production systems and that no potentially useful characteristic of the raw material is wasted.

The Metaphor of Growth

The curriculum is the greenhouse where students will grow and develop to their fullest potential under the care of a wise and patient gardener. The plants that grow in the greenhouse are of every variety, but the gardener treats each according to its needs, so that each plant comes to flower. This universal blooming cannot be accomplished by leaving some plants unattended. All plants are nurtured with great solicitude, but no

---

*Reprinted with permission from *Teachers College Record*, 72 (3), copyright © Columbia University, Teachers College Record, 1972.

attempt is made to divert the inherent potential of the individual plant from its own metamorphosis or development to the whims and desires of the gardener.

The Metaphor of Travel

The curriculum is a route over which students will travel under the leadership of an experienced guide and companion. Each traveller will be affected differently by the journey since its effect is at least as much a function of the predilections, intelligence, interests, and intent of the traveller as it is of the contours of the route. This variability is not only inevitable, but wondrous and desirable. Therefore, no effort is made to anticipate the exact nature of the effect on the traveller; but a great effort is made to plot the route so that the journey will be as rich, as fascinating, and as memorable as possible.

Section 6

Towards a Critical View: A Dissenting Statement

✳✳✳✳✳

26

Curriculum Criticism: Misconceived Theory, Ill-Advised Practice*

Rex Gibson
Curriculum
Cambridge University

There is a delusion abroad; a fantasy that has already misled some researchers in education and which seems likely to beguile even more who are attracted by "illuminative" methods. This chimera is known as "curriculum criticism."[1] It flourishes in the United States and is already gaining currency in British curriculum studies. Some of its leading proponents are Mann, Willis, Eisner and Jenkins.[2] Although it has a history of a dozen years or so, it is so new that a recent comprehensive review of educational research methods fails to give it mention.[3] I believe

---

*Reprinted with permission from *Cambridge Journal of Education*, Vol. 11, No. 3, copyright © Cambridge Institute of Education, 1981.

[1]Eisner, Elliot W. (1978). "Humanistic Trends in the Curriculum Field" *Journal of Curriculum Studies,* 10, 3, pp. 197-204.
Eisner, Elliot W. (1979). *The Educational Imagination: On the Design and Evaluation of School Programs.* Macmillan.

[2]Willis, George, ed. (1978) *Qualitative Evaluation: Concepts and Cases in Curriculum Criticism.* McCutcheon Publishing Corporation (see his own paper "Curriculum Criticism and Literary Criticism" pp. 93-111).
Mann, John S. (1978). "Curriculum Criticism" in Willis *ibid* pp. 74-90.
Jenkins, David (1979). "Business as Unusual: the 'Skills of Bargaining' Course at LBS" in Willis *ibid* pp. 345-369.

[3]Cohen, Louis and Manion, Lawrence (1980). *Research Methods in Education.* Croom Helm.

its theory and practice to be deeply flawed and urge that great caution is required lest a whole generation of teachers studying curriculum are encouraged to set off in pursuit of this mirage.

What is "curriculum criticism?" Fundamentally it comprises two basic assumptions: first, that the curriculum can be regarded as an art object, a literary object; and second, that the concepts and methods of artistic and literary criticism can yield deeper understanding of curriculum processes. Let the advocates speak for themselves. First, the curriculum as an art object; Mann, whose views have been seminal, begins:

> I will ask what is involved in talking about
> curriculum as if it were a literary object...I will use as
> an exemplum to be guided but not bound by —Mark
> Schorer's lucid treatment of the story...(he) focuses...
> firmly on the literary object itself...and I would like to
> propose that a curriculum can be regarded in the same
> manner.[4]

And within two pages Mann is unequivocally calling a curriculum "a work of art."[5] Willis supports him in seeing the curriculum as a "work," and asserting that a curriculum "shares the same functions of any work of art."[6]

The second assumption ("use the methods of literary criticism") has two versions: the first urges that certain concepts can be taken over from literary criticism and applied to education: "work" "author" "world" "audience"[7] or "metaphor" "point of view" "plot" and "theme."[8] However, the second version is much more radical; in Eisner's words:

---

[4]Mann *ibid* p. 75.

[5]Mann *ibid* p. 77.

[6]Willis *ibid* p. 109.

[7]Willis *ibid* p. 100 ff.

[8]Kelly, Edward F. (1978). "Curriculum Evaluation and Literary Criticism: Comments on the Analogy" in Willis *ibid* p. 116 ff.

the methods used must be artistically critical. The educational critic must be able to create, render, portray and disclose in such a way that the reader will be able to emphatically participate in the events described . . . (he) exploits the potential of language to further human understanding. The language she or he uses is expressive so that the kind of understanding the reader can secure is one that reaches into the deeper levels of meaning children secure from school experience. To convey such meaning, the artistic use of language is a necessity.[9]

What is being demanded here is not simply that the critic can be a critic; he must be an artist too. As we shall see, it is very difficult for the average human being to resist such a flattering and seductive invitation.

Now, what I shall show is that the first assumption is simply wrong: the curriculum is not an art object and it is exceedingly unhelpful to conceptualize it as such; and the second assumption is delusory, disclosing more the literary shortcomings of the curriculum critics than providing curriculum illumination. Thus, taken together the two assumptions have resulted in a rash of narcissistic, self-indulgent "research" or "evaluation" documents.

Before embarking on the critique, it is necessary to note briefly two claims of curriculum criticism; claims that, in any approach, invariably signify rhetoric rather than ideas. The first is that a "new language" is needed. Thus Mann advocates a move "Toward a New Language"[10] and Willis wishes to develop "a new language of curriculum criticism."[11] Certainly, some relief

---

[9]Eisner (1978). *ibid* p. 199.

[10]Mann *ibid* p. 88.

[11]Willis *ibid* p. 110.

from the older "scientific" approach is required but any call for a "new language" is simply bombast.

The second warning signal is the over-inflated claim of criticism's vital contribution to moral growth. Willis, for example, argues that the focal points, methodology and values within curriculum criticism will somehow have the result that:

> members of the audience become discerning and autonomous moral agents within the process of change. They make possible a similar kind of change for the curriculum worker himself, for in his role as maker of artistic choices he is also heightening his own moral vision.[12]

Such lack of modesty requires the cold-water treatment of David Daiches (1980) on similarly grandiose claims for literary criticism:

> The ability to read great writers with penetrating discrimination does not necessarily make one a better person or enable one to make morally better choices in real life.[13]

What's Wrong with Curriculum Criticism?

Curriculum criticism has three major defects: its assumption that a curriculum is a work of art or can be treated as one; its assumptions about literary criticism; and, resulting from these two, its practice. Let us examine each in turn.

A curriculum is not a work of art. The advocates of curriculum criticism are confident that a curriculum can be seen as a work of art:

> Curriculum criticism . . . enable(s) the curriculum worker . . . to see differences—especially ethical differences—between teaching predetermined subject matter and engaging in a professional discipline

---

[12]Willis *ibid* p. 108.

[13]Daiches, David (1980). "The Critical Voice in the Wilderness" *Times Higher Education Supplement*, 19, 9/80, p. 13.

involved in teaching curricula considered as works of art.[14]

But when the reasons are given for treating curricula as works of art they seem pretty strange, coming, as they do, from writers who claim particular sensitivity to language. For example, just why does Mann assert that a curriculum may be regarded as an art object? Because, it would appear, that curriculum, like fiction, is about selection, about choice. Thus, an artist selects "from a universe of possibilities," and "the selection made, considered against the infinite background of selections passed over constitutes an assertion of meaning."[15]

So, for Mann, what art appears to comprise of is that it involves selection, and has meaning. So, too, he argues does the curriculum: choice and meaning are central. But, so, too, the skeptic would retort, does all human activity: political, religious, economic, leisure pursuits: all involve choice and meaning. So, too, does this paper you are now reading, with these words, these ideas, rather than others. This, too, on Mann's criteria, is a work of art! It is evident that Mann and his followers use words and construct definitions in a very loose, all-embracing fashion.

What is lacking is an understanding that all life has meaning, because it is embedded in social practices. Mann makes much of the assertion that "raw life is formless, chaotic and without meaning until man-the-artist creates meaning by bounding it."[16] This is simply nonsense. Existentialism itself cannot break free of meaning: Sartre's La Nausee is strictly bounded, defined, meaning-full, not merely contingent. Every aspect of human life has meaning because man puts it there— indeed can't help putting it there—and he doesn't have to claim the pretentious title of "man-the-artist" to do so. When Mann claims that:

---

[14]Willis *ibid* p. 109.

[15]Mann *ibid* p. 75.

[16]Mann *ibid* p. 76.

> To listen to a chaotic, infinite universe and then
> answer with form, finitely, is to order chaos and to
> assert meaning. Such answering is the hallmark of
> man-the-artist: his answers are his works of art.[17]

We recognize rhetoric and flattery: it is paying every human being in the world the compliment of the title "artist." But it simply evacuates the word "artist" of all precision; it becomes merely a synonym for "man."

A further misunderstanding of curriculum critics relates to the nature of artistic activity. Mann claims that:

> Mallarmé stood in terror before the blank page: while
> it was blank it was infinite possibility, but to write a
> word upon it was to limit the possible meanings of the
> page.[18]

Mann appears to regard this statement as a literal fact. It's not and cannot be. It belongs to a fictional world where infinite possibilities exist. Further, it belongs to an untenable view of artist as transcendental genius. But all men, including those who are artists, are bounded, confined, subject to history and convention. Mallarme was restricted in what he might write by his society and its history, his own personal biography, the customs, manners, values and standards of his generation, and, crucially, by his thinking of himself as "poet." There is large freedom there, but it is not infinite. And what is true of Mallarme is even more true of "curriculum workers" (whatever that curious expression of the curriculum critics might mean). They are circumscribed by history, by material conditions, by convention —by man's meaning-seeking capacities themselves. Choice and selection is always limited, and such limitation must be acknowledged. "Infinite possibility" is a misleading dream even in art.

In addition to looseness of language and overestimation of artistic freedom, there are many other reasons for disputing the

---

[17]Mann *ibid* p. 76.

[18]Mann *ibid* p. 76.

claim that the curriculum can be regarded as an art object. Let us take literature as an example. A novel or a poem is, in a sense, "fixed": its "writtendownness" is, in a sense, all we have. Its interpretations and valuations will change over the years, but its words remain as the artist first set them down. Now not only does the "writtendownness" of a curriculum change over time, but its crucial dimension is *action:* pupils and teachers in classrooms *doing* mathematics or history or morality. Curriculum is a moving, changing, continuous process involving the interaction of many people; a play, novel or poem is realized by actors, spectators, readers, but all except the most arrogant participant recognize that the major, the fundamental contribution is provided by the words on the page, by the original artist. A work of art is just that: "a work"; a curriculum is "work." To put it bluntly: any fool can write "history" or "mathematics" on a sheet of paper and call it a curriculum. Only an artist of genius can write *Hamlet.* The "givenness" of *Hamlet* is of a quite different order from any curriculum "givenness." Its particularity makes it distinct from the generalities of curriculum characteristics or criteria. *Hamlet* is irreplaceable, no commentary is ever a substitute for it; it is the thing itself to be interpreted, analysed; but a curriculum is most vitally the *actions* of teachers and pupils, not the given text of a written curriculum. Not only does the writing of a work of literature require quite different qualities from those of writing of a curriculum, but, crucially, the participation of collaboration involved by others in the realisation of works of art or curricula are of quite different orders. Pupils and teachers are not called upon to write their own *Hamlet.* They work *at* it in present, joint activity.

Then, too, a work of literature is consciously a fiction; curriculum activity is not. One obvious sense in which this is true is that schooling involves actual children, and teachers, and thus important consequences, moral and cognitive, flow directly from their interaction. A work of art affords greater distancing, more opportunities for imaginative rather than actual participation. Another strong sense of this difference is argued by Frank

Kermode[19] who shows clearly that literature is ordered in a way
that reality is not. In brief, a work of literature has an *ending;* in
contrast everyday life inevitably goes on. In three hours or 300
pages the play or novel is completed. Such neatness has no
parallel in classrooms, in everyday life. There is no curriculum
equivalent of "Go, bid the soldiers shoot."

A work of art represents an act of sustained, imaginative
expression and heightened consciousness; a curriculum simply
cannot be thought of in this way. The practice that is curriculum
includes the mundane as well as the imaginative: boredom and
engagement, sheer slog and moments of inspiration. A work of
art, however produced, excludes those dogged, workaday, habitual
elements. In mundane contrast a curriculum covers more
ground, more time, more of the sheerly ordinary in human
experience. There is a great difference in the intensity embodied
in a work of literature from that in a curriculum. *Middlemarch*
may be about the everyday affairs of a midland town, but its
significances are differently, more consistently and intently
charged than the diffuse activities of life itself.

A further crucial difference, which curriculum critics are
all too prone to overlook, is that the aims and activities of teachers
and artists are rarely similar. The aim of the teacher is to
"educate"—however that word is interpreted —very few artists see
"education" as the main purpose of their activity, indeed, it is often
vigorously denied. Unlike teachers, artists do not think
primarily of particular children, at a particular age, to be affected
in particular ways: cognitively, emotionally, morally,
physically, socially. In spite of all the problems that attach to the
recovery of the author's intention, we can be sure that such
intentions are crucially different from those of teachers.

There are many other objections that could be raised to
treating the curriculum as an art object, particularly the place of
theory in relation to each, and the nature of the relationship of each
to the reality with which it deals.

---

[19]Kermode, Frank (1967). *The Sense of an Ending.* O.U.P.

Literary criticism and curriculum criticism. Although literary criticism may well have much to offer our understanding of curriculum, the promise of the self-styled curriculum critics is, as yet, unredeemed. Their large claims are often simply embarrassing in their pomposity:

> In doing so (adopting the aesthetic perspective) the curriculum worker may gain professional autonomy, become a discerning moral agent, and foster mental health.[20]

At least the "may" takes some of the edge off the pretentiousness. But the inflation hints at the defects in the literary: curriculum criticism analogy. First, Mann's original formulation seems, on close reading, to have little to do with literary criticism as such. In his very appropriate concern to focus on the processes rather than the products of education, in his attempt to provide an alternative to technological-rational approaches to curriculum, Mann advocates literary criticism as a model, but in fact is doing little more than arguing an ethical stance. He starts from the position:

> As with literary criticism, the function of the curricular critique is to disclose its meanings, to illuminate its answers.[21]

Leaving aside the highly arguable "answers," and the fact that many contemporary critics would deny their function as the disclosure of meaning, this is stating no more than the claims of social science or history. The elasticity of language is again evident. And this lack of precision continues:

> Meaning, then, abides in the design of selections . . .
> the critic discloses meaning by explaining designs.[22]

What is specifically *literary* about this? The argument goes on:

---

[20]Willis *ibid* p. 92.

[21]Mann *ibid* p. 77.

[22]Mann *ibid* p. 77.

to account for the choices in a work of art is precisely to
discover what the choices mean.[23]

Here, huge assumptions about intentionality are made,
and we have nothing that is specifically literary. And it is now
that Mann moves away from literary criticism (not that he seems
ever to have engaged with it) into a form of ethical theory.
Polyani's alluring "personal knowledge" is to become the basis of
the curriculum critic's theory and practice. It is the critic's
"personal knowledge" that will guide his choice of what to study,
will prevent subjectivity and will help him to discover significant
designs and meanings. And of what, we can ask, does the
curriculum critic's "personal knowledge" consist? Mann
grounds it in, "Knowledge about ethical reality."[24] Thus:

Personally held and universally intended knowledge
about good and evil or right and wrong stands as a
valuable guide to the processes of curriculum
critique.[25]

There is something very strange here. First, it would appear to
suggest that the best curriculum critic is likely to be a priest or a
moral philosopher; second, it implicitly plays down knowledge of
subject matter about curriculum; and third it has the
characteristic hubris of curriculum critics in implying that a
critic's "knowledge about ethical reality" is somehow superior to a
layman's or is more likely to issue in better choices. David
Daiches' strictures on this last point have already been noted.
Mann's proposals have far less to do with literary criticism than
with a claim to superior ethical knowledge. His concern for the
identification of designs does not constitute any advance on social
science or historical methods and his rhetorical, enthusiastic,
hurrah-type language ("new propositions" "new understanding"
"heuristic leap" "disclosure models lead without end to the

---

[23]Mann *ibid* p. 78.

[24]Mann *ibid* p. 80.

[25]Mann *ibid* p. 80.

unfolding of the world") collapses into banality ("a model is useful if it does disclose meaning and useless if it does not").

The second reason for dissatisfaction with the current state of curriculum criticism lies in its apparent lack of awareness about the fragmented state of literary criticism in the 1970s and 80s.[26] As much as education or sociology, literary criticism is characterized by competing schools, theories, fashions. Marxism, structuralism, new criticism, hermeneutics, deconstruction, formalism, archetypalism, receptionism, transactionism . . . the educational researcher greets the near-endless list with a wry smile of recognition. But generally curriculum critics seem unaware of the range of what counts as literary criticism. They seem tied to a narrow "disclosure of meaning" model. For such ignorance we must be thankful. What a curriculum critic with an acquaintance with Derrida or Lacan would produce is a frightening prospect. (It will, however, come.) At the present moment curriculum criticism both advocates and practices the unproblematic taking over and application of literary concepts (work, author, world, audience, metaphor, plot, theme) to curriculum. What would be welcome is far more caution with regard to the very different world to which literary concepts are applied.[27] To treat the teacher as "author" or the student as "audience" is more likely to obscure than illuminate.

As has been made clear above, the root of such unsubtle transfers is the erroneous assumption that the curriculum is an art-object. The error is compounded when the curriculum critic assumes it is his task to produce his own work of art. Although literary criticism may aid our understanding of curriculum, it is

---

[26]See for example: Watson, George (1978). *Modern Literary Thought*, Carl Winter. Bloom, Harold et al (1979). *Deconstruction and Criticism*, RKP. Eagleton, Terry (1978). *Criticism and Ideology*, Verso. Williams, Raymond (1977). *Marxism and Literature*, OUP.

[27]Kelly *ibid* is a notable exception here. A commendably cautious tone characterizes his paper.

a task calling for far more delicacy of treatment than has so far been evidenced.

Third, curriculum critics show little awareness of the problem of the relationships between language and what it claims to describe. This central problem, not only for literary criticism but for social science, indeed, for all disciplines, is unacknowledged. It is most evident in the writings of curriculum critics in relation to what might be called the theory of the artist. Thus, as between Aristotle's mimesis, the imitation of an action, and the romantic concept of art as expression, curriculum critics have seemed to plump for the latter. But this is to infer from their practice: the matter is simply never discussed, and the vital but uneasy relationship of language to reality remains a blank.

It is perhaps unfair to level charges of neglect of the diversity of literary approaches at such a comparatively new movement as curriculum criticism. However, if its promises are to stand any chance of being redeemed it will simply have to acknowledge the sheer variety of literary criticism. To mention only two: Marxist criticism (itself very diverse) provides a valuable antidote to simple-minded idealism and expressionism and the reduction of explanation to naive individual psychology; it provides a constant reminder that individual actions are embedded in a social structure. And second, greater attention to questions of content and form would not only supply useful conceptual tools for examining curriculum patterns, it would, like Marxism, very quickly reveal the genuine differences that exist between schooling and literature.

A final problem of the critical analogy inheres in the relationship between a work of art and a critic. Apart from such rare instances as Johnson or Eliot it is one of equality: the enterprise, the imaginative and expressive abilities of the artist far exceed those of the critic. However, for the curriculum critic the terms of the relationship are surely equal. But the development of curriculum criticism has been one of distortion. Those who aspire to be critics have been encouraged to see themselves *as* artists, to produce their own "literature," their own "works of art." In short, they have been deluded into believing that "the artistic use of language is a necessity."[28] To the sad results of this mirage we now must turn.

The practice of curriculum criticism. Some criticism, because of its restraint, is convincing;[29] much, because it strains after "the artistic use of language," is painful to read and carries little credibility. A quite classic example is Jenkins,[30] but before examining his study, a few examples from American writers show the defects of the method.

1. *A self-centred, narcissistic tone.* The egocentricity that the approach encourages makes the critic the real subject of the research, rather than the teacher or the pupils. After observing a difficult lesson Greer comments:

> I was drained after the tension of the interchanges I
> had just witnessed. Miss M. too, was weary.[31]

Miss M., poor devil, is only the teacher who has been involved in the "interchanges" witnessed. Grumet chooses a revealing image that places the tortured critic firmly at the centre of the research;

> I felt sorry for myself, victimized as I had felt during
> the discussion, seated in the centre of a circle of
> students, trying to hear them and to hold off the images
> of the stoning scene from *Zorba the Greek* that kept
> coming to mind. I am compelled to relate my response
> to this evening, not to make you cringe (assuming that
> you empathize) but to acknowledge the curriculum and

---

[28]Eisner (1978). *ibid* p. 199.

[29]McCutcheon, Gail (1979). "A Conflict of Interests: An Educational Criticism of Mr. Williams' Fourth Grade Class" in Eisner *ibid* pp. 245-260.

[30]Jenkins *ibid*.

[31]Greer, W. Dwaine (1978). "A Model for the Art of Teaching and a Critique of Teaching" in Willis I pp. 163-185 (this reference pp. 181/2).

my students' response to it as my situation and to
assume responsibility for what I may make of it.[32]
Well, the reader does cringe, but not because of empathy. This
case study is set very significantly in a two page opening from
Sartre's *La Nausee,* and a final three pages in which almost every
sentence is self-referential. Perhaps the "existential aesthetic"
that underpins the study is some explanation, but the whole essay
smacks of the narcissism of the curriculum critic's response with
a vengeance.

Pinar's study consists of extracts from his diary, giving
his responses to reading Sartre. Here, "I" is the prime word
throughout and he concludes:

personal knowledge . . . is not principally knowledge
about ethical reality as Mann maintains. It is about
ethical reality, but on a deeper level it is about life
history and direction, about biographic issues and
movement.[33]

However, the reader feels uncomfortably that the "life
history," "direction," "movement" referred to are purely personal,
solipsistic.   Much criticism reads more like therapy, like
personal disclosure. The self-absorption excludes any sense of
the social structure within which individuals act.

2. *Omniscience*. The self-centredness of the curriculum
critic can produce all-knowing judgements, frequently delivered
in the authentic voice of Mr. Pooter or A. J. Wentworth B.A.:

As I looked around rather pointedly at the mess, Miss
M. seemed to become more aware of it. At her rather
embarrassed comment, "And after my careful
preparation too," I couldn't help laughing at the
helplessness teachers so often feel in the face of the

---

[32]Grumet, Madeline (1978). "Songs and Situations: The Figure/Grand
Relation in a Case Study of Currere" in Willis *ibid* pp. 276-315 (this reference
pp. 311/12).

[33]Pinar, William F. (1978). "Currere: A Case Study" in Willis *ibid* pp. 318-
342 (this reference p. 340).

high spirits that had just spilled out into the courtyard.[34]

There is often a certainty that suits ill with the openness and provisionality of judgement so often recommended:

I had offered *currere* and some had returned the gift unopened.[35]

Again, the image of "the gift" is significant. Moreover, it is seen as foolproof:

Some had tried to use it but had not used the instructions and were understandably annoyed when the thing broke down.[36]

3. *Grandiloquent style.* Milner digs a pit for himself:

The analogy invoked here is that curriculum is like art and should be critiqued accordingly.[37]

And promptly leaps into it:

The Dionysian communalism of frenzy later passed to the abstract individualization of Apollonian remoteness.[38]

Time flowed through his being as it did for Rousseau or for Augustine.[39]

He arranged both form and content for his curriculum for the day so as to initiate the Judeo-Christian action. Not the pathetic modern action of

---

[34]Greer *ibid* pp. 178-179.

[35]Grumet *ibid* p. 321.

[36]Grumet *ibid* p. 321.

[37]Milner, Edward W. (1978). "The Amphibious Musician" in Willis *ibid* pp. 252-273 (this reference p. 266).

[38]Milner *ibid* p. 257.

[39]Milner *ibid* p. 259.

conformity, nor the tragic action of autonomy, but the
redemptive action of openness.[40]
If this reminds one most of Donald Wolfit, Pinar's "criticism"
echoes a pseudo-scientific Polonius:

This method which guarantees nothing (it is only a
tool you may or may not use effectively) is the
regressive-progressive-analytic-synthetic.[41]

4. *Dubious images: a self conscious searching for effect.*
In the straining after vividness, in an attempt to turn everyday
life into high drama, the effort shows:

As she looked up and saw me there was a fleeting
moment when she had the startled expression of an
animal interrupted when drinking.[42]

Dink's teeth sharpened into spearpoints when he
grinned.[43]

Eisner,[44] coiner of the unfortunate phrase "educational
connoisseurship," presents three examples of educational
criticism.   The first two, in their opening sentences reveal the
forced searching for the evocative image:

The classroom is almost a caricature of the society.
The curriculum is served up like Big Macs. Reading,
math, language, even physical and affective education
are all precooked, prepackaged, artificially
flavored.[45]

---

[40]Milner *ibid* p. 259.

[41]Pinar *ibid* p. 323.

[42]Greer *ibid* p. 175.

[43]Milner *ibid* p. 253.

[44]Eisner, Elliot (1979). *ibid.*

[45]Donmoyer, Robert (1979). "School and Society Revisited: An
Educational Criticism of Miss Hill's Fourth Grade Classroom" in Eisner
(1979) *ibid* pp. 229-240 (this reference p. 229).

> The splendid houses perched majestically upon the hills peek out from between the lush growth of trees and well-tended foliage that dress them. Many seem to snicker at the laws of gravity as they balance themselves so casually upon the slanted land.[46]

Eisner must bear much of the responsibility for such artifice, for he has encouraged his many students at Stanford University to believe that:

> Criticism itself is an art form.[47]

5. *The status of critical judgements.* Eisner's assertion coupled with a view of art as expression can result in the abandonment of any notion of objectivity. The status of critical judgement is undermined as the slide into mere subjectivity develops. In a revealing comment Grumet writes:

> One student demanded to know why I had not come to see him perform in a play . . . that had figured prominently in his early journal entries. I tried to show him that I was not there to share his experience as a close friend or a parent might, to confirm or contradict it with my interpretation but to listen to his interpretation. Had I seen his play, *all he would have received was my version, no more or less valid* than his own.[48] [my italics]

Now if a drama teacher's views are no more or less valid than anyone else's it raises the awkward question as to why should her views on curriculum be worth reading. The uneasy equation of criticism with merely personal response is an issue barely addressed by the curriculum critics.

Let us now examine a British case study, claimed to be "rich with detail and incident," "rather telling," with "elaborately

---

[46]Barone, Thomas (1979). "Of Scott and Lisa and Other Friends" in Eisner (1979) *ibid* pp. 240-245 (this reference p. 240).

[47]Eisner, Elliot (1979). *ibid* p. xiii.

[48]Grumet *ibid* p. 311.

drawn characterisation," where "disclosure of meaning flows directly from the observations of the narrator."[49] From such remarks it would appear to carry the seal of approval of the critical school. David Jenkin's study is of a one week residential course he attended at London Business School[50] in which he describes and analyses his experiences of curriculum, tutors, fellow students.

What are the failings of Jenkins' case study? First, its use of language. There is an inability to confine an image within any appropriate bounds. The labored effort to produce "literature" produces only poor journalism. Warning is given in Jenkins' own description of his study: an attempt

> to hold a narrative line side by side with an analysis,
> which is itself elaborately metaphorical, of the hidden
> curriculum, for example in seeing the competing
> pedagogies within the single course as a kind of re-run
> of Elijah versus the prophets of Baal.[51]

Such overdramatisation and grand analogies are invariably the mark of poor criticism. It assumes that the invocation of great names, transcendental themes, superhuman stories, will cause the mantle of literature to fall on weak writing. There are many examples:

> the wooden horse inside Andrew's Trojan citadel.[52]
> he deals, like Gospels, not in anecdotes but in
> parables.[53]

---

[49]Willis *ibid* pp. 243-244.

[50]Jenkins *ibid*.

[51]Jenkins, David and O'Toole, Bridget (1978). "Curriculum Evaluation, Literary Criticism and the Paracurriculum" in Willis *ibid* pp. 524-554 (this reference p. 540).

[52]Jenkins *op cit* p. 349.

[53]Jenkins *ibid* p. 352.

Philip's altar for calling down the divine fire was undoubtedly the simulation exercise.[54]

It was through this breach in nature that ruin entered.[55]

The MSc Course thus becomes the New Hampshire Primary in Philip's bid for the White House.[56]

the danger of epistemological overkill, the scorched-earth policy that undermines the manager's view that he has at least a commonsense understanding of what using words is all about.[57]

Once the rites of passage were over, with all attendant impurities and danger, work began in earnest.[58]

Along with such overdrawn images, mechanically strung together in an attempt to heighten the dramatic effect, to evidence the writer's erudition and grasp of great themes, goes a self-conscious style: a flashiness and quick, one-line put-downs. Flip and inaccurate metaphors are sprinkled around in the straining after vividness. The effect is however simply one of ostentatious display:

the facade is a set piece of stage decor for the CBS street theatre.[59]

Its problem isn't the excellence of the centre, but the centrality of the excellence.[60]

---

[54]Jenkins *ibid* pp. 355-356.

[55]Jenkins *ibid* p. 358.

[56]Jenkins *ibid* p. 367.

[57]Jenkins *ibid* p. 368.

[58]Jenkins *ibid* p. 351.

[59]Jenkins *ibid* p. 345.

[60]Jenkins *ibid* p. 346.

A kind of intellectual Kenwood Autochop turning the whole world to mince before your very eyes.[61]

almost inviting students to treat him as a body-on-the-barged wire.[62]

Philip's box 4 . . . is like a bank, which will lend you money if you prove you don't need it.[63]

Someone who could mastermind police tactics in the London Spaghetti Restaurant siege but who could not be expected to haggle over the provision of chemical toilets.[64]

Andrew's early warning system for this possibility is so sensitive that alarms ring at the first migrating Russian goose.[65]

To borrow Roy Lichtenstein's key concept, WHAM![66]

Each image is overdrawn, over-dramatic, self-consciously inserted. The result is to create disbelief; the reader simply is not convinced by the portrayal because he quickly becomes sated with mere flamboyance. The glittering surface does not conceal the poverty of the piece. In the characterizations of the course tutors all the pretentiousness of the style is evident:

Philip is an earthbound spirit, a hoverer, the earnest young man at the cocktail party.[67]

---

[61]Jenkins *ibid* pp. 353-354.

[62]Jenkins *ibid* p. 354.

[63]Jenkins *ibid* p. 354.

[64]Jenkins *ibid* p. 368.

[65]Jenkins *ibid* p. 369.

[66]Jenkins *ibid* p. 369.

[67]Jenkins *ibid* p. 355.

> young, watchful, nerve-racked and angular as a
> hairpin, but quite exceptionally bright.[68] [Angular as
> a hairpin!]
> Sylvia Maynard . . . long haired, theatrical, and
> rather beautiful in a whimsical kind of way.[69]

Nothing comes to mind more than Pope's "with every word a
reputation dies." And in the convoluted struggle of portrayal,
random pieces of information are offered with pseudo-
significance:

> His father is an inventive cartoonist.[70]

The reader can only wonder about his mother.

What this misuse of language conveys most vividly is the
second defect of curriculum criticism: its self-referentiality.
The curriculum takes second place to the critic. "Look at me" is
what comes through most strongly. Not only is the case study self-
consciously constructed as "a work" of "literature" (which it
certainly is not), it is all too obviously about the writer rather than
the course. Its value is in showing how crucial are the views and
perceptions of the case study writer, but in this instance shows how
much in question is their validity for the mannered writing
evidences an uncomfortable narcissism. Jenkins is always
centre stage, other people find him interesting, mysterious,
unclassifiable:

> On Wednesday evening in the bar Kevin (a
> charismatic character with real-life claims to fame
> as the Malcolm Allison of Gaelic football) got close to
> breaking my cover . . . 'It's funny' he said 'but your
> philosophy of industrial relations hasn't come
> through yet. You're the only course member that I
> can't place.[71]

---

[68]Jenkins *ibid* p. 346.

[69]Jenkins *ibid* p. 350.

[70]Jenkins *ibid* p. 346.

[71]Jenkins *ibid* p. 369.

Note that the "charismatic" Kevin is an interesting character too, but he is puzzled by, and interested in, the enigmatic Jenkins. And Jenkins "knows" people, "important" people:

> Roger Graef: "Knowing Roger, I had a dreadful fear that he would inadvertently blow my cover."[72]
> Philip Boxer (Course tutor) "I had made the mistake of relaxing too much . . . talking to Phil Boxer as if I knew him well (which of course I did . . .)."[73]

The case study writer has a God-like omniscience. Jenkins shares his secret knowledge of the inadequacies of the course's construction with a friend:

> "I wonder who Walter is filling in for?" queried an inside contact of mine.[74]

Note that "inside contact." Clearly, both Jenkins and his friend "know" Prof. Walter Reid has taken on a lecture brief beyond his competence. This image of omniscience has been noted in the American criticism above, but it is most marked in Jenkins. He always knows what is happening, why it is happening:

> Andrew (course director) entered at this point (I waved him across but did not explain what was happening for fear of breaking cover).[75]
> Where, I wondered, was the really wild card going to come from, the concept capable of giving a new purchase on problems.[76]

His evaluations read like Olympian judgments, with a barb in every line, damning with faint praise:

---

[72]Jenkins *ibid* p. 357.

[73]Jenkins *ibid* p. 369.

[74]Jenkins *ibid* p. 348.

[75]Jenkins *ibid* p. 360.

[76]Jenkins *ibid* p. 359.

> Philip is young . . . but quite exceptionally bright.[77]
>
> Andrew, who seems a natural teacher . . . is gifted at exposition and explanation (a skill surprisingly rare in teachers at any level) but clearly sees the knowledge component of the course as dormant knowledge to be handed on.[78]
>
> Although it's not a line I'd care to argue myself, it does have a certain zany appeal.[79]
>
> Andrew's . . . analysis was scintillating, fair, and (I felt) potentially useful.[80]
>
> [they] are excellent teachers *within their chosen modes,* although—[81]

And the put down, the condescending sneer, is ever present:

> 'Dear Rhoda,' I write, sending a postcard to my Mum in Cardiff, 'What a mental life do these people have.'[82]

All the defects of the curriculum criticism are present: the abuse of language in the search for a grandiloquent style, omniscience, narcissism, self-centredness. Criticism becomes display. Even the deception practiced to gain access to the course is turned to account. Jenkins "was pretending to be a negotiator from the Association of University Teachers."[83] He was in fact no such thing and throughout the study he speaks (in typical language) of his concern not to "blow my cover." Over and over he uses the same expression and when at the end of the course "cover

---

[77]Jenkins *ibid* p. 346.

[78]Jenkins *ibid* pp. 351-352.

[79]Jenkins *ibid* p. 352.

[80]Jenkins *ibid* p. 353.

[81]Jenkins *ibid* p. 369.

[82]Jenkins *ibid* p. 361.

[83]Jenkins *ibid* p. 350.

was blown," although he admits to "some embarrassment" he keeps himself, consistent to the last, centre stage in the final sentences of his case study. The course director, objectively and understandably found Jenkins' deceit "a shock and a disappointment." Jenkins did not attend the final session of the course but he ends by quoting from the course director's letter —

> 'Participant observation requires immense discipline and the ability to sustain this. I feel you just ran out of both, just when it looked as if you might be achieving a minor triumph.'[84]

The curriculum critic, not the curriculum remains the firm focus of attention. The attempt to redress the dehumanisation of positivist approaches to education has been overbalanced with egotistical subjectivity.

Conclusion

Do the strictures of the preceding analysis mean that the methods and concepts of literary criticism cannot be applied to curriculum? Is it the merely seductive will o' the wisp I have presented in this paper? My own conclusion is not quite as pessimistic as might be inferred for I believe that the method might yield some illumination of school and classroom processes. But it will only do so if far more thought and caution are exercised than is presently evident. Many of the issues requiring attention have been identified above, but finally—and all too briefly—I list, as recommendations, some items that need urgent consideration if curriculum criticism is to become a worthwhile practice.

1. The assumption that the curriculum is a work of art, or can be treated as one, must be abandoned.
2. The limits of the analogy: literary criticism=curriculum criticism, must be more fully appreciated. In particular, prospective critics must respect the different natures, practices, and functions of art and education.

---

[84]Jenkins *ibid* p. 369.

3. The language of curriculum criticism must guard against highsounding but empty expression. In particular, Eisner's assertion that "the artistic use of language is a necessity" should be seen for what it is: flattering but dangerously seductive; an ill-advised invitation that is more likely to produce purple patches of pseudo-literature rather than authentic portrayals.

4. If curriculum criticism is to draw on literary criticism, the sheer variety of the latter must be understood. In particular, close attention to (the varieties of) Marxist criticism would yield a valuable corrective to the notion of criticism as personal response and is more likely to ensure a due balance between psychological and structural factors.

5. Curriculum critics should resist the temptation to elevate all classroom processes into high drama. The analogy of the classroom as theatre is an attractive but flawed and seductive image. Reality includes the mundane as well as the exotic.

6. The validity of curriculum criticism requires far more grounding than it has yet received. Such an enterprise involves rigorous examination of the relationship between language and what it describes. If some objective criteria of judgment cannot be established, there is no reason why criticism should be taken seriously.

7. Curriculum critics should guard against narcissism and self-indulgence. Too many studies read like an exercise in personal therapy: the result both of too narrow a view of what constitutes literary criticism, and of Mann's exhortation to ground criticism in personal knowledge.

8. Curriculum criticism (indeed all research) should be more modest in its claims. Such modesty can be developed by reading more examples of literary criticism and literature, by regarding the word "new" with skepticism, and by the recognition that all critics and artists work within, and are constrained and aided by, convention and history. Albert Einstein was once asked what one should do with an original

idea. He replied after some thought "I don't know. I only ever had one."[85]

REFERENCES

Barone, T. (1979). "Of Scott and Lisa and other friends" in Eisner (1979). *ibid* pp. 240-245.

Cohen, L. and Manion, L. (1980). *Research methods in education.* Croom Helm.

Daiches, David (1980). "The critical voice in the wilderness" *Times Higher Education Supplement,* 19, 9/80, p. 13.

Donmoyer, R. (1979). "School and society revisited: An educational criticism of Miss Hill's fourth grade classroom" in Eisner (1979). *ibid* pp. 229-240.

Eagleton, T. (1978). *Criticism and ideology,* Verso.

Eisner, E. (1978). "Humanistic trends in the curriculum field," *Journal of Curriculum Studies, 10,* 3, pp. 197-204.

Eisner, E. (1979). *The educational imagination: On the design and evaluation of school programs.* Macmillan.

Greer, W. (1978). "A model for the art of teaching and a critique of teaching" in Willis, I, pp. 163-185.

Grumet, M. (1978). "Songs and situations: The figure/ground relation in a case study of currere" in Willis *ibid* pp. 276-315.

Jenkins, D. (1979). "Business as unusual: The 'skills of bargaining' course at LBS" in Willis *ibid* pp. 345-369.

Jenkins, D. and O'Toole, B. (1978). "Curriculum evaluation, literary criticism and the paracurriculum" in Willis *ibid* pp. 524-554.

Kelly, E. (1978). "Curriculum evaluation and literary criticism: Comments on the analogy" in Willis *ibid* p. 116 ff.

Kermode, F. (1967). *The sense of an ending.* O.U.P.

Mann, J. (1978). "Curriculum criticism" in Willis *ibid* pp. 74-90.

McCutcheon, G. (1979). "A conflict of interests: An educational criticism of Mr. Williams' fourth grade class" in Eisner *ibid* pp. 245-260.

---

[85]Watson, George (1978). *The Discipline of English.* Macmillan, p. 106.

Milner, Edward W. (1978). "The amphibious musician" in Willis *ibid* pp. 252-273 (this reference p. 266).

Pinar, W. (1978). "Currere: A case study" in Willis *ibid* pp. 318-342.

Watson, G. (1978). *Modern literary thought.*

Watson, George (1978). *The discipline of English.* Macmillan, p. 106.

Williams, R. (1977). *Marxism and literature.* OUP.

Willis, G., ed. (1978). *Qualitative evaluation: Concepts and cases in curriculum criticism.* McCutchan Publishing Corporation (see his own paper "Curriculum Criticism and Literary Criticism" pp. 93-111).

Winter, C., Bloom, H. *et al.* (1979). *Deconstruction and criticism*, RKP.

GLOSSARY

by Denis Hlynka

The purpose of this brief glossary is to highlight key terminology to be found in the various readings. The reference at the end of each term is to the article in this book, unless otherwise stated.

Art, Craft, and Science. Three key concepts integrally related. Davies points to Collingwood for a distinction between art and craft by noting that when distinctions (between means and ends, planning and implementation, raw material and finished product, form and matter) are maintained, we have a craft. When those distinctions are blurred, we have an art.

On the other hand, Fowler (1965) provides a classic distinction between science and art: "Science knows, art does; a science is a body of connected facts, an art is a set of directions; the facts of science are the same for all people, circumstances, and occasions; the directions of art vary with the artist and the task."[1]

Author-Text-Reader. The standard literary "formula" (often attributed to Roman Jakobson) which trichotomizes the relationship among the three primary components of written discourse. The author is the obvious source, the text is what we read, and the reader is the receiver. Having said that, the next step is to delve further into the significance of each concept. The term **author** is today considered to be far more ambiguous than initially thought. In an educational film, for example, who is the author? Is it the director, producer, scriptwriter, or a combination of these and more? Likewise the term **text** becomes a multiple system of signs with connotations and denotations which require careful reading. Finally, the **reader** is seen to do more than receive the text material. A reader interprets the text within his/her own experience. Roland Barthes (1985) writes that reading is "rewriting the text of the work within the text of our lives" (p. 101).

---

[1]Fowler, H. W. (1965). *A dictionary of modern English usage.* Oxford: Clarendon Press.

The relationship of this formula to the popular communications model of sender-message-channel-receiver is often noted. The communication model of Berlo and that of Shannon and Weaver are seen within a technical paradigm where the goal of communications is effectiveness, efficiency, and clarity. The aesthetic author-text-reader model stresses critical inquiry which focuses on alternative interpretations.

Connotation. The meaning which a reader gives to a message. This meaning may be partly emotional, partly cultural, partly political. See Hlynka,Muffoletto.

Critical Theoretic Orientation. A curriculum perspective which focuses on underlying root interests, root assumptions, and root approaches. Critical theorists tend to ask "Why?" Ends-Means theorists ask "How?" See Aoki.

Criticism. At the popular level, criticism implies negative judgment. This is not the meaning of criticism used in this book. Rather, criticism is a meta-discourse about discourse. Thus as literary criticism is talk about literature and art criticism is talk about art, educational criticism is talk about education. On another level, criticism is judgment, but also includes the pre-steps of description and interpretation (see Belland, Feldman). In educational technology, criticism is that study concerned with defining, expounding, and evaluating works and products of education.

Finally, Eisner contrasts the word "criticism" with the word "connoisseurship." Connoisseurship, he argues, is the art of appreciation; criticism is the art of disclosure. See Preface, Introduction, Belland.

Connoisseurship. See Criticism.

Curriculum Criticism. A critical examination of curricula based on the idea that a curriculum should be examined as an art object. Such an examination would then include aesthetic dimensions such as perception, analysis, interpretation, and portrayal. See Gibson.

Deconstruction. Contemporary literary and philosophic term derived from Jacques Derrida. It is generally assumed that texts "construct" or "reconstruct meaning." Derrida tries to show that in fact the opposite is the case, that careful analysis of a text shows its contradictions, its instability, its uncertainty. In fact, careful analysis of a text will result in its "deconstruction." By focussing on often trivial and marginal issues, Derrida shifts attention from the center to the parergon. In deconstructing, one normally searches first for binary oppositions, noting what is valorized. Then working from the margins, one shows that the oppositions fall apart, or that the oppositions may equally be valorized. When the valorization is reversed, the text falls apart and is deconstructed. Transcendental signifieds are shown to be false.

In education, scholars are beginning to apply post-modern and deconstructionist methods to curriculum theory. For example, Cherryholmes has deconstructed Bloom's Taxonomy, Schwab's "practical" and the Tyler paradigm in his 1988 book *Power and Criticism.*

Denotation. The literal or "dictionary" meaning of a message. See Hlynka.

Discourse. "What we say" as opposed to practice which is "what we do." Discursive practices refer to what we say and do. Discourse also seems to be related to particular "ways of saying." Thus we have scientific discourse, practical discourse, medical discourse, etc. In contemporary post-structuralist theories, especially the work of Michel Foucault, discourse is seen to be tied to power structures. In educational technology, post-modern studies would try to explore the discourse of educational technology in light of the way the field is structured and the paradigms which provide power and legitimization within the field.

Discursive Form. The language of science. The language of material thought which is accepted as the only bearer of ideas. Opposed to presentational forms. See Langer.

Ends-Means Orientation. A curriculum perspective which is reflected in the Tyler rationale, and in traditional educational technology. The ends-means model stresses efficiency, effectiveness, and goal orientation. See Aoki.

Generalization. The third phase of learning according to Whitehead. See Boyd.

Grounded Theory. Qualitative research term refering to theory grounded in the practical. From Strauss and Glasser. See Hudak.

Metaphor. Major aesthetic concept which requires the implied comparison of one object for another. The comparison may be explicit or implicit; it normally resides in the author, but a message may have metaphoric significance for a particular reader, and therefore reside within the reader of a text. Metaphors are useful in that they provide a way of seeing. However, metaphors are dangerous if they constrain thinking. For example, the use of computer icons which show the computer as an electronic filing system, complete with file folders, documents and even a trash can is a powerful metaphor indeed. However, the computer is *not* an electronic filing system, and thinking within that metaphor may prevent one from considering other functions beyond word processing and data bases. See Hlynka and Nelson.

New Pragmatism. A philosophical position opposing the scientific worldview. Advocated by Richard Rorty, new pragmatism is built on the assumption that all knowledge is a social construct, built by agreement and consensus, rather than demonstrable fact. See Taylor and Swartz.

Paradigm. This term was popularized by Thomas Kuhn in *The Structure of Scientific Revolutions* (1962). Hotly debated ever since, Kuhn suggests simply that: "in its established usage a paradigm is an accepted model or pattern" (p. 23). Kuhn then expands on that base, suggesting that while a paradigm normally permits replications, in science a paradigm is "an object for further articulation and specification under new or more stringent conditions" (p. 23).

Paradigmatic. Only indirectly related to the Kuhnian concept of paradigm noted above, paradigmatic is a semiotic term derived from Saussurian linguistics used in contradistinction to "syntagmatic." In the sentence, "He saw the cat," paradigms are the vertical selections which might replace each word. Paradigmatic alternatives (synonyms, antonyms, metaphors, etc.) for "cat" might be "dog" (a different animal), "tractor" (a metaphor), or "lynx" (a related animal). In media, syntagmatic and paradigmatic selections become a significant component in the development of meaning. See DeVaney.

Poetics. "Deals primarily with the question 'What makes a verbal message a work of art?' "(Jakobson, 1958, p. 350). By extension, a poetics of educational technology would ask: What makes an educational message a work of art?

Post-modern. Traditionally credited to Jencks in reference to architecture, it seems possible to find earlier uses of the term. Since then, the concept has become popular in a wide range of disciplines from literary theory to physics. For Jencks the key phrase is "a double coding." For physicist Prigogine (1984), the post-modern represents "a radical change towards the multiple, the temporal and the complex" (p. xxvii). Solomon (1988) writes that "The post-modern experience is best described as a perceptual montage (p 212). . . narrativeless flow and violent juxtapositions of discontinuous images (p 213). . . In the post-modern world, narrative has lost its sacred power. The post-modern myth has rejected the centuring structures" (p. 216). Others note that the post-modern aura includes a trace of irony and play. Derrida's deconstruction is post-modern; so are Eco's open texts. Lyotard defines post-modernism as "incredulity towards metanarratives."

What all these definitions share in common seems to be a recognition, acknowledgement and acceptance of not just one or two but of multiple world views. If modernism is certainty, post-modernism is uncertainty. If modernism provides meta-narratives, then post-modernism provides a disbelief of these. If modernism is singular, post-modern is plural. The early 1990s seem to present us with the ideal examples of post-modernism at work. The breakup of the Berlin wall; the fall of communism in Eastern Europe, coupled with a desire for national self-determination; the Quebec separatist leanings . . . all these are built on the breakup of what was thought to be monolithic, permanent structures. And these breakups are not by outside interference, but by internal inconsistencies finally coming to light. A Derridian deconstruction!

In educational technology, a post-modern view would challenge monolithic, technical and systematic models of instruction. Post-modern educational technology would see technical, practical, and critical models existing side by side, sometimes contradicting, but often complementing each other.

Precision. Second phase of learning according to Whitehead. See Boyd.

Presentational Form. Opposed to discursive form, presentational forms provide "first and foremost a direct presentation of an individual object" (Langer). Visual forms are not discursive, they are presentational. Visual forms, nevertheless, are just as capable of articulation as discursive forms, but via different means. Together, presentational and discursive forms provide two alternative ways of seeing.

Reader Response Criticism. Critical analysis term which stresses the role of the reader as opposed to the author in interpretation of a text. See DeVaney.

Romance. The first phase of learning according to Whitehead. See Boyd.

Semiotics. The study of signs and sign systems. See Muffoletto, Hlynka.

Sign. "A sign or representamen is something which stands to somebody for something in some respect or capacity. It addresses somebody, that is, creates in the mind of that person an equivalent sign, or perhaps a more developed sign" (Peirce, 1897, p.5). This statement by Peirce forms the fundamental definition in semiotics.

Signified. One of two components of a sign. (See Sign, Signifier.) The signified is the concept, or the meaning of a sign. In post-modern thought, a transcendental signified is an overarching, or ultimate meaning. However, one aspect of the project of deconstruction is to show that there are no transcendental signifieds.

Signifier. One of two components of a sign. (See sign, signifier.) The signifier is the "sound-image," that is the sign itself, the physical thing which represents an object.

Simulacrum. Literally, image. Plural, simulacra. The term has become a major concept in post-modern discourse, especially by Baudrillard. It is characteristic of post-modern society, that the simulacrum, the image, no longer follows reality, but in fact, displaces it. The four phases of the simulacrum, according to Baudrillard, are as follows: First the simulacrum reflects reality, then it masks reality, then it masks the absence of reality, and finally it deconstructs reality such that there is no relation between reality and its simulacrum.

For example, the television world begins as an image or reflection of reality; but concludes with its own reality which the real world tries to imitate. As this text goes to press, the current television craze is the Teenage Mutant Ninja Turtles. If Baudrillard is right, then while the Ninja Turtle phenomenon may have begun as an imitation of some sort of reality, in fact, the simulacrum has taken over and has become its own reality. Now the real world rushes into production toys and dolls and games to capitalize on the simulated world of the Ninja Turtles. "Henceforth, it is the map which precedes the territory, precession of simulacra." See Baudrillard.

Situational Interpretive Orientation. A curriculum perspective which is reflected in a pragmatic approach to analysis of curriculum development in light of inter-subjective communication amongst the specific players involved. Reflected in the writings of Schwab. See Aoki.

Syntagmatic. Semiotic term derived from Saussurian linguistics referring to its linguistic structure. Meaning is related to both syntagmatic and paradigmatic structures. Within a sentence, syntagmatic structures stress the relationship of words to each other in a linear or horizontal mode. In the phrase "He saw the cat," the relationship of each word to each other is a syntagmatic one. See also Paradigmatic. See Hlynka, Muffoletto, DeVaney.

Text. Term preferred by semioticists as an extension of "work." A work is passive; a text is active. A work stresses the contribution of the author; a text stresses the importance of the reader. A work is limited to the document under discussion; a text has many texts and messages including social texts, visual texts, literary texts, etc. See DeVaney, Muffoletto, Hlynka.

Worldviews. A "new pragmatist" concept which acknowledges alternatives to the scientific paradigm. See Taylor & Swartz.

REFERENCES

Barthes, R. (1985). Day by day with Roland Barthes. In M. Blonsky (Ed.), *On signs*. Baltimore, Md: Johns Hopkins University Press.

Cherryholmes, C. (1988). *Power and criticism: Poststructural investigations in education*. New York: Teachers College Press.

Jakobson, R. (1958). Closing Statements: Linguistics and Poetics. In T. Sebeok (Ed.), *Style in language*. Cambridge: MIT Press.

Jencks, C. (1987). *What is post-modernism?* New York: St. Martin's Press.

Kuhn, T. (1962). *The structure of scientific revolutions*. Chicago: University of Chicago Press (second edition, 1970).

Lyotard, J. (1984). *The postmodern condition: A report on knowledge*. Minneapolis: University of Minnesota Press.

Peirce, C. (1897). What is a sign: Three dimensions of logic. In R. Innis (Ed.) *Semiotics: An introductory anthology*. Bloomington: Indiana University Press, 1985.

Prigogine. I. (1984). *Order out of chaos: Man's new dialogue with nature*. Toronto: Bantam Books.

Solomon, J. (1988). *The signs of our time: The secret meanings of everyday life*. New York: Harper and Row.

Author Index

Subject Index